BF
698
.C68
1989
v.4
c.2

The Course of life / edited by Stanley I.
Greenspan, George H. Pollock. -- Madison,
Conn. : International University Press,
c1989-

    v. : ill. ; 24 cm.

    "Revised and expanded version"--T. p. verso.
    Includes bibliographies and index.
    CONTENTS: v. 1. Infancy -- v. 2. Early
childhood -- v. 3. Middle and late childhood
-- v. 4. Adolescence.
    Fisher Library and South Bay Library each
have vols. 1-4.
    ISBN 0-8236-1123-X(v. 1)
    ISBN 0-8236-1124-3(v. 2)
    ISBN 0-8236-1125-6(v. 3)
    ISBN 0-8236-1126-4(v. 4)
00029379   88-28465
921028

To Renew Books
Phone (925) 969-3100

THE COURSE OF LIFE

Volume IV

THE COURSE OF LIFE

Volume IV

Adolescence

Edited by

Stanley I. Greenspan, M.D.
George H. Pollock, M.D., Ph.D.

INTERNATIONAL UNIVERSITIES PRESS, INC.
Madison   Connecticut

This is a revised and expanded version of *The Course of Life: Psychoanalytic Contributions Toward Understanding Personality Development*, edited by Stanley I. Greenspan and George H. Pollock, published by the U.S. Government Printing Office, Washington, D.C., 1980.

Library of Congress Cataloging in Publication Data
The Course of Life.

  "Revised and expanded version"—T.p. verso.
  Includes bibliographies and indexes.
  Contents: v. 1. Infancy—   —v. 3. Middle and late childhood—v. 4. Adolescence.
  1. Personality development. 2. Psychoanalysis. I. Greenspan, Stanley I. II. Pollock, George H. [DNLM: 1. Human Development. 2. Personality Development. 3. Psychoanalytic Theory. WM 460.5.P3 C861]
BF723.P4C68 1991   155   88-28465
ISBN 0-8236-1123-X (v.1)
ISBN 0-8236-1126-4 (v.4)

Manufactured in the United States of America

Contents

vi

List of Contributors

Carl P. Adatto, M.D., Training and Supervising Analyst Emeritus, New Orleans Psychoanalytic Institute; Clinical Professor Emeritus, Louisiana State University Medical School, New Orleans.

Helen R. Beiser, M.D., Clinical Professor of Psychiatry Emeritus, University of Illinois College of Medicine; Emeritus, Faculty, Adult and Child Analysis, Institute for Psychoanalysis, Chicago.

Graham B. Blaine, Jr., M.D., Assistant in Psychiatry, Adolescents' Unit, Children's Hospital Medical Center, Boston.

Peter Blos, Ph.D., Teaching Staff (Retired), New York Psychoanalytic Institute; Faculty (Retired), Center for Psychoanalytic Training and Research, New York.

Hilde Bruch, M.D.,† Professor Emeritus of Psychiatry, Baylor College of Medicine, Waco, Texas.

Henry P. Coppolillo, M.D., Professor and Director, Division of Child Psychiatry, University of Colorado Medical School, Denver.

Aaron H. Esman, M.D., Professor of Clinical Psychiatry, Cornell University Medical College; Faculty, New York Psychoanalytic Institute.

Dana L. Farnsworth, M.D.,† Henry K. Oliver Professor of Hygiene, Emeritus, Harvard University.

Wendy M. Greene, M. Ed., Former Research Coordinator, Adolescent and Family Development Project, Harvard Medical School; Graduate Student in Clinical Psychology, Boston University.

Stuart T. Hauser, M.D., Ph.D., Professor of Psychiatry, Harvard Medical School; Co-editor, *Journal of Research on Adolescence;* Faculty, Boston Psychoanalytic Institute and Psychoanalytic Institute of New England East; Director, Young Adult Development Project, Harvard Medical School.

Richard A. Isay, M.D., Clinical Professor of Psychiatry, Cornell Medical College; Faculty, Columbia Center for Psychoanalytic Training and Research.

Eugene H. Kaplan, M.D., Professor, Department of Neuropsychiatry and Behavioral Science, University of South Carolina School of Medicine; Training and Supervising Analyst, University of North Carolina-Duke University Psychoanalytic Education Program.

Judith S. Kestenberg, M.D., Clinical Professor of Psychiatry and Analyst, New York University, New York; Co-Director, Center for Parents and Children sponsored by Child Development Research, Sands Point, New York.

Melvin Lewis, M.B., B.S. (London), F.R.C. Psych., D.C.H., Professor of Pediatrics and Psychiatry, Yale University Child Study Center.

†Deceased

Irwin M. Marcus, M.D., Clinical Professor of Psychiatry, Louisiana State University Medical School; Adjunct Professor, Tulane University; Founding Director of Child/Adolescent Program (now Emeritus); Emeritus Training and Supervising Analyst, New Orleans Psychoanalytic Institute, New Orleans.

Joseph L. Massimo, Ed.D., Chief Psychologist, Newton Public Schools, Newton, Massachusetts.

Joseph D. Noshpitz, M.D., Clinical Professor of Psychiatry, George Washington University, Washington, D.C.

Daniel Offer, M.D., Professor of Psychiatry, Pritzker School of Medicine, University of Chicago.

Milton F. Shore, Ph.D., Independent Practice; Adjunct Professor, Catholic University of America, The American University, and the University of Maryland.

Morris A. Sklansky, M.D., Training and Supervising Analyst, Chicago Institute for Psychoanalysis; Clinical Professor of Psychiatry, University of Chicago.

Erwin R. Smarr, M.D., Medical Director, Department of Psychiatry, Memorial Medical Center, Inc., Savannah, Georgia.

Herman D. Staples, M.D., Chief of Psychiatry, The Media Clinic, Media, Pennsylvania; Past-President, The American Society for Adolescent Psychiatry.

Heiman van Dam, M.D., Associate Clinical Professor, Psychiatry and Pediatrics, UCLA School of Medicine; Training Analyst and Supervisor in Adult and Child Psychoanalysis, Los Angeles Psychoanalytic Institute; Supervising Analyst in Child Psychoanalysis, Southern California Psychoanalytic Institute.

Preface

Perhaps the most illusive aspect of human development is the nature of man's innermost wishes, thoughts, and feelings. Until relatively recently, our limited understanding of this aspect of the mind has in part stemmed from a focus on the contributions of only a few developmental phases. Now, a wealth of observational, experimental, and clinical case studies at each stage in the course of life, ranging from early infancy to advanced ages, makes it possible to formulate a truly developmental perspective on mental functioning.

Each stage of development has its own special challenges, organizing properties, and unique meanings. Yet, each new stage builds on former ones, creating a developmental progression characterized by both continuity and opportunity. To understand the unique character of each stage of development, outstanding pioneers, clinical scholars, and researchers have prepared papers on each phase of development. Authors have been given an opportunity to update their original papers from the first edition of *The Course of Life*. Many have written new sections or entirely new papers. In addition, new contributions by outstanding investigators have been added for this revised and expanded edition. These papers have been organized according to stages in the course of life: infancy, early childhood, latency, adolescence, young adulthood, midlife, and the aging process. For each stage, each group of papers will illuminate the special challenges, potentials, and, most importantly, highly personal ways experience is organized.

1

The Role of the Early Father in Male Adolescent Development

PETER BLOS, PH.D.

Since it became plausible and indeed obvious that crucial determinants of personality development are to be found in early childhood, the search for them has passed through various stages. It is still vivid in our minds—either from participation or from reading—how changing foci have dominated at various historical times our thinking, research, and theory building in this field. What these changing foci had in common was the relative preeminence of influence on personality formation ascribed to each. They also shared the fact that they all represented consecutive stages in the development of object relations, starting long before this aspect of emotional life had become formulated as an independent theory. In retrospect we can state that each period of these selective emphases has made a distinct and lasting contribution to our understanding of child and adolescent development in an orderly progression.

Surveying historically the changing foci of which I speak, the first and most influential of them must be attributed to the discovery and elaboration of the oedipal stage and the Oedipus complex, because their clinical demonstration in neurotic illness opened a never ending inquiry into the early determinants of personality formation. With ongoing and expanding infant observation the focus shifted to the fundamental importance of early mothering and its critical impact on later life. Again a

This contribution is based on the Plenary Lecture delivered at the Congress of the International Society for Adolescent Psychiatry, Paris, July 22, 1985.

1

shift occurred when infant research moved forward to an investigation of the bridging years that lie between early mothering, merging, and bonding on the one hand and the fateful events of the oedipal experience on the other. It was here, in this neglected, transitional stretch of growth that the unique role of the preoedipal father was discovered as a developmental occurrence *sui generis*, representing a distinct phase on par with the one preceding it and the one following.

At present, interest in the specific role of the early father in the life of the child is very much alive. My own interest was kindled when my investigation of adolescent psychic restructuring, normal and abnormal, revealed that male and female adolescence follow basically different courses, courses neither anchored primarily in oedipal differentiation nor brought to their ultimate resolution by puberty. This fact made it imperative to explore male-female differences as well as similarities or, in other words, to study separately each gender-specific development. The discussion which follows is restricted to the neglected area of the early father experience of the male child and its specific normative influence on the male adolescent process.

When I was exploring the epigenesis of male object relations from infancy to maturity I became aware that the complexity of the boy's relation to the father of his infancy and early childhood had been codified in psychoanalytic theory in terms too monolithic to do justice to the clinical observations of child and adolescent development. If I might be permitted to anticipate the thesis I intend to develop, I will briefly state my proposition that the formation of the male personality and its deviations are not only and not even primarily influenced by the Oedipus complex (namely, the triadic state of object relations) but also and indeed decisively by the preoedipal (namely, the dyadic attachment emotions of the male child to the father). Considering both stages—dyadic and triadic—as comparable in their etiological significance, the uniqueness of the oedipal stage emerges as a period of consolidation which gives final organization and closure to this early period, readying the child for a confrontation with the new tasks of middle childhood. These tasks lie in the comprehension of the world by means of an ever expanding, socially shared, and communicable symbolism, generally identified with "school" and "learning" or with ego expansion and the consolidation of autonomy. Beseeched by these urgencies, the closure of this early period always remains incomplete. Unresolved residues of infantilism are repressed during the decline of the Oedipus complex, only to be revived and taken under final review at adolescence.

The triadic stage is traditionally referred to as the oedipal stage. The word "triadic" emphasizes the characteristic constellation of three partners always simultaneously involved in emotional interaction. From the child's point of view each partner pursues his or her aim of need gratification in a circular transaction. Gender specificity of the three partners represents an integral aspect of the oedipal stage and gives it its unique and stage-specific character. Due to this trilateral constellation and the presence of an antagonistic as well as an attractant affect aimed at one of the two partners in the child's simultaneous relatedness to both, this stage is called the triadic stage of object relations.

In contrast, the dyadic stage of child development refers to a time antedating the oedipal stage. The term "dyadic," employed to denote the earlier stage, emphasizes the significant interaction occurring between two partners—child and mother, child and father—both occurring in a linear interaction. What appears as significant for the dyadic stage are the attachment and avoidance emotions between two partners, infant-mother or infant-father, with the elective affective distancing at any time from one of them. This is in contrast to a three-partner constellation with its obligatory circular involvement and participatory presences which is characteristic of the oedipal stage.

Such rigid differentiations of stages as I have just described are not quite true to life. When I speak of a stage in the sequential order of progressive development, I am referring to preferential trends rather than to exclusive enactments, taking for granted that the blending and fusion of stages is the rule before a stage-specific mode is established.

The exclusive and earliest bonding is reflected in the mother-child unit, the oneness of the symbiotic stage. The dyadic stage continues the earlier one-to-one attachment which now is extended to both parents in an interchangeable dualism. Their gender difference is acknowledged but the attachment emotions are experienced equally in relation to each of the parents, usually one at a time. Their distinction, besides gender, is marked by the affect of pleasure or pain which one or the other parent evokes at various times in the dyadic child. A turn to one parent and the temporary affective exclusion of the other is the always available recourse in the child's pursuit of pleasure and avoidance of pain, frustration, disappointment, and fear.

My investigation in early, namely, dyadic object relations moved slowly but decisively into focus in my therapeutic work with adolescent boys and was a direct outgrowth of the puzzles and questions arising from therapeutic disappointments. Within the scope of male adolescence I investigated the developmental history of intergenerational, reciprocal integration between sonship and fatherhood. The ensuing propositions I will now share with you.

Every father has first been a son; arriving at fatherhood and having a son weaves the father's own sonship experience into the next context of a generational continuum. It seems to me that heretofore too exclusive an attribution of the little boy's sense of security and trust has been ascribed to the early mother and too much of the boy's aggressive self-assertion and fear of retaliation to the competition with the oedipal father. We have ample occasion to observe in the treatment of adult men the enduring influence of his early father, the father imago, especially when it remains fixated at the dyadic level and therefore remains excluded from the ongoing process of emotional maturation. At the termination of adolescence a new stage in the life of the growing boy appears, when the father's affirmation of the manhood attained by his son is conveyed in what we might call the father's blessing of the youth's impatient appropriation of male adult prerogatives and entitlements. This kind of passionate evocation of the good and strong father's spiritual blessing has been traditionally conferred on youth by a symbolic, sanctifying act which represents an acknowledgment by society of this stage in human development; its ritualization is found in all religions of the world.

I return to the discussion of the dyadic characteristics of the affectionate bond between son and father which proves to be of such lasting influence in the life of every man. One receives the impression from the psychoanalytic literature that the father complex declines by the sheer ascendancy of the Oedipus complex proper. Of course, we know that no developmental stage vanishes in such a manner. Yet until recently very little attention was paid to the process or the timing of this particular kind of same-gender attachment resolution which is to exert its fateful influence on adolescent object relations. We are presently justified in saying that a particular pathogenic specificity of the dyadic closure derives from an unaltered stage in the son-father relationship, the beginnings of which are to be found in a quasi-maternal bonding by substitution. When the little boy in his effort to distance himself from the symbiotic mother turns to the father, he replicates initially the same maternal dependency and closeness which he tries to transcend by the change of object. In order to endow the dyadic father with the protective power the little boy needs in order to resist his regressive pull to the symbiotic mother, the idealized imago of the dyadic father is created; one might speak here of an externalization of infantile narcissism.

I have arrived at an opportune moment to say more about the resolution of preoedipal and oedipal stages in the service of ongoing development. Whatever course the individual resolution of the other-gender or positive Oedipus complex will take, its achievement is reflected in the formation of a new structure: the superego. Dual parental, namely dyadic, determinants are always recognizable in the final superego structure; we refer to them as the archaic superego residues. They are built on the fear of loss of love and not yet on feelings of guilt and fear of punishment which we ascribe to the oedipal disharmonies of interpersonal affects. Quite to the contrary, the dyadic components in superego formation derive from a stage at which the father experience was not yet instinctually conflicted because it then belonged to a precompetitive, idealizing stage of the "good father," the "powerful father," the little boy's first "comrade in arms." Both father and mother complex operate at this early level more or less reactively and compensatorily rather than in an antagonistic libidinal entanglement. The prototypical dyadic split into pleasurable and unpleasurable parental figures precludes by its very nature the formation of an internal conflict but not of internal discomfort, experienced as anxiety. This preconflictual stage is further upheld by the attribution of pain to the external world, the "not me" realm of perception and the attribution of pleasure to the "me" experience, inclusive of the pleasure-providing object; within this dawning affective awareness lies the emergence of the self.

Observing the adolescent boy in normal and abnormal stages of regression, I came to realize that his same-gender or negative complex had not been subjected to as radical a transformation into psychic structure during prelatency as the other-gender or positive complex had been. In other words, its definitive transformation into psychic structure was delayed until adolescence. With the advent of sexual maturation at puberty arrives the biological imperative for a definitive, stabilized sexual identity; we do not refer to this position as synonymous with gender identity. The former presupposes sexual maturity, inclusive of sex-specific role competence, while the latter refers to the firm realization of being a boy or a girl. What had appeared to me earlier in my work with adolescent boys as the resuscitation of the positive Oedipus complex which, by deflection, transformation, and displacement turns in an apparently predetermined fashion to extrafamilial heterosexual object-finding, gradually acquired in my clinical judgment the character of a largely defensive operation. Here I have in mind the fact that the boy's dyadic father relationship, which has oscillated for at least a decade between submission to him, self-assertion vis-à-vis him, and sharing in his grandeur, is drawn into the sexual realm with the advent of puberty. The regressive pull to the dyadic father is counteracted by sexual gender assertion. I came to see ever so clearly that this defense springs into action in the wake of a resurgence of the boy's same-gender or negative complex, which reaches, at puberty, the apex of its conflictuality.

The defensive stage I speak of, namely, the male adolescent's heterosexual preoccupation, often bordering on monomania, is a transitory phenomenon. It declines with the definitive resolution of the dyadic father complex at the closure of adolescence. I am fully aware that this exposition does not tell the whole story, but I highlight here intentionally what appears to me a neglected stage in the ontogeny of mature male object relations and of the mature self as well. This particular comprehension of male sexuality at adolescence gained further clarity and plausibility for me from the analytic observation that inordinate, compulsive heterosexual activity or, conversely, anxiety arousal due to heterosexual inaction or passivity, subside markedly with the resolution of the normal father complex. I noticed that the decline of this conflict introduces a kind of heterosexual attachment behavior which possesses a different quality; to this we refer as a mature (or more mature) love relationship in which the defensive nature of the attachment has dropped away and recognition as well as appreciation can be extended to the partner as a whole person; her uniqueness of personality is not begrudged because it does not provide perfect need gratification but demands mutual adaptation as a creative act. When the defensive quality of the immature bonding between sexually mature partners has gradually dissipated, then the formation of the adult personality is reasonably assured. In saying this, I affirm my opinion that not until the closure of adolescence can the dyadic bonding of the boy to his father be transcended for good. Concomitantly I postulate that the structuralization of the adult neurosis cannot be thought of as completed until adolescence has passed.

In accordance with the oedipal schema just outlined and its dyadic antecedent stage as well, I am ready to say that the resolution of dyadic and triadic object relations advances in a biphasic fashion: the resolution of the other-gender or positive component precedes latency—in fact, facilitates its formation —while the resolution of the same-gender or negative component has its normal timing in adolescence when it facilitates the entry into adulthood. This schema was elucidated by my analytic observation that the flight of the male adolescent to his dyadic father is either silently disavowed or vigorously disclaimed by a negativistic involvement with his contemporary father; here it becomes defensively manifest in rising oppositionalism, hostility, and aggression. This behavior is commen-

surate with the intensity and urgency of the son's need for a
protective closeness to the dyadic father vis-à-vis the magnetic
and mysterious female to whom he is irresistably drawn with
the biological advent of puberty. We recognize here the toddler's turn to the father as an ally in his effort to grow up or,
in other words, to resist the regressive pull to the reengulfing,
symbiotic mother. This adolescent drive constellation just mentioned is too frequently and readily identified with a homosexual trend or with homosexuality as such; this simplistic
interpretation demands a strong disclaimer. What we observe
is the male's defensive struggle against passivity in general, not
against homosexuality in particular.

I must admit at this point my omission of some well-known
and relevant facts about the adolescent boy's competitive and
rivalrous struggle with the oedipal father, which is part and
parcel of his global forward move toward the stabilization of
sexual identity. We are well aware that adolescence is the stage
in life when the universal polarities of active and passive are in
conflict and in final collision on a Promethean scale.

In any form of psychotherapy or psychoanalysis of the
adolescent boy it becomes imperative that the double-faced defensive struggle—against submissiveness and passivity as well
as against the symbolic patricide of uncompromising self-as-
sertiveness—becomes disentangled. Should this effort fail, both
sides of the struggle will obstruct and confuse the progression
to emotional maturity. It is a commonplace observation in the
treatment of the adolescent boy that his stubborn perseverance
on the conflict with the female—be this mother, sister, girlfriend, or simply the female "sex object"—keeps his affectionate, i.e., libidinal father attachment effectively in abeyance. The
patient himself usually does his best to keep the focus of attention on heterosexuality by preoccupation and avoidance, while
the therapist too tends to keep the so-called central adolescent
problem of heterosexuality the focus of attention. At any rate,
the adolescent's incessant alternation between defensive and
regressive object involvement is profusely demonstrated by his
proverbial shift of mood, attitude, and general behavior. It did
not escape my attention that the regressive emotional, nonsexual pull of the adolescent boy to the early father imago—forcefully

obscured at this age by repression or reversal—is a manifestation of unsettled residues of the universal father complex, aggravated at this age by the powerful hold which the female acquires on his emotions and sexual drive. The following treatment episode will exemplify this point.

A late-adolescent boy had reacted for some time to my interpretations of his violent behavior toward his parents, especially the father, as proof of my taking sides with them and as an expression of my judging his accusatory and demeaning comments about his parents as "amoral and demented." This reaction reached paranoid proportions. I abstained from interpreting his acting out in the transference because I knew that interpretations inflamed his defensive rage toward submissiveness. During a session, which I shall now describe, the patient accused me in a highly agitated state of thinking of him as a helpless and weak child who is scared to stand up against his father. He was obviously trying to pick a fight with me. When his shouting mounted and he was on the verge of losing control altogether, I told him firmly and in a loud voice that he had to stop telling me what is on my mind or get out. His attack suddenly subsided; he became calm and pensive. After a long silence, he said quietly:

"I just remember a dream I had last night. I am wrestling with my father, not fighting, just wrestling. Suddenly I feel that I'm coming—I cannot control it—I get panicky and I yell: 'no, no—I don't want to make up with you.' I repeat these words again and again in my dream, getting more and more panicky. I can't stop the orgasm. I have it." After the recall of this dream neither patient nor analyst had much difficulty in recognizing son and father engaged in sporting playfulness, a rare and painfully missed occurrence in the boy's early and middle childhood. He said: "I hardly ever played with my father. He was not there—especially when I was afraid of my mother. I saw just enough of him—or perhaps more than enough of my mother—to know how much I missed him." The dream reflected the son's present struggle between a murderous defense against submission and a passionate yearning for paternal acknowledgment of his manhood. The paranoid reverberations of his past, examined in the struggle of his adolescent life,

helped to free the young man from the fixation on the dyadic
father and mobilized his advance toward the oedipal position.
Alongside this developmental progression the compulsive and
defensive need for "having sex" gave way to a wish and a budding capacity to form a relationship of a sexual as well as a
personal, emotional, and romantic nature with a girl. This kind
of relationship became his ego-syntonic model of a heterosexual
partnership, an attainment slow in arriving and even slower in
trusting, considering the moments of rejection and disappointment which intimate relationships always entailed.

The regressive pull to the father of the dyadic period becomes apparent when the adolescent boy is viewed in a developmental continuum as outlined above. As I pursued this
course of thinking in the therapeutic work with the adolescent
boy and adult man, it became apparent to me that the loved
and loving father of the dyadic and triadic period ascends to
a paramount conflictual position at the terminal stage of adolescence. Once alerted to this phenomenon, I became increasingly aware of the omnipresence of these affects as a normal
constituent of the male adolescent process. With this realization
I began to desist from relegating the manifestations of these
inordinate passions solely to the realm of oedipal psychopathology. Rather, these affects as they arose affirmed to me that
the normal adolescent formation of male sexual identity was on
its way. Further, they confirmed that the emotional vagaries of
this period comprise the infantile affects and the expressive
manifestations of the normal father complex in the stage of its
decline. It is therefore no surprise that identity issues of a homosexual modality are universally, even if not manifestly, present
at the stage of adolescent personality consolidation. We should
here recall that a father assumes for the little boy early in life
a charismatic quality in his physical presence which differs in
its constitutional disposition and bodily responsiveness from
that of a mother. The respective quality of the way the father
or the mother hold the infant or the little child or play with
him demonstrates well the disparity of which I speak. The
father of the dyadic period is indeed a facilitator who, in conjunction with the mother, activates the individuation process
and finally becomes for his son a savior from the beckoning

regression and the threatening reengulfment during the rapprochement interlude. The dyadic father has been called "uncontaminated" due to the fact that he has never been a full-fledged symbiotic partner. He belongs to the post-differentiation, preambivalent, idealizing stage of early object relations. Jealousy is indeed noticeable in the larger context of immediate object-availability or quest for total object possession. The son's turn to the dyadic father is not yet affected or burdened by sexual jealousy, patricidal conflict, and traumatic retaliation anxiety. These emotional disharmonies belong to the father of the oedipal era. It is my opinion that the dyadic father-oriented emotions and their imagery are never buried or totally absorbed in derivative psychic formations until the closure of adolescence.

At this point I have to introduce a correction in the portrayal of the dyadic son-father relationship of which—so I fear—I have given too idyllic a picture. What has to be introduced are the father's ambivalent emotions toward his infant son which throw dark shadows over his infantile exuberance and lust for life. Quasi-paranoid reactions in the son are powerfully muted by his idealization of the father. Even when love, pride, and devotion are the father's manifest and self-avowed emotions, negative feelings are bound to drift into the relationship unless, as in some instances, they are defended against by a blinding idealization of the son. As a rule, these negative feelings remain unacknowledged by the father; they remain unconscious and, if not neutralized to some degree, they affect perniciously the early son-father attachment experience. The father who harbors feelings of envy, resentment, and death wishes toward his son is dramatically represented in the Greek myth by King Laius, who set out to kill his infant son, Oedipus, by abandoning him in the wilderness. The inference that the unnatural deed committed by Laius was evoked by the voice of the oracle bespeaks the ubiquitous danger of hostile emotions which the birth of an infant son evokes in the father. The oracle had spelled out the King's unconscious misgivings about his son, thus leaving the moral responsibility of murder to the gods, who had given the father a warning in good time to secure his own safety by resorting to infanticide. Should the father's negative emotions be acted upon as real and valid, as in the myth of Laius, then the father becomes a primary accomplice in the son's fulfillment of the projected role in which he has been cast, resulting in revolt or submission, symbolic patricide or actual suicide. Normally, negative paternal emotions are reduced to insignificance under the onrush of joy and elation elicited by paternity. However, such benign compromises hardly conceal the fact that fatherhood arouses emotions from the father's own dyadic sonship experience which have to be brought into intergenerational harmony with the actuality of having become a partner—the senior male partner, to be correct—in a new family constellation.

I have been vexed for some years by the question of why the role of the so-called "negative," i.e., dyadic Oedipus complex during male adolescence has received so little clinical and theoretical attention, given its evident importance. It remains a matter of record that the clinical phenomenon of the dyadic attachment emotions to the father, when reanimated in adolescence, remained allocated to the Procrustean bed of the Oedipus complex and assigned to the conflicts of either heterosexual or homosexual incest. We have good reason to be astounded by the effectiveness with which the analytic work with the adolescent boy's father complex brings about a noticeable advance in the young man's heterosexual identity and in his adaptive resourcefulness in general. It is the analytic work on the resolution of the libidinized dyadic father complex—a most "positive," namely, phase-typical attachment experience—which occupies during male adolescence, recurrently and often precipitously, the center of the therapeutic stage on which the drama of the inner world—the process of psychic restructuring—is played out. In other words, the resolution of the "complete" Oedipus complex finds its ultimate completion at adolescence in the resolution of the preoedipal, dyadic father experience and its affectionate bonding. This statement does not alter or invalidate the importance of the boy's competitive conflict with his oedipal father, but addresses itself to an intrinsic dyadic component as the bedrock of the male father complex as a whole.

Every adult male who has failed in the course of his emo-

tional development to resolve his father complex suffers from
the consequences of an aborted adolescence. Should he be in
treatment, the pathogenic effect of his developmental failure
will be starkly laid bare within the nexus of his neurosis. What
we observe in such adult cases enlightens us about the patient's
own adolescent process and where it went critically astray. It
also demonstrates the intimate linkage and transmission of
father fixations in this transgenerational continuity. I shall illustrate this phenomenon of a three-generation interlocking
son-father pathology from the analysis of a middle-aged male
patient. This man derived excessive pleasure from the caretaking ministrations to his infant son, which gratified the father's
overwhelming need for tactile proximity to his son. His little
boy responded to the father's need by becoming a nightly visitor
to his father's bed, always bypassing the mother. No disciplinary
interference could influence the now 4-year-old child to stay
in his room at night. The little boy kept responding to the
father's unrelenting, unconscious wishes for physical closeness
to him. When the patient's deprivation of physical and emotional closeness to his early father emerged in the analysis, and
was relived and resolved in the transference, then surprisingly
the little boy began to hear and listen to his father's request that
he remain in his room. The nightly commuting to his father's
bed faded away with the patient's mounting realization that he
gratified vicariously his own dyadic "father hunger" via his little
son's bodily closeness. This vicarious gratification had blinded
this sensitive, caring, and sophisticated man to the inappro-
priateness of his behavior. The lifelong emotional distance between father and son never extinguished the flame of his
yearning for father contact. With tears and sobbing, this man
came to realize how much and how hopelessly he had loved his
dyadic father.

Returning to our focus on adolescence, our attention is
aroused by the boy's conflictual (specifically, active and passive)
father engagement and disengagement. This should not surprise us if we contemplate that puberty, the time of sexual
maturation, deals with the deflection of sexual libido from both
primary love objects onto one gender. This adolescent urgency
has been preshaped by the dyadic and triadic constellation of

early childhood. At both stages, prelatency and adolescence, conflictual and repressed drives as well as transient ego identifications are transformed into psychic structures. At the entrance into latency the superego is consolidated, and at the end phase of adolescence I recognize in the adult ego ideal the resolution of the same gender attachment emotions and dependencies. These psychic structures immortalize, so to speak, vital primary emotional involvements which cannot be transformed into harmonizing object relations. The infantile ego ideal, in its proximity to archaic object idealizations, represents a primitive source of the child's sense of security and safety, physically and emotionally. In contrast, the adult ego ideal is an agency of autonomous choice and aspiration; as such it is guarded as a cherished and beloved personality attribute; its origin in the male lies in dyadic father attachment, in the same-gender complex. The high drama of the adolescent's inner world centers most fatefully and forcefully in the process of deidealization of self and object. By the achievement of this gigantic task, the sense of reality is established for good and mature object relations to move into the reach of the late adolescent.

The proposition of a biphasic resolution of the Oedipus complex (dyadic and triadic) leads to the logical conclusion that the definitive organization of the adult neurosis can have its timing only after the termination of adolescence. What is to become the adult neurosis remains incomplete until the closure of adolescence, because this moment declares that the psychobiological period called childhood is irrevocably passed. Whenever a derailment of the phase-specific differentiations in psychic structures or their abnormal consolidation occur during childhood, the developmental injury meets a last chance of spontaneous healing during adolescence. What continues to loom large as a developmental challenge of male adolescence is the loosening of the son's libidinal tie to his father. Simple displacement along same-gender lines is observed only when a durable fixation prevents libidinal modulation from advancing in puberty toward a heterosexual identity. Simple displacement onto object attachments along the father series of the dyadic type endangers the son's heterosexual identity formation during adolescence, weakening and possibly preventing its formation and its irreversible constancy.

The struggle of the adolescent boy to free himself from the same-gender dyadic, regressive pull is well known to us. Behavioral observation has taught us that the adolescent boy possesses a particular sensitivity to social situations or interactions which contain potential entrapments into submissiveness to males or dependency on them. The same adolescent entrapment fear in relation to the female is well known. The boy's leanings toward libidinized passive compliance in relation to same-gender figures is counteracted and sublimated in his active turn to male hero worship. We are also familiar with the many ways submissiveness or dependency, real or imagined, are fought off by the adolescent boy as, for instance, via oppositionalism and pugnaciousness. However, we should not overlook the many ways in which submissive modalities, directly or symbolically, are overtly or covertly sought by him. These trends can take the form of admiration, gratitude, followership, idealization, and the need to please. These trends, however, if they are steps toward psychic autonomy, represent characteristic adolescent stages in the ontogeny of mature object relations. Compromise formations appear to be the best possible outcome of the struggle. We can trace certain disharmonious object relations in the adult to developmental failures which received their final and lasting imprint—for better or for worse—during adolescence; one source of these I described earlier in this paper when I discussed the dyadic father experience of the little boy. As always when developmental continuities are disrupted and shunted irretrievably onto a dead-end track, a deviant kind of adaptation takes over. In such cases we witness deviances such as delinquency, characterological, social, and sexual pathologies, the eruption of a neurosis, or a psychotic break.

I have traced in my deliberations the mutual influence of drive and ego development throughout the male child's dyadic and triadic father relatedness as it proceeds within a changing soma and social surround during the first two decades of life. I have made the effort to conceptualize the normal developmental progression in male adolescent personality formation with explicit references to the fate of the boy's dyadic father relationship as well as his "negative" Oedipus complex in general. In a broad sense, I have dealt with the reciprocal integration between sonship and fatherhood throughout the adolescent process. The fact that every father has first been a son weaves his own sonship experience into the context of a generational continuum. These considerations, restricted as they are in scope and gender, assign to the dyadic father complex a distinct, universal, and conflictual presence in male adolescence. Further, I assign to the dyadic father complex in the male a nuclear role in normal development as well as in neurosogenesis; more specifically, I recognize in the early son-father experience an essential etiological factor which represents a significant component of most forms of psychopathology in male adolescence and, indeed, throughout the male life cycle.

2

Eleven, Twelve, Thirteen: Years of Transition from the Barrenness of Childhood to the Fertility of Adolescence

JUDITH S. KESTENBERG, M.D.

The ages 11 to 14, like all periods of transition, are difficult to characterize and label. They mark an era of growth and change in the internal and external sex organs. As years of impending fertility, they are most illustrative of the psychoanalytic tenet of the relationships between biological characteristics and psychological experience (Freud, 1905). From this perspective, we can view the principal developmental task of this phase as an integration of reproductive inner genitality with external and internal manifestations of sex-specific sexuality.

In this presentation I shall refer to the ages 11 to 14 as *prepuberty*, and I shall try to define and elaborate its dynamic, somatic, cognitive, and social aspects, placing special emphasis on the progressive changes in organization that proceed from diffusion to reintegration (Kestenberg, 1967a, 1968b).

Some Problems in Nomenclature

Diverse terms and age-ascriptions cloud both the psychological and endocrinological literature concerning adolescence.

Peter Blos, Aaron Esman, Kurt Eissler, Melvin Grumbach, Roger Short, and James Tanner supplied supplemental data. Mark Sossin added bibliographical data and conducted an informal survey about the onset of ejaculations.

Some of the differences are basically semantic, while others stem from the difficulty in pinpointing the time when fertility is established.

The word *Adolescenz* is rarely used in German. In all his writings, Freud referred to puberty as the time when genital primacy was established. Since Hall's famous book, *Adolescence* (1916), this term has been firmly established in American literature. Anna Freud (1936) and Helene Deutsch (1944) looked upon prepuberty as the time in which latency organization is dissolved but changes in primary and secondary sex characteristics have not yet become a challenge to the ego. Anna Freud (1949), Erikson (1951), Blos (1958), Harley (1970), and others have referred to this phase as preadolescence.

For researchers in somatic development, puberty generally means the attainment of fertility, but many authors use the term to indicate that sexual maturation is progressing toward this attainment. Some authors call this preparatory or transitional period "pubescence" and the time after fertility ensues "postpubescence" (e.g., Schonfeld, 1943). In the most general sense, prepuberty connotes all the years of childhood prior to the substantial release of steroids effecting the growth of primary and secondary sex characters. In a narrow sense of the word, prepuberty is a synonym for pubescence, and it is in this sense the term will be used throughout this chapter. The term *adolescence* will connote the growth that occurs between childhood and adulthood, which can be divided into the subphases of prepuberty and early and later puberty (Kestenberg, 1967a, 1968a, b).

Ages and Stages

The difficulty in assigning developmental phases to specific ages is compounded by the wide range in individual rates of maturation, by the social and cultural changes that occur from decade to decade, and by differences due to ecological variation, socioeconomic status, and family size. Well-nourished children are now taller than they were a few decades ago. The mean age of menarche dropped from 13½ in 1965 (Wilkins, 1965) to under 13 in 1975 (Cone, 1976). According to Hamill (1974), the difference in maturation between boys and girls has diminished from two or more years to one and a half or less. At the same time, the span between menarche and fertility has shortened. From research on childbearing in adolescence, it has become evident that at times menarche is followed immediately by an ovulatory cycle (Fineman and Smith, 1977; Hansen, 1978). Kinsey, Pomeroy, and Martin (1948) put the mean age of the first ejaculation at 13.88. Tanner (1962, 1970) reports that the first ejaculation occurs a year after the onset of accelerated penis growth at the mean age of 12.85. Sperm has been detected in the urine of boys as young as 12, with the mean age of first spermaturia placed at 13.3 or less (Richardson and Short, 1978); neither spermaturia nor ejaculation, however, is an indicator of fertility.

All researchers agree that phases and ages need not coincide. In order to study phase development within the context of three-year periods, one has to rely on averages rather than individual differences. The ages between 11 and 14 are considered average in identifying landmarks of prepuberty progression (see Table 1).

Suggested Correlations Between Stages of Physical and Psychological Development

Very little headway has been made since Freud's first attempts to correlate soma and psyche, but new discoveries in endocrinology tend to confirm many of Freud's basic hypotheses.

Freud's theory of biological bisexuality has received confirmation from the discovery that gonads produce not only sex-specific hormones but also hormones of the opposite sex (Freud, 1905). The immature reproductive organs are sensitive to hormones, and both estrogens and androgens are secreted in small quantities in childhood (see Table 1). This may well be the physiological basis of infantile sexuality. Puberty is no longer looked on as the result of a "sudden activation of a previously

TABLE 1
Stages of Sex Maturation

AGES	BOYS	GIRLS
Fetus	FSH and chorionic LH are detectable at 68 days of gestation. From 84–150 days FSH rises, falling in late months of gestation. LH decreases in newborn (see Table 2 for abbreviations and definitions).	
	Secretion of androgens by the fetal immature Leydig cells.	Higher concentration of FSH & LH than in boys.
Infancy		
First	Initially rapid, then slower decreases in estrogen.	
3 days	Testicular activity present.	
1–12 mos.	Higher levels of FSH and LH than in childhood.	
	Gradual increase of testosterone at 3 mos.; gradual decrease until 7th month.	
	At 3–6 mos. LH elevated, decreasing to low levels until the age of 6 yrs.	
Up to 2 yrs.		Bursts of FSH secretion may be characteristic of female infancy. The disappearance of episodic secretion of FSH after the age of 2 yrs. may be the result of increasing ovarian function (Winter and Faiman, 1972).
2–4 yrs.	Testosterone drops.	
3 yrs.	Small amounts of estrogen & 17-ketosteroids in urine, the former higher in girls & the latter higher in boys.	
4 yrs.	Testosterone rises. Androsterone & androstenedione in urine.	
3–9 yrs.		Ovaries similar to adult's, but smaller & have no corpora lutea. Uterus growth.
Latency		
5–10 yrs.	Urinary FSH & LH increase, the latter by intermittent spurts.	
7 yrs.	Gradual increase in ketosteroids & estrogen excretion.	
9–10 yrs.	Increase in serum FSH & LH is followed by *testicular growth*.	Initiation of adolescent growth spurt.
10–11 yrs.	Dehydroepiandrosterone, an adrenal androgen, increases.	
	Rise in 17-ketosteroids excretion, more so in boys.	
	Most rapid increase in muscle cells which continues more gradually until end of third	Considerable, rapid rise in estrogens. Maximum size of muscle cells. With an abrupt

TABLE 1 (*Continued*)

AGES	BOYS	GIRLS
	decade. *Prostate & testicular growth.* Incomplete spermatogenesis.	rise of FSH, *ovaries reach 20%* of adult weight (60% at the age of 16).
Prepuberty 11–12 yrs.	Considerable increase in FSH and LH, gradual in the former & abrupt in the latter. 20-fold rise of testosterone. (Circulating LH & testosterone continue to rise until 17 or later, while FSH reaches a plateau earlier.) Initiation of adolescent height & weight spurt. *Growth of penis, of seminal vesicles, & the bulbourethral glands. More rapid testicular enlargement. Thinning of scrotum.*	Large FSH increase heralds onset of female sexual maturation. Plasma estradiol & estrones augment. The relative scatter of estradiol may indicate *episodic ovarian* function before menarche. Urinary excretion of testosterone & epitestosterone increases. *Accelerated growth of external & internal genitalia.* Remolding of the bony pelvis & accumulation of fat. *Vaginal secretion,* Ph changes, cornification & glycogenization. Increased proliferation of vaginal epithelium & irregular cell sizes. Some of these changes are cyclic. *Pubic hair over mons &* labia pigmented. *Breast budding.*
12–13 yrs.	*Episodic secretion of GH & LH, with mean levels higher during sleep.* Further increase in testosterone. Decrease & stabilization of estrogen excretion. *Pubic hair,* sparse, long, downy, somewhat pigmented. Accelerated growth of penis, continued enlargement of scrotum.	Continued enlargement of *breast* and areola. Pigmented *nipples. Pubic hair dark, coarse, & curly.* Peak *height & weight velocity* precedes menarche (highly correlated with bone age). *Menarche* appears ½–1½ years before ejaculation in boys. Acceleration of fat deposits reaches maximum at 13.
13–14 yrs.	Progressive rise in testosterone. *Rapid testicular,* penal and scrotal enlargement. Pubic hair darker, coarser, still sparse. *Active spermatogonia,* Leydig cells may be present, but they are of puberal rather than	Rise and stabilization of androgenic substances. Adult type hair on mons. Axillary hair & perspiration odor. Voice changes. Thyroid hormones rise after previous decline. Postmenarcheal serum

TABLE 1 (*Continued*)

AGES	BOYS	GIRLS
	adult type (Wilkins, 1965). Increased pigmentation of scrotum. Subareolar node on nipples (not in all cases). Spermaturia (Richardson and Short, 1978). *Ejaculation* (Kinsey, Pomeroy, & Martin, 1948).	LH increases. Progesterone rises & is becoming cyclic. *Earliest pregnancies* (still earlier impregnation unusual).
Puberty 14–15 yrs.	Serum LH mean quantity still higher during sleep but waking LH concentration on the increase (adult LH levels are constant).	
	Great rise of testicular androgens. Voice changes noticeably. Peak height velocity. Size of muscle cells reaches maximum. Axillary hair. Odor of perspiration. Further growth of testicles and penis, rapid growth of prostate. Down on upper lip. Pubic hair resembles adult type but no spread to thighs.	FSH & LH, estradiol & testosterone reach normal adult ranges, but no comparable progesterone level in the luteal phase of the menstrual cycle. Ovaries grow more quickly. Pubic hair spreads to thighs.
15–16 yrs.	Thyroid hormone rise. Marked rise of testosterone. Considerable increase of FSH & LH reaching adult levels. Beginning of facial & body hair. Acne. Adult-type genitals. *Mature spermatozoa* (Wilkins, 1965).	High cyclic progesterone levels. Ovulatory cycles frequent, as progesterone rises to adult levels in appropriate phase of cycle. Mature breasts. Voice deepens. Acne.
16–17 yrs. plus	Testosterone levels continue to rise well into the 3rd & 4th decades. Bone maturation completed. Period of rapid growth almost completed. Muscle cells still enlarge and increase in number, much more than in females.	Arrest of skeletal growth. Ovulatory cycles stabilize. Size and weight of reproductive organs still on the increase, reaching adult levels at 18–20.

Source: Compiled from Botstein and McArthur 1976; Boyar, Roffward, Kapen, Weitzman, & Hellman, 1972; Jenner, Kelch, Kaplan, & Grumbach, 1972; Kestenberg, 1967a, 1968b; Kulin & Reiter, 1973; Lamberg, Kantero, Saarinen, & Widholm, 1973; Marshall & Tanner, 1969; Reiter & Root, 1975; Richardson & Short, 1978; Root, 1973; Sonek, 1967; Tanner, 1962, 1970; Wilkins, 1965; Winer & Faiman, 1972, 1973; from *Gonadotropins*, ed. Saxena Beling, & Gandy, 1972; and from *The Control of the Onset of Puberty*, ed. Grumbach, Grove, & Mayer, 1974.

TABLE 2
Abbreviations and Definitions

FSH—Follicle-stimulating hormone; in appropriate quantities it promotes the growth of ovarian follicles or testicular tubules.

LH—Luteinizing hormone; in appropriate quantities it induces ovulation or stimulates Leydig cells in the testicle to produce testosterone.

These hormones act synergistically to stimulate estrogen production. They are controlled by the hypothalamic-releasing factors. First signs of pubescence are said to appear when there is a negative feedback between FSH & LH & gonadal steroids. The change in feedback sensitivity begins prior to the onset of puberty, & the process continues through the early pubertal years. The ability to release LH following estrogen stimulation may be attained only in mid-puberty (Kulin and Reiter, 1973).

Chorionic LH is secreted by the placenta.

GH—Growth hormone.

Leydig cells are said to secrete testosterone.

Androsterones & androstenediones are precursors of testosterone.

Dehydroepiandrosterone is an adrenal androgen. It is said to be responsible for the growth of hair in adolescence, especially in the girl.

Estrones & estradioles are estrogenic hormones, the latter being most responsible for the growth of female target organs. It becomes cyclic in prepuberty & increases until it has an effect on the endometrium to produce bleeding.

Progesterone is a corpus luteum hormone. It is responsible for the maintenance of the corpus luteum. Cyclic production of estrogens & progesterones in appropriate quantities is responsible for ovulatory cycles.

Testosterones affect the growth & differentiation of male target organs. They promote growth of body & hair. The feedback mechanism between the hypothalamus, the pituitary gonadotropins, & testosterone is not yet clarified. The secretion of male hormones is said to be tonic rather than cyclic.

dormant system" but as the "gradually increasing function of a system that has been continuously active from the in utero stage of development" (Root, 1973, p. 14; Table 1). Thus, the psychoanalytic theory regarding the intrinsic continuity between childhood, adolescence, and adulthood (Jones, 1922) received corroboration from modern endocrinology.

In childhood there exists a high sensitivity of the hypothalamus to the secretion of small amounts of hormones. Thus, when gonadotropins rise slightly, they effect a fall in the quantity of gonadal hormones. Conversely, a small rise in the latter effects a fall in the former. In prepuberty there is a significant decrease in hypothalamic sensitivity, which continues until the final attainment of a new set point of the hypothalamic gonadostat. Through the mediation of gonadotropine-releasing factors in the hypothalamus, large quantities of steroids can be secreted before the feedback is set in operation through which a pituitary secretion of gonadotropins effects a lowering of gonadal hormone output. In prepuberty the irregular production of hormones seems to indicate that the hypothalamic gonadostat has lost its childhood sensitivity but has not as yet attained a new equilibrium. The change in sensitivity "seems to correlate with the attainment of a critical level of the CNS and general somatic maturation that correlates with skeletal age" (Grumbach, Roth, Kaplan, and Kelch, 1974, p. 127). There appears to be a comparable change in the regulation of the "affectostat" of the psyche. Drives and affects rise and fall episodically in transition from the equilibrium of latency to the creation of a new equilibrium before adulthood is attained.

The change in sensitivity in prepuberty is reflected in an alteration of day and night periodicity. The growth hormone (GH) and the luteinizing hormone (LH) are secreted in several pulses during the night, with the mean average of quantities considerably lower during sleeping than during waking. In latency as well as in adulthood, the average quantity of secretion is constant during sleep and waking (Boyar, Roffwarg, Kapen, Weitzman, and Hellman, 1972; Finkelstein, Roffwarg, Boyar, Kream, and Hellman, 1972). We are confronted here with changes in periodicity which begin in the prepuberty of both sexes and can be understood only within the framework of the beginning transformation of bodily rhythms generally (e.g., food intake, body temperature, heart rate and blood pressure, responses to light and darkness). A new periodicity of drives and a changed reactivity of the psyche reflect the new somatic rhythms. These are balanced by the maturing, cortically controlled cognitive structures (Kestenberg and Robbins, 1975, p. 416). Psychoanalysts look upon latency as steady and upon prepuberty as unpredictable. Endocrinologists contrast the steady (tonic) level of hormone secretion in childhood with the episodic and cyclic modes of secretion in the beginning of adolescence.

The growth of reproductive organs precedes the appearance of secondary sex characteristics in prepuberty. The increase in mass and volume of the uterus and ovaries and the prostate and testicles creates the internal somatic basis for the acceptance of inner genitality in preparation for a new sexual and reproductive functioning in puberty. The need for a representation of the inner genital in prepuberty led me to designate it the "prepuberty inner-genital phase" (Kestenberg, 1967a, 1968a, 1975). Most of the external changes, other than the estrogen-dependent breast development, are influenced by the increase in androgenic substances (e.g., pubic, axillary, and body hair). Testosterone, rising much more in the boy than in the girl, also enhances body growth and the increase in size and quantity of muscle cells. It is more than likely that androgens, especially testosterone, have a bearing on the considerable increase in aggression in prepuberty (Anna Freud, 1936). The imbalance between the internal and external changes effects episodic shifts of libidinal and aggressive cathexes from inside to outside and vice versa. Moreover, prepuberty diffusion is not limited to drives. Ego and superego structures break down, not only under pressure of irregularly increasing drives, but also because of a decrease in hypothalamic sensitivity and perhaps because of a decrease in cortical inhibition.

In prepuberty, the disruption of the body image is counteracted by each successive step in the acceptance of new somatic landmarks, both internal and external. In all likelihood, the task of prepuberty to reintegrate inside and outside is correlated with a reintegration of hormone secretion on the basis of a new timelock in the hypothalamus. A related change in the CNS seems to influence the progression toward a new organization via the newly acquired cognitive structures (Inhelder and Piaget, 1958).

Table 1, which schematizes the stages of sexual maturation, serves as a reference for the correlation of psychic and hormonal changes. The inclusion of anatomical and endocrinological data before prepuberty and after should be looked upon as a framework for the appraisal of *prepuberty as a psychobiological phase*.

Transition Into and Out of Prepuberty

There is a continuity in the development from latency into prepuberty and from this phase into puberty, differences becoming apparent when progressive changes in organization become the subject of scrutiny.

Changes in Organization as Seen in Masturbation Fantasies

A successive change in masturbation fantasies of a boy at 10, 12, and 13 years of age, as reported by Wermer and Lewin (1967), elucidates the transition from early to later coping with internal genitality.

At the age of 10 Johnny dreamt about a house with all kinds of electronic equipment and a central switchboard, like the family's hi-fi system, which he was forbidden to touch. The house was owned by a queen who was everybody's boss. In the basement was a bomb factory and next to it a vault in which the queen's money was kept. The queen let the boy play with the controls of the bomb factory; when he pressed a button the periscope went up. However, he was careful and did not let any bombs fall out; he stopped playing with the buttons when the "lady" told him to.

At 12 Johnny had pubic hair but did not like it. At this time, he had the analyst participate in his fantasy rather than the queen-mother. Driving together, they backed into a cliff overlooking the ocean. "When they try to leave, they find that their rear wheels are stuck in the sand and begin to spin, causing sand and rock to be cast off in the ocean." The ocean engulfs the territory where the cliff used to be, inundating more land and killing a multitude of people.

After Johnny had experienced ejaculations, at the age of 13, he experimented with syringes and tubes he emptied and squeezed out. He began to think for hours about the shoes and boots in his mother's closet. Feeling an erection, he had the wish to rub his penis inside the shoe.

When he got older, Johnny replaced the fetishistic fantasy with a fantasy about sex play with his sister and later with a daydream about girls he knew.

At 10 Johnny had had forebodings of what a 12½-year-old patient of Erna Furman (1973) referred to as explosions and clandestine night activities. He represented his rectum as the money-storing vault which adjoined the bomb factory (the prostate?). The construction of his inside as an electronic device belonging to his mother and his obedient touching of the button with permission only, as well as his caution not to let the bombs explode, reflect his orderly and stable latency oganization. By the time he was 12 he no longer sought his mother's permission, but used the analyst as his alter ego—an object of mirroring. Stuck together and spinning together, they caused an erosion, an avalanche, and a mass killing through engulfment. The breakdown of latency organization is depicted in the fantasy, as are the overwhelming sadistic excitment and the fear of losing a substantial part of his body. It is understandable that he did not welcome the external symbol of his new sexuality, the pubic hair. However, the experience of ejaculation had a mitigating effect on his fears. He began to concentrate on the mechanics of ejaculation, and he hoped to achieve control over the ejaculatory reflex. His fetishistic fantasy expressed the wish to contain on the outside what was exploding from the containers in his inside. Throughout the fantasies we can see the influence of anal-sadistic drives on genital drives, but their organization (through continuity and order in latency, through the escape from genitality into thoughts of the toilet in prepuberty, and through a seeking of an external container for his new discharge in late prepuberty) proceeds from latency stability through prepuberty diffusion and regression to prepuberty reintegration between inside and outside. Concomitant is the progress from latency dependence on the mother to the seeking of sameness in prepuberty and the shift toward the oedipal mother before puberty begins.

It is interesting to speculate that 10-year-old Johnny's representation of an inner electronic system reflected the growth of his testicles and his prostate, which adjoins the rectum (see Table 1, ages 9–10 and 10–11). The flood and avalanche fantasied by the 12-year-old correlate with the twenty-fold increase of testosterone at that time. The reorganization following ejaculation may correspond to the more uniform increase of testosterones at this stage. Only when he reached puberty—the age of fertility—could he develop an affective commitment to an object which evolved from growth of excitement and deep feelings, based perhaps on the new organization of sex-specific hormone production (of LH secretion becoming equal in sleep and waking time; see Table 1, age 14–15).

Sequential Changes in Attitudes as Seen Through the Rorschach Test

Statistical studies such as those by Gesell, Ilg, and Ames (1956) and his followers (Ames, Metraux, and Walker, 1971) provide a means of reflecting changes in attitude from year to year, without consideration for the process of transformation, as stressed by psychoanalysis. No doubt, the two methods complement each other.

On the basis of many Rorschach tests administered to children and adolescents, Ames, Metraux, and Walker (1971) described *ten-year-olds* as concrete and seeking order, using isolation of parts to make sense of shapes but becoming diffuse when their defenses break down (p. 129). I believe that their interest in anatomy and maps reflects latent attempts to cope with what is going on in their bodies.

Described by their parents as belligerent and argumentative, *eleven-year-olds* lose their 10-year-old calm. Girls more than boys become diffuse and repetitious, their verbalizations approaching a stream of consciousness:

> On the other side of the mountain, away from the dinosaurs, looks like a couple of—sort of cow—with a cow's

head and a kangaroo's body, big long horns—and they are running down between the mountains, about to land on top of the dinosaurs. . . [excerpt from an 11-year-old boy's response to card X, pp. 147–148].

The *twelve-year-old*, according to Ames, Metraux, and Walker, appears to be in an equilibrium, but his emotions are unmodulated and shapeless. He tends to conform to a peer group, showing few individual differences. However, his tendency to put "all parts into a whole" to counteract disintegration is so strong that it surpasses his ability to make combinations. Contaminations and confabulations make images flow into one another, and displacement wins out over coherence. He abounds in responses about cut-off or split-open parts of the body and frequently sees fires and explosions.

At the age of *thirteen*, there seems to be a greater mobilization of force to pull things together and to think about things (Ames, Metraux, and Walker, 1971, p. 180). At the same time, 13-year-olds display many body responses, such as grimaces, frowns, sighs, and tongue-play. Things appear queer, weird, jagged, bloody, and wild. Despite the high number of explosion-responses and a sometimes "diffuse and vague sense of self" (p. 186), there is a gradual approach to adult forms of thinking and relating. Prepuberty reorganization prepares the adolescent to withstand the onslaught of "boundless exuberance and energy" (p. 201) he will experience as a *fourteen-year-old*.

Rorschach responses confirm conclusions drawn from analyses. Prepuberty is a period of diffusion and reintegration of psychic structures. Late latency forebodings about the feelings inside the body are superseded in prepuberty by regressive responses to the irregular increases in sexuality and aggression. Inner-genital drives and interests help to reintegrate regressive infantile drive components under the aegis of the new adolescent genitality, and newly developing cognitive structures become the foremost tools for the reorganization of ego and superego.

The Development of Abstract Operations in Prepuberty

Just as childhood inhibitions are removed and massive regression becomes the first line of defense against the new sexuality, a novel way of thinking comes to the rescue of the young adolescent (Piaget and Inhelder, 1969).

The 10-year-old conceives reality via the use of concrete operations; the 11- to 14-year-old grasps and assimilates reality in terms of imagined and deduced events. The new structures are part of a developmental continuum; the early sensorimotor structures are followed by internalization of actions through symbol formation and then by a grouping of internalized actions into coherent reversible systems, such as joining and separating. Built upon these achievements is the 11- to 14-year-old's ability to test hypotheses. He takes many factors into consideration all at once. He begins to use abstract propositions such as implication (if-then), disjunction (either-or, or both), exclusions (either-or), and incompatibility (either-or, neither-nor). Schemes become operative which take into account proportions, the double system of references, understanding of hydrostatic equilibrium, and certain forms of probability. The newly won ability to manipulate propositions via combinations and transformations calls for precision in the use of language, a precision which counteracts prepuberty diffusion of thought. Piaget and Inhelder (1969; Inhelder and Piaget, 1958) indicate that the older adolescent becomes progressively more proficient in the use of symbolic logic and acquires the capacity for the creation of his own hypotheses, which lead to new ideas and new value systems.

Emerging cognitive structures play a decisive role in the rebuilding of the body image in prepuberty, based as it is on a combining of representations of the inside with those of the outside of the body. All previous fantasies about the inside of the body were based on concrete images of bodily products and on externalized impulses to touch and nurture (Kestenberg, 1975). Rejected as unreal and repressed in the past, they are revived now and reorganized through transformations and combinations, as well as deductions, based on observations of one's own functioning and that of others.

Metapsychological Assessment of Prepuberty Through the Interpretation of Movement Profiles

The solid and dependable latency child looks proportionate and symmetric. His trunk seems to be hewn from one piece and is isolated from the mobile limbs. In prepuberty the waist becomes loose and flexible and the limbs shoot out every which way. The girl becomes clumsy (Benson, 1937), and the boy seems in continuous danger of losing his balance and breaking things. These derailments are counteracted by an inhibition of flow in the pelvis, where the center of gravity is located (Kestenberg and Robbins, 1975). Experimentation with shifts in weight (toward a restoration of balance) becomes the vehicle for the release and containment of shifting pelvic sensations.[1]

Rhythms of Drive Discharge

Rhythmic changes in tension from free to bound flow and vice versa characterize the motor patterns for drive discharge. Whereas in latency there is an even distribution among well-differentiated pregenital and early genital drive components, prepuberty brings on a disorganization, with various drive-discharge forms vying for dominance and interrupting and derailing one another. In addition to oral play, anal-type twisting and straining, and urethral restlessness, prepuberty brings on a preponderance of inner-genital modes of languid stretching and an admixture of phallic-type leaping and dropping. The inner-genital drive expressions assume leadership over others, as they are capable of absorbing them without complete loss of their own distinctive quality. Toward the end of prepuberty and with beginning puberty, we see an increase in combinations between inner-genital and phallic modes of discharge, which

[1] It is not possible to give here the data from movement studies which warrant the conclusions presented above. Movement notations are of the same order as the immunoassays from which the hierarchic changes in hormone production are derived, as the raw data of the Rorschach Test administered by Ames, Metraux, and Walker (1971), and as Piaget's experiments, on which their respective formulations are based. Movement notations of a subject are scored and the results are used for the construction of a movement profile (MP) devised to correlate with Anna Freud's developmental assessment (1965). Recommended works on movement studies on which profiles are based include Laban, 1960; Lamb and Turner, 1969; Kestenberg, 1965, 1967b, 1975, 1980a; Kestenberg and Buelte, 1977; Kestenberg and Marcus, 1979; Ramsden, 1973; Kestenberg and Sossin, 1979.

very likely constitute the beginning of adult genital modes (Marcus, 1966).

Prepuberty regression to earlier forms of drive discharge is accompanied by rapid shifts of narcissistic cathexis, from one body part to another and from the body to objects. Rapidly changing moods are reflected in exaggerated facial expressions, such as frowning, grinning, pouting, and scowling. Reactivity to stimuli is either too high or too low. Every little touch can produce pain, but at the same time there may be a conspicuous lack of response to a punch or a slap. A rapid sequence of grimaces and odd gestures may herald the emergence of a hebephrenic disorder, but more often inappropriate responses to stimuli and rapid shifts in positioning, gesturing, and grimacing are transitory phenomena of prepuberty. Through them, the youngster becomes acquainted with all body parts in such a way that a relocation and reevaluation of libidinal and aggressive cathexes can take place. From such practices there evolves the image of the whole body, which becomes the core of the body ego in puberty.

Movement observation often reveals the sources of complaints by parents and teachers that their children are lazy or in a daze. When kids are sprawling, unable to mobilize themselves, and wanting to be left alone, their bodies seem to lose elasticity and plasticity, and they appear to be in abnormal states of consciousness. These states must not be confused with passivity, which invites actions by others (Kestenberg and Marcus, 1979). They are probably responsible for what adolescents in this phase call "feeling like nothing" or "feeling dead." They can develop into states of depersonalization or alienation. Various means are used to recover alertness. One of them is a restless moving about to remobilize oneself; another is taking drugs in order to experience vivid feelings instead of feeling empty and depressed. Hypercathecting body parts which were "lost" during the inert states can be a prelude to hypochondria. Young adolescents who suffer from learning disabilities seem to have more frequent states of inertia than do average 11- to 14-year-olds. However, they are never as all-pervasive and long-lasting as in catatonic episodes. In the normal youngster of this age, they come and go, perhaps in conjunction with drops and rises in hormone secretion.

More conspicuous than the passing states of inertia are the variety of conflicts that are acted out in movement. Conflicts between activity and passivity, between aggression and libido, and more specifically between pregenital, inner-genital, and phallic-drive components run rampant. For that reason the integrative influence of inner-genital drives, which brings harmony into disorder is particularly significant. Integration is reinforced by the renewal of identifications with the preoedipal mother. Maternal attributes, derived from sublimation of inner-genital drives (Kestenberg, 1975), are instrumental in the many ways in which the young adolescent mothers himself and thus becomes independent of his mother. Young adolescents cater to their bodily needs and tend to soothe their frequent "hurts" by staying in bed or eating. Underneath their rough exterior there hides a gentleness which reveals itself in the way they cuddle pets and soft animals or care for their machines—their radios and guitars—both of which are their transitional objects and their babies (Kestenberg, 1968a, 1971). Underneath a hateful grimace may hover an unexpressed feeling of lowered self-esteem. Clashes between withdrawal and approach are many; shrinking away from someone on whom one has a crush is a commonplace occurrence. Gradually, these clashes become mitigated by identifications with idolized heroes and heroines—substitutes for the idealized preoedipal mother.

Compounding the intrasystemic conflicts in the id are the intrasystemic conflicts in the ego and the superego (Hartmann, 1939). There is an almost continuous conflict between externalization and internalization. Defenses serving the taming of drives clash with those directed against external dangers. A breakdown in the superego expresses itself in conflicts between its punitive and permissive aspects, and between the ego ideal and archaic intolerant attributes of the superego. Family and peer loyalties are pitched against one another, but acting out by trying new solutions is the vehicle by which the ego and the superego are rebuilt. In this process, becoming like one of the in-group and being popular fill the void created not only by the

loss of the preoedipal parent, but also by the loss of the former
self.

   Nowhere is it more noticeable than in prepuberty movement studies that regressions and disintegrations, resulting
from too many conflicts, are followed rather quickly by a reorganization at a higher level of functioning. Each regression
becomes a challenge for refitting and rebuilding the old into
new attitudes and functions (Eissler, 1958; Geleerd, 1964; Kestenberg, 1967a, 1975). Prepuberty has at its disposal two principal organizers of ego and superego functions:

   1. *New ways of problem solving, not only by the use of multiple
combinations and transformations, but also by a phrasing of actions
and thoughts which matures at this time.* Trial actions are followed
by a total commitment to a given attitude, and these are followed
by a limitation of the commitment to a realistic degree. In terms
of thought (modeled after movement), we can speak of phrases
in which one thinks something over, then becomes totally engaged in the theme, ending the process by finding the appropriate degree of acceptance for the given attitude. Conflicts
between the ego and the superego are expressed by adopting
attitudes contrary to those suggested in the trial action or in the
ending of a total commitment by an acceptance of its opposite.
Through many variations of such conflicting sequences, the 11-
to 14-year-old finds a solution which brings him peace.

   2. *A capacity to adopt structures from external models. A successful
conflict-free performance is more likely to occur if and when a formal
demonstration is provided by a parent, a teacher, or an admired idol.*
The clumsy, conflicted 11- and 12-year-old girl becomes grace-
ful during a dance lesson where she can model herself after the
harmoniously integrated adult teacher. The boy of this age who
horses around with his peers may perform superbly when engaged in sports under the guidance of a coach or in emulation
of an admired sports hero. Similar types of unexpected solutions of problems are encountered in intellectual functioning.

   The process of adaptation through problem solving in prepuberty can be progressive, but more often it is interrupted by
resurgences of regressions. Under optimal circumstances, the
14-year-old has integrated drives and ego and superego functions in such a way that the past becomes an important com-

ponent of the present without an undue pull toward infantilism and dependence. He leaves his prepuberty, prepared for the onslaught by the enormous upsurge in drives and the equally enormous societal challenge that requires him to give up old objects while seeking new ones.

Genetic Roots and the Nature of Prepuberty Regression and Reintegration

Despite changes in growth patterns and social organization through the ages, prepuberty remains much the same. Aptly called *Flegeljahre* (fledgling years) in German, it is defined by *Cassell's German/English Dictionary* (Breul, 1955) as a time of indiscretion, insolence, clownishness, and impertinence.

Psychoanalysts agree that prepuberty revives preoedipal problems (Deutsch, 1944; Blos, 1962), but oedipal strivings are revived as well, sometimes in a crude undisguised form (A. Freud, 1949; Harley, 1970). There is further consensus that prepuberty is initiated by a pregenital regression, more striking in boys than in girls (Blos, 1962). There is no doubt that there is a quantitative increase in drives (A. Freud, 1936, 1949), but a more important characteristic of prepuberty is the drive diffusion and drive dedifferentiation which become the springboards for the progressive reintegration of pregenital and genital drives.

I look upon the period between 11 and 14 as an inner-genital phase whose developmental process can be subsumed under the heading "From Diffusion to Reintegration." It is that subphase of adolescence which initiates and carries through a major portion of the reorganization that is necessary to achieve adulthood (Eissler, 1958). This reorganization, achieved by means of a regression to all of the prelatency phases (Jones, 1922), is given a special direction by the recognition of inner-genital sensations and representations. Its immature prototype is the "inner-genital" phase in childhood that follows the pregenital and precedes the phallic phases (Kestenberg, 1967a, 1968b, 1975, 1980a).

The Early Inner-Genital Phase

In transition from the pregenital to the early genital phase, pregenital representations come into the service of making an illusory baby out of the insides of the child and the mother. The externalization of inner-genital impulses and their transformation into maternal forms of sublimation go hand in hand with an all-encompassing identification with the preoedipal mother. The formation of images of the inside and the creation of sexual theories (Freud, 1923) are aided by the new ability to symbolize and verbalize. The mother and her accessory, the father (Kestenberg, 1971), act as external organizers who provide explanatory models for what the child is trying to understand and who teach the child words and phrases with which to communicate. Inner-genital drives act as internal organizers, with sensations and wishes contributing to the rebuilding of the body image (Kestenberg, 1989).

When drives rise too high and sublimations fail, the child of 3 or 4 responds to the nagging "funny feelings" inside by nagging, arguing, or otherwise passing excitement on to the mother (Kestenberg, 1973). The girl thinks that her baby was "deadened" when she feels depleted of inner-genital excitement. Disappointed and disillusioned with baby substitutes, such as dolls and teddies, both sexes now turn to the external genital for solace. The boy generally does this much earlier than does the girl. Phallic impulses increase in intensity and frequency, achieving dominance in the phallic phase.

The Phallic-Narcissistic and Phallic-Oedipal Phases and Latency

Denial of the internal genital and overcathexis of the external one marks the beginning of the phallic-narcissistic phase. When, in the phallic-oedipal phase, oedipal wishes to be penetrated threaten the undoing of the denial, repression sets in. At the end of the phallic-oedipal phase and in latency the repression of inner-genital wishes is fortified by a projection of these wishes onto the opposite sex. When awareness of the introitus persists into latency (Fraiberg, 1972), the impact of the reawakening of inner-genital sensations in prepuberty is weakened. Consequently there is a lesser need to regress.

Prepuberty Regression

With the end of latency and the beginning of prepuberty comes the reawakening of long-forgotten "funny feelings" that radiate from the inside outward. Baffled by these cryptic sensations, the child tries to connect them to external organs. The nipples and the growing clitoris act as stimulators, transmitters, and resonators of the girl's internal genital sensations (Kestenberg, 1968a). Some boys experience similar sensations in the nipples. Most boys have an inkling of something mysterious going on inside them which they interpret in pregenital or phallic terms. Sublimations of inner-genital drives via externalization exist side by side with explorations and manipulations of the changing sex organs. Playing with the pubic hair and the mons and rubbing the breasts produce sensations which overflow inside the body. Producing erections, shifting the penis, pushing it inward, hiding it between the legs, and pulling on the scrotum stimulate a variety of sensations—from anoprostatic and scrotal inner-genital waves to urethral tingling and phallic onrushes of genital tension.

At first new sensations and new secretions are experienced in terms of pregenital ideation. Trying to cope with the strange happenings in the pelvic-genital area, youngsters hold back or drip urine, retain feces, or expel gas in public. All inferior things are referred to as "crap," and words with sexual connotations are used as dirty. The breakdown of defenses against regressive anourethral genitality leads to an abhorrence of washing. The odor of perspiration merges with genital smells. The discovery of new secretions and play with them may revive the old habit of eating nasal and genital mucus. All these and similar activities are new editions of the genital-pregenital confusion of the 2- to 3-year-old. Old fears of touching reappear; they may lead to symptoms, such as compulsive washing, or to transitory exaggerations of reaction-formations. Overeating and food fads may be followed by an attack of anorexia nervosa or by less rigorous dieting, such as the avoidance of meat as a defense against coprophagic and genitophagic wishes.

Considerable quantities of object-libido are withdrawn from parents and invested in the body, in the self, and in peers.

Mutual explorations culminate in transient homosexual episodes. The accumulated aggression is directed outward, with
parents as the principal recipients. Nagging, arguing, and the
passing-on of excitement, revived from the early inner-genital
phase, mix with anal-sadistic provocations. Oral-sadistic, sar-
castic descriptions of parental shortcomings alternate with confusing tirades (flowing like urine or tears). Oratory mixing
logical and diffuse thinking confuses parents. They may become incensed by manifestations of a regressive mixture of
phallic intrusiveness and sign of separation-individuation. In
the quest for independence, the 11- to 14-year-old practices
and explores; at the same time he is offended when his mother
is not available for refueling. Like a toddler in the rapprochement phase, he shadows his parents (Kestenberg, 1971; Mahler,
Pine, and Bergman, 1975). He spies on them to find evidence
of their wrongdoings; e.g., they are greedy, possessive, unfaith-
ful, liars and cheats, criminals, or prostitutes. The more he
repudiates his own sexuality, the more he finds fault with his
parents for their lack of restraint.

The Regressive and Progressive Aspects of Ejaculation, Menstruation, and Masturbation

Cottle (1972) described vividly how, at the age of 12, he
and his friends had forebodings of ejaculation—forebodings
they interpreted as pregenital and yet elevated to a superior
phallic position. They pondered the problem of whether it was
normal for the heart "to kind of flutter or beat unevenly" during
urination. The heart, which symbolizes sexuality and love, became an internal measure of excitement through its externally
monitored beat. Its connection to the "stomach" and to pelvic-
genital sensations is revealed in the following observation of
Cottle (1972): "Some of the boys agreed the fluttering happened . . . how foolish they looked pulling up their shirt to
examine their stomachs. . . . But most importantly the thought
had been born, namely, that on the inside of the body, extraor-
dinary connections, some rather delicious, but most rather terrifying were becoming evident" (p. 295).

Forebodings of ejaculation and menstruation, and even more so the actuality of experiencing them, have a double effect. Expecting them as signs of maturation makes the adolescent exuberant when they finally come, but there is nevertheless the feeling that something is wrong. Thirteen-year-old Tony anticipated his wet dreams; faced with his ejaculation, however, he associated it with an illness—the stomachaches that had plagued him for some time (Blume, 1971). Thirteen-year-old Kitty Foyle knew that menstruation was a sign of growing up, but she thought of it at first as a tubercular hemorrhage, more serious because "it has gone the wrong way" (Morley, 1939, p. 37).

When a youngster experiences ejaculation for the first time in a waking state, and without masturbation and fantasies, he is struck by the "delicious feeling" that overrides all other considerations (Steffens, 1931). It is rare that girls speak of their menarche as a sexual experience, even though there is engorgement of the vulva and vagina. Boys masturbate deliberately, sometimes for a long time, to achieve ejaculation. Girls frequently use menstrual pads as masturbatory props, but they may not even know they are masturbating. Sometimes good sensations are openly associated with menarche. For example, Ann Frank (1947) noted, "I have the feeling that in spite of all the pain, the unpleasantness and the nastiness, I have a sweet secret" (p. 115).

Blood and pain become symbols of female sexuality, constituting a preparation for defloration and delivery. At approximately the same time, boys become initiated to pain experienced in the testicles, due either to "a kick in the balls" or to prolonged erections. However, shame underlies efforts to hide evidence of erections and ejaculations. Unlike girls, who are usually carefully prepared with regard to personal hygiene during menstruation, boys have to invent their own ways of disposing of their "come."

Menarche revives and intensifies feminine fears of losing one's insides. However, these fears may become submerged by the ambition to excel, as the peer group puts a premium on "getting it first." Popular cliches such as "you have now become a woman" also obscure the girl's real emotions. Feeling sticky from blood, she may not look forward to that kind of womanhood (Kennedy, 1953). She may feel disappointed by the appearance of blood instead of a baby. Each girl in this phase has to resolve the conflict between wanting a baby and postponing motherhood until she becomes a woman. Some feel driven to be impregnated as soon as possible, hoping to get love from the baby, to revive their own babyhood (i.e., to be mothered), and to feel full rather than lonely and empty (Fineman and Smith, 1977).

First anovulatory periods are often painless. In addition, there is currently a great deal of social pressure to disregard the pain and tiredness accompanying the menses and the irritability of the premenstrual period (Delaney, Lupton, and Toth, 1976). If accepted, prepuberty cyclicity, effecting changes in sensations and moods, becomes a rehearsal for puberty. After ovulatory menses bring on cramps and blood clots, and a new feeling of receptivity emerges in the luteal phase of the cycle (Benedek, 1952), the full meaning of feminine periodicity can begin to be understood. Menarche and subsequent menstruation mark the introitus as the opening from which blood emerges. As a result, denial of the introitus can no longer be maintained, and the repression of inner-genital wishes is lifted. A massive regression revives the confusion between the inner genitals and the adjoining bladder and rectum. Experimentation with retaining stool and urine is often used to differentiate between nongenital and genital sensations and to effect a separation-individuation of genital organs. When the inner genitalia begin to assume a central role in the formation of sexual identity, both sexes, but girls more than boys, give up pregenital habits and through externalization from the inside to the outside of the body, become excessively interested in their appearance. Under normal conditions, the affirmation of the uterus and vagina as organs of containment and passage counteracts fears and paves the way for feminine identification (Erikson, 1951, 1959, 1964). Tension in the ligaments of the Fallopian tubes and ovaries helps to make these organs real and acceptable. During prepuberty girls learn to anticipate the changes in sensations, tensions, and moods which are part of feminine cyclicity. There develops a feeling of organ constancy that persists despite the waxing and waning of inner excitement.

In our culture, adults rarely prepare boys for the advent of ejaculation (Kestenberg, 1968a). Advance information that makes a youngster look forward to his first wet dream is often supplied by siblings or friends. At first he looks at his ejaculate as an excrement and a proof of incontinence revived. Once he understands it, however, the emergence of the seminal product frees the boy to acknowledge his previously denied and repressed inner genitality and to cope with the involuntary nature of the act of emission. In analysis, boys hardly ever describe the experience in terms of the consistency and volume of the ejaculate, and it is only a rare analyst who discovers the connection between a youngster's drawings and his attempt to construct the image of his insides. A notable exception is R. Furman's account (1973) of Frank, a 13½-year-old boy who, during his analysis, abruptly began to draw helicopters. For a month, he focused on more and more details and elaborations of weapons systems and living quarters on board, without ever being satisfied with the result. When he stopped drawing, he confessed that he "thought" he had had ejaculations. With the help of his analyst he understood that his drawings were attempts to deal on the outside with feelings he had inside. He could not describe what he felt, and the drawings did not fully represent it. Some months after, Frank told the analyst that he had finally achieved ejaculation by masturbating. He could now describe his first ejaculations as coming upon him without warning and leaving small amounts of a sticky substance at odd times—for instance, when he was reading. His self-induced ejaculations were voluminous, but, more important, he could now "feel it coming," whereas before he was not aware of inner-genital sensations.

Adults tend to forget the degree of explosivity and the frequency of contractions of their first ejaculations. Some recall worrying about the velocity and distance of the seminal trajectory. Both sexes, but boys more so than girls, tend to distort inner-genital sensations by attempts to immobilize and visualize them as static. They unconsciously depict their unseen inner genitals as a stage or a scene they can view, and both sexes allot space in their insides to their mother. In the rare instances when the first wet dream is remembered, its manifest content appears to be a representation of the internal and external genital complex. A colleague reported his first wet dream as follows: "I was looking at something. There was a long lamp on one side and a woman holding it. On the other side was a small dog, a Scotty, holding it also." He did not remember any contractions, but had a feeling of something "pulsatile," while at the same time he agreed that the dream was like a stage. The women in his dream most likely represented the internal keeper of the penis (Kestenberg, 1968a), and the Scotty may have been a symbol of a child, probably condensed with the pubic hair in which the penis seems "rooted." Being held and contained within the stillness of the picture has the reassuring quality of boundaries preserved and kept in place, a reassurance needed to counteract the fear of the penis flying away during orgasm.

As was mentioned above, boys at first look upon their seminal fluid as an excrement, a cross between urine and fecal mucus. In the midst of wondering where it came from and how it was ejected, they become keenly preoccupied with the method of its disposal. The unconscious wish to eat it (the equation of semen and milk) is sometimes realized. Smell and consistency, as well as taste, are distinguishing characteristics that help the boy separate the ejaculate from other excretions. As he transforms his pregenital wishes into genital ones, he practices ways and means of containing it—e.g., in the cupped hand, in a handkerchief, in the toilet. His preoccupation with hiding his new sexual activity from his mother is pregenitally tinged but does betray his wish to show and even give it to her. Differentiating his inner-genital apparatus from the bladder and the rectum, he looks upon his genitals as a weapons system, and he measures how "loaded" he is by applying principles of ballistics to his genital machinery. Fears of being robbed of his hidden arsenal, of becoming depleted, of misfiring and hurting himself and others alternate or condense with fears of anal penetration or entry through a wound (by castration). The immature, impatient urethral or phallic impetuosity which calls for a rapid discharge, with little concern for the receiver of the product, is at the core of juvenile ejaculatio praecox. The cathexis of the male inner genitals as a precious, life-giving, living organ-system is requisite for the transformation of pregenital representations into the image of the semen as a valued gift. The concomitant transformation of homosexual (oral and anal or urethral) into heterosexual (genital) fantasies in prepuberty prepares the boy for his future role as a generous provider and depositor of good things in the girl's vagina.

Both sexes gain mastery over their genitals by hidden or overt homosexual play and masturbation. Girls do not masturbate less than boys, but their methods are hidden and often unconscious. Tensing thighs, "squeezing," and closing off all sphincters are associated with contractions of vaginal and pelvic muscles. Holding excitement for a long time is a female control mechanism that leads to feeling full (being pregnant or having an inner penis). Lubrication, secretions, and the "disappearance" of the clitoris during orgasm gradually change their pregenital and phallic connotations to become models for the anticipated heterosexual experience of receiving the penis and keeping the ejaculate.

Masturbation as a regressive phenomenon is maintained by genital practices and fantasies, with sadism prevailing in boys and masochism in girls. By fostering the dominance of genital libido, masturbation exerts an integrative effect upon drives (Kestenberg, 1967a; Laufer, 1968; Sarnoff, 1976). Genital masturbation fantasies bring harmony into the precarious balance between narcissistic (masochistic) and object-related libido and aggression. They form the base of secondary masturbation fantasies in individual and shared daydreams. Daydreams, usually disclosed to the analyst, are precursors of sublimations and creativity. Girls repetitiously spin yarns about preparation for dates and the locales of encounters; boys depict their exceptional achievements (as athletes, inventors, generals, scientists) in the hope of inducing feminine admiration. Both sexes dream of being performers, popular and thus desirable. Daydreams effect a transformation of homosexual into heterosexual interests, and first heterosexual group experiences become the next step in the transition from a narcissistic seeking of sameness to an appreciation of complementary differences between sexes.

Prepuberty Reintegration

Prepuberty regression gives the growing adolescent another chance to work out unresolved problems and to use new

solutions as a bedrock for the reformation of psychic structure
(Geleerd, 1964; Blos, 1967; Kestenberg, 1967a, 1971; E. Furman, 1973). By reintegrating his drives under the aegis of adolescent genitality, forming new combinations of defenses and
transforming old ways of coping with reality into new ones, the
11- to 14-year-old fortifies both id and ego. Only some of his
defenses have a temporary value. Shallowing of affect, deani-
mation, and their opposites (e.g., giggling, horsing around, and
mirroring gestures and postures) serve the restoration of equilibrium from day to day and hour to hour.

The breakdown of stable relationships effects an increase
of secondary narcissism, which in turn combats self-destructive
tendencies. But there is more to narcissism in prepuberty than
this. The libidinization of the whole body is important for the
formation and persistence of a positive body image and sense
of self. The narcissistic investment in new organs and functions
is comparable to the primary narcissism of the young infant.
Cottle (1972) described the experiential aspect of a primary
erotization and valuation of the new body as follows: "As we
saw it, the organism which was of course our simple self was
extraordinarily complex, and lovably, thankfully incomprehen-
sible to anyone but ourselves" (p. 229). Like a young infant, the
young adolescent does not discriminate between himself and
others. From this basic matrix, self- and object representations
(Jacobson, 1964) are built anew, but at this time there is a decisive shift from primary objects to their new editions in peers.

In prepuberty, the lack of stability in body contours, size,
and configuration brings on fear-inducing shifts in outer and
inner boundaries. However, the new capacity to combine variations in shape and in space-, weight-, and time-orientation
into mobile and cohesive units, and the ability to grasp and
foresee reversibility of positions are all aspects of an arising
cognitive mode that counteracts fears of loss or distortion of
body parts.

Boys are afraid that their testicles will be stuck in the groin
or will increase their asymmetry. They personify the movements they feel inside into skeletons, monsters, or robots. They
attempt to identify with these internal aggressors and to gain
mastery over them by thinking of themselves as dangerous and

by gaining control over "outer-space creatures" in fantasy. Girls are particularly afraid of losing excitement. They try to perpetuate it as a sign of the intactness of inner organs. Fantasies of phallic substructure in boys (such as electronic equipment or tree roots) and an inner phallus in girls are usually unconscious. However, pregnancy fantasies are played out in a jocular way, with boys hiding their penis and sticking out their pelvis and girls putting pillows under their dresses (Deutsch, 1944). Boys are keenly aware of the growth of their phallus, which they compare with that of others, and girls speak openly of how "we must increase our bust" (Blume, 1974, p. 72). Both sexes worry about the penis being too big or too small for the vagina. Each of the many prepuberty worries becomes the basis for a new conceptualization. Paramount in this process is the externalization of inner-genital impulses and a thorough investigation of objects to be used as models for a schema of the body. Externalizations of the inner and outer genitals lead to daydreams about machines and inventions, about constructions and animations of the inanimate. They stimulate interest in maps and mazes. Clothing like sweaters and shirts is used to give an outer shape to internal organs. Machines are of greater interest to boys; clothing to girls. Boys have fantasies of touching girls (brushing against them or holding them), and girls dream of being touched. Pushing, shoving, and tripping are not only fantasied but are a real pastime. Whether in fantasy or in reality, these contacts give a liveliness to the outstanding landmarks of the sexual body. What is going on in the body is understood by a matching of internal and external experiences and by a linking of past, present, and future (Kestenberg, 1968a).

Constructions related to erections and ejaculations are many, in support of symbol formations and as an incentive to hypothesizing and feeling "brainy." Boys at this time are beginning to exceed girls in schoolwork. Interest in internal movements combines with an investment in the growing muscular system to provide an outlet for aggression. Watching and listening are the passive counterparts of real activity.

Boys are primarily interested in the reproduction of the movement mechanism they feel; girls are much more touch- and shape-oriented. Girls are more interested in enclosed structures, while boys use space to build things up and out (Erikson, 1951). A girl's interest in dolls and in large, soft toy animals frequently persists well into adulthood. However, real pets are the most sought-after recipients of maternality in both sexes, with girls nowadays being more interested in horses than are boys (A. Freud, 1965; Kestenberg, 1975). Despite the recent spread of feminism, girls usually use sports with boys as a platform for reaching them. However, a fixation in the negative phallic-oedipal phase may motivate girls to want to be stronger and better than boys in every endeavor.

External Organizers in Prepuberty

The regression in prepuberty is not only a source of annoyance and dismay to parents; it also gives them another chance to deal with such basic problems as training for cleanliness, developing good eating habits, and nurturing a tolerant (not seductive) attitude toward sex.

Intimidated by their children and their public advocates, harassed by their own problems, parents often miss the opportunity to reminisce with their youngsters and to help them connect today's disappointments with yesterday's hurts and tomorrow's challenges. A beautiful example of a mother who knew what to say to her daughter, but could not say it, is Mollie (Kennedy, 1953). When her daughter Valerie, upon her menarche, had been told the usual cliches, she ignored them and said: "It's an awfully sticky feeling." Mollie wanted to say that "when a man makes love to you sometimes that's a sticky feeling too. So was eating candy when you were a baby, or sweating when you gave birth to one. Sticky wasn't bad. Being immaculate . . . isn't the key to a clean and happy life. Sticky with living can be something good" (p. 287). What Mollie eventually could say was: "It will make you even prettier and allow you to feel wonderful things you never felt before." Even this encouraging and truthful statement is the invention of a male author. Men, fathers, brothers, and "boys who like me" can all help the girl feel desirable, and vice versa; women, mothers, sisters, and "girls who like me" make a growing boy feel good about himself.

Where relationships with primary objects were too tenuous, the breakdown in prepuberty may be lasting, without any prospect for the resolution of an unsuccessful separation-individuation or a traumatic inner-genital phase. The road is open then to the deepening of an anaclitic depression or to delinquency as a mode of life.

Under average expectable conditions (Hartmann, 1939), parents now reinforce socially acquired taboos but are capable of giving praise and recognition to developmental advances. A parent who cannot say, "You hurt my feelings," will respond with depreciation that lowers the youngster's self-esteem. Fortunately, through relationships with young adults and peers, in groups and in pairs, the overwhelming libidinal and aggressive wishes toward parents become diluted. Disappointment in friends and feeling unpopular plague adolescents in prepuberty. They revive the mourning of the loss of the mother (and later the father) and the loss of the self—both now past and gone—that characterize the passing of each developmental phase. The current mother is frequently called upon to sympathize with the rejected daughter or son, and thus has a chance to repudiate the hurts she had inflicted on her child in earlier times, especially in prelatency. Quite often, older siblings become a source of solace and encouragement, especially as parents often turn out to be "brutes," as they themselves strive for the achievement of "letting go" that eventually makes them "childless parents" (Kestenberg, 1970).

Teachers, older siblings, and friends, and parents also, can be of great help in encouraging "tertiary masturbation fantasies" in which intricate problems are solved in science or feelings are expressed in poems. Acceptance of the youngster's contribution is not enough. Help in organizing his creative thoughts is crucial at this time. Youth leaders and teachers may have a lasting, unforgettable influence on an individual's development in prepuberty.

With the experience of menses and ejaculations, there begins a renewal of identification with parents that superimposes itself on childhood identifications. Maternal moods, parental relationships, and their concerns begin to be better understood. The current reality of a gentle father who can be affectionate without being overbearing, and of a mother who truly admires the father without being subservient, are far removed from prepuberty fantasies of sadism and masochism as the basis of adult relationships. There follows a need to see parents united and loving one another and an ensuing desire to form a similar relationship with a peer. The ego ideal of courtship and love contributes to the mitigation of narcissistic relationships and fosters true friendships.

The breakdown and rebuilding of the superego proceed through fluctuations of relationships, competition and generosity, envy and altruism. A community of interests fosters identifications as a model for new solutions of conflicts and for internalization of new values, now less family- and more community-oriented. The sense of social justice which had begun to be incorporated in the superego during latency (Kestenberg, 1975, Chapter 10) goes far beyond the confines of fairness in treating siblings and friends. Parents are reinvestigated from the viewpoint of their behavior toward their friends and associates. Building triangles at home, in school, and within larger groups of friends, deserting some in favor of others, or provoking desertion goes hand in hand with weighing issues and changing viewpoints. These prepubertal experiments transpose oedipal configurations into a larger social context. The new social framework prepares the ground for the development of true friendships and of intimacy. Persistent feelings of isolation and alienation in later adolescence and in adulthood are based on a failure to lay a proper foundation for a structured social role in prepuberty.

Therapy in Prepuberty

I have highlighted the development of pathology in prepuberty in terms of exaggeration of normal tendencies. A failure in reintegration in prepuberty lays the ground for future disturbances. In the brief discussion of therapy in prepuberty that follows, I shall focus not on specific pathologies but rather on special problems of therapy during prepuberty. In doing so, I shall rely more on the concluding case presentation than on theoretical considerations.

The problem of analyzing adolescents has been a subject of attention for many years (Katan, 1935; A. Freud, 1937, 1958; Deutsch, 1944; Spiegel, 1951; Eissler, 1958). Fraiberg (1955), in a comprehensive study of psychoanalysis during prepuberty, focused on problems involving early resistance, on the establishment of a positive transference, on the dangers of acting out, and on knowing how to interpret and how deeply to analyze.

The 11- to 14-year-old, suspicious of adults, fears that the analyst may be in cahoots with his parents (Katan, 1935). Being made to come for analysis evokes masochistic fantasies; shame over the developing affection for the analyst leads to silences and crude behavior in sessions. Playing the role of a chum (Deutsch, 1944) may work with some children, but it may also lead to accusations of insincerity and putting on airs incompatible with one's age. Perhaps a grandparently attitude is the least innocuous approach at this time (Deutsch, 1967). It puts the therapist above the parents and promises greater success for the child's expectation of getting his parents to change their behavior toward him.

If treatment has begun during latency, the previously developed trust carries over into prepuberty, but beginning analysis at this time is not an easy undertaking. The choice of a same-sex analyst for the 11- to 14-year-old usually makes the course of analysis smoother (Katan, 1937). A good friend who has been in treatment will induce some young adolescents to seek therapy, even when parents approve only reluctantly. The resistance of parents to have their children analyzed at this age is considerable. In many cases it is necessary to prepare them for the treatment of their 11- to 14-year-old children. Either their own behavior has been so extreme that the child's problems have become obscured, or they find it doubly difficult to share their child with the analyst at a time when they are being excluded from the child's confidence.

The most difficult problem in analysis with this age group is the patient's fear of his own regression, his shame, and his reluctance to talk about it, lest it will make him even more babyish. Recollections of childhood events may be shunned, as if there were a danger of shrinking into an infant if one thinks about having been one.

Perhaps the most important guidelines for the analysis of prepubertal patients are:

1. Follow the child's interests in whatever direction they take, without probing and without losing patience.
2. Introduce confrontations and interpretations at the time when reorganization is being sought, in a form that most befits the ongoing process of reintegration.

At first the analyst may be baffled by the frequency and unpredictability of regression from day to day and from one part of the session to another. Careful attention to the patient's typical changes in periodicity makes it possible to keep in tune with his moods, fears, and pleas for help in solving problems. Playing games rather than speaking or talking incessantly about trivia is less boring to the analyst, as he can study the ways in which affects rise and fall and how resistance follows a brief period of receptivity. Treating this age group demands a great amount of versatility in the analyst. It presents a special challenge to the psychoanalyst's ego to regress in the service of therapy without losing sight of therapeutic goals.

Case Presentation

The salient points of this chapter are illustrated in the following brief account of the psychoanalysis of a girl from the ages of 9 to 13.

Margie and her brother, two and a half years her junior, were both adopted. A trauma at 9 affected Margie so that she began to demonstrate prepuberty behavior relatively early. At this point she reported a frankly incestuous dream, as might be expected of an 11-year-old. Against the backdrop of the dream's fairy tale setting, however, was content more characteristic of latency.

She and her brother were kidnapped by a king who kept them "until I would say that I'd be his princess. So I was his princess and my brother was his prince and we got married and lived happily ever after. After a few weeks we got a baby, half boy and half girl. We did not like the baby, so we decided that we will divorce and get married to someone else." The dream, and its themes of kidnapping, divorce, and abandonment stemming from parental disapproval of the baby's sex, reflected Margie's fantasies about adoption.

Veering from concerns about her mother's illness to fears of robbers who would take her away, Margie would jump rope ceaselessly, preventing my talking by insisting I count her jumps. When her preoedipal attachment to her mother (and, in the transference, to me) threatened to break through, Margie shifted to negative oedipal fantasies, still within the framework of fairy tales. She was writing her own version of *Sleeping Beauty*. When I commented that Sleeping Beauty wanted her mother to love her, she added, "Her mother loved her so much that she hated the king and got married to Sleeping Beauty."

Margie's latency defenses were breaking down quickly, and she regressed to the time when her brother had been adopted. In a long, confused, and ever shifting story, she told me first that she had a baby sister and a baby brother, and then that she had no brother, just a sister who was her baby—Mary, who was 2 or 3 years old (Margie's own age when her brother came into her life). Margie thus restored herself as a toddler and played the role of both mother and older sister to a female baby. Her regression to the inner-genital phase was in full swing. However, the influence of premature prepuberty led Margie to invent another Mary-sister-daughter, two years older than Margie was at this time.

Soon Margie's body attitude changed, and she looked like an "S," sticking out her belly and wobbling her pelvis. In addition to talking about her two sisters or children, she became preoccupied with mazes. I suggested that she wanted to know what was inside of her and how a baby fit in; she drew a maze, placing little Mary at the entrance. The end of the maze carried the inscription: "Help little Mary find her way to Dr. Kestenberg's house." Not until several years later was it possible to show Margie that she wanted to be my child.

There followed a period of resistance in which Margie yawned, went to sleep on the couch, and complained of headaches, stomachaches, and dizziness. She was grateful when the doctor to whom I sent her found her free of physical illness. She told me that I must like kids better than parents. This promising rapprochement was followed by endless play with paper dolls and Barbie dolls, getting dressed and ready for dates. When I asked her once what they were all doing, she replied: "Nothing. They are talking privately, nobody can know. I don't even know." Margie's boring repetitiousness and shallowness of affect served as a defense against the exciting secret of sexuality. About the same time, she began to defend herself against any good feelings she had toward me and especially her mother. She was undergoing a transformation from a silent and resistive child to a rude, irritable "Flegel" who threw things around to annoy me. She opened each session with the persistent demand, "I am hungry," and she ended by leaving me with a mess. Her personal appearance deteriorated. She refused to wash, comb her hair, or do her homework. She fought relentlessly with her mother and impressed both parents as stupid. Occasionally she would give me glimpses of her secret life with little Mary and big Mary, but their conversations became repetitious and diffuse, difficult to listen to.

In a way I was glad that she turned to playing games. She began to cheat and invented new rules. At home she got into arguments with girlfriends by refusing to obey the rules of games they played. However, though she was abrasive and crude, her paintings began to reveal that something much subtler was unfolding within her. Flowers were opening up, displaying languidly spreading reddish colors. A small child emerged from the flowers.

By the time Margie was 10½ she went through a brief renewal of latency. She drew houses and roads, coloring them in various shades. After a while she would interrupt this routine with outbursts of anger, or she would lapse into inertia. She did not want me to talk about anything that was not trivial; she matched each question or confrontation with a shrug of her shoulders and a stereotypic phrase: "I don't know." At home she was provocative and annoyed her father with clumsy, annoying advances. No one seemed to like her now. When she tried to be physical with me, interpretations were of no avail, but I could control her by a decisive "no" which was respected, resented, and yearned for at the same time.

At 11 her physical development proceeded by leaps and bounds. Her breasts and pubic hair were a source of shy pride, but also a burden. She got into people's way, fought with her brother, and seemed to want to get feelings from mechanical stimulation during acts of aggression or awkwardness. Sometimes she was easily offended by her friends during play outside, upon which she would trod home. Her mother could not stand looking at her sour, depressed face, so she would aggressively send her back outside. Margie felt rejected by her mother and found less solace from little Mary. Talk about chasing boys became almost her only source of exhilarated pleasure.

At 11½ Margie had numerous fantasies about associating with groups of children who had no interest in her. Both little and big Mary grew older by a year and became part of the group. She controlled her imaginary friends, making up for her helplessness in relations with children who would not listen to her. Her mother became once more the prime recipient of her nagging discontent. Margie tried to master in the present the traumas her mother had inflicted on her when she was a child under 4. At that time her mother used to ignore her and talk to her women friends. Margie then attempted to alienate her mother from some of her friends by starting quarrels with their daughters.

There then began a long phase in analysis during which Margie veered from acting out her mother's past to mirroring current idiosyncrasies of both parents. She became silent because her father was moody; soon afterward, she began to look out of the window while I talked to her. During a conference with her parents, I discovered that her mother behaved identically. Upon inquiry, I heard that this had been her characteristic when Margie was young, and the current alienation was only a small revival of the past. I was able to describe to Margie how she felt when her mother turned away from her because

I had experienced it myself when Margie treated me that way. She looked at me when I told her how much she yearned for contact with her mother, both now and in the past.

Margie began to cooperate with me in our common endeavor to improve her handwriting. Studying her movements and consulting photographs, we discovered that Margie's cramped position during writing was a carbon copy of her mother's position when she held Margie as a baby. This opened up a scrutiny of Margie's infancy and toddlerhood and led us back to her third and fourth years, in which she had failed to integrate her baby past with her big-girl self. She began to present me with material indicating thoughts about babies. Some were connected with her growing awareness of breast sensations ("bosom babies flying out") while others were anal ("the baby got into me like doodie"). Penis envy, apparent for some time, receded, but images of babies were condensed with primal scene fantasies and theories of adoption (e.g., babies flying out of their houses and fighting at night or being kidnapped).

Margie began to draw houses with girls looking out windows and with various objects inside visible to the outside. I suggested that she might want to find out what was inside her. Reluctantly, out of the corner of her eye, she looked at drawings and books about the body; at least, she admitted her interest in the route of delivery. In the midst of this unearthing, she began to renounce her imaginary sisters, projecting them upon her parents. This solution gave bizarre results which caused me a great deal of concern. Margie began to hear voices at night—voices of her parents' "real children," who came out at night but were hidden during the day. Talking about the scary noises and voices that frightened her, Margie began to draw concentric circles, as if she needed to conceptualize several layers from the outside to the inside. When we clarified that the night children represented the hidden genitals of her parents, whose noises and voices she heard, nights became more peaceful. Now she revealed in a dream that her sexual feelings were so strong that they threatened to consume her and many others unless she was rescued by a boy before her father had a chance to help her.

The new sexuality was soon followed by renewed or intensified bouts of regression. Margie was trying to seduce me with
odors in the double meaning of pregenital and genital smells.
I had to tell her that she could not come to my office literally
stinking. My interdiction had an organizing effect on the whole
regressed family. Margie's pregenital aggression had become
contagious to her mother, and both seemed to respond to an
inner excitement by nagging each other and arguing who
should clean the house. Now things became cleaner, clearer,
and less seductive. Margie's attention turned from her parents
to her peer group, both girls and boys.

Preoccupied with kissing games and finding out who
smoked tobacco or marijuana, Margie secretly yearned to belong to the group of "smoking girls" who had boyfriends. When
at 12 years and 3 months she had her first period, without pain
and without fuss, she once more denied all previously admitted
sexual knowledge. It seemed impossible at this time to approach
any subject directly. A whole group of girls and boys became
engaged in a matchmaking fever, carrying messages about a
youngster's interest in going out with a friend of the messenger.
In this manner, Margie acquired a boyfriend, one year younger
than herself.

Margie had proven by this time that she was capable of
strong feelings. She was worried when I took sick, and she
helped her mother organize things at home. However, when
she got close to being loved by a boy, she regressed and humiliated him in front of her assembled girlfriends. Her desire
to be admired by the girls overrode her feelings for the boy.
She seemed as callous as she had previously been to her mother
and brother. After the loss of the boyfriend, Margie fell back
into a degraded position in which no one liked her, and girls
humiliated her publicly. Soon she began to drown her sorrow
over the lost boyfriend in a sea of names which grew in number
as she entered junior high school. She reverted to being uncooperative at home, and her disappointed parents wanted to
discontinue her treatment.

For some time Margie complained that her mother forced
her to come see me. Faced with the choice of coming for treatment or not, with her parents offering her another chance

without insisting on it, Margie somewhat shamefacedly admitted that she wanted to continue. She embarked on a period of months in which she participated wholeheartedly in the analytic work. Her schoolwork improved, and her perennial "I don't know" was transformed into its opposite. Her body attitude had changed after menarche, and now she began to look like a young, almost fully grown woman. She wore clothes well and took care of herself. At the same time she was convinced that boys would like her if she could outwrestle them and beat them up. This did not mean she wanted to be a boy ("If I was a boy I could not have a boyfriend"). In her daydreams and in the plays she wrote, she returned to the kidnap theme, but this time she yearned to be forced to associate with groups of similarly imprisoned peers.

The theme of wanting to improve her relationship with the mother of her infancy and toddlerhood was repeatedly worked through, but the need to show her mother how deserted she was seemed to continue. I suggested to her that she should not let her mother know how she felt, as that type of restraint might help us understand her problems with peers. At once she became friendly, even gleeful. Her new behavior really brought her closer to her mother, who now enjoyed being with her. Soon she began to complain that her mother had been intruding into her social life and into her innermost feelings. True enough, her mother called me repeatedly, giving me accounts of how she questioned her daughter about her girlfriends and did not allow her to conceal her rejections. I helped her to understand the value of restraint and reported this to Margie. It became clear that Margie yielded to her mother's encouragement and would produce scenes of a rejected child in need of a mother's help. Margie began to describe her parent's squabbles with a benign condescension and tolerance and did her best to organize the family, giving them directions and helping them find adult-type solutions.

As Margie's thirteenth birthday approached, she came closer to acknowledging her sexual desires and her fears of involvement with one boy. She daydreamed about becoming a popular singer, loved by all, and rejecting all but two. She could not commit herself to one, but now she was not marrying the king and her brother, as she dreamed at the age of 9. Now she chose two contemporaries to escort her. She avoided older and more forward boys who smoked and got into trouble.

All along, Margie felt no cramps during periods and had not seen any blood clots. However, two weeks before her birthday, she reported a long dream that became the source of a continuous daydream. In one of the sequences, she and a group of boys and girls went up in the air in a plane. There was a window in the bottom of it and on top. Some boys on the ground threw a ball up and broke the lower window. Margie was afraid of falling out and fainted. Somehow, through closed doors, she came close to the opening and was rescued in time by the boy she currently liked. She pointed out that another boy, who was closer to her, would not help. When I asked Margie whether she had her period, she immediately understood that the dream related to having gotten it the night before. She looked away from me when I remarked that she was worrying about the blood coming out of her hole and connected it with her feelings about boys. In the next session, the location of her sexual excitement became the topic, and she drew question marks on a drawing of female sexual organs. She did not want to have a period and did not want to be a boy, but she would rather keep her period because she wanted babies. I had the impression that something had changed about Margie's period, that she now felt that her "hole" existed and looked upon menses as a result of penetration. The boy who did not rescue her in the dream signified her father, who had refused her advances. Margie was now close to puberty, if not in it. The removal from her oedipal father had proceeded from a fear of sexual excitement (in the previous rescue dream) to a disappointment in his reliability as a reliever of genital needs. She was becoming ready to face her mounting excitement and her fears of injury, death, and rejection.

This excerpt from a long analysis illustrates the numerous regressions and progressions of prepuberty. It begins with the transition from latency into prepuberty and ends with the transition from prepuberty into puberty. It highlights the changing vicissitudes of the young patient's preoccupations with her inside and her ways of coordinating her maternal wishes with her new genitality.

References

Ames. L., Metraux, R. W., & Walker, R. N. (1971), *Adolescent Rorschach Responses*. New York: Brunner/Mazel.
Benedek, T. (1952), *Psychosexual Functions in Women*. New York: Ronald Press.
Benson, S. (1937), *Junior Miss*. New York: Doubleday.
Blos, P. (1958), Preadolescent drive organization. *J. Amer. Psychoanal. Assn.*, 6:47–56.
——— (1962), *On Adolescence: A Psychoanalytic Interpretation*. New York: Free Press.
——— (1967), The second individuation process of adolescence. *The Psychoanalytic Study of the Child*, 22:162–186. New York: International Universities Press.
Blume, J. (1971), *Then Again Maybe I Won't*. New York: Dell.
——— (1974), *Are You There, God? It's Me, Margaret*. New York: Bradluns Press.
Botstein, P., & McArthur, J. W. (1976), Physiology of the normal female. In: *Medical Care of the Adolescent*, ed. J. R. Gallagher, F. P. Heald, & D. C. Garell. New York: Appleton-Century-Crofts, pp. 519–528.
Boyar, R., Roffwarg, H., Kapen, S., Weitzman, E., & Hellman, I. (1972), Synchronization of augmented luteinizing hormone secretion with sleep during puberty. *New Engl. J. Med.*, 287(12):582–586.
Breul, K. (1955), *Cassell's German/English Dictionary*, revised & enlarged by J. H. Lepper & R. Kottenhohn. 12th ed. London: Cassell.
Cone, T. E. (1976), Secular acceleration of height and biologic maturation. In: *Medical Care of the Adolescent*, ed. J. R. Gallagher, F. P. Heald, & D. C. Garell. New York: Appleton-Century-Crofts, pp. 87–92.
Cottle, T. J. (1972), The connection of adolescence. In: *Early Adolescence*, ed. J. Kagan & R. Coles. New York: Norton, pp. 294–336.
Delaney, J., Lupton, M. J., & Toth, E., eds. (1976), *The Curse*. New York: Dutton.
Deutsch, H. (1944), *The Psychology of Women*. Vol. 1. New York: Grune & Stratton.
——— (1967), *Selected Problems of Adolescence with Special Emphasis on Group Formation*. New York: International Universities Press.
Eissler, K. (1958), Notes on the problems of technique in the psychoanalytic treatment of adolescents: With some remarks on perversions. *The Psychoanalytic Study of the Child*, 13:223–254. New York: International Universities Press.
Erikson, E. H. (1951), Sex differences in the play configurations of preadolescents. *Amer. J. Orthopsychiat.*, 21:667–692.
——— (1959), *Identity and the Life Cycle*. New York: International Universities Press.
——— (1964), Reflections on womanhood. *Daedalus*, 2:582–606.

Fineman, J. B., & Smith, M. A. (1977), Some effects of lost adolescence: The child mothers and their babies. Unpublished paper.

Finkelstein, J. W., Roffwarg, H. P., Boyar, R. M., Kream, J., & Hellman, L. (1972), Age-related change in the 24 hour spontaneous secretion of growth hormone. *J. Clin. Endocrinol. & Metabolism*, 35:665.

Fraiberg, S. (1955), Some considerations in the introduction to therapy in puberty. *The Psychoanalytic Study of the Child*, 10:264–286. New York: International Universities Press.

——— (1972), Some characteristics of genital arousal and discharge in latency girls. *The Psychoanalytic Study of the Child*, 27:439–475. New York: Quadrangle.

Frank, A. (1947), *The Diary of a Young Girl*. New York: Doubleday, 1952.

Freud, A. (1936), *The Ego and the Mechanisms of Defense*. London: Hogarth Press.

——— (1949), On certain difficulties in the preadolescent's relation to his parents. In: *The Writings of Anna Freud*, Vol. 4. New York: International Universities Press, 1968, pp. 95–106.

——— (1958), Adolescence. *The Psychoanalytic Study of the Child*, 13:255–278. New York: International Universities Press.

——— (1965), *Normality and Pathology in Childhood*. New York: International Universities Press.

Freud, S. (1905), Three essays on the theory of sexuality. *Standard Edition*, 7:125–245. London: Hogarth Press, 1953.

——— (1923), The infantile genital organization: An interpolation into the theory of sexuality. *Standard Edition*, 19:141–145. London: Hogarth Press, 1961.

Furman, E. (1973), A contribution in assessing the role of infantile separation-individuation in adolescent development. *The Psychoanalytic Study of the Child*, 28:193–207. New Haven: Yale University Press.

Furman, R. (1973), Excerpt from the analysis of a prepuberty boy. Presented at the Baltimore/D.C./Columbus/Cleveland/Philadelphia Psychoanalytic Congress, June 1972. Abstracted in: *Bull. Phila. Assn. Psychoanal.*, 23:259.

Geleerd, E. R. (1964), Adolescence and adaptive regression. *Bull. Menn. Clin.*, 28:302–308.

Gesell, A., Ilg, F. L., & Ames, L. B. (1956), *Youth: The Years from Ten to Sixteen*. New York: Harper.

Grumbach, M. M., Roth, J. C., Kaplan, S. L., & Kelch, R. P. (1974), Hypothalamic-pituitary regulation of puberty in man: Evidence and concepts derived from clinical research. In: *The Control of the Onset of Puberty*, ed. M. M. Grumbach, G. D. Grove, & F. E. Mayer. New York: Wiley, pp. 115–166.

Hall, G. S. (1916), *Adolescence*. 2 vols. New York: Appleton.

Hamill, P. (1974), Discussion: Somatic changes in puberty. In: *The Control of the Onset of Puberty*, ed. M. M. Grumbach, G. D. Grove, & F. E. Mayer. New York: Wiley, pp. 471–472.

Hansen, K. (1978), Sex: How to explain it to the kids. *New York Daily News*, January 31, 1978.

Harley, M. (1970), On some problems of technique in the analysis of early adolescence. *The Psychoanalytic Study of the Child*, 25:99–121. New York: International Universities Press.

Hartmann, H. (1939), *Ego Psychology and the Problem of Adaptation*. New York: International Universities Press, 1958.

Inhelder, B., & Piaget, J. (1958), *The Growth of Logical Thinking from Childhood to Adolescence*. New York: Basic Books.

Jacobson, E. (1964), *The Self and the Object World*. New York: International Universities Press.

Jenner, M. R., Kelch, R. P., Kaplan, S. L., & Grumbach, M. M. (1972), Hormonal changes in puberty: IV. *J. Clin. Endocrinol. & Metabolism*, 34:521–530.

Jones, E. (1922), Some problems of adolescence. *Papers on Psychoanalysis*. 5th ed. London: Bailliere, Tindall & Cox, 1948.

Katan, A. (1935), From the analysis of a bedwetter. *Psychoanal. Quart.*, 4:120–134.

——— (1937), The role of displacement in agoraphobia. *Internat. J. Psycho-Anal.*, 32:41–50, 1951.

Kennedy, J. R. (1953), *Prince Bart*. New York: Farrar, Straus & Young.

Kestenberg, J. S. (1965), The role of movement patterns in development, I & II. *Psychoanal. Quart.*, 34:1–36; 517–563.

——— (1967a), Phases of adolescence, I & II. *J. Amer. Acad. Child Psychiat.*, 6:426–463; 577–614.

——— (1967b), The role of movement patterns in development, III. *Psychoanal. Quart.*, 36:356–409.

——— (1968a), Outside and inside, male and female. *J. Amer. Psychoanal. Assn.*, 16:457–520.

——— (1968b), Phases of adolescence, III. *J. Amer. Acad. Child Psychiat.*, 7:108–151.

——— (1970), The effect on parents of the child's transition into and out of latency. In: *Parenthood: Its Psychology and Psychopathology*, ed. E. J. Anthony & T. Benedek. Boston: Little, Brown, pp. 289–306.

——— (1971), From organ-object imagery to self and object representations. In: *Separation-Individuation: Essays in Honor of Margaret S. Mahler*, ed. J. B. McDevitt & C. F. Settlage. New York: International Universities Press, pp. 75–99.

——— (1973), Nagging, spreading excitement, arguing. *Internat. J. Psychoanal. Psychother.*, 2:265–297.

——— (1975), *Children and Parents: Psychoanalytic Studies in Development*. New York: Aronson.

——— (1980a), Ego organization in obsessive-compulsive development in the Rat Man. In: *Freud and His Patients*, ed. M. Kanzer. New York: Aronson.

——— (1980b), The three faces of femininity. *Psychoanal. Rev.*, 67:313–315.

——— (1989), Two-and-a-half to four years: From disequilibrium to integration. In: *The Course of Life*, ed. S. I. Greenspan & G. H. Pollock. Madison, CT: International Universities Press.

——— Buelte, A. (1977), Prevention and infant therapy, and the treatment of adults: I. Towards understanding mutuality; II. Mutual holding and holding oneself-up. *Internat. J. Psychoanal. Psychother.*, 6:339–396.

——— Marcus, H. (1979), Hypothetical Monosex and Bisexuality: A Psychoanalytic Interpretation of Sex Differences as They Reveal Themselves in Movement Patterns of Men and Women. In: *Psychosexual Imperative*, ed. M. C. Nelson & J. Ikenberry. New York: Human Sciences Press.

——— Robbins, E. (1975), Rhythmicity in adolescence. In: *Children and Par-*

ents: Psychoanalytic Studies in Development. New York: Aronson, pp. 411–460.

———— Sossin, M. (1979), *Movement Patterns in Development II.* New York: Dance Notation Bureau.

Kinsey, A. C., Pomeroy, W. B., & Martin, C. E. (1948), *Sexual Behavior in the Human Male.* Philadelphia: Saunders.

Kulin, H. E., & Reiter, E. O. (1973), Gonadotropins during childhood and adolescence: A review. *Pediatrics,* 51:260–271.

Laban, R. (1960), *The Mastery of Movements.* Rev. ed. London: MacDonald & Evans.

Lamb, W., & Turner, D. (1969), *Management Behavior.* New York: International Universities Press.

Lamberg, B. A., Kantero, R. L., Saarinen, P., & Widholm, O. (1973), Changes in serum-thyrotropin, thyroxine and thyroxine-binding proteins before and after menarche in healthy girls. *Acta Endocrinologica(kbh),* 177(suppl.):302.

Laufer, M. (1968), The body image, the function of masturbation, and adolescence: Problems of the ownership of the body. *The Psychoanalytic Study of the Child,* 23:114–137. New York: International Universities Press.

Mahler, M., Pine, F., & Bergman, A. (1975), *The Psychological Birth of the Human Infant.* New York: Basic Books.

Marcus, H. (1966), Personal communication.

Marshall, W. A., & Tanner, J. M. (1969), Variations in patterns of pubertal changes in girls. *Arch. Dis. of Children,* 44:291.

Morley, C. (1939), *Kitty Foyle.* New York: Grosset & Dunlap.

Piaget, J., & Inhelder, B. (1969), *The Psychology of the Child.* New York: Basic Books.

Ramsden, P. (1973), *Top Team Planning: A Study of the Power of Individual Motivation in Management.* New York: Wiley.

Reiter, E. O., & Root, A. W. (1975), Hormonal changes of adolescence. *Med. Clin. N. Amer.,* 59(6):1289–1304.

Richardson, D. W., & Short, R. V. (1978), The time of onset of sperm production in boys. *J. Biosocial Science,* 10(Suppl.):15–25.

Root, A. W. (1973), Endocrinology of puberty. *J. Pediatrics.* 83:1–9.

Sarnoff, C. (1976), *Latency.* New York: Aronson.

Saxena, B. B., Malva, R., Leyendecker, G., & Gandy, H. M. (1972), Further characterization of the radio-immunoassay of human pituitary FSH. In: *Gonadotropins,* ed. B. B. Saxena, C. G. Beling, & H. M. Gandy. New York: Wiley, pp. 399–416.

Schonfeld, W. A. (1943), Primary and secondary sexual characteristics: Study of their development in males from birth through maturity. *Amer. J. Disturbed Children,* 65:535–549.

Sonek, M. (1967), Vaginal cytology during puberty. *Acta Cytologica,* 11:41–44.

Spiegel, L. A. (1951), A review of contributions to a psychoanalytic theory of adolescence: Individual aspects. *The Psychoanalytic Study of the Child,* 6:375–393. New York: International Universities Press.

Steffens, L. (1931), *The Autobiography of Lincoln Steffens.* New York: Harcourt, Brace & World.

Tanner, J. M. (1962), *Growth at Adolescence.* Oxford: Blackwell.

————— (1970), Physical growth. In: *Carmichael's Manual of Child Psychology*, Vol. 1, ed. P. H. Mussen. 3rd ed. New York: Wiley, pp. 77–155.

Wermer, H., & Lewin, S. (1967), Masturbation fantasies: Their changes with growth and development. *The Psychoanalytic Study of the Child*, 22:315–328. New York: International Universities Press.

Wilkins, L. (1965), *The Diagnosis and Treatment of Endocrine Disorders in Childhood and Adolescence*. Springfield, IL.: Charles C Thomas.

Winter, J. S., & Faiman, C. (1972), Pituitary-gonadal relations in male children and adolescents. *Pediatric Res.*, 6:126–135.

————— (1973), Pituitary-gonadal relations in female children and adolescents. *Pediatric Res.*, 7:948–953.

3

The Pubescent Years: Eleven to Fourteen

MORRIS A. SKLANSKY, M.D.

Adolescence may be said to begin with pubescence. In no other phase of development is the direct correlation of the physiological with the psychological as obvious as it is here (Kestenberg, 1967). Pubescence or puberty is a critical physical maturational process that profoundly affects personality development and initiates adolescence. Hormonal secretions produce physical changes and psychological reactions which, though universal, are novel and remarkable to the growing child. Reactions to pubescence—both by the child and by others—are crucial and in part determine the subsequent course of personality development and life.

The physiological process of pubescence occurs approximately during the first two to four years of the second decade of life, within the range of 9 to 14 years of age. It begins with the secretion of hormones that specifically differentiate the genders. According to a maturational timing, the hypothalamus secretes gonadotrophin-releasing hormones which act on the pituitary to effect the secretion of gonadotrophins. In turn the gonads are activated to produce testosterone in males and estrogens in females. There is evidence that testosterone, in much smaller proportion, is produced also in girls. The pituitary also releases the growth hormone, whose effect is to produce the well-known "growth spurt" of pubescence (Karp, 1977, p. 25).

Although pubescent physical changes and some specific psychological reactions to them will be presented first, it should be kept in mind that these reactions are best understood in the context of the total psychological development that takes place at this time. Reactions to body parts are meaningful only in the framework of the early adolescent's self-image, which includes his body image.

Other aspects of early adolescent development must be looked at in the same overall context. Pubescence produces profound changes in the nature of object relations, in drive intensities, and in the narcissistic equilibrium in the self. These modifications lead the early adolescent into a deidealization of parental imagos, instigating a shift to extrafamilial objects, including peers, and to heterosexual object relating. Throughout pubescence, the young adolescent experiences an intensified drive for autonomy which, though essential for maturation, may lead him into maladaptive behavior.

Physical Changes and Psychological Reactions

The first sign of pubescence in girls is the beginning of tumescence ("budding") of the breasts; in boys it is testicular enlargement.

The characteristic physical changes are traditionally categorized as primary and secondary sex characteristics. Primary characteristics are those directly involved in coitus and reproduction: the internal reproductive organs and the external genitalia. Secondary characteristics do not definitively differentiate the sexes; they may be shared in varying degree by both genders. Thus, enlarged breasts may occasionally occur in boys, and facial hair may grow thickly for some girls. Normally, however, the differences between the sexes in both primary and secondary sex characteristics are great enough to be universally acknowledged and to arouse psychological reactions to them in all adolescents.

In describing these pubescent changes and the psychological reactions to them, one recognizes that the hormonal increment exerts a disequilibrating effect on the relatively cohesive personality integration of latency. The latency structure is loosened, and there are frequent breakthroughs into consciousness of previously repressed impulses and fantasies: the "return of the repressed" (Freud, 1939). The new experiences, so bodily in content, are experienced with primary process quality and are accompanied by pregenital phase associations.

When menarche occurs, adolescent girls commonly react with dystonic affect. The first menses may come as a surprise and be embarrassingly evident to others—e.g., blood on clothing. The girl feels, to her embarrassment, that she has revealed a previously prohibited function or behavior. Commonly what is thought to be revealed is the arrival of mature femaleness with all its sexual implications. The adolescent girl feels that through her menarche she exposes that she is now capable of sexual acts and childbearing—oedipally prohibited wishes. An infantile castration fantasy underlies the anxious thought that she may be wounded in some unknown way. A resurgence of the primitive maternal superego is evident additionally, in thoughts of suffering a disease or of now being afflicted with "the curse." This common phrase denoting the menses, while often acknowledged as only a figure of speech, nevertheless indicates an age-old history of anxiety, awe, and prejudice related to this primary female function. Cloacal fantasies from the anal phase are evoked and arouse reactions of revulsion and disgust at the menstrual flow. Not infrequently young girls at first hide the evidence of their menses. Occasionally there may be unconscious denial of the menses. For a smaller number of adolescent girls, menarche may be greeted with a sense of achievement and fulfillment (Kirstein, 1977). Clinical experience in psychoanalysis and psychotherapy would indicate, however, that such positive reactions are still rare, and even when one is observed the possibility of a counterphobic defensive orientation must be considered. It may be that a favorable change in the cultural attitude toward women will ultimately effect a more positive attitude in girls toward their menses.

The pubescent male's first ejaculation is reacted to similarly. It, too, may occur as a surprise (e.g., in exercise, as a noctural emission, or as a spontaneous emission in masturbatory acts). While most boys have already learned (usually from their peers) of the nature of ejaculation, the sudden sequence of spasms in the genitourinary system, the wetness, and the viscosity of the ejaculate are all subjectively unfamiliar, and previously repressed fantasies of bleeding or damage (castration) and disgust reactions to the "excretum" (anal phase association) may occur. For each adolescent the pregenital associations depend on his unique history, though a certain commonality of such fantasies is revealed in clinical experience. (When the adolescent is unenlightened by accurate information, whether from parent, school, or peers, fantasies of pregenital origin are the only information he has, and are usually accompanied by anxiety. Misconceptions about the nature of semen, menses, conception, and pregnancy abound among early adolescents, are reactivated in this phase, and may exist side by side with facts gleaned from sex education courses.) Yet for some boys, this proof of adult masculinity is a phallic narcissistic gratification.

Regarding the external primary sex characteristics, the early adolescent girl is less aware of changes than is the boy. Her comparatively greater difficulty in visualizing the external genitalia and an almost complete lack of correct anatomical information foster the continuation of infantile and childhood misconceptions and imagery. Education for little girls about their anatomy is minimal. Few are aware of the changes in the labia, the enlargement of the introitus, and the changes in the character of the mucous membrane of the vulva and the vagina. Nevertheless, in early adolescence girls respond with "wetness" to excitatory fantasies and contacts. Orgasmic spasms may occur. At first, such responses produce anxiety. Not uncommonly, as for the first menses, the girl wonders if she has had a loss of urinary control or a discharge due to some disease. But the early adolescent girl soon becomes fully aware of the pleasurable sensations in the genital area. Conflict over sexual excitation will of course result in shame over sexual wishes. Preoedipal and oedipal phase fantasies about the nature of their genitals are common in girls—e.g., the universal cloacal fantasy of a common outlet for urine, feces, and babies, and castration fantasies of a lost penis, a damaged little penis (the clitoris), a penis torn from its roots, etc.

Few adolescent girls admire their genitals, as boys do theirs. For many, penis envy is literal and specific (Ritvo, 1976). Commonly, adolescent girls react to the thought or the sight of their genitals with degrees of disgust varying from dislike to revulsion. These affectively laden attitudes derive from the disgust of the anal phase. These attitudes may exist concomitantly with pleasurable excitations felt in the genital area. They become clinically significant when they lead to frigidity or when they are part of a more general debasement of the self as woman.

The pubescent boy, by contrast, is fully aware of the changes that take place in his genitals. He can readily visualize these changes, both directly and in the mirror. The penis becomes elongated and widened. The scrotum becomes looser and longer, the testes larger. While most pubescent boys take pride in this development, it may be accompanied by embarrassment if the unconscious (or conscious) implications of potential for masturbatory and coital pleasure are conflicted. The penis is now highly sensitive to stimuli, both intrapsychic and external. Ejaculations, both spontaneous and masturbatory, are now frequent.

Young adolescent males are much preoccupied with the size of the penis, and comparisons are made regularly, whenever exposure and examination are possible. For most adolescent boys these may be conscious though unspoken. But many adolescents are raucous and teasing about this highly cathected subject. Those whose penises are small may be subject to ridicule, as may those whose penises are viewed as too large, the latter implying excessive masturbation. The unconscious concept that the large paternal penis is more satisfying to the woman lingers on into adolescence, carried over from the oedipal phase and its competitive strivings. Knowledge of the accommodative capacity of the vagina and of the more complex relationship interests of the female is not achieved until later in adolescence and in any case does little to dispel this phallic narcissistic concern, even in adult males.

For most young adolescent boys the phallic narcissism involved is maintained, if necessary, by isolation of the distressing affects or by compensatory mechanisms in the development of alternative phallic skills—athletics, intellectual interests, etc. When he feels his penis is too small, the young adolescent does not yet compensate for his sense of masculine inadequacy by an exaggerated heterosexuality; rather, he is more likely to avoid sexual encounters and exposures for fear of rejection and ridicule.

Concern about penile adequacy becomes of clinical significance when it causes the young adolescent to isolate himself from peers, to avoid gymnasium, swimming, and other possible occasions for exposure. As the young adolescent begins to develop heterosexual interest and to seek encounters, an anxious preoccupation may be sufficiently intense to prevent this next developmental step. Frequently the preoccupation is simply a focal point within the area of a broader narcissistic vulnerability, indicating low self-esteem and a defective sense of self. Upward displacement to the nose of the unconscious fantasy of the small (castrated) penis may lead a young adolescent boy to request rhinoplasty even when his nose is not misshapen. Such requests should be carefully investigated for the possibility of psychopathology. The small penis complaint may indicate a persisting unresolved oedipal conflict or a situation in which a passive oedipal resolution is maintained.

Pubescence is usually followed by the onset of genital masturbation or an increase in its frequency (Sklansky, 1958, 1965). It is now acknowledged that girls masturbate in latency as well as in adolescence (Clower, 1976). Nevertheless, adolescent girls, like latency girls, masturbate less frequently than do males. Manual clitoral stimulation and the use of phallic-shaped items for insertion are common methods. Adolescent boys masturbate frequently, usually manually. Once a source of the greatest anxiety, condemned by church, medicine, other helping professions, parents, and peers (Hall, 1904, p. 432), masturbation is today practiced with greater equanimity, at least by a majority of boys. Shame and guilt reactions are still common, however, because the fantasies accompanying masturbation are unconsciously oedipal.

Specific reactions to masturbation depend on individual psychosexual development. Girls may masturbate to resolve penis envy (Ritvo, 1976), overcome castration fantasies, indulge masochistic fantasies, or discharge less specific tensions associated with narcissistic personality problems. Similarly, boys usually masturbate with heterosexual fantasies in mind. But compulsive masturbation may occur, in both sexes, out of a sense of narcissistic defect, castration anxiety, gender confusion, etc. Autoerotic excitation provides some reassurance against fragmentation (in seriously disturbed adolescents) or personality disintegration (schizophrenia, psychosis). Masturbation in all instances is the individual's attempt to provide a maximum erotic sensation experience, to provide pleasure, and to discharge tensions of varying origin.

The secondary sex characteristics, readily available to public inspection and commentary, are the basis of common interest, attention, and concern to the pubescent child. Peer approbation has been important from the latency years on, and now the narcissistic mirroring (Kohut, 1971) or reflective-appraisal (Sullivan, 1953) previously provided by the parents is sought from peers. Being accepted by them, being one of them, and being "popular" with them are conscious wishes of great significance. Consequently, peer opinion of secondary sex characteristics is the basis for the adolescent's reaction to them. In eary adolescence, an interest in being desirable to the heterosexual object is present, though with conflict, and the quality of the secondary sex characteristics as part of the ideal, sexually desirable body and of the self-image carries grave import. Thus, intensified sexual impulses provide the underlying motivating force which engenders the concern about the secondary sex characteristics. In addition, the rapidity of physical changes is disequilibrating to the previously formed body image and creates experiences of anxious unfamiliarity or even fragmentation in vulnerable adolescents. Tensions, adequately contained by prior body and self-image formations, are reactivated.

Although secondary sex characteristics in general differentiate the sexes, they are, as indicated above, not definitively differential, but rather only statistically so. Hence, in many instances they may be common to both sexes. This observation is important in alleviating the anxieties some adolescents may have about characteristics which they are convinced are signs of the sex opposite their own.

The earliest change in secondary sex characteristics is in the breast. Usually, of course, the greater breast changes occur in girls. There is local enlargement of the glandular tissue, the accumulation of fat, and change in the elevation of the areola surrounding the enlarged nipple. In some males, too, in early pubescence, there is some change in the breast—usually slight tumescence—due to the precipitous hormonal imbalance. Because unresolved gender identity may continued into adolescence in some children, these boys are often made anxious by the change, thinking they might "turn into a girl." There is, however, a rapid realignment in hormonal proportions, so that no further enlargement takes place. Boys tending toward obesity may have the appearance of female breast formation. In older adolescent males, gynecomastia (female breast formation) may develop from the extensive use of marijuana. But only a true physiological hermaphroditic male would have breasts with glandular tissue capable of lactation.

Adolescent girls suffer from having breats whose size is at variance with the acceptable style of any particular period. These styles may change cyclically from voluptuous to flat to voluptuous, etc. Early maturing girls may have enlarged breasts prior to their age mates, and boys in early adolescence or pre-adolesence react with embarrassment and tension to these girls. Short girls with large breasts are unhappy about this feminine attribute. But later, in middle and late adolescence, the girls who are flat-chested are the ones who feel unhappy. Of course, it is not its nurturant significance but, rather, the breast as sexual symbol in our culture that underlies this distress. Some girls in pubescence deny the development of breasts, even when they are obvious to all, and refuse to wear bras. Others wear extra sweaters or tight shirts, hoping to hide the development. But there are also eager adolescent girls who long for adult status and may plead for bras and wear them long before this is necessary.

Hair is another characteristic of great significance for adolescents. Hirsutism, hairiness on parts of the body other than the head or pubes, is sometimes distressing to girls who feel they have too much of it. Not only is it considered unattractive, but it may arouse bisexual anxieties. A similar problem exists for adolescent boys; those whose facial hair is sparse may feel themselves lacking in masculinity. Some adolescent boys, fearing growth into adult sexuality, deny their beard and avoid shaving. Occasionally, adolescent girls may deny the presence of facial and body hair, or feel that to remove such hair cosmetically is to give in to male chauvinist views of femininity.

The pubic hair appears simultaneously with the first bodily changes. Although not insignificant as a psychological sign of maturation and sexuality, it is mentioned infrequently in analysis and therapy. The shape of the "escutcheon" is different in males and females but is seldom discussed.

Another change is that in the "scent" and sweat glands. The genders share these changes almost equally. The apocrine or scent glands develop to function more profusely in the genital area in pubescence and are occasionally problematic. However, it is the sebaceous glands that are of greater concern to adolescents. For when these glands enlarge and their pores remain small, the accumualted secretion is subject to infection and darkening at the surface. "Blackheads" and "pimples"—acne vulgaris—may be the result. Adolescents, concerned as they are about sexual attractiveness, go to great lengths to cure this condition. For some, acne carries the connotation of excessive masturbation, of "unclean" sexual thoughts and feelings, now revealed for all the world to see.

The voice changes in both sexes, but the enlargement of the larynx and the lengthening of the vocal cords are greater in males, so that the pitch of their voices is much lower. In any case, even high-pitched male voices differ in quality from most female voices. There are many jokes among adolescent boys about high-pitched voice, castration, emasculation, and femininity—all to be feared.

A sudden increase in height takes place early in pubescence. This "growth spurt" is due to the effect of the increased secretion of pituitary growth hormone. In girls it usually occurs somewhere between 11 and 12; in boys, a little later, about 14 to 15. The rapidity of the growth spurt is in itself disturbing to the body image and may explain the physical awkwardness of some adolescents. However, height has phallic-narcissistic significance for both sexes. In Western culture, especially the United States, a premium is placed on height, and studies have shown that tall men are statistically more successful in achieving executive and leadership positions, as well as being considered more sexually attractive to females. Consequently, short adolescent boys suffer feelings of inferiority on this account alone. Girls generally prefer to be shorter than their male companions. However, each generation of girls tends to be taller than the previous, and being a very short girl may be as much a source of narcissistic vulnerability as being too tall. Generally, the oedipal configuration of little girl and big daddy is preferred.

With growth comes increased strength as well as change in muscle and bone structure. Although it is now postulated "that the female has the same potential for strength development as the male of comparable size" (Douglas and Miller, 1977), after puberty there is still a widening disparity between males and females in athletic ability and strength. It is not altogether settled whether this disparity has a strictly physiological basis or is the effect of a stereotyped image of femininity engendered in little girls. Although the women's liberation movement has brought about some change in this area many girls at puberty are still likely to relinquish athletic interests, while boys continue and even increase their interest in athletics. It will be of interest to note the effect of the ongoing cultural press toward equalization of the sexes.

Adolescent males, with few exceptions, value muscular prowess. Their preoccupation with muscular development and with athletics is often as constant as it is with sex. We can see in weight lifting, an activity rarely of interest beyond the adolescent years, a concomitance of two interests—prowess and body shape. The interest in all this muscle power and appearance is often an upward displacement from concern with the potency and size of the penis. Certainly the adolescent male is interested in his sexual attractiveness, and his female compeers are naturally attracted to the shape, size, and tautness of his muscles. Small adolescent boys suffer painfully if they are lacking in this area, and frequently they compensate by developing their muscles excessively. If this is not possible, they then compensate in nonphysical areas of achievement. Adolescent boys who are fearful of appearing feminine because of shape and size or who are reactive to latent homosexual tendencies may defend themselves by exaggerated development of their muscles. Girls by and large are not so much interested in the long muscles of their own bodies. A girl with boylike musculature may be concerned about inadequate femininity and gender identity. Homosexual girls may be happier with such a physique or be attracted to girls who have one. Girls with these physiques are often latently or overtly homosexual, but by no means always. Differences in body shape due to the size of the muscles, fat distribution, and widening of the pelvis all go to define the gender aspect of body image, and if the difference is insufficient or extreme, one may expect untoward psychological reactions in the adolescent, sometimes of clinical significance.

The anxiety of insufficient gender difference in the young adolescent is based on the unsettling of the specific gender identity established in latency and the pubertal stirring of the bisexuality of prelatency development. The definition of self-image includes gender definition, and a narcissistic investment in the specific gender contributes to cohesion of the self. Unconsciously, intrapsychic bisexuality continues from infancy throughout development. In most children the specific gender definition is maintained with concomitant anticathexis or defense against opposite-sex aspects of this pregenital bisexuality. Latency, preadolescent, and early adolescent boys taunt girls, even avoid their company, and fear being labeled "sissy." Girls who pride themselves on their achieved femininity and who have repressed their penis envy act similarly to protect their gender identity prior to development of heterosexual longings. When body changes do not fit the essential gender body images, as described, the anxiety of insufficient gender difference is aroused in pubescence.

The implications may be far-reaching. Regression to bisexuality and other gender positions may evoke a regressive passive relationship to the same-sex parent, temporarily for most adolescents, and a regressive fixation for some, with pathological consequences. Passivity longings may include infantile regression of a preoedipal nature with an even more maladaptive quality. Fortunately for most adolescents, there are sufficient defensive and adaptive mechanisms to foster maintenance of cohesion and maturation.

In early adolescence the stress of puberty undermines the security of previously established gender identity. But defenses set in quickly to prevent disintegration into bisexual components and homosexual resolution. Commonly boys engage in nonserious homosexual play. There is also some homosexual activity among girls. Neither is necessarily an indication of a homosexual outcome. Concern about being too much like a member of the opposite sex does intrude into consciousness. In response, girls may exaggerate their behavior into a pseudofemininity; boys, into machismo. At camp, early adolescents may engage in homosexual liaisons, usually of a temporary nature. Periodically, those destined to have a homosexual outcome in character development may find the partner and the experience which introduce them to it and thus serve to satisfy essential personality and relationship needs.

While these specific psychological reactions to pubescent changes are in themselves highly significant in adolescent development, they are to be understood more fully in the context of the adolescent's self-image. The adolescent's awkwardness and discomfort with a "new body" in its various aspects are an outcome of the incongruity between a previously developed image as a latency child, including the modified infantile and early childhood self-images, and this new image. The image of the body and its parts comes to be part of the total self-image, both as to gender and ideal self. It is that aspect of the total self-image which is presented to the world to see. For adolescents that image may represent, adequately or not, their gender, their worth, their sexual and social self, and their ambitions in the world and in relation to others. We shall discuss these further below.

Object Relations and Drive Increment in the Young Adolescent

Pubescent physiological changes are comparatively sudden and upset the relative hormonal homeostasis of latency and preadolescence. The relative drive quiescence of latency (Sarnoff, 1976) and the characterological equilibrium in the personality are affected by this hormonal increment. Included among these effects is the nature of object relations. The latency equilibrium is brought about by the repression of the Oedipus complex (Freud, 1905, p. 178). That complex involved the parent of the opposite sex as the object of sexual strivings, and ambivalent feelings for the rivalrous parent of the same sex. Sexual interest in the same-sex parent was active, though transient. Identification with the latter parent and the superego attitudes of that parent became part of the defensive and characterological outcome in latency personality formation.

The intensification of drive in pubescence acts upon the latency personality structure to loosen it and to cause once again a surge of intensified libidinal investment in the repressed oedipal objects. Young adolescents may experience transitory conscious erotic fantasies and feelings about the oedipal parent (Werman, 1977). Often these incestuous fantasies appear in dreams. When they are quite conscious and explicit, they arouse reactive anxiety, shame, or guilt, and are almost immediately defended against by denial, rationalization, humor, etc., and are quickly repressed again. Sometimes they appear in masturbation fantasies and are similarly defended against. Adolescent behavior is evidence for this reactivation of the oedipal conflict. Girls begin to find it quite uncomfortable to sit on Daddy's lap or even to be touched in a friendly fashion by their fathers. Aware of the father now as a male sexual being, they are uncomfortable about his sexual expressions with them or with others, including their own mothers. Suppressing their own great curiosity, they prefer that the parents keep their sexual lives private.

There are, however, some adolescent girls who, by use of defensive mechanisms, can permit rather close physical contact with their fathers. We imagine that such defensive safeguards permit the pubescent to get through this sensitive reincarnation of the Oedipus complex and that many girls go on to further maturation and "normal" development. When such girls come to analysis, they reveal that the defensive stand was not perfect, and their rediscovery of intimate feelings and fantasies is accompanied by reactive distressing affects.

The situation is similar for boys. They may "kid" with their mothers, make innuendos, and suggestive remarks, always denying (to those who ask as well as to themselves) that they have any sexual interest in their mothers. Defensively, they find their mothers "old-fashioned," dressing "funny," etc. They may also, like the girls, react with easy irritability to any interactions which suggest too much involvement with the parent as oedipal object.

Nevertheless, boys are more comfortable with their mothers than with their fathers during this phase of adolescence, reflecting a sensitivity to paternal superego and castration anxiety. Some adolescents in this early phase fear their mothers (Blos, 1970). The image of the mother is split into the mother as pregenital object and the mother as sexual object. The pubescent boy, like the oedipal boy, sees his father as a potential rival and castrator.

Pubescent girls relate ambivalently to their mothers. The mother is reacted to as rival and depriver of autonomy, and intruder on developing adult femininity. The constant bickering with the mother seen in many pubescent girls is a derivative of the reawakened image of the oedipal mother as a superego image.

Erotic excitation in young adolescents is always on the edge of awareness, yet in contrast to older adolescents they deal with it tentatively and defensively. Young adolescent males become suddenly conscious of the turn of a woman's ankle, her explicitly sexual configuration, and her physical attractiveness as sexual object. Young adolescent boys are aroused by sexual imagery, and they burn with longing for sexual contact. But these feelings and thoughts are commonly kept secret. To others, including peers, they may contain the intensities by common peer group defensive modes—teasing, joking, bragging, etc. The young adolescent is not yet comfortable with members of the opposite sex, though usually there is not total avoidance. There is much interaction at a distance. Heterosexual contacts which are approved of socially, by peers or adults, may be engaged in ambivalently.

In most of the subcultures in our society there is a more suppressed sexual interest among young adolescent girls. They, like the boys, subjectively take note of the opposite sex—their faces, their musculature, their hips, and their genital area. They are curious about the nature of sexual experience. But there is less talk about sex among girls than among adolescent boys, and in early adolescence there is still a major sublimatory press in girls, who are consequently more involved in scholastic and creative interests than are their male age mates.

However, girls more readily indulge in romantic fantasies about heterosexual objects and begin to elaborate fantasies of fulfillment in the future. For some adolescent girls, object involvement takes priority over scholastic and vocational interest, and for these girls a decreasing interest and success in school become evident. Exceptions are always found among those for whom sublimations were already active or in the process of development prior to adolescence. Freud (1929) thought of women as having little capacity for sublimation. But it may be that the cultural relegation of girls to "küche, kinder, und kirche" of the Victorian period was the basis for his observation and conclusion. How much the recent change in cultural attitudes (toward an expectation that girls may achieve intellectually, academically, vocationally, etc., as much as boys) will indeed bring about psychological change in girls remains to be seen.

However, for both sexes in this phase of adolescence, the object shift from familial to extrafamilial persons is evident though still tentative, while the detachment from the parents as oedipal objects is a phase-specific issue.

Narcissistic Equilibrium in Early Adolescence

Young adolescents begin to suffer the narcissistic vulnerability characteristic of the entire adolescent phase (Spiegel, 1951). Again we may attribute the onset of this disruption in the cohesion of the latency structure to the hormonal increment of pubescence. The altered physiological state intensifies drive tensions. Tension-regulating mechanisms achieved previously are no longer adequate to the task of maintaining the integration and cohesion of the personality. The narcissistic equilibrium is upset concomitantly. Young adolescents have yet to experience an adequate assessment of their own talents and capacities and rely on the opinions and evaluations of their elders at home and at school. Few of them have specific educational and vocational goals to reify ego ideal and identity.

Consequently, they are subject to the variations in mood which result from unstable self-definition. Compensatory grandiosity in fantasy and behavior alternates with periods of low self-esteem and a sense of fragility. Irritability, argumentativeness, and withdrawal from offending objects are common. Adolescents fortunate enough to have a consuming talent, a definite goal, or a preadolescent history of constant positive narcissistic internalizations will be less vulnerable than others. But few adolescents are so cohesive in their integration and so stable in their narcissistic gratifications that they are without some degree of vulnerability in their sense of self (Kohut, 1971).

Deidealization and Its Effects on Personality Structure

In this early phase of adolescence, deidealization of the parent comes to the fore. During latency the infantile grandiosity attributed to the parent (idealization) had found its denouement, along with the resolution of the oedipal conflict, in its transmutation by identification with the same-sex object, superego internalization, and ego ideal formation. The latency child maintains his actual parent in the necessary position of being the object for externalization of these internal imagos. Yet the actual parents are related to with an optimal degree of neutrality, so that the conduct of the routines of latency life at home, school, etc., is relatively stable.

But in early adolescence cognitive maturation, increased experience with other adults, and an internal repellent force against the infantile and oedipal objects combine to make it possible for the adolescent to react to the limitations and faults of the parents with annoyed disappointment. The reaction is to the incongruity between the real parent and the internal idealized parent imago. For most adolescents this deidealization is in the service of ego development and autonomy. For some the reaction may be one of depression, loss of self-esteem, or even diffusion in the sense of identity. That the deidealization serves an intrapsychic growth process, rather than being simply an accurate assessment of the reality of the parent, is evident from the frequent exaggeration of parental faults and the amount of affect that accompanies the faultfinding. Of course, parents naturally do not react amiably to this process of deidealization, especially if they are unaware of its significance as part of the adolescent growth process.

The deidealization of the parent in the early adolescent phase often makes for familial disharmony. But it makes it possible for the adolescent to reevaluate and restructure the latency superego, to modify the ego ideal, to include a larger variety of new, extrafamilial values, and on this basis to develop, in late adolescence, a more adaptive character synthesis (Gitelson, 1948).

The deidealization leaves the adolescent character structure temporarily in a state of disequilibrium. The latency superego and ego ideal gross and unsophisticated as they may have been, had served for ego control and goal setting. The positive narcissistic affects aroused in their successful function provided the necessary motivation. Now with these structures deidealized, controls and direction are temporarily nonfunctional, and the adolescent character integration is in some jeopardy. A solid sense of cohesion and narcissistic fulfillment is absent. The state of disequilibrium is highly dystonic and can be endured for only short periods. Consequently, a variety of ego mechanisms are quickly activated to prevent its continuation and further disintegration or fragmentation. These ego defensive mechanisms may be regressive and maladaptive. Yet it must be recognized that they may be ultimately in the service of individuation and autonomy (see below).

The adolescent in this early phase has a nonspecifically defined sense of self. Having momentarily put aside the specific latency attributes of superego and ego ideal, he has little settled content as to the values and goals which are his own. Periodic indulgence in infantile gradiose fantasy alternates with compliance to parental and other adult-imposed values and rationales for compliance.

The identity of the young adolescent (Erikson, 1956, 1959) is still very much defined by the same specific familial and cultural factors that had contributed to the child in his latency years. His values are those of his parents. His ego ideal and superego encompass the internalization of representations from his relationship to them throughout the first decade of life. The immediate surround of the community provides the definition for social identity. And yet the seams of character structure, integrated sense of self, and the inner definition of identity are being pulled at by the stress of the burgeoning instinctual increment of pubescence. The effect of pubescence and the psychological effort to maintain the personality structure in the face of it account for the psychology of the early phase of adolescence.

The regression to grandiose fantasy may be in the service of maturation in some adolescents by motivating them to engage in pursuits that ultimately will be of characterological value. These adolescents may become creative, scientific, studious, athletic, political, etc. But when the grandiose fantasy is resorted to without attempts at fulfillment in activity, or when they are so far out of the realm of the realizable, pathological disorders, including even psychosis, may be the outcome.

The Significance of the Peer Group

The deidealization of superego in conjunction with peer group influences may lead to instinct gratification of a maladaptive nature, as in the group delinquency so common in this early adolescent phase.

Peer group values are highly influential, filling the gap left by the abrogation of previous parental values. Sometimes, under fortunate circumstances provided by the social environment of the adolescent, such peer group influence may be socially desirable—athletic teams, music groups, religious activities, and various scouting, hiking, artistic, and other groupings. But the peer group, even among very well-brought-up adolescents may sometimes influence the individual to engage in socially abhorrent activities—mischief, destructive acts, drug abuse, etc. Peer-prescribed activities, however, tend to provide a system of values and modes of behavior for a large number of young adolescents. Indeed, Bronfenbrenner (quoted in Byrne, 1977) asserts that a large proportion of American adolescents are more influenced by the peer culture than by the adults in their lives. While he attributes this phenomenon to an insufficient participation of adults in the life of the young adolescent, it should also be recognized that the intrapsychic restructuring which takes place during this period presses the adolescent to choose his peers over the adults in his life.

Without the previously formed ego ideal to direct and motivate his activities, the young adolescent may find himself disinterested in activities the adult world has established to prepare the young person for adult life, especially education. That vacuum may also be invaded by peer group influences. However, the young adolescent may turn to others as well. Various adults in reality or in fantasy and fiction may become alternative ego ideals—teachers, scout and church leaders, therapists, and heroes in literature, on television, and in the movies. These figures may be idealized, usually for several years during the adolescent period.

Both superego and ego ideal are revised during later adolescence and take on a more adaptive and reality-determined form.

While the infant, oedipal, and latency child depended largely on parental empathy, approval, and admiration for narcissistic gratification of the self, the young adolescent begins to displace this function onto extrafamilial objects as well. He is still susceptible to the effect that his parents may have on him, but he turns now more to other adults and, of course, his peers.

To be popular among his peers is a major goal for the young adolescent. Not being accepted by an idealized peer group can be excruciatingly painful and a blow to the adolescent's narcissism. It is therefore obvious that the group now serves the function of providing an admirable sense of self and self-esteem. Rejection by the peer group may be a sufficient trauma to lead to depression and isolation. During these years, the empathic, admiring responses of the real parents may be helpful but insufficient, for the displacement of the self-admiring function onto peers has taken priority. Age and sex equality make for easier identification and mutual empathy among peers. The peer group phenomena in early adolescence serve compensatory, defensive, and often adaptive purposes.

Adolescent Love

The extrafamilial object shift which now becomes intensified ultimately leads to adolescent love. While love during the course of adolescent development is among the most passionate experiences of life, in actuality it undergoes several modifications during the adolescent phase before crystallization into young adult heterosexual love. In analysis love is revealed to be a highly complex affect state which imbricates narcissistic, sexual, and aggressive drives. The object of these drives may be a composite of object imagos from all or several phases of development or one chosen from an intrapsychically preferred object imago from a specific phase.

In early adolescence it is possible to observe love in its still unamalgamated drive and object components. Early adolescents are often aware of a desire to be in love, the object not yet chosen. They may also be more specific and feel intense erotic desire, with the character of the object nonspecific. Following the effects of deidealization of the parental imagos, we observe that the need for continued idealization of an object can be fulfilled in the love experience.

Idealization may thus be displaced now onto extrafamilial loved objects. In early adolescence, secret and unspoken love affairs may include an idealization of the loved one which may be more intensely felt than the erotic longing for the object. For boys of this age, this can rarely be admitted to peers, and the boys act toward girls in the teasing and avoiding manner described above. Girls, too, avoid the loved one but are more able to sustain thoughts and fantasies of a love relationship and to describe them to friends, diaries, and therapists. While the object is idealized, sexual desire may be suppressed as inappropriate to feel for the exalted person, reminiscent of the repression of sexual impulse in the oedipal phase. These relationships may be very intense and preoccupying, yet the sexuality is not conscious. Witness the idealization of rock stars in the present era and of the heroes of story, stage, and screen in the past.

Nevertheless, the libidinal component in the love affairs and infatuations, repressed though it may be, lends an affective intensity to the idealization, so that one finds it difficult to separate the affects of exaltation from those of erotic involvement in these young adolescents. Neither unmitigated sexual desire for the object nor the acceptance of sexuality as a necessary component of a heterosexual relationship is fully acknowledged in this early phase of adolescence (Sklansky, 1977).

Within the past decade, there has been an increase in sexual behavior among adolescents generally. While adolescents in the early phase of this period have also been subjected to this cultural "permissiveness," their increased sexual behavior is more in conformity with peer group expectation and challenge than it is with a true inner longing for heterosexual involvement. Consequently, increased sexual activity in early adolescence can be understood as a narcissistic issue rather than an object-instinctual drive necessity. The young adolescent wants to be accepted and admired by his peers and engages in the sex act to fulfill that need.

In vulnerable adolescents the need for the maintenance of a sense of worth and self-cohesion may force them into sexual activities in which they may experience compensatory contact, warmth, and admiration from the sexual partner (Sklansky, 1977).

Autonomy

In early adolescence, intrapsychic separation from the parental objects of infancy and the assertion of autonomy begin a process of individuation which will not be complete until late adolescence or young adulthood. For this reason among others, Blos (1967), adopting Mahler's apt description of a developmental process of early childhood (1963), has called adolescence "the second individuation phase."

The assertion of autonomy is manifested in a variety of independency behaviors in inappropriate and bizarre forms. It also continues to alternate with recurrent infantile forms of behavior in these young persons. Autonomy as a conscious subjective experience for the adolescent is the feeling of being self-determined in action. The conative ego function of willing one's own behavior is narcissistically prized, is highly ego-syntonic, and excites transmuted grandiose affects of self-satisfaction, pride, and self-esteem. The adolescent experiences the longing for autonomy intensely and equates it with becoming an adult—being *his own man* or *her own woman*. (In our culture, it is felt as being only fair and right that an individual be allowed to be himself—a feeling of entitlement, a constitutionally guaranteed right to equality with the adult.)

The longing for the sense of autonomy is so strong that it may motivate the adolescent into disobedience, rebellion, and sometimes delinquent and pathological behavior. Commonly the disruption of familial peace and harmony over trivial matters is an expression of the assertion of autonomy—the bad manners, messy room, disobedience, rising late, forgetting chores, not doing homework, dallying at play or the TV set when asked to do something, etc.—all are evidence that the young adolescent is no longer willing to be the good, loving, and compliant child and wishes to assert his independence.

However, in the early phase of adolescence the young person cannot afford a total disruption in the relationship with the parents, who are still necessary for material gratification and primary need satisfaction (food, shelter, clothing, protection). All the structures to be formed from interaction with these objects are not yet internalized. Specific intrapsychic structures remain incomplete—definitive superego controls, ego ideal definition, educational, vocational, and social identity. While the sexual impulses may no longer be ego-syntonically directed toward the parental object, the shift to extrafamilial objects is still incomplete. The young adolescent still depends on the parents for structure formation. The assertion of autonomy entails a risk of loss of the object for the young adolescent. Consequently, there is an irregular alternation between the assertion of autonomy and childlike behavior in relation to the object. Nevertheless, the wish to be autonomous will become increasingly stronger and its modes of assertion more constant with adolescent maturation.

The sense of autonomy is a subjective preconscious and conscious experience. Structurally and developmentally, no *actual* autonomy can exist psychologically, for structure implies the internalization of object-related need gratifications and frustrations from earliest self-object merger to postoedipal superego formation for identification. The parental objects have served from earlier infantile psychic development for the internalization of evolving structure and continue to do so in adolescence. Inexorably, it is the specific quality of this structure which determines the specific quality of the sense of autonomy the adolescent will experience. Adolescents who as infants and young children developed no adequate positive sense of self (Bernstein, 1963) will probably not have been able to undertake the infantile separation-individuation and will therefore suffer in adolescence a continued need to depend on parental objects to fill the persistent defect in autonomy, remaining excessively compliant to their parents or developing similar infantile attachments to parental substitutes. No true sense of autonomy is experienced by them.

Young adolescents who in their earlier development were forced into a passive compliant relationship to the object out of a defective sense of self, from a difficult anal phase training, or punitive superego development, may develop in early adolescence a fear of autonomous striving accompanied by unconscious hostility toward the parental object. This is then manifested by passive-aggressive behavior at home and at required tasks at school, often resulting in underachievement and failure. Rather than experiencing the ego-syntonic sense of autonomy, these young adolescents are distressed over the continual helpless failing that takes place. These adolescent cases are difficult to treat and require a thorough psychoanalytic approach.

Even more extreme and pathological forms of adolescent behavior may contain this striving for autonomy. In the adolescent's search for self-fulfillment or self-actualization, he may be induced by peer influence and what is contemporaneously available in the environment to join groups and engage in behaviors totally abhorrent to the parental value system. While becoming obviously dependent on the leaders and members of exotic theologies, philosophies, and ideologies, the adolescent feels he has made his own decision, asserted his own will, and chosen his own way of life. Clinical observation, however, reveals the continued need for objects that fulfill infantile needs, as well as the striving for autonomy.

The adolescent sense of autonomy begins its evolution in the positive experiences of self-function in the nuclear self-object matrix of earliest infantile experience. From these arise a confident sense of self in tension regulation, body mastery, and adaptation to the childhood milieu. Adequate infantile separation-individuation leads to further integration, cohesion, and confidence in self in relation to objects. In pubescence, then, striving for even further autonomy in separation from the actual parents and in functioning as a self-determined individual becomes a dominant behavior, one characteristic for the phase.

Adolescent Aggression

What happens to aggression during early adolescence? Theoretically one may assume that an increase in aggression takes place on a hormonal basis, as does sexual drive. But what hormones are involved in aggression? Testosterone increases in both sexes during pubescence, but proportionately the increase is many times greater in boys (Conger, 1973, p. 119). It has also been observed that early adolescent boys are more aggressive than girls. One observes that adolescent boys have a greater tendency to act out their hostility, more frequently engaging in delinquent acts and physical combat than do girls (Henderson, Davidson, Lewis, Gillard, and Barkie, 1977). How the intensified aggressive impulse is managed will depend then on ego mechanisms used to handle aggression from prior phases of development, the pressure of peer and other influences in the environment, and the specific superego attitudes, faltering though they may be during this phase of development. Of course, aggression may be discharged in sublimations and near sublimations like athletics. Increase in muscular strength makes it more possible for adolescents to discharge aggression via this route and causes a considerable modification in the relationship between the adolescent and his parents. The increase in aggressive drive may be seen in neutralized and sublimated forms in the playful jousting and boisterousness of young adolescents, in the vigor of self-assertion and demand for autonomy, and even in the energetic involvement in intellectual endeavor. Often vigorous activities within a peer group are mistaken for vandalism and delinquency, but much of the available hostile aggression may be expressed in antisocial destructive and rebellious behavior which is the actual delinquency frequently encountered in this age group.

Character Structure and Pathology in Early Adolescence

The cohesiveness of the early adolescent character structure is maintained largely through characterological dynamisms formed in the prepubescent years, especially during latency. Technically these dynamisms must be looked upon as regressive when reasserted under stress, or as fixations if continued from the earlier phases. Often it is difficult to differentiate them without close observation. Because they are used so readily and so repeatedly, the character of the early adolescent does not seem as fragile as the impression given by psychoanalytic study and description. But the sensitivity, hyperreactivity, easy irritability, restlessness, frequent "obstreperousness," and surprisingly unpredictable behaviors are all evidence that the solidity of the integration is not as constant as it appears. However, there are individuals who in the years when most young persons are undergoing the "adolescing" process maintain a rigid preadolescent character structure. They may be labeled generally as preadolescent characters of the preadolescent developmental phases—latency, phallic, anal, oral, etc. For them the adolescent process is foreclosed. In the analysis of adults who have had such preadolescent character formations, it is remarkable how much the qualities of anal character formation have continued into the character structure—stubbornness, obsessive-compulsive traits, perfectionism, efficiency, etc. These young persons may not suffer "the turmoil" of adolescence, but they also miss its maturational benefit and the enrichment that may accrue from it.

Interestingly from a clinical point of view, such adolescents will not be sent for treatment, for, if they are highly adaptive to the adult-defined value system, no parent or teacher would find fault. Such adolescents do well at school and are quite compliant with their parents' wishes. They may even be successful achievers in school, in acceptable groups, etc. Their peers may find them a bit stuffy and superior, but they are not sources of referrals to psychoanalysts. From a psychoanalytic point of view they are immature and therefore abnormal.

Such preadolescent characterological styles which persist into adolescence may indeed protect the early adolescent ego from intensified drives and disturbing intrapsychic regressions. But by midadolescence the character structure of the latency and preadolescent years may be adaptively insufficient, and the adolescent process is then engaged (Richmond and Sklansky, 1984).

The young adolescent ego capacity to contain intensified drives and to withstand the alternation between regressive pull and maturational push which characterizes this phase will determine the clinical picture. Alternation of defensive and adaptive mechanisms, when extreme, is distressing subjectively and maladaptive in the parental and school environment, but an alternation of lesser amplitude can be tolerated and is recognized as typical teenage behavior. It is evident here that a quantitative or comparative basis is used for the determination of pathology.

Persisting regression and persisting "pseudomaturity" are both characterological defensive positions which may bring the young adolescent to clinical attention. Let us consider regressive positions first. Young adolescents who suffer from severe anxiety over separation from the maternal object, as in school phobia, are unable to engage the adolescent object-shift or adapt to the several necessary achievements in school and among peers for that age group. It is a common observation that the beginning of the first high school year is a precipitant of early adolescent psychopathology (Sklansky, Silverman, and Rabichow, 1969, p. 24). This new environment is one highly laden with anxiety. Some adolescents regard high school life as meaning sexual freedom or at least the opportunity for it. Others react to achievement requirements as an impossible barrier to self-esteem maintenance. For still others, the change from a familiar grade school or junior high school, with well-known teachers and peers, is a disturbing intrusion on their intrapsychic integrative boundaries, with a consequent sense of anxious fragmentation.

The regression to the infantile bad mother (breast) image results in the adolescent's inability to get along with his present mother and female teachers, on whom this image is displaced. The clinical presentation then is that of quarreling at home, recalcitrance, disobedience, refusal to do homework, and misbehavior at school, including truancy. A variant of regression to anal phase ego mechanisms is seen clinically in adolescents who are remarkably compulsive in activities unapproved by either parents or school, combined with passive-aggressive defenses to those that are. For example, a young adolescent girl was an avid collector of dolls, doll clothes, doll houses, furnishings, etc. She was meticulous and detailed in the way she set them up in her room and spent most of her playtime with this "hobby," but she could not find time for her schoolwork, was failing her subjects, and was involved in constant angry bickering with her parents over chores, etc. Such anal-compulsive, regressive integrations seem, however, to be more common among boys.

In early adolescents who use anal compliance and compulsive behavior to establish a "pseudomaturity," we observe that their adaptation to adults, and their successful application to school and home requirements, goes on parallel with a tendency toward social isolation and the avoidance of peers and heterosexual relationships. They get no pleasure from the play activities appropriate to the age group, except in institutionally prescribed activities, where they are sometimes favored by the adults in charge. They suffer from emotional constriction and, often, arrogance.

Although we have yet to discover the definitive etiology and therapy for anorexia nervosa, it seems evident that pubescence and its psychological significance is a precipitant of the disorder (Bruch, 1975). The female sexuality of adolescent maturation, its pregenital and oedipal implications, its alterations of the body image, and its threats to the infantile maternal object relationship are all observed from a psychoanalytic orientation. The condition is one of the most life-threatening disorders that come under the clinician's purview of this age group.

This review cannot encompass the numerous disorders that are seen in this developmental phase. Suffice it to say that, clinically, young adolescents develop pathology when the ego mechanisms for managing the real and imagined stresses of the phase result in behaviors that are maladaptive. Inability to cope with pubescent stress may lead to loss of interest in schooling, which, except in a few subcultures, is considered a sign of maladaptation by parents and teachers alike (Sklansky, 1984). Disobedience and passive-aggressive noncompliance at home, a source of constant and common difficulty, may eventually result in psychiatric and psychoanalytic referral. In "good" families, delinquency and sexual activity of a precocious nature will bring young adolescents to clinical attention. Depression and psychotic reaction are seen less frequently in early adolescence than in mid- and late adolescence. It may be that the permission to continue functioning as a child protects against the inevitable pressures from within and without to undertake the role of adult, with all the anxiety-producing implications of that role in the youngster's mind.

Psychoanalytic Treatment of the Young Adolescent

Analytic treatment in early adolescence requires not only conflict resolution but the abatement of mechanisms interfering with the ongoing adolescent process. The young adolescent patient transfers phase-specific, need-fulfilling objects onto the analyst which cannot go unfulfilled. The analyst must undertake the parameters which make this maturational evolution possible. Any therapy must take into account the specific dynamics of the early adolescent phase of development—namely, that the stress of puberty requires ego mechanisms for integration of the instinctual drives; that conflict is an outcome of the individual adolescent's attempt to integrate those drives; that adolescence means the development of mechanisms for becoming autonomous as an individual; that there is a necessary distancing from infantile and childhood (oedipal) objects; that adult character formation requires substructures like self-image, identity, ego ideal, and superego, *still incomplete in development* in early adolescence. Therapy of adolescents, then, cannot be only undoing and analytic, but must also facilitate the development of the essential character substructures. Usually the latter means the modification of the preadolescent structures, rather than the creation of these structures *de nouveau*. This requirement applies to analysis as well as psychotherapy for this phase of development. The nature of the adolescent personality structure, not the imposition of the therapist's technical preference, will determine the process.

Transference in adolescence includes transference of those object and superego imagos that are included in whatever conflict the adolescent child may have. But there is also transferred onto the therapist or analyst those essential structures in development for which the parental object is used developmentally: the self-object for mirroring and idealization; the object of dependency gratifications; the modified superego and ego ideal of adolescence. Consequently therapy cannot be only analysis of the conflict but provides, whether the therapist is aware of it or not, these substructures of personality that make for growth and development. The adolescent developmental need forces the adolescent to place the therapist *in loco parentis*, and he projects onto the therapist the transference images mentioned above. This process goes on throughout the therapy with an adolescent, along with whatever insights, direction, reassurance, etc., may be necessary. Indeed, if the adolescent does not transfer onto the analyst or therapist a sufficient idealization, the therapist's words will fall upon psychologically deaf ears. Furthermore, to divest these personality-developing transferences of their emotional significance by a premature "analysis" of them empties the therapeutic relationship of its effectiveness. It would be like giving a hungry man the chemical formula of the components of bread.

It is a rare adolescent in this age group who can participate in a prototypical analysis. A true therapeutic alliance, directed primarily toward insight accumulation, rarely develops. The young adolescent is amused by the clever insights of the analyst.

Only occasionally does he make them himself. The introspective capacity, for most adolescents, is only now beginning to develop. Therapy and analysis are not given the necessary priority in the adolescent's life. The therapist finds himself more active with adolescents generally than with adults, but especially so in the case of early adolescents. Prolonged silence without intervention is definitely contraindicated in the therapy of adolescents. They often mistake it for disinterest, hostility, or peculiarity on the analyst's part.

Alleviation of conflict makes it possible for the adolescent process to proceed unimpeded. But only theoretically can one say that no crises will arise later. How the adolescent will react to later critical events, what their meaning will be to him in advanced phases of development and life is unpredictable. Whether a stress is a crisis will depend on the maturation that has taken place in the total personality and on the specific meanings that stress has for that personality at the time (Sklansky, 1971).

Determination of Pathology in Early Adolescence

The determination of pathology in adolescence is sometimes complicated by the mix of phase-specific mature and regressive behaviors manifested during adolescence. Consequently, behavior even in "normal" adolescents may appear highly deviant, though it may be only transitory. Such deviant behaviors, when they are investigated analytically in neurotic adolescents, may have as their basis dynamics similar to those underlying deviant behaviors seen in highly disturbed adolescents. For example, the resistance to doing homework in an "ordinary" adolescent and in a delinquent may in both cases be a manifestation of the drive for autonomy. Manifest behaviors in "normal" populations do not reveal the dynamics of neurotic adolescents seen clinically (Offer and Offer, 1975, p. 163).

Of course, no adequate clinical evaluation is based on the observation of single symptoms and behavioral manifestations. It is the total developmental history and clinical picture which will differentiate pathological from normal. Pathogenicity from earlier phases of development usually exists in the serious disturbances of early adolescence. The earlier the onset of the pathogenic factors, the greater the likelihood of pathology in adolescence. A history which indicates inadequate ego mechanisms for conflict resolution and adaptation prior to adolescence will suggest a greater degree of pathology when pubescence takes place. Developmental difficulties in infancy and early childhood inadequately resolved prior to pubescence prognosticate pathology during adolescence.

In the manifest clinical picture itself, the *persistence* of maladaptive behavior and symptoms over an extended period of time—let us say several months—is an indication of pathology, for it indicates inflexibility in the ego or the inability of the ego to utilize more adaptive and defensive mechanisms. The *intensity* of a symptom—difficult as it may be to ascertain, except comparatively—is also a measure of pathology. For example, an anxiety severe enough to prevent an adolescent from taking a school examination should be considered more pathological than anxiety prior to an examination that does not inhibit taking it. *Recurrence* and *frequency* of maladaptive symptoms and behavior are additional measures of pathology. Behavior which is self-destructive or destructive of others requires investigation for protection of the individual and others, though it may turn out that the overall picture of pathology may not be as grave as the behavior itself suggests. Regression in libido and forms of object relating are less pathological than are regression in ego processes and in cohesion of self. Actual loss of ego boundary, hallucinatory experience, and distortion of reality perceptions are indicative of potential psychosis.

Parents are loath to think of their children as psychiatrically disturbed. They hope the adolescent child will "grow out of it." In many cases, spontaneous remission and integration with maturation do occur, but it is better to assess the situation during adolescence than to wait until a resolution of a more maladaptive nature develops. Later integrations are not as readily modified as those formed during adolescence. A characterological integration in late adolescence or young adulthood may remain rigidly cohesive for several reasons. Maladaptive though a cohesion may be from the point of view of others, subjectively it serves to allay both structural conflict and fragmentation anxiety. Selected and preferred object choices as part of the intrapsychic resolution come to be absolutely essential in later adolescence. They are adhered to in some cases with a feeling of such necessity as to make alternate choices impossible, even when reality would dictate otherwise. Finally, ego mechanisms, defenses, and adaptations, which serve these specific purposes in the context of characterological integration, are held with a force that yields only with the greatest difficulty, if at all. The older adolescent manifests the inner process with the conscious conviction of dogmatic belief. These later possible character crystallizations suggest that assessment and therapy in early adolescence would be of great benefit in their prevention.

However, there are early adolescents who are themselves fearful and resistant not only to treatment, but even to psychiatric interviewing, and it may be necessary to wait until introspective capacities, self-observation, and personal suffering motivate the young person to seek help. While a young adolescent may be fearful of seeing a psychiatrist, often it may be possible for him to accept consultation with a school social worker, counselor, or psychologist.

The Parents of the Early Adolescent

While we have emphasized the psychology of the young adolescent, several points must be made briefly about the parents.

There is a developmental lag in the psychology of the parents compared to the accelerated psychological changes that take place in the pubescent child. Parents tend to continue to regard the 12-year-old child as they had their 10-year-old. Consequently, they find it disruptive to their own psyches to observe the previously cheerful and compliant or cooperative child now behaving in the moody, unpredictable, and rebellious manner described above. Few parents modify their expectations in accord with the psychological changes in the pubescent child.

Another important consideration is the effect of pubescent changes on the psychological equilibrium of the parent. The parent has, after all, mastered his own adolescence more or less successfully. Whatever distress he may have had during adolescence, he has found ego mechanisms for relative resolution in the late adolescent or young adult character formation. He has himself undergone the complex process described for adolescence at least two decades previously. Observing now the adolescent process repeated in his own child, with whom he is in all likelihood identified and about whom he has elaborated a variety of expectations, there is aroused in him anxiety about the process he himself experienced. Once again there is a reaction to the return of the repressed—the unacceptable impulses, the struggle with superego, and the questioning of the values in the ego ideal. All of this creates anxiety in the involved parent, an anxiety which the empathic clinician will take into consideration. From the point of view of the parent, psychological developmental lag and reactivation of his own adolescent process account for much of the "generation gap."

In benign relationships and happier circumstances, parents may not only enjoy their adolescents' development, but even profit from it psychologically. Because of the identification with the adolescent child and empathy with his psychological struggles, the parent may appreciate and enjoy the narcissistic pleasures of admiration and pride in his child's mastery over conflict and disturbing affects, and in his child's maturational achievements and successes. Thereby, the parent himself may add to his own maturation during the adolescence of his child.

References

Bernstein, H. (1963), The reality of the sense of the self and identity. Paper presented at the Chicago Psychoanalytic Society.

Blos, P. (1967), The second individuation process of adolescence. *The Psychoanalytic Study of the Child*, 22:162–186. New York: International Universities Press.

——— (1970), *The Young Adolescent: Clinical Studies*. New York: Free Press.

Bruch, H. (1975), Anorexia nervosa. In: *American Handbook of Psychiatry*, Vol. 4, ed. M. F. Reiser. New York: Basic Books, pp. 787–809.

Byrne, N. S. (1977), Nobody home: The erosion of the American family. *Psychology Today*, May.

Clower, V. (1976), Theoretical implications in current views of masturbation in latency girls. *J. Amer. Psychoanal. Assn.*, 24(suppl.):109.

Conger, J. (1973), *Adolescence and Youth: Psychological Development in a Changing World*. New York: Harper & Row.
Douglas, J., & Miller, J. (1977), Record breaking women. *Science News*, 12:172–174, September 10.
Erikson, E. (1956), The problem of ego identity. *J. Amer. Psychoanal. Assn.*, 4:56–121.
————— (1959), Identity and the life cycle. *Psychological Issues*, Monograph 1. New York: International Universities Press.
Freud, S. (1905), Three essays on the theory of sexuality. *Standard Edition*, 7:130–243. London: Hogarth Press, 1953.
————— (1929), Civilization and its discontents. *Standard Edition*, 21:59–145. London: Hogarth Press, 1961.
————— (1939), Moses and monotheism. *Standard Edition*, 23:3–137. London: Hogarth Press, 1964.
Gitelson, M. (1948), Character synthesis: The psychotherapeutic problem of adolescence. *Amer. J. Orthopsychiat.*, 18:422–431.
Hall, G. (1904), *Adolescence*, Vol. 1. New York: Appleton.
Henderson, S., Davidson, J. A., Lewis, D. C., Gillard, H. N., & Barkie, A. G. (1977), An assessment of hostility in a population of adolescents. *Arch. Gen. Psychiat.*, 34:706–711.
Karp, M. (1977), Diagnosis and treatment of delayed puberty. *Drug Therapy*, June.
Kestenberg, J. (1967), Phases of adolescence, with suggestions for a correlation of psychic and hormonal organization. *J. Amer. Acad. Child Psychiat.*, 6:426–463, 577–614.
Kirstein, L. S. (1977), Ages, menses and adolescent development. Paper presented at the Sixth World Congress of Psychiatry, Honolulu, September.
Kohut, H. (1971), *The Analysis of the Self*. New York: International Universities Press.
Mahler, M. (1963), Thoughts about development and individuation. *The Psychoanalytic Study of the Child*, 8:307–327. New York: International Universities Press.
Offer, D., & Offer, J. (1975), *From Teen-age to Young Manhood: A Psychological Study*. New York: Basic Books.
Richmond, M. B., & Sklansky, M. A. (1984), Structural change in adolescence. In: *Late Adolescence: Psychoanalytic Studies*, ed. D. D. Brockman. New York: International Universities Press, pp. 97–121.
Ritvo, S. (1976), Adolescent to woman. *J. Amer. Psychoanal. Assn.*, 24(suppl.):127–138.
Sarnoff, C. (1976), *Latency*. New York: Aronson.
Sklansky, M. (1958), The management of puberty and sex in adolescence. In: *Emotional Problems of Childhood*, ed. S. Lieberman. New York: Lippincott, pp. 71–86.
————— (1965), Impulse experience and control in adolescence. *J. Amer. Acad. Child Psychiat.*, 2:495–503.
————— (1971), Panel report: Indications and contraindications in the analysis of adolescents. *J. Amer. Psychoanal. Assn.*, 21:134–144.
————— (1977), The alchemy of love: Transmutation of the elements in adolescents and young adults. *Annual of Psychoanalysis*, 5:77–103. New York: International Universities Press.

———— (1984), Some observations on learning inhibition in college students: A developmental failure in the sense of autonomy. In: *Late Adolescence: Psychoanalytic Studies*, ed. D. D. Brockman. New York: International Universities Press, pp. 213–255.

———— Silverman, S., & Rabichow, H. (1969), *The High-School Adolescent*. New York: Association Press.

Spiegel, L. (1951), A review of contributions to a psychoanalytic theory of adolescence: Individual aspects. *The Psychoanalytic Study of the Child*, 6:382–395. New York: International Universities Press.

Sullivan, H. (1953), *The Interpersonal Theory of Psychiatry*. New York: Norton.

Werman, D. (1977), On the occurrence of incest fantasies. *Psychoanal. Quart.*, 46:245–255.

4

Ages Eleven to Fourteen

HELEN R. BEISER, M.D.

Children from 11 to 14, when compared to younger children, are not as uniform a group, either physically or psychologically. There are marked differences between boys and girls in age of onset and rate of development of prepubertal changes, as well as among individuals of either sex. Although girls generally mature two years before boys do, there are early and late developers in both sexes, and some early-developing boys overlap late-developing girls.

Psychological changes usually parallel the physical ones, but not necessarily. Consequently, some prepubescent children act as if still in the latency phase. In the literature, papers relating to this period may be found under the heading of "late childhood" or "the last phase of latency." Some authors consider this age an introduction to adolescence and therefore speak of "preadolescence." A distinction is often made between the ages 10 to 12, considered preadolescence, and the ages 13 to 15, called early adolescence and usually including puberty. If the physical changes leading to puberty are emphasized, this phase may be called "prepuberty." By 14 most girls have achieved menarche, their first menstrual period, which should close the preadolescent phase both physically and psychologically; many boys of that age, however, have not yet had their first ejaculation, considered the point of puberty for males. In what follows I will concentrate on the psychological changes that take place in preparation for adolescence proper, usually marked by the physical onset of puberty, as this event has a considerable psychological impact on the young person.

Review of the Literature

Although writings on adolescence appear in the psychoanalytic literature from early on, specific consideration of the preadolescent period is a later development. Freud (1905) does not mention it at all, moving directly from latency to adolescence. Although some papers on the topic were published in German in the 1930s, the English literature does not deal with preadolescence until the 1940s, when translations of these works began appearing. Redl (1943) describes preadolescents who border on the delinquent with great clarity and complexity, though in a deceptively "adolescent" jargon. In a chapter on puberty, Anna Freud (1936) alludes to the indiscriminate increase of libido during this period. The first chapter of Helene Deutsch's *The Psychology of Women* (1944) is entitled "Prepuberty." She, as well as Josselyn (1952), saw this period as the last phase of latency; both stressed the drive toward reality, ego development, and the relative tractability of these children as compared to adolescents.

There were important contributions in the 1950s, beginning with Erikson's classic study (1951) of the differences in the play patterns of boys and girls at this age. Blos (1958) published his concept of the drive organization of preadolescents, later included in his *On Adolescence* (1962). Sullivan (1953) included a chapter on preadolescence in his *The Interpersonal Theory of Psychiatry*. In the nonanalytic literature, Gesell, Ilg, and Ames (1956) published a detailed cross-sectional descriptive study of boys and girls in each year between 10 and 16. Inhelder and Piaget (1958) added to our understanding of cognitive development, while Galenson (1964), reporting a panel on "Puberty and Child Analysis," summarized psychoanalytic thinking to that point.

In the biological area, the studies of Connor and McGeorge (1965) and Money and Alexander (1969) of children with early puberty call into question the correlation between hormonal and psychological changes. Kestenberg (1967), by contrast, develops a very careful and detailed relationship between physical and psychological changes at this time. Gardner and Moriarty (1968) studied the cognitive development of middle-class, nonurban children, confirming that cognitive development, at least in this population, approaches that of adults. Wolff (1977) has studied the cognitive differences between early and late developers, which may explain some of the differences between boys and girls.

Harley (1971) and Kaplan (1976) have added to our understanding of the psychology of the preadolescent girl and suggested that Blos's original formulations may reflect his experience with passive boys and the fact that girls typically do not express their aggressive and anal preoccupations with male therapists. Finally, it is interesting that Sarnoff (1976) includes preadolescence and even puberty and early adolescence in his book on latency.

Physical and Cognitive Development

Physical changes can be classified into internal changes (both hormonal and in the internal sex organs), the development of secondary sex characteristics, and general bodily changes such as height, weight, and facial features. There is a definite sequence for boys and girls, girls usually starting at age 9 or 10, and boys 2 years later. Details are available in the works of Gesell and Kestenberg. Although the sequence is the same, there is considerable variability in the age of onset. This means that any group of 11-year-olds will contain children who show no evidence of prepubertal changes, as well as children who are fully pubertal. Girls will in general appear more mature than boys, at least in this culture (Wolff cites some evidence that Chinese and Japanese children do not show this time lag between the sexes).

It may be that increased hormones are responsible for an observed restlessness in both sexes, but it is harder to explain the impression of awkwardness and incoordination on this basis, as formal tests actually show an increase in strength and skill during this period. It may well be that psychological changes have an effect on body movements. In other words, awareness of bodily changes, especially sudden changes in height, make children of this age unsure of their physical boundaries, especially when not focused on a specific goal.

Cognitively, interesting changes take place. Although Piaget establishes age 11 as the age at which concrete thinking shifts to formal modes, this change is not sudden and probably takes several years. I have observed, however, that children in treatment are by this age able to conceptualize formal perspective in drawing and to accept the innate properties of substances. Simple tests, for example, will prove that clay in oil will melt in heat, and clay in water will harden. These children will also experiment with new ways of playing games. Their growing awareness and developing skills seem to precede the ability to express this new knowledge in words; many children in this age group are unable to carry on an abstract conversation for very long, though they have some idea of what an adult conversation is like. There is a self-consciousness, but little ability for introspective reporting.

Gross Personality Characteristics

Children of this age were described long before any psychoanalytic explanations were available. Their restlessness and awkwardness have already been mentioned, as well as a difficulty in verbal expression. Even those whose physical development may be slow give a message to the adult world that they are no longer to be treated as children. Nevertheless, they cannot act in an adult or even an adolescent way. An education professor of mine once explained the difficulties of teaching junior high school students: "They are too big to respect adults, but not big enough to have attained self-respect." Often they have poor body hygiene, and dress is determined more by peer fads than by parents or teachers. Groups form, even gangs, which cannot be penetrated by even concerned and friendly adults. Although there is not quite a war on adults, they tend to be excluded, except when they can be used to improve various physical and intellectual skills. This can be particularly frustrating to adults, parents or teachers, who may previously have had a pleasant relationship with a friendly and respectful latency child. Now the same child may voice an idealization of a rock star, an actor of questionable morals, or older children or peers with values different from those of the child's family.

Depending on the population under consideration, there is great variation in these patterns. In a tightly controlled, homogeneous culture, children this age may still act like children, even though their physical and cognitive development may proceed on schedule. By contrast, in a disorganized culture with high crime rates, resistance to authority may actually become delinquency. Among psychoanalytic patients a group of children may be observed who have had trouble becoming part of a peer group and who may as a result be overly friendly with authority. As they improve, these patients often give us important insights into the psychology of this age group. Historical and social changes, including the prolongation of adolescence by compulsory education, have produced important changes in the attitudes of both children and adults. The utilization of psychoanalytic knowledge has changed the behavior and some of the psychology of children, who are given far more information about expected sexual changes than in previous generations and far more freedom in various spheres.

Boys

Aside from the general characteristics, specific differences may be observed between boys and girls. At the beginning of this age period, boys tend to be dirty personally, and sloppy with their possessions, and yet may spend hours on a hobby such as stamp collecting. They prefer groups of boys with similar interests and are not interested in girls until late in this period. They tend to tell dirty jokes and to use anal language among themselves, with the jokes taking on a sexual tone as the boys become older. They are interested in the workings of things—in machines, models, science—as well as sports. They may have a special friend, or a group of friends who are almost identical, although there may be experimentation with friends who seem markedly different. If such friendships become intense, which is more likely in less active and group-oriented boys, there may be overt homosexual behavior as well as feelings. Sullivan (1953) feels that this is the first real "love" relationship. According to Money and Alexander (1969), boys with precocious puberty do not show homosexual interest, even though they receive offers from the older boys with whom they have been associating. Although a period of homosexuality has been considered normal for preadolescent boys, the social situation of pressure to accept homosexuals as "normal but different" may produce a different attitude toward this phase, in both the boys and in their parents and teachers.

Girls

There is considerable variation in the observed personality of girls of this age. Some seem like little women, actively involved in learning household arts and preparing for marriage and motherhood. Even these "old-fashioned" girls, however, may question their mothers as ideals and may instead learn from neighbors or various models from books or magazines. A variation of the feminine type is the girl who is mostly involved in enhancing her appearance, experimenting with the latest fashions in clothes, hair, or makeup. The effect may be somewhat less seductive than the girl expects, due to the immaturity of her body, the directness and aggressiveness of her exhibitionism, and a tendency to an incoordination of her attempts. I recall a flat-chested girl of 12 who arrived for her treatment hour with plunging neckline, spike heels, dangling earrings, and a floppy hat—in *her* eyes, the ultimate in adult sophistication. Other girls may be active in other ways, as in athletics, or be especially fond of horses. Some want to perform with animals, others to take care of them. It is these girls who may be more like the boys their age, with poor personal hygiene and an interest in dirty jokes.

All girls of this age, however, tend to share secrets of a sexual nature with friends, and to giggle. Girls tend to have strong friendships which, if intense, may have homosexual aspects. Small groups tend to break up and re-form as those who cannot keep up with the more knowledgeable are excluded. Progress in physical development is compared, as well as ability to attract older boys. Blos has called the 12- and 13-year-old girl "Diana on the hunt." I have observed even tomboyish 13-year-old girls to be markedly aggressive sexually, throwing themselves at men and putting down the less mature boys of their own age. Battles with the mother may start over care of clothing, cleaning their room, and limitation of social activities.

It should be mentioned that the behavior of girls this age has shown considerable change over the years. At the beginning of this century it was not unusual for them still to be playing with dolls. Deutsch (1944) mentions girls playing at being pregnant by putting pillows under their dresses. Early in my practice, it was more usual for girls to imitate adult women in their clothing and makeup. Now it is unusual to see a girl in a dress, and pants are no longer the sign of a tomboy. Girls now seem to want the privileges of adolescents, choosing their own styles and friends, and coming and going as they please. In the same timespan the ideal of the preadolescent girl has shifted from teachers to movie stars to popular singers.

Internal Psychological Changes

Etiology

Although the psychological changes of preadolescence usually take place along with the hormonal and other physical changes of prepuberty, there is not a complete correlation. Certainly the increase of sexual hormones may directly relate to the indiscriminate increase in activity noted at this time. However, in children with precocious puberty, although cognitive development seems to be stimulated, and these children are both bigger and smarter than same-age peers, they still act like children until age 11. Under certain circumstances, latency attitudes persist beyond puberty, in spite of the expected hormonal and physical maturation. In fact, I have treated married adults with families who continue to act like latency children.

The *fact* of preadolescence, usually occurring in the prepubertal period, seems then to be a psychological preparation for adolescence. Its *form* depends on many factors. First, there is a difference between boys and girls. Second, there is a variation depending on previous personality development. An expectable sequence is to be found in children who have solved preoedipal and oedipal conflicts adequately and used their la-

tency years to develop dependable coping and defense mechanisms. If these are too rigid, preadolescent loosening may be
delayed or inadequate. If these have never been adequately
developed, or if major conflicts have not been resolved, the
loosening may bring pathology to light. Of course, this previous
personality development has been influenced by parental attitudes which may also influence the process of preadolescence.
Harder to evaluate as factors, although certainly influential, are
society and its changing mores. I have already mentioned the
increased availability of sex information, including contraception. Of considerable importance are the various civil rights
movements for women, blacks, and homosexuals, which have
increased the range of adult roles available. One could look on
technological advances in the same light. Another influence is
the prolongation and glorification of adolescence, so that *it*
becomes the goal rather than adulthood. But with all these
changes, one that has not changed is the psychological impact
of the peer group. Does the individual see himself or herself
as one of the early developers and as therefore superior? Or
does late development lead to a sense of inferiority or bitterness,
with fantasies of revenge? How does the early development of
girls as compared to boys influence heterosexual object relations
at different ages?

General Tasks of Preadolescence

Before one can become an adult, one must stop being a
child. A negative step of this sort seems to precede each forward
step in development. If one superimposes Mahler's observations
of the preoedipal child (Mahler, Pine, and Bergman, 1975) to
the postoedipal period, one could say that the latency period,
with its good adaptation of the child to the environment, resembles the symbiotic period of infancy. Preadolescence, then,
is like the first subphase of separation-individuation, that of
differentiation. I doubt if all the Mahlerian subphases are re-
capitulated, but certainly the negative precedes the positive, as
separation precedes individuation, which is the task of adolescence. This requires that children change their internalized
concepts of the parents, as well as of the self. Children at this
stage do not seem to say, "I am not a child anymore"; in fact,

they may resent any adult who comments on how much they have grown. Instead, they criticize adults or avoid them. In either case, these children are saying that adults do not understand them, or that they are old-fashioned or repressive. In other words, preadolescent tensions are projected onto adults, who are blamed for the child's own change in attitude. Similarly, these children do not introspect on their need for a new identity now that they are no longer children, but instead search for an identity in the mirror of their peers. This explains the often intense, but possibly changing, relations to peers of the same sex. The true friendship or object relatedness of preadolescent peer attachments is doubtful, although it may develop into such friendship after the search for the self in the mirror of the other is complete. In cases where peers seem quite different from the child who selects them, there is probably an extension of the need to separate from the values of the parent. On the other hand, the child may have to search for different aspects of the self, both good and bad. As criticism of the parents may leave the child feeling without support, there is a tendency to experiment with finding ideal adults, often quite different from the parents, who at least provide fantasy support. Often the parents of friends seem much better, and there may be a fantasy ideal family. Such substitutions are an indication of the difficulty the child has in giving up the close, dependent relationship to the parents, especially the mother. In case of illness, the dependency is reestablished, and the real increase of dependency in chronic illness may interfere with the preadolescent process.

The other task of preadolescence is to anticipate the future. This might be compared to Mahler's "practicing" subphase. It is the variations in this that give such a wide range of individual behaviors. The practicing has an awkward or uncoordinated feel to it, as with my 12-year-old patient in spike heels and floppy hat. Although these attempts are more realistic than those of the oedipal child who parades around in the parent's clothes, or wants to be a fireman, there is still an aura of fantasy about them. For example, when I asked my patient what her idea of adulthood was, she replied that you could smoke, drink, and go to the race track. It seems to be the hedonistic aspects of adulthood that are desired most, and much more learning and testing are necessary before a realistic work identity can be internalized. It is for this reason that the real anticipation of the preadolescent is for the bodily changes of puberty and the social life of the adolescent. Here there are considerable differences between boys and girls.

Boys

Blos (1958) states that the drive organization of preadolescent boys regresses to an anal or at least preoedipal level. This seems the preferred method of loosening the tie to the mother or declaring independence from childhood—by becoming like a much younger child. It is using an old mechanism to be negative. Blos also emphasizes that the boy must deal with the castration threat from the phallic mother. I think that to free himself from dependency and childhood, the boy must not risk the erotic feelings that were possible in the oedipal period, as this would pull him back into dependency, felt at this time as castration. At this age, he usually refuses physical affection from his mother *and* his father as childish, but the boy's sloppiness may actually require a lot of care from the mother, which can be tolerated because it is seen as an unnecessary imposition.

Although it is most important for the boy to see himself as not dependent on his mother, he may not have a good relationship to his father either, even though it would seem desirable to learn from him about the changes going on in his body, as well as his approaching puberty. This, too, seems dependent, and he prefers to learn from older boys, as well as peers. Many boys go through a stage at which they are chubby and undergo some breast changes. Such physical changes, along with the severing of their dependency on reliable adults, allow boys to play with ideas of femininity and to express their dependency through a homosexual desire toward an older or stronger boy. Others may develop a strong attraction to an older woman, usually a teacher.

The boy's strong interest in how things work, as well as his own body, gives him sublimated interests in sports, mechanics, and science. These are ego supportive and also allow him relationships with a variety of teachers.

As parental dependency ties are loosened, superego values are also questioned. New values are experimented with, sometimes in a dangerous way. Gangs provide a group superego often at variance with that of the parents and the culture. If boys have had inadequate dependency, the peer group will give it, and an individual child will take on the superego values of the gang in order to get the support he wants. In less dangerous ways, boys will temporarily overthrow parental or cultural values in pairs or small groups, which aid in loosening the childish superego.

Although most writers talk about the ease with which boys accept their sexuality, given how clear and external their genitalia are, this ease seems doubtful when one comes to know the concerns of the preadolescent. Although he has no true object-related heterosexuality—in fact, will avoid or dislike girls—he has to deal with erections that occur without his control; and when puberty and the first ejaculation finally arrive, he has another function which may occur without control, and at embarrassing times. In many ways, the preadolescent boy seems even less sure of his ability to deal with the future than does the girl of the same age.

Girls

There is some question as to whether girls regress to a pregenital drive organization as boys do. Blos (1962) sees them rather as pressing on to early sexual drives. However, women analysts such as Harley (1971) feel that girls reveal their regressive side to women therapists, whereas male therapists stimulate their sexual feelings. It is possible that when motherhood was the only acceptable goal for females, its anticipation was predominant in preadolescence and served as a sufficient mode for the girl's separating from a dependent relationship with her own mother. With the wider range of adult roles now open to females, the male mode of changing from the child's dependence on parents may be seen increasingly in girls. Rather than purely anal defiance, however, shifts in the oral level may be observed, as well as a greater tendency to bisexual experimentation than in the boy.

Whereas oral greediness may serve the boy in a regressive

way, it can also serve the fantasy that he will grow faster. The girl, who is already growing rapidly, may experience her increased oral drives in a more conflictual way. If she sees orality as continuing her dependence on the mother, she may fight this by dieting. If this reaches pathological proportions, it may even foster the fantasy that she can control her development and *not* grow up. Before puberty, she can still fantasy that a penis will yet grow, or at least can be substituted for by riding a horse, or owning a large and powerful animal. This path, though it fosters separation from the mother and combats the temptation to remain in childish dependence, may interfere with a comfortable femininity. What should be seen as the last gasp of "normal" penis envy may also be seen in the aggressive put-down of immature boys the same age.

Although girls tend to have best friends to mirror their interest in themselves and their own development, these relationships do not seem to have as much of the homosexual component as in boys. This may be because girls develop early and are able to direct their heterosexual feelings to older boys. Groups of girls, rather than forming semidelinquent gangs, tend to share sexual interests and brag about their usually fantasied conquests of older boys or men. They also anticipate menarche and compare notes on development, causing some slow developers to feel there is something wrong with them. It is now more usual to look forward to the first menstrual period, although the more compulsive girls may still suffer from feelings of dirtiness and loss of control relating to the menstrual flow. Certainly this is one area where education and the technological development of more esthetic modes of handling menses have allowed girls to welcome the event as positive evidence of their maturation and not as a "monthly sickness" or "the curse."

Ego development in the girl of this age is similar to the boy's, although she may have different areas of interest. Rather than machinery and science, she enjoys dramatics, music, and art. I have seen the wish to perform that Erikson describes but not the interest in closed spaces. Except for the anticipated menarche, girls seem more interested in enhancing their outward attractiveness in preparation for heterosexual relations.

Also, the superego of the girl may not undergo the same testing as does the boy's. If experimentation does take place, it is less in the area of violence and more in the area of sexual contact and running away, or a combination of both.

Implications

Phase-Specific Pathology

In general, children who cause concern at this age fall into two main groups: those who move into adulthood too quickly and those who are fearful or reluctant to face growing up. Some have shown disturbance earlier, but there are many whose disturbance first appears with the specific problem of approaching adolescence. Some of the attendant suffering is not really the result of pathology, but occurs, in children, parents, and other adults, because of phase-specific changes in the child's personality.

First, adults, the mother in particular, must deal with the child's wish for greater independence, which is often manifested in disobedience, sloppiness, and a refusal to accept affection, enjoy family outings, or even be given sex education. Particularly disheartening can be the child's idealization of adults representing a totally different value system than the parents'. Even well-informed parents may experience this change as a narcissistic blow and can use professional support to tolerate the negativsm, as well as suggestions as to when to place firm limits on the experimentation.

There is also a certain amount of expectable pain for children in this age period. The loosening of ties to the parents without yet having adult object relations leaves the young person feeling isolated and unsure of himself. Although activity and peer relations handle this to a large extent, the restlessness and instability of interests and friends indicate that the process is painful. Another area of distress is in comparing oneself to others. Very early developers may feel like monstrosities, but this is rare. It is the late developers who more commonly feel the pain of being left behind or wondering if they will ever develop. This is particularly true of boys, where even the normal delay (vis-à-vis girls) in the growth spurt causes feelings of inferiority and anxiety. Those who experiment with adult dress or skills find that their wishes exceed their abilities, and they may feel depressed by failures or find themselves teased by older and bigger young people, or even adults.

Professional judgment as to what constitutes a real problem requiring treatment is often taxed, as not all parental concern or unhappiness in the child can be dismissed as "just a phase." Valid concerns that may first come to light at this age, although having roots in the past, relate to children who want to grow up too fast. This wish shows up as delinquent behavior in boys and excessive early sex interests in girls. Often these are children of busy parents who have provided a great deal of material goods, but inadequate relationships. Such children do not want treatment, but freedom, and it is necessary to provide control and supervision first. The girl who is delayed in her sexual interests usually does not cause concern at this age, but the immature boy does. He is usually passive and may be a bit fat. He prefers younger children and, rather than belonging to a peer group, is often the butt of teasing. He has usually been too close to his mother and, if bright, may have been a favorite of women teachers. Treatment can be a valuable experience for mother and son, the treatment process itself loosening the bond, often by encouraging the boy to come to sessions himself, interesting him in competitive games, and helping him to deal with his sadistic fantasies in a constructive manner.

More serious problems in the precocious developers cannot be treated in ordinary psychotherapy. Parents are rarely cooperative, and it usually takes a well-coordinated community team or a supervised, controlled institution to protect both the child and the community. It should be mentioned that delinquency is easier to control at the preadolescent stage than later in adolescence. At present, drug abuse is probably the most frequent problem in this area.

Problems relating to fear of adolescence or adulthood are more commonly dealt with in psychotherapy. Anorexia nervosa or school phobia represents dependency problems or severe conflicts with the mother. Obesity is the opposite side of the anorexia coin. A more common problem, one less serious, is poor schoolwork. This is not a "learning problem," which usually has been present throughout the school years, but an inability to work toward a goal or set a direction for the future. This is sometimes accompanied by disobedience, but in the more compulsive child there may be compliance with assignments but a failure to set personal goals. Another common problem, usually voiced primarily by the child, is lack of friends. Here again, the problem is long-standing, as attachment to the parents prevented the usual latency peer relationships; now at preadolescence, with its strong peer attachments, it becomes more apparent and painful.

Many authors describe an increase in somatic symptoms at this age. These may take various forms (e.g., tics) relating to increased motor restlessness. Awareness of bodily changes promotes expression of anxiety through hypochondriasis. Those with the constitutional predisposition may also develop psychosomatic symptoms such as asthma, ulcers, or migraine for the first time.

The Preadolescent in Treatment

I would like to describe briefly the problems for psychotherapy specific to the preadolescent personality. Early in the period the treatment process is much like that of the latency child. An immature predolescent especially enjoys being the sole focus of attention of an interested adult. Boys especially still enjoy a wide range of play activities, board games, models, drawing, etc. They may bring their collections to the hour for demonstration and talk about sports heroes or the latest feat of their favorite athletic team. Direct interpretation of symbolic material is met with disavowal and even flight from treatment, but alternate solutions couched in metaphor will be adopted. Play is sometimes used for expression and exploration, and sometimes for symbolic representation of conflicts. One very small 12-year-old boy confided in me that he had found a way to make money by cutting paper currency in half and turning in each half for a new bill. It was his way of trying to make something valuable out of what he saw as a defect. I informed him that it was necessary to have five-eighths of a bill to get a replacement, but we discussed other ways of making money. Some boys will experiment with new techiques for playing checkers, being willing to risk losing while testing them out. At this age this represents exploration, not masochism.

Girls this age are in many ways harder to treat than boys. It is probably no accident that there are fewer play materials available for girls of this age than there are for boys. Girls are likely to refuse play activities at an earlier age than are boys, although some may draw and play games; they are then left with the problem of verbal communication at an age when introspection and abstract thinking are not sufficiently developed. With women therapists, the girl also has the problem of her conflicted relationship with her mother, especially at the time of puberty. I have sat many times with a silent, hostile 13-year-old girl, totally unable to communicate. I have come to the conclusion that such girls do better with a nonseductive male therapist. The closer relationship of problem boys to their mothers may be an advantage in starting therapy with a woman.

With both sexes, therefore, it is best to start when they are a little immature, so that the positive relationship can carry the process at least partially through the preadolescent and early adolescent phases. Even this cannot be accomplished without strong support from parents and usually also from the school. After age 12, the more motivation from the child himself, the better. Because a disturbed child has a strong need to assert independence from adult authorities, it is difficult to discriminate resistance from improvement, and termination as evidence that an immature child is ready to deal with separation. Again, as regards content of the therapy hours, it is best if some play material can be accepted early, and flexibility of play and conversation is established. Play may aid the physical restlessness of the preadolescent, and he may be able to talk *while* playing, rather than use play as a vehicle of communication.

I have already mentioned the problems involved in the content of preadolescent conversation. In an analyst's office, the subject of the couch also comes up. Highly sophisticated children, who intellectualize, come from homes where parents have been in analysis, or who have read about it, may lie down on the couch. This more often leads to sleep than to free association. These same children may be able to talk about dreams and fantasies like adult patients but, strangely enough, do not seem to change. Their pseudo-adult talk is a symptom and is split off from an infantile part that resists integrated maturation. Actually, children in the preadolescent phase do not act like *good* patients, either of the childhood type or the adult. With patience and persistence, however, therapists can treat at least some preadolescents and have the satisfaction of watching the change from playing children to introspective early adolescents. If one wants them to behave like adults, one is asking for pathology.

Implications for Future Pathology

It is interesting to speculate on the influence of the preadolescent period on adult personality. I have long thought that it is the basis for many problems between the sexes. The early development of girls, with their search for older boys as the objects of their first heterosexual strivings, seems to carry on in the custom of women being younger than their husbands. It might also make men uncomfortable with women their own age. It may be that this preadolescent phenomenon may be more influential than an unresolved oedipal conflict, which has been the usual explanation. Of course, the phenomenon is not universal and probably depends on how much of a problem was actually encountered. Girls who have socialized very early and who then find themselves without a source of older boys, such as in the senior year of high school, may become depressed as their age mates are being actively sought by younger girls. Very late developers may maintain their sense of inferiority into adulthood, and it is certainly something to keep in mind in the treatment of adults.

Some of the problems that arise in preadolescence may not be resolved during the course of adolescence and persist into adulthood. Drug abuse and delinquency may seriously affect the individual's adult life if not successfully treated. Similarly, if defense mechanisms against delinquency, such as tics or hypochondriasis, are not handled, they too may persist as adult problems.

Problems indicating a fear of growing up, if not resolved,

may interfere with adults' achieving their full potential; such adults appear as neurotic or as having character disorders. I worked with one boy throughout his preadolescence until we finally uncovered his fear, based on the early deaths of a number of male relatives, that he would die or become sick if he passed the age of 13. He had no learning disability, but read only to feed omnipotent fantasies and not to attain a life goal.

A more interesting speculation relates to the idea of fixation in latency or preadolescence as a way of dealing with the fear of growing up. Fixation in latency would avoid the risks of preadolescence and adolescence. I believe this used to be a fairly common occurrence in girls, and the compliant little-girl personality was often mistaken for ideal femininity. It usually was very successful in attracting a husband, but such immature women had a hard time dealing with the problems of marriage and motherhood when compliance did not solve all problems.

I have felt that the "hippie" generation was fixated in preadolescence. Rather than remaining as compliant children, they rebelled from childhood, but could not set realistic adult goals. Instead, they criticized the available adult models, regressed anally to poor personal hygiene, and had poorly defined sexual identities. The emphasis was on sensuality rather than on object relations.

Implications for Home and School

In an individualistic, democratic culture or society, adolescence is considered a desirable phase of development, necessary to produce the most autonomous adult. Preadolescence is then a necessary prologue. The adolescent opportunity to question the values and relationships of childhood and to construct a new personality means that the representatives of society must bear the brunt of the questioning.

Schools have reacted to increased activity patterns by allowing movement between classes and different teachers. This makes it easier for students to keep a distance and for teachers to avoid too much attack by the same students. It also prepares for more specialized learning during adolescence. Perhaps what has not been taken into consideration is the faster preparation for adulthood by those who do not want a prolonged educational experience. This is complicated by compulsory school laws and the democratic ideal of equality. Compulsory school attendance during the teen years is not a true adolescence, and students who do not use it to increase their knowledge tend to behave like preadolescents, resenting being treated like children but unable to move toward valid adult goals.

By contrast, young people who are likely to have a long educational experience, in which they are really preparing for a complex, adult work identity, tend to be flooded with vocational information and advice at earlier and earlier levels. It is possible that this frightens the bright students, and they feel that they cannot really learn or aspire to anything so difficult. This situation may influence young people to a fixation in preadolescence or adolescence.

The home has perhaps been less able to prepare for the immediate accommodation of the preadolescent. It is strange how many parents think that they were misunderstood by their parents at that age and that their different methods of child rearing will prevent rebelliousness or withdrawal in their own children. Most finally make the adjustment, but there might be a fight which keeps the child in the latency period for a time. On the other hand, some parents give up and do not fight with the child for the control needed for his basic protection. A battle won so easily is not worth the victory, as it may be dangerous.

Other parents push for maturation. Some do this by early and excessive sexual information, some by inordinate and specific demands for adult goals. It is not easy to keep lines of communication open without demanding confidences or to dose information to that which is immediately pertinent and looks just enough to the future to give a general direction. Parents who have had to struggle against family attitudes and financial troubles to get their own education are frustrated that their children refuse the same goals made easy for them. Luckily, the activity drive of the preadolescent is so strong that it cannot be easily turned off by the need to demonstrate independence from parents and society. Perhaps the biggest problem to this generation is that there are too many alternatives, too many roles available to them, and it is hard to give up any of them in the process of making a choice.

118   HELEN R. BEISER

References

Blos, P. (1958), Preadolescent drive organization. *J. Amer. Psychoanal. Assn.*, 6:47–56.

—— (1962), Preadolescence. In: *On Adolescence: A Psychoanalytic Interpretation*. New York: Free Press, pp. 57–71.

Connor, D. B., & McGeorge, M. (1965), Psychological aspects of accelerated pubertal development. *J. Child Psychol. & Psychiat.*, 6:1161–1177.

Deutsch, H. (1944), Prepuberty. In: *The Psychology of Women*, Vol. 1. New York: Grune & Stratton, pp. 1–23.

Erikson, E. (1951), Sex differences in the play configuration of preadolescents. *Amer. J. Orthopsychiat.*, 21:667–692.

Freud, A. (1936), The ego and id at puberty. In: *The Ego and the Mechanisms of Defense*. New York: International Universities Press, 1966.

Freud, S. (1905), Three essays on the theory of sexuality. *Standard Edition*, 7:173–231. London: Hogarth Press, 1953.

Galenson, E. (1964), Prepuberty and child analysis: A panel report. *J. Amer. Psychoanal. Assn.*, 12:600–609.

Gardner, R., & Moriarty, A. (1968), *Personality Development at Preadolescence: Explorations of Structure Formation*. Seattle: University of Washington Press.

Gesell, A., Ilg, F., & Ames, L. B. (1956), *Youth: The Years from Ten to Sixteen*. New York: Harper.

Harley, M. (1971), Some reflections on identity problems in prepuberty. In: *Separation-Individuation: Essays in Honor of Margaret S. Mahler*, ed. J. B. McDevitt & C. F. Settlage. New York: International Universities Press, pp. 385–403.

Inhelder, B., & Piaget, J. (1958), Adolescent thinking. In: *The Growth of Logical Thinking from Childhood to Adolescence*. New York: Basic Books, pp. 334–350.

Josselyn, I. (1952), Psychological growth patterns. In: *The Adolescent and His World*. New York: Family Service Association of America, pp. 9–25.

Kaplan, E. (1976), Manifestations of aggression in latency and preadolescent girls. *The Psychoanalytic Study of the Child*, 31:63–78. New Haven: Yale University Press.

Kestenberg, J. (1967), Phases of adolescence, I & II. *J. Amer. Acad. Child Psychiat.*, 6:426–463; 577–614.

Mahler, M., Pine, F., & Bergman, A. (1975), On human symbiosis and the subphases of the separation-individuation process. In: *The Psychological Birth of the Human Infant*. New York: Basic Books, pp. 41–122.

Money, J., & Alexander, D. (1969), Psychosexual development and absence of homosexuality in males with precocious puberty. *J. Nerv. & Ment. Dis.*, 148:111–123.

Redl, F. (1943), Preadolescents: What makes them tick? *Child Study*, pp. 44–48.

Sarnoff, C. (1976), Sexual development during the latency age: Cognitive development. In: *Latency*. New York: Aronson, pp. 37–146.

Sullivan, H. S. (1953), Preadolescence. In: *The Interpersonal Theory of Psychiatry*. New York: Norton, pp. 245–263.

Wolff, P. (1977), Development of behavioral sex differences. Paper presented at the Chicago Institute for Psychoanalysis.

5

Disturbances in Early Adolescent Development

JOSEPH D. NOSHPITZ, M.D.

One of the difficulties in evaluating the clinical status of a troubled adolescent is distinguishing between the more dramatic vagaries of normality and the warping impact of true psychopathology. The fluid, changing state of character during rapid growth and transition makes evaluation uncertain and prediction a trap for the unwary. Even a simple delineation of the clinical conditions likely to be found among any population of adolescents poses difficulties.

In an attempt to deal with this situation, the material in this chapter has been organized along hierarchical lines. At the outset there is a brief account of the events associated with normal puberty, followed by the minor adjustment reactions of the time, then by the more serious syndromes, and finally by those with the gravest prognosis. At each level comprehensiveness has been sacrificed for an illustrative sampling of some of the conditions that beset young people. The afflictions are numerous and, in some instances, unclassified. Thus the psychological implications of dental braces, the meaning of premature baldness, the simple realization of having an unattractive face or an unpleasing figure—or for that matter of beauty and voluptuousness—are topics that have been little studied. The sexual identity issues of adolescence, the variety of antisocial patterns (in spite of all the study, much remains to be learned about this realm), the work inhibitions, the pathological religiosity—in short, a great many fairly serious dimensions of adjustment—also remain in a sort of professional limbo. There are indeed practitioners who know a lot about them, but the field as such has only partially assimilated them, and there is no recognized, generally held therapeutic approach for their management.

Since there is much here that is ambiguous, pronouncements in these areas cannot be made with apodictic certainty. The emphasis here is on a brief account of a few of the typical problems of early adolescence. The need is for far more extensive study.

Highlights of Pubertal Development

Biological Factors

There is no precise point at which puberty begins, nor is it certain why it begins. Somewhere in the brain, and particularly in the hypothalamus, a biological clock marks the appointed hour, and a series of neuroendocrine changes ensue. The pituitary is alerted. Its many tropic hormones begin to pour into the bloodstream; adrenarche follows, the secretions of the adrenal cortex adding themselves to the pituitary liquors, and at last the sex hormones as such begin to pour out of testes and ovaries to add their moiety to the heady endocrine soup that is now bathing the body tissues. Growth follows according to the templates laid down in the basic genetic code, and, given adequate nutrition, a host of bodily changes occur. As these become visible, the youngster is said to have entered puberty.

In any sizable population of youngsters, the onset of this phase will be evident in girls some one and a half to two years before it is manifest in boys (Tanner, 1962). Both the age at which changes begin and the rate at which they proceed are highly variable. Certain youngsters, not all, show a prepubertal fat stage—they become plump or chubby as they approach puberty. For the majority of girls, the first tufts of pubic hair and the earliest areolar changes and breast budding occur about 10 or 11. Menarche follows within one and a half to two years. Increase in the length of the long bones, widening of the pelvis, and rotation of the neck of the femur come in their turn, along with a redistribution of subcutaneous fat and the alteration of facial contours.

Presently the flat latency girl's body is transformed into that of a shapely young woman, while the maturation of the ovaries and uterus initiates the menstrual cycle and prepares the way for fertility. The boy undergoes parallel changes, although they usually do not appear until age 13 or 14. The first hints of puberty are again the appearance of pubic and axillary hair, increase in the size of the genitalia, and, presently, a considerable lengthening of the long bones. The boy begins to have frequent erections, becomes very alive to sexual stimuli, and experiences his first nocturnal emissions. In short order, he elaborates viable sperm in adequate number, and he too is physically ready to reproduce. Collectively these changes are known as the appearance of the secondary sexual characteristics (the primary characteristics, present prenatally, define the child's gender). These changes continue over a period of five to six years, although some of them, e.g., deepening of the boy's voice and the growth of the beard, may not begin until later in the process.

Cognitive Factors

Piaget (Inhelder and Piaget, 1958) places the initial appearance of the stage of formal operations in thought at about age 11. Increasingly there is a capacity to think abstractly, to draw ever finer distinctions, to see essential consistencies despite superficial differences, to hold a chain of cause-and-effect sequences firmly in mind, and to use concepts as manipulable entities. The youngster begins to think in abstract formal propositional terms; no longer is he bound to the concrete occasion. He reasons more effectively in academic pursuits and argues ever more trenchantly in his altercations with parents, teachers, and other authorities. Presently he can invest himself in such abstruse concepts as religion, ethics, truth, etc.

Affective-Dynamic Factors

Pregenital arousal. Along with the new maturational capacities occurs a major disruption of the relatively quiescent instinctual life of latency, a vigorous reawakening of the pregenital

and phallic-oedipal phases. The early drives are swept up with
the pubertal advances and begin to make themselves felt in a
variety of forms. Behavioral changes commonly ensue: the
youngster begins to gorge or grows finicky, changes food preferences, and eats only natural foods or only junk. Some young
people go through minor anorexic periods and are said to be
"off their feed" for a while. Orderly children may become careless and defiantly sloppy; there are major hassles about maintaining one's room. Others become protective, secretive, and
lock their doors, protesting vehemently if anyone enters their
area. Occasionally the pendulum swings toward their becoming
excessively, obsessively neat and orderly. Temper outbursts are
common. Language characteristically changes to reflect both
cognitive advances and the recrudescence of anal interests.
Sometimes street terms formerly confined to peer interactions
now burst forth in teacher-student and parent-child contexts.
There is often a far greater interest in money—making it, saving
it, hoarding it, and spending it—than previously.

Phallic-oedipal instinct pressures. The phallic-oedipal drives
are soon much in evidence, with many dirty jokes, questions
about sex, bumptious inquiries into the intimate practices of
adults (including often enough the parents), grandiose assertions of one's own sexual mastery ("I know all about that"), and
the flaunting of sexually related materials such as underclothes,
sanitary napkins, jock straps, *Playboy* magazine, or bits of erotic
"art." For many boys and girls, active sexual behavior begins
at this point. Their newly mature bodies become objects of
considerable interest to sexually experienced individuals in
their immediate environment, leading to all manner of seduction and sexual abuse; and their own interactions with one
another may all too easily spill over into various forms of sexual
expression. Boys become much involved with looking and girls
with showing. There is commonly some experimenting with
body manipulations; coitus is by no means uncommon. As a
rule, the more direct experiences of sexual response to the
bodies of the parents are quickly warded off. They are suppressed and repressed. A pattern of distancing reactions may
follow; the parents may come to be regarded defensively as old,
disgusting, and altogether unattractive. There follows a deter-

mined plunge into peer group interests. Even at home, moody withdrawal or hours spent on the phone with friends may speak volumes of the need to fend off oedipal impulses, and patterns of willful and unreasonable opposition to parental values and stances may well ensue.

The final phase of early adolescence involves the work of separation-individuation (Blos, 1967). The youngster must accomplish the task of achieving true autonomy, no longer the partial way station of yore, but the beginning march toward the end of the adolescent process, adult independence. The particular task at puberty is the detachment of the affective bonds, both erotic and aggressive, from the persons of the parents, and their reworking, displacement outward, and reattachment to the variety of nonincestuous objects available in the larger world—in particular, their investment in peers and near peers.

There are many ports of call on this voyage. Initially, the experience of bodily transformation arouses a passionate interest and intensely sensuous excitement. The new muscles, the new height, the new bosom, the new genital size, the new contours, the new face, the new possibilities offered by clothes, makeup, hairdos, gestures, modes of speaking, facial expressions, and all manners of posturing are explored in detail. The body is felt, studied, tested. Not infrequently there are grandiose thoughts about one's attractiveness, sexual prowess, strength, beauty, handsomeness, intelligence, talent, and the like. Masturbation figures in the life of almost all boys and probably a majority of girls. Fantasy is rife, and masturbatory fantasy in particular plays a profound role in the psychic life of these youngsters. The cumulative experience of the formative oedipal and pregenital interactions now crystallizes in the form of powerful interests and dispositions which thrust themselves into the awareness of the boy or girl, and with which each must cope. Sometimes the fantasy life involves whipping or beating. At times overt images of sexual interaction with a family member may appear; even the encounter with relatively "normal," well-defended images (such as a boy's seeing an unknown woman taking off her clothes as he masturbates) can cause reactions of considerable dismay.

Superego changes. The instinctual stirrings of puberty arouse the superego to excited activity. It was precisely to deal with such oedipal issues that this agency of the mind was created, and with these newly energized wishes now hammering at the gates of consciousness, it is radically alerted. Guilt feelings, moodiness, a sudden distaste for parents, an inability to speak to them (despite excellent relationships in earlier years), and indeed a readiness to accept everyone's opinion but theirs tell something of the effects of the superego alarm system. The injunction is: Thou shalt not think of oral clinging, of anal sensuousness, and especially not of genital incest. The ego must find ways to carry out this injunction. At the same time, the youngster's newly acquired sense of intellectual competence leads him to look at the superego in a new way. Perhaps for the first time he begins to study its proscriptions, to question its values, to evaluate its stances, and presently to challenge something of what he finds. He is suddenly finding fault with his parents—with their ethics, their politics, their religion, their prejudices, their entire weltanschauung. Their faults go all the way from demanding proof that there is something wrong with staying out till 1:00 A.M. to their chuckling over a racist joke.

Identity. One of the major issues youngsters face at this time is the nature of their identity (Erikson, 1959). They can no longer think of themselves as children or accept that social role. At the same time, clearly they are not yet adults. But they begin to ask why not: how come they aren't and what's the difference anyway? The organization of self as a latency child is fragmented; into the breach leap all manner of posturings and fantasies. There are grandiose moments when they feel infinitely more on top of things than their fuddy-duddy parents. And yet, there are moments when the comforts of being in the relatively safe state of knowing who one is, of being someone's child, dependent and taken care of, are remembered. From time to time, they can regress and be the compliant "good" child of yore, but at best, this regression can only be a temporary state, perhaps a response to stress, and the resurgent yearnings of puberty rise up again, and once more the great uncertainty looms ahead.

The solution found by most youngsters is to create a new persona in fantasy, to try on identity roles, and thus, through experiment, to discover who one is and what one does best. Identity must be worked at, and many, many such experiments must be carried out. Indeed, it usually takes several years before a stable sense of self becomes set (GAP, 1968). The first truly major step into adulthood involves the establishment of a reasonably stable and consistent organization of this sort. The nature of the organization may be infantile; indeed, it may be a state of protracted adolescence. But once the experiments are over, once it is clearly set, the outcome is adulthood.

Unusual Talents and Abilities

The presence of some special gift is often evident even in early latency; in a few rare instances it is obvious from the very beginnings of personality development. But it is quite common for talents to blossom with puberty. Indeed, this period of life makes many an average person feel talented. New intellectual worlds are opening. Suddenly the youngster understands all manner of things heretofore hidden and obscure; without warning emotions are felt whose sweetness and intensity seem like radically new discoveries, something no one could have felt before. It is a time of life when many youths write poetry because they must, perhaps never again to do so. It is not surprising that a latent capacity for some form of creativity, be it singing, boxing, or abstract mathematics, now comes to fruition and finds concrete expression. One rather special development that might not necessarily be designated a talent functions in a somewhat similar way. This is the appearance of unusual beauty or handsomeness. Psychologically it plays an analogous role.

A genuine talent is a remarkable phenomenon. It has the quality about it of changing reality. Money, status, recognition, adulation, sexual favors, bids for friendship, opportunities for travel and for training, and many other rewards may come the way of the gifted, and many doors open for them in a manner calculated to affect the self-concept and social orientation of anyone. It is no exaggeration to say that it takes rather a fortunate personality organization and an unusual degree of maturity to cope with talent. All too often, brilliant and talented young people arc across the sky of their social surround and burn out like meteors so that by the time they reach adulthood they are lost and no longer able to achieve. In some instances the unusual factor is precocity rather than genuine talent. A youngster may perform in an amazingly competent fashion much earlier than do others the same age; when the others finally catch up, however, the precocious one may no longer be outstanding. In many instances, however, quite a different combination of events ensues.

Dynamics

The resolution of narcissistic issues can be radically interfered with by such factors (Kohut, 1971). The original grandiose residues of symbiotic fusion must gradually resorb during the separation-individuation phases so that by the time of oedipal resolution the last flare-up of grandiosity is seen in the structure of the oedipal fantasy itself. It is after all a very considerable presumption on the part of the child to dream of sexual rights with one parent or the other and to contemplate the destruction of the rival. As this wish-fantasy construct is gradually given up, the superego, with its principles and prohibitions, is formed. The grandiose idealization of both self and parent is slowly converted into the ego ideal, a part of the superego that continues to evolve and develop into an ever more mature presence in the mind, a part of the self that holds up a model for striving and self-realization.

Such a complex sequence of developmental events is clearly vulnerable to the many vicissitudes of growing up. In particular, inadequate resolution of the work with the grandiose elements of childhood thinking leaves a youngster with a distorted self-concept and an uneven and hazardous quality regarding the estimation of significant others. All these factors undergo an explosive recrudescence at puberty. As pregenital and phallic-oedipal concerns are once again aroused, these grandiose elements are rekindled, resonating with a normal increase in fantasies and searching attention regarding one's changing body and mind, and an outburst of narcissistic preoccupation can ensue.

Evidently a state of unusual talent will set up many reverberations within this grandiose system. Or, more precisely, the normal tendency toward overestimation of the self will be reinforced by the adulatory regard of the surrounding human environment; the consequence is a tremendous enhancement of this aspect of the self-concept. One sees oneself as larger than life; all sorts of advantages belong to one by right. No criticism of one's work can be tolerated without a tremendous flare-up of resentment, a feeling that one is being personally attacked. Self-centeredness becomes exaggerated to the point of distorting the appraisal of reality, and there ensues a state of heightened expectation of the self and a vulnerability to any breath of criticism that may pave the way toward failure. For such people, competition is excruciating (How can they compare themselves to me?), and failure to be first, best, the chosen one, is catastrophic. Under such circumstances, peer problems can be considerable; prodigies often think of themselves as having no need for "those clods" or, worse still, may develop an entourage of followers sufficiently awed as to abandon the usual peer interactions that in most instances help individuals recognize the implications of their actions and the nature of social reality. As these youngsters become more and more isolated, they rely increasingly on their talent to carry them through, and often it is insufficient to the task. Not understanding what is going wrong, they become angry and depressed. In due course comes the burnout that blights the careers of so many promising and talented adolescents. They fall into states of confusion, depression, work block, and failed productivity that leave them wounded and able to work at only a fraction of their actual potential.

There is no technical name for this condition; labels such as worker's block and work inhibition fall far short of conveying the personal tragedy and the serious loss to the culture of such a chain of events. Narcissistic dysrealization of talent may express in capsule form what has occurred here. On the other hand, when the combination of genetic endowment and wise environmental management has avoided the fostering of such narcissistic fixations, gifted youngsters can have a remarkable adolescence, full of rich and challenging experience, replete with many gratifications, and thoroughly preparatory for a magnificent adulthood.

Problems of the Normal Adolescent

Turmoil

When Offer and his associates (Offer and Offer, 1975) sought a group of normal average adolescents to study, they found that their subjects fell into three categories. There was a relatively conflict-free cohort who did not get into difficulties with their families, who performed well at their studies, who appeared to enjoy many activities and social relationships, and who seemed stable and happy. Another group seemed by contrast to be relatively anxious, depressed, at odds with their world, and plagued by numerous behavioral problems. An in-between group felt troubled but did not ordinarily allow the emotional upset to invade their behavioral adjustment. In brief, Offer suggested that the majority of adolescents do not demonstrate overt behavioral or emotional disturbance and that of those who do there are many who still fall within the norm. It seems safe to assert that all adolescents are probably shaken by emotional storms and troublesome floods of impulse (A. Freud, 1958); for many, these experiences are transient and readily mastered, whereas for a minority the same issues occasion far more serious reactions.

Anna Freud's observation about the normalcy of adolescent turmoil is probably as accurate a statement as one can make. Erupting instincts and the fragmenting of latency identity create conditions of disequilibrium. In effect, the adolescent ego is under considerable developmental stress. The capacity of this ego to cope with these pressures is a function of its genetic endowment, strengths and weaknesses that have emerged during personality formation in the early years of life, the kinds of trauma to which the youngster may have been exposed, the identifications that have been made, and the character and firmness of superego formations. The strength of the drives is a factor that defies measurement but that thrusts itself into every discussion of this time of life. And finally, the family constellation in which puberty takes place and the attitudes of the parents toward the changes in the youngster and toward the drives themselves are factors of central importance in the way this developmental stage unfolds.

In any event, the predictable state of affairs for any given youngster is a condition of episodic turmoil, sometimes ensuing because of guilt over forbidden fantasies, sometimes because of frustrated yearnings for ever greater degrees of autonomy and independence; sometimes because of confusion and uncertainty about who one is and who one is expected to be; sometimes because a momentary imbalance between impulsive and controlling forces has led to some impulsive, explosive act whose consequences have to be adjusted to; and sometimes because the shifting of defense structures and identity patterns has given rise to feelings of confusion and depersonalization that are as frightening as they are unexplainable. In short, there are myriad sources of that sense of profound disturbance which is usually designated as adolescent turmoil.

The one virtue of this state of affairs is that the actual experience of turmoil is usually short-lived; in one way or another, most of the time the youth copes with the imbalance and adjusts. The adjustment too may be short-lived, but it does occur, and the basic stability of life is preserved. In less fortunate situations, the turmoil is not so much episodic as chronic, and the youngster may enter a state of depression, agitation, and excessive reactivity that can have serious implications. Occasionally such stressful sequences can lead to running away or suicidal gestures as the youngster attempts to escape an unendurable and continuing sense of crisis. On the other hand, most adolescent turmoil is probably never visible; the young person copes by talking things over with a friend or a respected adult or, by use of abreaction and identification, finds a way to resolve the issue without overt dramatics.

Rebellion

Of all the phenomena associated with this time of life, rebellion is probably the most often described and discussed. Pressures toward separation-individuation, toward giving up a lifelong dependency on the parents, toward the achievement of ever greater degrees of personal autonomy, toward seeking and finding new objects for social and sexual interest, and toward becoming a self-determining individual with the ability to make one's own decisions often set a youth on an inevitable collision course with the adult environment. The intensity of the drives toward independence can be great, as can the resulting challenges to, and differences with, parents, teachers, coaches, and law enforcement officers. To make matters worse, the immaturity of the pubertal youth frequently leads to stands and assertions which are at best illogical and which to the adult ear may sound downright ridiculous. Ensuing interactions may well aid the youth in defining a separate identity, but they are emotionally costly to everyone concerned. Many a young person resorts to attitudes of pitiless defiance and even of arrogance in insisting on some valued position. Its value may rest chiefly in its ability to evoke parental reactivity.

For more troubled youngsters, this need to achieve autonomy by defying various authority figures represents an early form of seeking self-definition. It is the simplest means of separating from a source of dependency. One has been attached all of one's life; now the quest is on for full individuation. The easiest way to get there seems obvious: to take each point of parental value and deny it or challenge it. By differing with the parents, one has asserted a kind of independence of them.

In particular, the rebellion of this time is a reflection of the renewed encounter with the superego. The need to challenge, to rebut, to explore, to test out the dictator that heretofore has reigned unquestioned within the youngster's personality comes into a kind of resonance with the search for autonomy. The outcome is a sense of rebellion that can take many forms. There can be a series of fantasied denunciations and devastating attacks on parents and teachers that are never verbalized by a youngster who is outwardly accepting and compliant. There can be alternating episodes of stubborn opposition and cheerful acceptance of rules. There can be a chronic nasty, negative attitude, with sullenness and surliness within an overall context of basic good behavior. And there can also be overt hostile refusal to comply with the most elementary requirements of age-appropriate adjustment coupled with destructive outbursts, school failure, running away, and all manner of personal challenges to authority figures.

The nature of the early adolescent process is to experience the world and to react to it in forms that tend to be extreme. The youngster is head over heels in love, suffused with rage, covered with confusion, drowned in embarrassment, filled with maudlin sentimentality, or overwhelmed with concern—the only common factor among these states being the totality of the emotion. Nuances will come later, as adolescence advances; now the state is close to all or none. This emotional style gives rather a specific coloring to the interactions of the period, a mixture of intensity and childishness that speaks for the transitional character of the time. It also makes the moments of rebellion particularly difficult to bear.

Reaching Outward: The Great Displacement

Generally speaking, the types of adjustment seen as part of this time of life are not given diagnoses. They are considered part of the fair wear and tear of growing up, the phenomenology of puberty, but it is important to note some of the more common varieties in greater detail.

Young love. In the interpersonal sphere, there are unaccountable loves and hates. The emotions are callow to be sure, but no less intense for their immaturity. Affection, newly displaced from idealized parents, is likely to be reattached to overvalued distant figures such as pop stars, TV idols, movie actors, great athletes, racing car drivers, and the like. When a figure closer to home fills the form needed by this youngster, a crush can ensue, taking the form of an inordinately intense attachment to a teacher, a neighbor, a coach, or some other older person. It is as though the vivid idealization formerly reserved for the parent has become tinctured more and more by defensive devaluations and the need for distancing. The positive feelings are then transferred wholesale to some other parental person, of either sex, and for a while the youngster feels drawn toward this individual, hangs on the person's every word and gesture, feels thrilled by every look or touch, and literally adores the person. Only after some time does this emotional bondage loosen. Often enough this happens abruptly, so that the object of this attachment is sometimes bewildered at being first so pursued and now so abandoned. In the normal course of events, the affections sooner or later turn away from the idealized adult and attach instead to a peer of the opposite sex, perhaps a classmate or a next-door neighbor. Again the initial emotions are typically intense and overwhelming; the youngsters moon over one another, dream of one another, feel thrilled to the very core when they catch each other's eyes, and often treasure some trivial object handled by the other. This is called puppy love and has a peculiar poignancy; it is often remembered with special wistfulness for a lifetime.

Hedonism. In some instances the new capacities for pleasure, both in masturbation and in other forms of sensuous experience, cause a child to give himself up to a surge of sensation seeking. Latency defenses have crumbled, and there has not been time for the establishment of a new organization. The young ego falls prey to the pressure of the instincts, and a pattern of instinctual abandonment follows. Dancing, smoking, sex play with others, masturbation, attempts at drinking, experimenting with drugs, joyriding, gorging at meals and stuffing junk food between meals—all manner of bodily pleasures temporarily dominate the life of the young person. Inevitably such a pattern exposes the youth to the many dangers associated with ungoverned expression of instinct. Accidents occur, the police are often involved, pregnancy is a potential complication, and tempestuous parent-child relations are predictable. Usually there is some history of overstimulation in the background of such young people, and the reencounter with previous memories and fantasies of flooding emotional experiences throws the youngster into a state in which he wants to make them all happen again, this time with himself as initiator rather than as passive victim. If no truly catastrophic event ensues, in many instances the sensation hunger does not persist, the old trauma is mastered, the youth settles down, and development proceeds.

Romanticism. At times the hedonic tendency is more dilute and more idealized. Even at the beginning of puberty the boy or girl may be forever falling in love, forever swooning over some matinee idol, peer, or both. Newly aroused erotic capabilities create a state of emotional disequilibrium, but here the ego strength is greater than that of the hedonic youth. Such youngsters write poetry, lose themselves in loud music, live in states of impassioned fantasy, take many people into their confidence swearing each to secrecy, and never quite touch earth. Schoolwork may go on as usual but often enough suffers as the youth's cognitive processes are temporarily derailed by the invasive romantic fantasy. There is usually little acting out of the yearnings and dreams; things stay on the level of wish and compromise. Again the state is temporary and gradually gives way to a more realistic and balanced appraisal of self and other. The ego is basically competent, and no very dramatic behavior occurs. Occasionally, wish-fulfillment yearnings are sufficiently powerful to cause a youngster almost to believe a fantasy and to tell tall tales of an encounter with some famous, longed-for "star."

Moodiness. Where the affective charge is powerful but superego strictures more powerful still, many a youth becomes moody, irritable, and mildly depressed. The depression is complex; it is compounded by the feelings of loss associated with the decathexis of the parents plus the sense of guilt associated with the powerful aggressive and erotic yearnings that the superego condemns so roundly. The loss experience can be intense; after all, the parents have been from the outset major figures in the child's life. To give them up at one fell swoop is no minor matter; one has abandoned the closest and most supportive attachment one has ever known. But they must be given up nonetheless, and a sadness without source steals over the youth's life. People about him note that he is peevish and morose "for no reason." Occasionally such youngsters will have flashes of anger and lash out bitterly and inexplicably at some family member. Occasionally they will be glowering and depressed until a phone call comes from a good friend; then they brighten up and become different people. This fluid and fickle emotionality is typical of this time of life; the moody adolescent is no rare variety.

Boredom. A defensive position adopted by many youngsters is to repress incestuous longings and rages; to make sure the repression holds, they move into asceticism. It is important to distinguish this from anhedonia. The latter is a state of inability to experience pleasure; the ascetic is capable of pleasure but eschews it. Ultimately his pleasure comes from the renunciation of pleasure or from the mastery of his own yearnings for pleasure. This is not a trivial distinction. The individual who obtains gratification from the sense of worthiness that derives from giving up the pleasures of the flesh is on the high road toward moral masochism. This is the studious youngster who looks down on the dirty words, dirty jokes, sexual teasing, and accounts of sexual achievement of his peers. His gratification comes from his sense of righteousness and worthiness; he gives up on the frightening possibilities hinted at or, in fantasy, frankly offered by his resurgent pubertal id in favor of the warm glow of goodness and approval tendered him by his newly alerted, frowning superego. There are occasional falls from grace in the face of temptation, which send him into paroxysms of guilt, annealing a resolve never to sin again. A certain melancholy intellectualism hovers over such youngsters, and they often drown themselves in a sea of work and activities in order to shore up the sense of doing the right thing and to keep themselves distracted from the nagging inner voices of the id.

This type of asceticism (A. Freud, 1936) differs in basic ways from the youngster who glories in his mastery over his appetites. Here is the larval anorexic, the proud virgin who boasts that he has never masturbated, the youngster who often enough covers up a terror of loss of control by becoming a supreme master of control. As a rule, there is also a second tier of defense. Merely keeping impulse at bay is not enough; one needs to do more. Such youngsters may become expert in some discipline involving the body—anything from running, tennis, or gymnastics through ballet or horseback riding. The sense of mastery of the body, of disciplining the self so that the body obeys utterly and totally the dictates of the mind, of forcing the recalcitrant flesh to submit and obey, is the high point of pleasure for such youths. It confirms and reinforces their supremacy over the terrifying threats of id eruption and may become the single dominant focus of their lives. There are a multitude of "syndromes of normality" which may characterize early adolescence. These varieties shade over into more clearly diagnosable conditions, although many complex constellations of troubled adolescent adaptation defy any conventional categorization.

The Encounter with a New Physique

Appearance

One of the most obvious shifts in behavior between latency and adolescence is the increase in the interest youngsters now experience in their own body. Boys tend to study their musculature; girls their faces and figures. They may spend hours in front of the mirror, or they may avoid mirrors or look at the mirror out of the corner of their eyes, and tell themselves that they do not really care about the changes and how they look—but, in reality, they are all vitally concerned.

Deviations in Height

The short youth has often looked eagerly forward to springing up in height, with all sorts of associated fantasies of strength, command, domination, superiority, sexual attractiveness, and prowess. When the movement into puberty fails to bring about the long anticipated advance, a considerable element of stress is often added to the work of development, and a sense of real mourning ensues for the person one hoped to be. The youngster may have to cope with many angry jealous feelings; a considerable measure of narcissistic injury is inflicted on him. That life is unfair may reverberate in his thoughts for many days, and a tendency toward overcompensation may emerge. He may become quarrelsome, loud, or provocative; he may start to strut, or to clown. He may seek to develop some special capacity like good school work or playing an instrument well; or he may seek to ally himself with bigger, stronger youngsters, even to the point of becoming delinquent (with them and, in a sense, for them). Girls are less vulnerable than boys in this respect, but unusually short girls may also be affected by this factor.

The sense of shortness is often experienced as a form of castration (indeed the joke is to call such a youngster "sawed off") (Rotnem, Genel, Hintz, and Cohen, 1977). The nicknames and teasing that may fall to his lot confirm the sense of lack, of injury. Sometimes the readiness of people to view him as younger than his age causes the youth to react vigorously; behavior may become precociously mature in an effort to deal with the threat. Occasionally a boy or girl may prefer to take advantage of his childlike appearance and the uses of infantility, helping him ward off the sense of incompetence engendered by the advances of puberty. A common sequence is for the teenager to keep hoping that growth may come later; this hope becomes particularly poignant when thinking ahead to dating and socializing.

The unusually tall youth, on the other hand, has quite a different problem. The girl will often bemoan her height and feel gawky and undesirable. The childhood sense of injury that had come with the discovery of sexual differences may be rekindled. She may feel cheated, unfairly treated, and lacking the comely form that others possess. Anxiety may pervade the formation of her sense of an attractive self, which at this stage of development is a formation of critical and sensitive proportions. The narcissistic injury of not feeling lovable reverberates in mutually augmenting fashion with the earlier anal-phallic theme of feeling castrated. The sense of personal deformity, of lacking congruence with an idealized image of femininity, can "dog" the awareness of many an impressionable young pubertal girl. Growth itself feels like the body is out of control, and a certain helplessness is sometimes injected into the youngster's emotional state. Some girls attempt to adapt by stooping or somehow contracting their posture to deemphasize their height. Others, of course, make realistic adjustments and keep an eye out for tall boys with whom they will feel comfortable and who won't feel uncomfortable with them.

The tall boy has a different problem. Throughout childhood the unusually large boy is always at risk. Again and again he is warned that he must not be aggressive, that he is bigger and therefore should not attack others or even hit back if attacked. The entire development of the aggressive component of personality can be skewed by such a rearing. Inhibition, anxiety, fear of loss of control, and chronic resentment at being picked on and always in the wrong, tinged with an uneasy sense of guilt, are likely to characterize the childhood of such a boy. Where the strictures are less harsh and the child uses his strength at will, tendencies to preserve a grandiose self-concept cannot be adequately resolved and serious deformations of peer relationships may ensue. He can all too easily become an aggressive bully who achieves a form of self-realization through terrorizing other children by his sadism and who harbors megalomanic fantasies of power.

Such large children are constantly assumed to be older than their peers, and various social expectations are directed toward them prematurely. For the child with a more competent ego, such expectations can serve as a spur to growth. For some youngsters, however, it means a crushing sense of inferiority, as they are forever asked to perform at a level beyond their capacities; for others it acts to augment an inclination toward grandiosity. The large child, like the small one, can be genuinely vulnerable.

Problems in Breast Development

For girls, the earliest evidence of puberty and a primary expression of femininity is the growth of their breasts. Culturally vested with enormous power to arouse the passions of males, and hence central to the entire mystique of femininity, breasts are regarded by the growing girl with intense interest and not a little concern. Their shapeliness is an important issue, but far more important is the simple element of quantity. Breast development, like height, can go awry, either through too little or too much. Somewhat similar dynamics are at work, but with the special quality of being closely tied to the sense of gender identity. It is not unusual for a girl to seek to compensate for small breasts by padding her clothes or to reduce the too large bosom by surgery. The presence of some imperfection in this aspect of her body can wound her sense of competent femininity to a serious degree. The invidious comparisons to other family members may heighten oedipal tensions; the teasing of peers can generate feelings of inadequacy, even of ugliness. To some extent, the breasts compensate for the former encounter with castration concerns. The body-phallus equation to which so many girls turn after their initial sense of disappointment and the feeling that all of the body is beautiful, sexual, exciting, and very much worth displaying become resurgent with puberty. The development of the body contours is watched anxiously to be sure they retain and increase their allure. Anything which detracts from this therefore counts heavily against the girl's sense of competence as a lovable sexual being in general, and as a female in particular. The flat-chested girl may feel castrated, deprived, and masculinized. The heavy-breasted girl may feel sloppy, freakish, a slob—even ugly and deformed. Occasionally body problems feed into other difficulties a girl may harbor and lead to attempts to overcompensate by sexual willingness. Sometimes such girls become "boy crazy," "throw themselves at boys," and feel that no one will like them if they are not sexually available. Given a somewhat different basic personality organization, a profound shyness and self-consciousness may ensue, with some feeling that everyone is noticing and looking at their "problem."

Squeaky Voice

A similar but by no means identical problem for the boy is change of voice. Unlike breast development, which ushers puberty in, voice change tends to come at the close of pubertal transformation. Again, unlike breast development, it is subject to some measure of voluntary control. For example, a youth with excessive attachment to his mother did not lose the squeaky high-pitched quality of his vocalization until he left home and went off to college, where quite literally overnight he spoke in a deeper and more masculine voice. A childish voice clings at once to the image of self as child and to the sense of self as effeminate. With it, one need face neither the rigors of independence nor the responsibilities of masculinity. Nor has one separated from the mother; one has her voice (and thus her presence) with one constantly. The adult male voice is the father's phallus; it is potency; it is an instrument of penetration, of self-assertion, of aggression. The failure to achieve depth and an adequate measure of loudness means castration, effeteness, and infantility.

Acne

Perhaps no other physical problem of adolescence is as ubiquitous as a distressing skin condition. For many youngsters it is experienced as a mark of shame, a signal of badness. It has at times been held to betoken masturbation, the hidden inner secret that suddenly blossoms forth for everyone to see. More often it is experienced as something that mars, defaces, and makes ugly, something that injures one's sense of narcissism. With it comes the sense of a botched self, someone no one could really care for, which permeates the youngster's social experience. For the vulnerable youth, either a compensatory or a withdrawal reaction may follow.

Unusual Physique

Physical differences may play a very considerable role in the ease and comfort of pubertal adjustment. In particular, large buttocks may become a focus of intense concern and enormous preoccupation. A boy may experience them as suggesting homosexuality or effeminacy; he watches anxiously to note whether anyone's eyes fix on this part of his body; he fantasies what he might look like from behind or, perhaps worse still, from the side. It is as though all the growth fears of pubertal change become concentrated in this one area. A strong regressive element is present, the phallic phase issues of the time are too much, and the interests of the boy take an anal form. At some level he feels like a youngster whose pants are full after an anal accident and who fears discovery; this kind of fear is actually a compromise with the greater fear of oedipal challenge and retaliation. Guilt gives way to shame; one is less concerned with castration and more worried about the humiliation of being looked at and laughed at. Paradoxically, a certain number of young people who go through such an experience seek surgical relief. They invoke a cutting off of the feminine parts to protect the masculine self, a sort of castration in the service of preservation, or giving up the feminine part of the self in order to maintain the masculine core.

In general, any blemish, any deficiency, any aspect of the body that is deemed unattractive or that challenges the sense of gender identity evokes a host of reactions which will take their character from important early fixation points.

If oral phase symbiotic stress has been a significant factor in development, a sense of narcissistic injury may be paramount.

The flawed symbiotic unity leaves its trace in a sense of unresolved grandiosity coupled with excessive fragility. The perfection of the self is a constant issue that alternately puffs up to unreal proportions and radically collapses into a sense of painfully deflated worthlessness.

The cognitive intellectual functions may or may not be caught up in this process. If they are affected, a stubborn type of pseudo-mental retardation may emerge along with major difficulties in relationships. If they are spared, the picture is one of an intelligent child who is too vulnerable, self-centered, and grandiose to have any sort of adequate peer relations. Puberty is likely to be a particularly hard time for such youngsters, as they can tolerate no criticism, need desperately to believe in their own perfection and superiority, and yet are confronted constantly by the discrepancies between what they would like to believe and the way reality in fact presents itself. If puberty brings with it any of the conditions noted here, these youngsters are likely to be in a chronic state of panic regarding this marring of their perfection.

Anal phase children going through the rapprochement stage of object relations are particularly vulnerable. They can be profoundly affected by stressful experiences, and any sufficiently traumatic event results in fixation at this level. It is a time for consolidating a sense of autonomy, of making the first tentative explorations into what independence is all about, of constructing an initial body image, however shadowy, and of the beginning establishment of a sense of self as actor and doer; but all of these processes are new and fragile and may be radically compromised. The result may be an inclination toward passivity, a sense of futility, and a chronic need for clinging attachment which easily becomes hostile dependency.

Disturbances of Development

Gender Identity Problems

The pubertal period is a critical moment for the consolidation of gender identity. For some children, the initial assumption of a sense of gender is accomplished by 12 months;

for all children it is certainly achieved by 24 months. Gender differences are clearly recognized and responded to by 18 months. In many instances, patterns of disturbed sexual identity are recalled or can be recognized by 3 or 4 years of age. Before they even approach adolescence, many children are already known as tomboys or sissies, or as otherwise somewhat atypical in their expressions of sexual identity. Puberty itself, with its major addition of phallic interest, can sometimes provide a paradoxical masculinity or femininity to a child who is basically confused in orientation. With the injection of reinforced phallic drive, the passive sissy becomes more like a regular boy or the tomboy more conventionally feminine, at least for a while. As young adulthood is reached, however, the extra input tapers off, and the basic equilibrium is likely to be reestablished.

But many sexual and gender problems surface in puberty for the first time. Incest may be triggered by the developing sexuality of the boy or girl. Impulsive acts of public masturbation, exhibitionism, or voyeurism may be functions of newfound sexual pressures encountering an undeveloped ego. Precocious sexual experience and pregnancy are the result of a variety of individual, social, and cultural factors; the sexual exploitation of younger children by the teenager is likely to first manifest itself at this time, and in some cases prostitution is initiated. Some children have engaged in frankly homosexual practices since relatively early childhood, but many a boy or girl who has formerly had no hint of such interests now begins to notice sexual responsiveness to the bodies of same-sex peers (in locker rooms, showers, swimming, etc.) for the first time. If mild in degree, this can be a very common complication of normal development (stemming from earlier negative oedipal experience). But in many cases youngsters are not prepared and such feelings may have enormous meaning, often begetting morbid concerns about being homosexual.

There are also instances in which homosexuality as a primary source of gratification now becomes manifest. Sometimes a latent pattern is triggered by a homosexual seduction; sometimes heterosexual experiments turn out to be strangely disappointing, and a "chance" encounter reveals the predominant pattern. There are instances in which powerful homosexual fantasies are pushed aside for a long time, and a determined effort is made to be as heterosexual as possible, to assert one's gender by vigorous action. The youngster becomes sexually hyperactive, "macho," or "boy crazy." Such excesses may have their own complications, and complex patterns of adjustment can ensue.

Precocious and Delayed Puberty

Of particular interest are the circumstances attending precocious and delayed puberty. The girl who shows breast development at 8 and begins to menstruate at 9 is radically out of synchrony with her friends and classmates. She is often painfully self-conscious, confused, and embarrassed by what is happening to her. She doesn't understand it, nor, even after it is spelled out to her, can she readily explain it to others. Parental support and guidance, help by teachers, and explanations, education, and reassurance by family physicians can be of incalculable value here, while anxious peers who express their tension through sadistic teasing can be a source of pain. The peer group often needs some help if the girl is not to be excluded or in some way exploited. Paradoxically, the full gamut of pubertal emotions does not coincide with biological transformations. Strong sexual interests and the moodiness or tempestuous quality of the time may not come until a few years later. Without considerable support, such children can have radical misconceptions about what is happening to them. They may feel sick, wounded, different. They fear they may bleed to death. The sense of things being out of control is pervasive, and the latency ego is shaken; sometimes such children become anxious or depressed. They fancy what is happening is a punishment or the result of something they have done wrong. The increased vulnerability of such children to exploitation is always a factor; if a seduction does occur, guilt and confusion are surely heightened.

Given adequate management, this kind of precocity need not be a significant disturber of development; lacking that, it can cast a cloud over the sense of self that will take many years to dispel.

In boys, precocity has its own problems. Here sexual issues

are perhaps less prominent than aggressive ones. The big boy, as noted, is always marked as a potentially destructive fellow in the rough and tumble of latency peer interaction and, to the extent that he internalizes warnings, experiences himself as dangerous and threatening, a sort of monster. He can deal with this by identification with this image and become a bully; or he can try to undo it and become inhibited and paralyzed. Again, appropriate parental support and competent management at school can avoid these problems and allow development to proceed normally.

Delayed puberty, on the other hand, carries quite a different weight of emotional stress. Feelings of inadequacy tend to prevail, and a sense of unfairness—one lacks what everyone else has; one is left out, left behind. The boy worries about the size of his genitals; he is patently smaller than his peers, and castration anxiety begins to mount. In some instances the youngster has had many conflicts about growing up; under such circumstances the delay may bring with it a measure of relief. But the partial peer exclusion that prevails, along with the constant experience of being treated as though one were younger, is a strong goad to make development an object of great concern. For the girl the situation is different but not much better. It is baffling and frustrating to the adolescent to feel that she is lacking in this essential dimension that so preoccupies her peers, and she often feels alarmed and woebegone. Moreover, the childhood castration complex which would presumably have been laid to rest long ago is now reawakened, and a tremendous envy is felt toward those who are "ahead."

Dynamically, a sense of punishment is often present. Oedipal pressures cause these youths to experience what is happening as the outcome of wrongdoing or as victimization at the hands of antagonistic and vengeful parents. In particular, the loss of the ticket of admission to the sexual and social framework of adolescent relationships means a dismaying sense of exclusion from a critically important peer experience.

Accidents

Accidents are one of the major causes of death in adolescence. They are less an issue during puberty than in middle and late adolescence, but the groundwork is laid down at this time. No single etiological sequence makes for this class of events. Instead, a concatenation of developmental factors works synergistically to create a state of accident proneness.

To begin with, the acquisition of a mature body is a heady thing, a seductive and evocative experience that leads one to want to use that body, to do things with it. Reflexes are quick at this time of life, and pleasure is taken in their exercise. The newly augmented sensuous capacities of this age (for the first time the capability of orgasm is present) lead to a kind of sensation hunger; young adolescents, especially boys, are possessed by an urgent need to feel. Excitement, thrills, novelty—every kind of stimulating experience—beckon invitingly, and avid youngsters of this age respond, seeking opportunities for stimuli-rich encounters, thrusting themselves into situations of high risk. In effect, they are unlimbering a whole new range of ego functions which they seek to exercise and master. And the pleasure of such mastery is intense.

The superego is barking out warnings, commands, and prohibitions, and the youngster is bridling at these and beginning to heed an inner tendency to challenge warnings and test out the forbidden. Why shouldn't one do what one feels like doing?

The superego is also sending out castration messages—the punishment for rivalrous self-assertion is exactly that. The youngster must deal with this beacon of anxiety and may do so by a series of counterphobic maneuvers. He turns toward the anxiety signal and says in effect, "I do not fear you; I will not let myself be panicked. No, on the contrary, I like you; you give me a thrill. I will seek you out; I will beard you, just to show you you don't scare me; just to show everyone how I like to play with you." The youngster provokes authorities, races past the policeman, dives into the quarry pool, climbs the dangerous mountain—to prove something.

In boys this is often associated with a sense of ordeal, with proving one's manliness. What the exhibitionist seeks to establish crudely and directly, most young people need to demonstrate in more sublimated and socially appropriate fashion. But it does involve doing manly things, and the fear of teasing if one avoids such acts is one of the powerful shapers of childhood and youth. The wish to prove one's manliness is thus an important impetus to danger-seeking behavior and can be observed in everything from a bar mitzvah ceremony to a hazing. The ordeal is to perform a feat before a large audience or before a group of one's peers. A test of one's manhood is present throughout.

Finally, the general increase in emotionality during this period leads to a greater tendency to act out impulses, a proclivity which is one of the distinguishing features of this time of life. Personal tension, anxiety, guilt, sensation hunger, and general pressure of instinct combine to sweep adolescents toward various forms of tension discharge. Action obviously is a most efficient channel for such expression and is part of the normal economics of the epoch. There may, in addition, be more direct factors in the neurological and hormonal rearrangements of this time of life that might lead to this proclivity.

It is a complex matter to identify the "specific" cause of accidents or to distinguish the potentially accident-prone youth from the "safe" one. Statistically, insurance companies have found that they had better raise rates when an adolescent is added to the family's roster of drivers, but that adolescents who are doing well in school tend to have fewer accidents and hence need pay lower premiums. Youngsters whose basic orientation is toward externalization rather than internalization are more likely to be caught in patterns of adaptation which make for such literal impacts with surrounding reality. A variety of diagnostic categories fall into the column of the accident prone.

Adolescent Depression

Varieties of depression appear at this time of life. Some are indigenous; they reflect the adolescent process and are specific to it. Others are carry-overs of earlier depressive constellations, with their specific forms now shaped by the dynamic configuration of puberty. Still depressions have their onset at this time of life and continue into adulthood.

Exogenous Types

Identity structures and characterological defense patterns that have stood the test of time and served the child well for years now shatter, fragment, and lose both form and function. These include the identity of self-as-child (the hallmark of latency) and a body-image pattern that forms part of that identity but contains outlines and definition of its own. Now the sense of connectedness to one's past is lost; continuity of growth seems interrupted and one feels estranged from one's immediately preceding life. Bonds to the parents are affected by distancing devices that are hard at work fending off oedipal wishes (both incestuous and destructive) and protecting the still immature ego from the lashings out of the newly aroused superego. In addition, one's relationship with the larger world shifts radically as development progresses, aided by the culture's decision in many instances to transfer youngsters from grade school to junior high and then to high school on the basis of age or academic achievement rather than in response to attained level of development.

In addition to these disruptive factors, many new and threatening areas of exploration open up. The shift from a homosexual to a heterosexual orientation toward peers is exciting, inviting, and frightening. The ability to understand and grasp the abstract and the conceptual usually brings enrichment, but it can also entail discomfort. Suddenly one understands what has been going on all these years, and it is shocking. This can be experienced in connection with politics, religion, racial issues, the father's role at work, or family relationships. In brief, there is a loss of something, innocence if you will, a loss of continuity and the safe structure of things as they have always been.

And this loss begets pain. The pain is expressed as sadness, moodiness, a kaleidoscopic shifting of emotions. Youngsters at this age pass through dark spells and display all the evidences of an ego under stress. They manifest irritability and touchiness; are restless and full of vague inexpressible longings for they know not what. They may become listless, bored, apathetic, and uncommunicative, and schoolwork may suffer. Or the shift may take a more explosive turn and they may become quarrelsome, cantankerous, and easily upset. Apathy and gloom may settle over the youngster for a time. Avoidance can be a particularly serious complication.

Where the depressive mood is truly developmental in origin there is usually a cardinal sign present—the youngster's unhappiness is immediately relieved by peer interaction. No matter how deep the blue funk, if a friend comes calling or even phones, the youngster brightens immediately. This is a syndrome soluble in peer group interaction.

Psychophysiological Reactions

Many youngsters going through puberty experience their distress in part at least in terms of bodily sensations and malfunctions. Two of the most common forms of such difficulty are headache and vague abdominal pains. In more vulnerable youngsters, the sheer stress of growth and change seems by itself to be cause enough for such reactions. Add to that the many individual encumbrances which converge on that moment in life, and there is no lack of challenge posed to the adaptive mechanisms of the ego. Internalizing adolescents will often experience psychophysiological symptoms under the same circumstances that drive externalizers toward confrontation with their environments. In either instance, the person encounters a set of circumstances that prove too much to handle. Feelings of helplessness, of being out of one's depth and unable to cope, of being hurt or shamed or embarrassed or humiliated, with no way to relieve the intense discomfort—all these together generate enormous internal pressure. A series of disturbing affects—rage, anxiety, depression—flood the ego and are experienced as intolerable. An overflow phenomenon then occurs, a siphoning off of these tensions into the autonomic nervous system. The biological genetic constitution determines what happens next; in the vulnerable individual there is a *locus resistantia minoris*, a readiest pathway for discharge. This may result in a variety of physical complaints, at which point conditioning and social supports for symptoms become powerful discriminating forces.

One way to construe these events is in terms of limbic

system imbalance. A series of positive feedback loops in the emotion-associated limbic pathways leads to a flow of neural pulses of progressively increasing intensity. Presently these can no longer be contained within existing pathways and shoot out into adjacent structures. In internalizers, the constitutional tendency is such that they pour downward into the hypothalamus. This part of the brain is capable of both secretion and neural discharge. It may therefore impinge upon the pituitary, and thus the endocrine system, or instead seek to pour energy into the autonomic nervous system directly. Or it may do both. At each juncture the anatomical and physiological history of the individual determines which pathway is facilitated, which organ targeted. There may also be special vulnerabilities present in respect to some aspect of body image which influence the choice of path of discharge. Thus a history of early nurturant problems may precede vague abdominal pains at a later period. Problems with superego formation may pave the way for later headaches, or the overall dimension of ungovernable stress may cause nonspecific symptoms that are more or less chronically present and unrelated in time or circumstance to identifiable precipitating causes. In any case, the resulting pain or dysfunction may set up eddying currents in the ego, foci of preoccupation, cathexis, and body image disturbance that alter the economics of the psychic apparatus. These in turn act as additional hindrances to adjustment and complicate the youngster's problems. They may generate secondary adaptations and be employed as excuses to avoid stressful situations such as school or dates. All sorts of subtle cueing within families may facilitate the choice of one symptom pathway over another. With sufficient reward and reinforcement of given problems (e.g., the mother has herself experienced severe dysmenorrhea and becomes especially concerned about her daughter's recurrent stomachaches even when these are unrelated to her menses), special sensitivities may ensue which increase the likelihood that one particular form of discomfort will be complained of, especially when there is a test at school, or when grandmother comes to visit.

Often these events are part of adaptation syndromes in which the youngster lacks good coping methods. There is a sense of social incompetence, of intellectual inability, of defeat in trying to make one's mark in the family or in the world—and the body becomes the bearer of the message: I hurt. This sequence needs to be differentiated from conversion reaction, whereby a symbolic compromise solution to an intense unconscious conflict causes a certain dramatization of a fantasy to be lived out in connection with body image configuration. The conversion reaction is usually found, along with other neurotic symptoms, in association with a hysterical personality structure. The distribution of the disability defies any known neurological, anatomical, or physiological pathway. The psychophysiological reaction, by contrast, may occur with almost any type of personality organization (including the hysterical). Commonly (but by no means always) specific target structures are involved that show evident changes: flushing, blanching, swelling, etc. Treatment of the conversion reaction may require careful working out of the underlying neurotic conflict. For the psychophysiological disorder, treatment must be addressed to the overall adaptive stresses the youngster is undergoing. Supportive measures are often of considerable benefit.

The Minor Alienation Syndrome

A substantial group of youngsters seek solutions to familial and personal problems by action within the larger social framework. They find and join a cultural entity radically at odds with the matrix within which they have been reared. Although very diverse developmental sequences may give rise to this form of behavior, certain common elements seem present in all cases. Usually there is a background of troubled family affiliations. Perhaps one parent has died, and the other has had a hard time coping; often marital discord, separation, and divorce have marked the parental relationship, sometimes complicated by the insistence of one parent or the other on a particular form of group adherence, be it ethnic, religious, or national. These youngsters' efforts to deal with the oedipal issues of puberty are compounded by this marital disruption; it seems all too real to them that they are responsible, that their forbidden incestuous and murderous fantasies have influenced the lives of their parents. They cannot use available cultural structures to expiate this sin, as they are part and parcel of the parental realities. If their parents would send them to a priest or rabbi, they turn to atheism or to another faith; if the parents encourage psychotherapy, they seek out any of several convenient religions that specialize in beckoning to the disenchanted. A great many group-oriented religious structures have emerged: Scientology, Reverend Moon's disciples, the Hare Krishna movement, the "Jesus believers," and many smaller communal groups which offer haven and some sort of alternative to family life for such needy young people. In a sense, a peer group is created with adult leadership that promises a chance for a new affiliation in a guilt-free environment. A strong selling point for all such groups is that by the very act of joining one sheds the burdens of the past and finds a way to proceed in life with a sense of belongingness, acceptance, and a maintained sense of distance from the past. Of crucial importance in all this is the new ideology. One is no longer the guilty begetter of divorce; one is instead part of a larger, loving entity that understands all, forgives all, and shows how best to proceed.

Dynamically, the issues here are largely superego oriented. The peculiar vicissitudes of pubertal superego development lie at the center of this problem. Blos (1958) has indicated how in prepuberty the presence of the pregenital mother dominates the inner life of the child, through both the yearning for infantile satisfactions and the fear of the oral, devouring punisher. As puberty proceeds, this presence subsides and is eclipsed by the mounting pressure of the castrating father, at once punitive and ethical. At the outset such formations are at best undeveloped and primitive, and youngsters must explore them and rework them over months and years. Gradually, with additional identifications, ever more value-oriented and mature structures emerge which are closer to consciousness and allow for greater freedom to choose ethical stances and appropriate courses of action. In the course of these developments, considerable use is made of experimental value structures often worked out within the context of peer group interactions. Group attitudes have about them a certain moral force; they are closely akin to the basic psychological nature of superego structure. Normally, these do not altogether replace the internalized familial figures as guides and limits to behavior; they merely allow for richer experience. There is an ongoing testing out and a measuring of one's own superego elements against those of other youngsters with similar dispositions. When growth proceeds in a healthy way, group values are used to the extent that they enrich and enhance existing superego positions. The youngsters seek to give their moral, ethical, and value stances increasingly precise definition, to apply them to all sorts of new situations in order to see how they work, to compare them with the views and values of others, and perhaps to add additional dimensions of structure as they are discovered.

Where the superego formation has been deformed by the nature of the experience with parents, youngsters may feel as though they harbor an internal enemy. There is a terrible pressure that emanates from this inner presence. The messages that come in from this quarter say: shame! evil! wicked! pay! suffer! The devouring mother has not been put to rest; instead this presence joins the castrative destroyer to create a sense of intolerable threat. Such youngsters fend these off as best they can, but clearly it is an impossible position. Either they get depressed, perhaps even committing suicide, or they externalize the entire sequence and strive to live it out in some way. They may try to flee from it into group affiliations that will help blanket these inner experiences—hence the all-too-ready affiliation with superego-oriented social structures that seem to have so much appeal to so many youngsters.

Rage, frustration, and hurt are evident in such a syndrome. These children are intensely troubled by serious internal conflicts and by the pain engendered by this inimical inner presence. They blame their parents for this distress and feel deeply wounded by the parental failure to protect them from this dismaying experience. The youngsters feel it is their own fault that things went wrong, but somehow it is the parents' fault too. They want to disaffiliate themselves from these pain engenderers, to distance themselves from what they stand for, and they want to get even. The consequences of this alienation are often of catastrophic proportions. The parents have been hav-

ing enough difficulty; suddenly their problems are compounded. There is a peculiar pleasure in the act of parenting
that comes from seeing one's values transmitted. Parents offer
their children the beliefs, attitudes, and traditions that they
themselves hold most dear. These each child must decide to
accept or reject. When things go well, acceptance seems auto-
matic, inevitable. The youngsters certainly see other models,
but these seem curious, eccentric. They can't really imagine
behaving other than as their parents do and as their culture
would have it; it is the only way that makes sense. Here the
superego is well integrated, without that quality of hostile and
critical assertiveness that is the case with more troubled youths.

Often enough, however, as adolescence gets under way,
youngsters begin to question the old ways and to explore alternative values. Parents observe this process with concern.
There are always occasional notes of anxiety as their children
question some tenet of faith or experiment with alternative ways
of life. And then there is the intense gratification when such
experiments end with a return to the basic value position. This
transmission of values, if successful, is one of the most positive
rewards of parenting and is associated with moments of intense
conscious pleasure.

But when the transfer of values does not work well, the
distress felt by parents is intense. There is a mixture of feelings
stirred up by such an event: a profound narcissistic injury that
the self, offered here in its most ideal form, has been judged
and found wanting. There is a deep sense of guilt that one's
responsibilities as a parent have not been met—one has failed
in a major way to pass on one's traditions. Some sense of the
extent of parental reaction can be arrived at by noting the
frequency with which oral themes are reported by such parents.
In this new guise their child sickens them; they are disgusted
by the new appearance or attitudes. Aside from what this situation does to the quality of parent-child interaction, it is often
appalling in its effects on parental self-concept and self-value.
In generating these feelings, alienated youngsters take their
revenge. Occasionally parents respond by totally disaffiliating
themselves from such children, disowning or disinheriting
them. But the dry ashes of that "victory" are small solace in the

face of the object loss, the narcissistic injury, and the superego pain they experience.

Group Delinquency

A somewhat different form of alienation occurs when the superego pathology leads youngsters not so much toward cultural disaffiliation as toward aggression. These adolescents do not turn away from the value set to embrace another; rather they turn toward it and attack, thereby entering the complex and difficult world of antisocial behavior, about which more is written and less understood than almost any other aspect of adolescent maladjustment.

Of the many categories of acting out, only one will be discussed here: youngsters who do not seem individually to commit depredations, but who take part in activities initiated by a group of peers. Such youngsters seem weak and easily led; they seem to seek companionship and peer acceptance rather than revenge or an outlet for rage. It would appear that they want to keep up, to avoid being shamed or teased or left out, and they join in gang activities for that reason. When caught, they seem fearful and guilty and promise never to do it again, but often enough are back with the gang immediately and continue as before.

In such cases the dynamic element is typically a combination of ego and superego pathology. Among other things, there are present a basically low sense of self-esteem and a chronic low-grade rage that remains masked and seldom surfaces as such. Phenomenologically it is far more likely to appear as passivity or sullenness. Feelings of attachment to parents are weak; somehow such youngsters have grown up with no great feeling of being loved or valued, and with a considerable sense of having been cheated. Much of this is quiet; they do not say a great deal or think about parents in quite these terms. Instead, these youngsters seek out and find angry youths and groups who will speak for them. The operating superego here is without clear values; indistinct and ambiguous, they lack the introjected quality of authority of which Sandler (1960) speaks. These values are, nonetheless, experienced as threatening and inimical, making these youths feel oppressed and pushed from within. The relief obtained by joining a group and letting its mores take over the superego function is experienced as heaven-sent. No longer must one knuckle under; as part of the group one has joined a functioning superegolike entity, and doing what everybody else does somehow makes it okay. The group catalyzes the expression of otherwise suppressed impulses and is sought out for precisely that reason. All these youngsters have the opportunity to join nondelinquent groups, but they don't feel as good with other, less angry children. Their sense of self is one of having little to offer, certainly nothing anyone would want very much. They anticipate rejection and failure and can conceive of success and acceptance only as a result of participating in the acting out. Predators may not be loved, but they are always respected. By letting it be known that they have shared in such exploits, they will be valued; only then will they find relief for what hurts inside.

Treatment of the group delinquent is not necessarily easier than that of the individual delinquent; the problems are not superficial. But a greater element of control is present. There is a measure of compromise reached—antisocial behavior is made contingent on the external factor of the group rather than taking form as a simple, direct expression of antisocial impulses. On the whole, there is more to work with.

The Adolescent with Minimal Brain Dysfunction

This syndrome is usually diagnosed in latency in connection with school difficulties. The youngsters display characteristic patterns of hyperactivity, distractibility, poor attention span, difficulties in certain patterns of movement, and, in many cases, specific learning deficits. They seem to have egos which are constitutionally incapable of mastering the drives. Even when well socialized, these youngsters show a good deal of difficulty in "putting on the brakes," especially when excited. Their restlessness and awkwardness evoke teasing and many negative social pressures; when their attention and learning deficits lead to poor school achievement, they are regarded or regard themselves as "dumb." They incorporate a picture of themselves as peculiar, weird, spastic, stupid, or, at best, different in some unfortunate way.

On the basis of EEG, neurological and laboratory studies, several varieties of MBD have been defined. There is a group who display minor physical anomalies (Waldrop and Halverson, 1971; Rapaport, Quinn, and Lamprecht, 1974); a group who give evidence of low arousal on EEG (Satterfield, 1973); a group with soft neurological signs (Werry, Minde, Guzman, Weiss, Dogan, and Hoy, 1972); a group with reduced levels of monoamines in urine or platelets (Wender, 1969; Rapaport, Lott, Alexander, and Abramson, 1970; Coleman, 1971). Family studies suggest at least some evidence of a genetic factor, as in reports of similar findings in parents and siblings (Millichap, 1973; Satterfield, Cantwell, and Satterfield, 1974).

As these youngsters move into adolescence, the hyperactivity seems to diminish, but the awkwardness may persist. More than that, the "attention deficit disorder" remains and continues to plague these youths' attempts to cope with school. A pattern of failure or, at best, of academic inadequacy has been in the picture throughout; now, in adolescence, the demands are greater than ever and the pressures more painful. Who wants to date someone like that? Who wants him at a party? As a result, accumulated feelings of low self-esteem bear heavily on these youngsters. They become depressed, morose, and often irritable and resentful. Their constitutionally weak impulse control apparatus sometimes results in serious eruptions. It has been estimated that many such youngsters (perhaps a quarter of them) drift into delinquency, and about 10 percent have police records. Long-range follow-ups have suggested that some MBD youngsters become seriously emotionally ill (Menkes, Rowe, and Menkes, 1967; Wood, Reimherr, and Wender, 1976).

Ego pathology is central to this disorder. Many ego functions are affected: perception is distorted; short-term memory is often weakened; the integration of perceptual and expressive patterns is deficient; the regulation of attention and concentration is seriously awry; the ability to screen out extraneous stimuli and to keep figure distinct from ground is abnormal; the management of emotions is poorly accomplished; and the inhibition of impulse is faulty. Motor patterns may be affected. A dysregulation of motor integration is often present, with the youngster appearing jerky, awkward, and twitchy. In many such cases the saving grace seems to be that superego organization is not necessarily defective, and many of these boys and girls do reasonably well. Perhaps the largest cohort becomes part of that broad group of youngsters who do not shine at school but who struggle by one way or another, who are regarded more or less as "oddballs," yet who are not so deviant that they fail all social inclusion, and who eventually are lost in the general population.

Anorexia Nervosa

This condition is found characteristically as part of puberty. It may occur earlier—it has been reported as early as age 4 (Sylvester, 1945)—or later, but the large majority of cases are diagnosed at this time. It occurs far more often in girls than in boys (in a ratio of 20:1) and can be most serious. Indeed it has been reported to have a mortality rate between 7 and 25 percent. By and large, it is a condition of the middle class, the relatively affluent, and appears to be increasing in frequency.

It has been studied and reported most intensively by Bruch (1973), who divides the condition into primary and secondary varieties. In the secondary forms, the primary condition may be hysterical, phobic, borderline, depressive, psychotic, or due to some other personality aberration; in such instances the failure to eat is merely a surface symptom. Thus, a hysterical youngster who vomits on the basis of a conversion reaction, a psychotic child with fantasies of devouring and being devoured, and a phobic compulsive youngster afraid of germs all may avoid eating.

The primary form of the condition, on the other hand, has a unique dynamic configuration and typical symptom picture. The child generally has a history of good behavior, compliance, neatness, and adequate school performance. Somewhere around the beginning of puberty the youngster becomes interested in issues of overweight and diet. Occasionally this comes after an illness, sometimes there is an account of being teased about being fat, or perhaps a coach or hygiene teacher has made some remark about weight. In any case, the child decides to go on a diet. In a short time the dieting takes over the youngster's life and a condition of near starvation ensues. There are occasional gluttonous food binges, followed by even more intensive efforts to lose weight. Meanwhile, the youngster's activity patterns also change. There is an increasing effort to exercise (this may take the form of calisthenics, running, ballet, or gymnastics) which before long assumes a driven character as it is alleged to help with the weight problem. Coupled with the marked aversion to eating is a great deal of interest in what others eat. Some anorexic youngsters love to prepare elaborate meals for their friends and families. There is also an almost panicky reaction to the notion of gaining weight, which is watched with sedulous care.

In its more severe and life-threatening forms, this condition will go on until the patient is physiologically overwhelmed by the combination of overexertion and lack of nourishment, at which point any one of several forms of physiological failure can follow. As the biological imbalance gets under way, a characteristic finding is cessation of menses. Blood pressure falls, body temperature drops, pulse and respiration slow, and in some cases a light downy hair appears over the extremities. Emaciation is striking and stands in sharp contrast to the patient's continuing protest about being overweight.

Bruch (1973) has described three characteristics that define the anorexic. First, there must be a profound disturbance in body image and concept; the cathexic patient, down literally to skin and bones, speaks worriedly of being too fat. Second, there is a distortion in the way the patient perceives stimuli from within the body. Hunger is not felt, or the patient eats almost nothing and feels full, although in the earlier stages, the patient was much concerned with hunger (Bruch, 1978). Third, the patient feels like a passive, ineffectual puppet in the hands of some all-powerful master. A pervasive sense of helplessness permeates these patients' lives, and it is to cope with this profoundly distressing feeling that they develop anorexia. If they can master nothing else, they can at least control their own bodies and urges. The excesses to which this striving leads them constitute the anorexia syndrome.

Sours (1969) sees three clinical courses as typical of the illness. The first group are girls who develop their symptoms early in puberty. In effect, they are at war with their own pubescence. They seek to stifle sexual form and sexual feeling, to hold back development. To further this, they regress to a mixture of oral and oedipal levels, and the anorexia serves in part to protect them against fantasies of oral impregnation. However, the regression exposes them to a reencounter with the engulfing images of early experience; by not eating, they seek to master these as well.

The symptoms of the second group tend to appear in middle and late adolescence. These are girls who most closely meet Bruch's criteria for primary anorexia. Primitive defenses such as splitting, projecting, denying, and acting out predominate. Body image distortions and disturbances in inner perception are marked. In particular, the sense of personal ineffectiveness is the hallmark of their adjustment.

The third category comprises anorexic boys. Prepubescents or young adolescents, usually rather chubby, they fear their newly burgeoning oedipal yearnings. They strive for masculinity by overcoming maternal dependency feelings, or tendencies to merge, and they do so by stopping the intake of nourishment.

There are many secondary characteristics associated with all these young patients, regardless of the subgroup to which they belong. Often they are manipulative and deceptive, finding many ways to put off eating or to convince their caretakers that they have eaten when in fact they have hidden their food or flushed it down the toilet. They argue, bargain, accuse, complain, and are by no means easy to deal with. Careful, precise pediatric management, coupled with close observation and a stringent routine, is basic to their initial biological recovery. Psychotherapeutic intervention is essential, and family involvement is a critical factor for longer range psychological healing. Behavioral therapy has been tried and is currently felt to be undesirable (short-term improvements are readily achieved at the expense of long-term recurrence), but there is no guaranteed or "standard" means of cure. Recovery comes rapidly in some cases, but many others drag on as chronic problems, regardless of the approach.

True Neuroses

The neuroses are usually assumed to take form in latency. Prior to that, the immature ego can develop neurotic symptoms as it strives to cope with some of its conflicts, but it does not have the necessary organization to construct a true neurosis. The presence of the superego supplies the component heretofore lacking; it allows the full structure of a neurosis to be elaborated.

In particular, this condition speaks for a failed ego operation. It begins with an id impulse contained within an ego defense. But the protective measures of the ego are insufficient, and the resulting configuration partially conceals and partially reveals the forbidden impulse. There is always a measure of success achieved by efforts to keep the impulse at bay; this is evidenced by the fact that awareness of the impulse is successfully curtailed (the factor of unconsciousness is here paramount). The element of failure lies in the fact that the patient is not functioning well in some area. Symptoms appear which are troublesome and inconvenient: "paralysis," loss of voice or memory, obsession by some troublesome thought, compulsion to perform some symbolic action, anxiety "for no good reason," depression "for no good reason." In brief, the patient develops some thought, feeling, or behavior which is limited in scope, which is felt to be unpleasant and foreign to the smooth functioning of the self, and which spares the rest of the ego.

Hysterical symptoms, anxiety attacks, and neurotic depressive reactions are particularly likely during early adolescence; they represent the initial struggles to keep a cap on the newly emergent erotic and aggressive impulses. Occasionally, these are organized into full-blown neurotic conditions that are stable over time.

The Depersonalization Syndrome

Among the common phenomena that characterize pubertal experience is the state of transient depersonalization. Many pubertal youngsters pass through such states for a few seconds or a few minutes at a time. As a rule, these episodes are fleeting; on coming out of such a state one can scarcely say what has happened, or where one has been. Occasionally, however, the transformation is not momentary; the youngster gets "stuck" in such a frame of mind and cannot "come back." This disturbing experience gives rise to intense feelings of dismay. It is immensely distressing, sometimes to the point of engendering ideas of suicide. Resolution of the condition is usually spontaneous, but in many instances psychotherapy is necessary to carry the youngster past the sense of despair and to help relieve the symptoms.

The actual experience involves several dimensions. To begin with, the sensory world is altered. Vision seems strange, sometimes all perception is hazy, and the images seem far away. When the youngster stretches out an arm, it appears to be elongated; a hand seems much more distant than the actual length of the arm. Sound, too, is altered; there is a harsh, or brassy, or tinny quality when people speak. Sometimes it seems as if they are talking through some barrier, and always as if from a distance. Distantiation is characteristic of the syndrome.

Feelings about one's body are also very different. It is as though the body belonged to someone else; it has a wooden or a dead feeling. There is a distinct sense of estrangement here, a quality of occupying a body that is in some vital way not one's own. The relationship of thoughts has also undergone a transformation. One's thoughts have a kind of independence; they march across the field of awareness as if generated outside the self, as if one were a hapless spectator as thoughts and actions proceed on their own. Finally, the feelings are fundamentally changed. They seem muted or absent. One feels unrelated to one's emotions or altogether distant from them. Sometimes they are described as leaden or as gone. The whole sense of self is transformed; identity is split. One lives one's usual life, but one is also a small helpless figure who stands at the side and observes that other person react, who reaches vainly for contact with others and with that self, who feels barred from access to one's world, and who can do nothing to get back. The condition seems to be a form of hysterical dissociation, one that operates defensively at a time of major identity fragmentation and reconstruction. The more transient and commonplace moments of depersonalization seem to emerge from the ego's efforts to integrate all the new elements of ego function and character formation. In a sense, the fleeting experiences of estrangement reflect the occasional slips that occur on the way to assembling this complex array in a balanced and symmetrical fashion.

Occasionally, however, there is a more major disruption in the assemblage of these parts. The ego's integrative functions cannot quite make elements match—some affective valence is too intense; some forbidden unconscious conflict too invasive. Things have to be kept apart for a while until the defensive structures can knit a firmer webbing and reconstruct a tighter seam. Instead of uniting the various fragments and functions, they need to be kept isolated for a while, and the syndrome follows.

A major problem is to distinguish between this temporary neurotic solution and the beginnings of a far more serious and persistent psychotic process. Certain schizophrenic syndromes also begin with a state of depersonalization, but in these instances the degree of disturbance is usually far more severe and tends to be progressive. Bizarre notes creep in. Delusions are almost always present. Hallucinations are common, and the quality of the affective state is far more empty as a rule than is true for this syndrome. Occasionally, a period of observation is necessary in order to be certain about the diagnosis.

Problems in Adolescent Sexuality: Pregnancy, Promiscuity, Incest

The process of transforming the self into a young man or woman is seldom simple. Gender role is assigned by the nurturing environment; gender identity is achieved by the work of separation-individuation. As one leaves the initial unity of self and mother, and the later involvement between self and oedipal couple, a certain element of each is retained. The child incorporates the messages and the models of the circumambience within which he grows and develops. Where these are discordant and cacophonous, the identity that is presently forged, including the sexual identity, will be askew in like proportion. The youth may find himself prey to conflicting models or impulses and ideals that are radically at variance one with the other. The inner signposts which guide behavior and relationship point simultaneously in different, and opposed, directions. There is no inner compass that points the way, that tells one who to be and how to act.

The needs for nurturance and for the elementary protections against primary loneliness may never have been met. The deepest yearnings of a young developing life may center on just such issues; compared to these needs, all other drives are of secondary force. Thus, one basis for adolescent pregnancy is formulated again and again by teenage girls who speak of the baby as the answer to all the pain of early privation. In fantasy, the infant becomes someone all their own, to whom they can show all the love and care that they seek so urgently for themselves, someone who will need them, love them, and will not leave them. It is a possession treasured beyond all other treasures, something so uniquely one's own that it is a part of the self. Impregnation and gestation may become the primary goals of such a life. The girl child may dislike the act of copulation, fear it, have frightening fantasies about it, about pregnancy, and especially about childbirth. In spite of all these, she will be driven by an aching inner emptiness to seek to fill herself with life and thus relieve the profound depressive void bequeathed by her impoverished childhood. Neither reasoning nor education offers her much protection; the hunger is too great.

Another force at work in many pregnant teenage girls is the unrelieved stress of the unresolved castration and oedipal complexes. A girl may have been the one female of four siblings; she is bracketed by older and younger brothers, and her mother fails to understand her plight and help her with her burgeoning femininity. The girl may grow up always feeling the outsider, deficient and incomplete. With her entry into puberty, however, her position changes. Suddenly she is regarded differently; she can command the eyes of male peers. She has something to offer. She has the power to excite, to make conquests. She can find worth in the previously despised femininity itself. Her own uncertain gender identity, her wish to be a boy like the others, her fantasy at times of really being a boy except for not having a penis, all give way to the need to assert herself as a girl, to prove that she is fully female. There is no more certain way to achieve that state than being pregnant. In contrast to the first group, such girls often can benefit from sex education courses, from rap sessions, from counseling, or from work with the family.

Under certain conditions, powerful cultural and familial vectors can come to bear on the pubertal girl and move her toward pregnancy. A mother may send many covert messages to the budding young woman that she is grown up now, that mother has lost her baby. The mother recollects with a sigh how when she was 13 she had her own first baby and never loved anybody like she loved that baby. As a matter of fact, the mother remarks, she had been Grandmother's baby when grandmother was still in *her* teens. Thus, in this or in some analogous way the family and the culture it represents impinge on the pubertal youngster and head her in this direction.

Like most conditions, early pregnancy has its primary and secondary forms. Some youngsters do not seek pregnancy as such. They may wish to trick a boy into marrying them or seek an excuse to get out of their homes. They may desire principally to spite a parent, compete with a rival, or demonstrate that nobody can tell them how to behave. Pregnancy, then, is only one of many ways by which to achieve that end. Some youngsters are overwhelmed by the encounter with the sensuous. They seek the sexual experience as such and have no wish to be pregnant; carrying the gestation to term may come about because they are so busy denying and concealing what they are doing that their condition is recognized only when it is too late for an abortion. The large majority of such secondary syndromes are far more susceptible to preventive or early intervention than are the various kinds of primary pregnancy.

The role of the boys who impregnate is beginning to receive

a certain amount of attention. Much of their behavior is a result of the sensation hunger of adolescence, the exploratory interest in gratifying bodily yearnings. They have little or no interest in impregnation. There is a definite subgroup, however, whose emotional situation involves a profound concern about masculinity. They have a pressing need to prove their manliness to themselves and their world. In line with this, they seek to get as many girls pregnant as they can and take pride in the achievement. This often helps shore up a fragile sense of maleness forever tottering on the brink of effeminacy or infantilism; they need this visible demonstration of their manliness to undo their hidden inner weakness.

Similar dynamics are at work in certain forms of promiscuity. Both boys and girls are likely to discover that their sexual apparatus is a means of bringing people close; it is like a beacon, drawing interest, attention, attempts at conversation, and acts of friendliness. On the part of one partner, these may all be means to an end; but for the deprived, depressed, relationship-starved youth, the bargain is a good one. Instead of a void, there is a presence; instead of emptiness, there is sensation; instead of loneliness, sex play. Words of love are bandied back and forth and gestures of affection exchanged. Perhaps it is all a trick to obtain sexual advantage, but for the moment, at least, it offers the illusion of caring that serves as an anodyne to the pain.

The later forms of promiscuity are often connected to phallic oedipal issues. There is a constant striving to undo castration, to prove one's sexual capacity, to reaffirm the intactness of one's own body, or to overcome a gnawing sense of defect. This necessity drives many a boy and girl to extremes of sexual hyperactivity that make for very disturbing patterns. The need to overcome the hurt and fear of oedipal encounter can act as a continuing goad and may spur protracted attempts to recoup. But each reassurance, each bit of "success," lasts only briefly. The nagging need reappears; the unmastered tension mounts once more and must again be dealt with. One young girl with a history of extensive sexual activity described an affinity for married men. During intercourse she would think to herself:

What would his wife say if she knew he was doing this? Thus, the youngster's oedipal hunger would be slaked by a momentary "victory" whose effect was as evanescent as the act itself, and she then would need another "victory," and yet another. The permutations and combinations of such needs often lead to intricate patterns of love-hate relationships that enmesh young lives in complex transactions that are even more destructive than they are involved.

Perhaps the most potentially dangerous pattern of this kind is that associated with the direct acting out of oedipal impulses in the form of incest. This behavioral sequence typically embraces a number of elements. Its most common form includes a newly pubertal daughter, an unconsciously compliant mother, and an unstable father. The father is sexually drawn to the daughter's budding sexuality; he begins to explore her body and presently involves her in intercourse. The mother manages to remain oblivious to this or even to foster it, and the pattern, once established, may persist for years. Numerous studies have indicated that both mother and daughter may lend themselves to the maintenance of the arrangement. The child herself is often caught in the midst of conflicting yearnings. On the one hand are the sexuality of puberty and the realization of the oedipal wish; on the other, the full weight of the superego presses on her with a nagging and insistent sense that she is doing something shameful, wrong, forbidden. Often the situation is not revealed until the child begins to tell school friends or neighbors. Sometimes her attempts to report it to her mother lead only to disbelief and punishment. For that matter, this can happen with community people as well.

The long-range prognosis was long held to be dismal, but in recent years studies indicate that a wide spectrum of developmental consequences may ensue. Thus, there are instances where a history of incest is reported by apparently well-adjusted adult women or where the subsequent effects appear only mild. But in the light of the many severe reactions that do occur, it is well to regard it as a serious stress for the child's work of development, one that carries with it the possibility of catastrophic personality disturbance.

Delinquency

One of the most common forms of emotional disturbance in adolescence takes the character of antisocial acting out. Although the subject of intense research over many decades (Martin and Fitzpatrick, 1964), it continues to defy easy formulation. Here only a limited number of aspects are presented.

Etiology

Antisocial behavior has been variously ascribed (1) a given set of social conditions that would affect any population subjected to them (Burgess, Lohman, and Shaw, 1937); (2) an array of personal and behavioral traits characteristic of lower working class populations (Miller, 1958); (3) limited peer group models which require a child growing up in poor neighborhoods to mingle with and, ultimately, emulate the tough kids (Sutherland, 1947); (4) the frustrations attendant on lower class youths who are tempted by middle-class advantages yet lack any means by which to achieve them (Cohen, 1955); (5) the rage engendered by the lack of opportunities for upward mobility in a society which demands such progress (Cloward and Ohlin, 1960); (6) a lack of affection during early developmental periods (Bowlby, 1944); and (7) the transmission of covert instructions to act out because of familial superego lacunae (Johnson, 1949).

There is a clear socioeconomic dimension here; statistically, delinquency is associated with poverty. Many factors are present at once, such as emotional exhaustion of single parents; lack of adequate care and nutrition during pregnancy and the postnatal period; alcoholism and drug abuse among caretakers; adolescent parenthood; households characterized by the coming and going of many people, in which interpersonal relationships are attenuated and primitive; emotional instability among significant adults; unpredictable eruptions of violence and brutality; child abuse and sexual exploitation of children; wildly inconsistent management of children; much passing of care responsibilities among caretakers; an absence of stable and wholesome identification models; frequent moves, and chronic lack of adequate funds to ensure a sense of safety and stability in the home. In varying combinations these lead to a childhood characterized by a lack of trust; a paucity of opportunities for forming stable identifications; a ground-in sense of being small, weak, and inadequate in the face of an overwhelming and unpredictable world; a defensively maintained status of infantile grandiosity; chronic rage at the frequent frustration of the need for care and attention; recurrent depressive reactions because of shifts from home to home and caretaker to caretaker; periodic episodes of flooding overstimulation as a result of sadistic abuse and sexual exploitation during the infantile period, along with lack of adequate stimulation of cognitive functions; patterns of spotty health care that might fail to deal with early lead intoxication; the effects of undiagnosed and untreated petit mal, temporal lobe, or even grand mal epilepsy; and undetected disturbances of vision and hearing, along with a variety of other physical disorders.

The result is a suspicious, distrustful child who experiences a sense of basic unfairness in the very fabric of things. The youngster cannot develop good impulse controls and faces life in a state of chronic rage. Again and again he must deal with the consequences of loss of control. Later on he cannot concentrate or learn in school. If he has the ego strength, the street teaches him to become wily, manipulative, and an excellent dissimulator. He learns to be devious and opportunistic, and he never learns to be other than totally self-centered. Social and sexual relationships are exploitative and exhibitionistic. He is early attracted to the "rackets" and gets used to lots of money. And a sizable fraction of his youth will be spent in various lockups and industrial schools.

The less gifted youth is likely to lack the ego capacities to become an adequate manipulator; his fate is therefore to be read in the annals of the violent and the vandalistic. He is filled with anger, bitterness, and self-hate and can be merciless and vicious in his depredations. In the course of an interview, he is likely to be silent and monosyllabic, often sullen and negative, and usually lacking in the ability to express fantasy. Fixations are at a level where anal sadism and power struggles dominate his horizon.

The more sensitive or more vulnerable youth is likely to add the dimension of drug abuse or alcoholism to his lifestyle. This becomes a major begetter of delinquent behavior in its own right, as well as a source of destructive medical complications.

Often the attempts such youngsters make to help themselves are aborted by their organic difficulties. The residue of lead poisoning and the malnourished brain, the chronic interference of undiagnosed seizure potential (petit mal or psychomotor temporal lobe discharges), the disruptive effects of MBD or low-grade chronic brain syndromes, the stress of trying to adapt with subnormal vision or hearing, or the vitiating effects of other chronic diseases which are not properly cared for—these may singly or in combination pose insuperable hurdles for even the well-motivated child to overcome. The acting-out pattern appears during the early years at school and continues throughout childhood and youth. By the time puberty arrives, the youngster is wise in the ways of the street and firmly locked into his characterological set. In brief, certain forms of socioeconomic stress seem to be prime breeders and maintainers of a state of antisocial adjustment.

It is all too evident that many other forms of delinquency exist. Dynamically, the approach to etiology is couched in somewhat different terms. In order to give some sense of the way these syndromes are constructed, three etiological factors are described along with some of the prime ego mechanisms that are typically present.

The etiology of these conditions seems primarily environmental. Various genetic theories have been advanced, but none has really fulfilled its promise. The environmental factors that seem especially important include emotional deprivation—a lack of adequate emotional nurturance in the first year of life leaves the individual with a seriously diminished capacity to empathize or even identify with others (Bowlby, 1944). As a result, adequate superego formation does not take place, impulse control mechanisms develop awry, and the potential exists for the formation of an "affectionless character." In a sense, youngsters who emerge from early deprivation in this way are the lucky ones. The rest become cases of failure to thrive, mental retardation, schizoid character, or frank psychosis. There are, of course, numerous variants in terms both of constitutional differences and of evironmental management. Thus, one youngster can flourish on even minimal emotional nurturance, whereas another remains frustrated and unfulfilled with even a solid and adequate maternal input. Similarly, one environment is characterized by minimal care for the baby in the hands of a 9-year-old sister; another by passing the baby back and forth among a host of transient caretakers (some of whom give more, some less); and a third by a disturbed mother who punctuates extended periods of neglect with transient moments of excessive holding and loving. In each case, it is the individual equation of what shaping factors were present, when, and for how long, that lends the resulting personality its unique coloring.

Overstimulation

The essence of traumatic experience is the flooding of the ego and the overwhelming of its defenses by emotional arousal of excessive intensity maintained for too long a time. For certain children, the erotic and sadistic attentions thrust upon them make their early lives one chronic prolonged trauma. Some react by withdrawal, in effect puckering up their sensory world to shut out this torrent of input and making themselves into dulled, constricted, empty people in the process. Others, however, adapt to this "aggressor" by identifying with it. They become sensation-hungry, chronically excited, hyperalert, and hyperactive. They are forever into things, as invasive of others as they have themselves experienced invasion, and constantly probing and manipulating their environment. Inevitably they are reacted to as destructive pests. They are repeatedly being yelled at, chased away, or punished, and intense negative self-feelings ensue. This adds to the accumulation of trauma, and the youngster reacts with even more activity and hostility. As a rule, it is the encounter with school that brings these problems to a head. Labeling occurs early—these are bad children. Soon they have an image, and they feel pressured to live up to it. As a result, these youngsters often learn deftness, and during latency they become expert thieves, liars, and vandals.

At puberty, shifts in drive and affect tend to intensify the entire constellation; this phase magnifies the difficulties. It also lends these young people a host of physical and intellectual strengths, new resources that become harnessed to their now highly developed antisocial proclivities. Shoplifting and purse snatching may give way to more organized housebreaking and the more serious kinds of street crime. Such youngsters can become dangerous people.

Lack of Limits and Overgratification

This is the spoiled child syndrome. Here are youngsters who are denied nothing by their parents, who ask for and get the moon if they wail long and loud enough. As a result, they are simply unprepared to deal with the vicissitudes of normal give-and-take among peers, with the predictable moments of frustration that enter the average life. The end result begins to be visible in the latency years but truly comes to a head in puberty. The aroused oedipal yearnings of this time of life cannot be satisfied in any direct way, and in these low-tolerance individuals, the experience is galling. They become filled with rage and feel intense vengeful resentment toward their parents, sometimes splitting off part of their lives and living out all sort of antisocial patterns sub rosa. In other cases, the child becomes a sort of mortal enemy of the parents, overflowing with vindictive spleen, heaping endless accusations of deprivation and unfairness on the mother or father, and seeming to work night and day to punish them even if destroying oneself in the process. Underneath all this there is often a veritable sea of guilt on which the entire syndrome floats and into which the youngster cannot peer.

To have gotten one's own way and been given more than one's fair share is gratifying—but it places great burdens on personality organization. In particular, it begets conscience problems, disturbing feelings of something wrong. To avoid any encounter with the tormenting superego, the entire problem is externalized; along with the parent, the teacher is seen as the enemy, as is the policeman, the employer, or anyone with the aura of authority. The youngster takes up cudgels against them all; they are all unfair, all frustraters, depriving the child of entitlements. Such children feel justified in employing the most egregious measures to redress the balance. The more guilty they feel, the more violent they become. It is a situation rife with paradox.

Although relatively few in number, the mental mechanisms basic to these syndromes form in their many permutations and combinations the core of much of what passes for adolescent delinquency. The four most prominent mechanisms are converting passive into active, the counterphobic defense, identification with the aggressor, and externalization. As do most defenses, they indicate that an attempt at repression has failed; the conflicting forces will not stay in the unconscious. The nature of what is repressed varies, however. Converting passive into active implies a state of earlier trauma that has left an ineradicable residue within the personality. There is a haunting feeling of painful helplessness that will not be identified and cannot be forgotten. The pain can be relieved, however, by doing to someone else what one has suffered oneself—for a while at least, one can be doer and not victim. But it is only for a little while, for the need for relief is endless. The sexually exploited girl becomes a seductress or prostitute. The victim of child abuse becomes, in his turn, an abusing parent. The tough, rapacious, street wise youth was once a terrified youngest child cruelly dominated by a whole hierarchy of destructive and envious older siblings. The child subjected to early object loss and later castration threats becomes a shoplifter, a thief. Each in his turn has tried to swallow a bolus of trauma that has lodged in his throat, and all his adaptive resources are marshaled to dislodge it. His delinquency is an endless reliving of the original state of helplessness in reverse. Now it is he who renders the other helpless, dominated, humiliated, castrated, deprived of his precious possession, and crushed physically and spiritually. Some very vicious behavioral patterns indeed are fueled by this mechanism.

Identification with the aggressor is somewhat similar in function and effect. The source of the trauma in this instance can usually be specifically identified, as the youngster is reliving and reworking a relationship with a known person. The conflict here is perhaps somewhat closer to consciousness. It tends to occur in more mature individuals whose traumatic experience has not been as massive and has occurred later; the mechanism itself is less diffuse. It is a more specific response to interaction with particular individuals; an explosive, narcissistic mother; an alcoholic, battering father; or some other figure with like force in one's life.

Externalization has several forms. In its simplest version it involves the turning of some neurotic fantasy onto the environment. The child gives to a teacher the value of some early version of mother or father. The principal at school is another in the archaic pantheon. Peers are perceived as the primordial siblings. Loves, hates, suspicions, dependency attachments, fearfulness, revenge impulses—all are distributed in keeping with the unconscious assignment of roles. The behavior then follows this scenario: there is an unexplainable and inordinate reactivity toward one person or another, with violent flare-ups, baiting, provocation, and all manner of seemingly causeless behavioral disturbance. The nature of the provocations is calculated to evoke the proper responses from the significant others; presently the child re-creates about him the entire constellation of the early traumatic experience and continues to relive and replay it endlessly.

Another, somewhat more specialized, version of this adaptive style is the character Freud (1916) described as "criminal from a sense of guilt" (pp. 332–333). In this pattern the chief conflict is between a cruel and attacking primitive superego and a defending ego unable to cope effectively with this onslaught. The ego tries to repress and sequester the superego, but this is not easily done. The inner voice is too harsh and powerful. A compromise formation is then arrived at: the superego is repressed, and that portion which will not remain unconscious is externalized. Various environmental figures, especially authority figures, are invested with the quality of hostile, unrelenting, and inhumanly vicious predators. They are all versions of the implacable, unloving conscience. One must take up arms against them and seek by every possible artifice to evade, outwit, and defy them. Since they are seen as knowledgeable and dangerous, one must be even more wily and more destructive to stay ahead. In the end, one's efforts are doomed to failure; sooner or later the others will win.

When some given depredation succeeds, the transient sense

of elation is considerable. There is a pervasive quality of guilt associated with all this; these individuals are in a real sense trying to ward off a depression by their antisocial acts. The compromise therefore serves them well. The superego is omniscient; it knows everything one thinks, all of one's evil intentions, every twist and turn one might make to evade the assault. The outside world is much less dangerous; one has a chance. One can hide, dissimulate, get a lawyer—there are many possibilities.

Ultimately, these youngsters tend to get themselves caught or punished. The nature of the psychopathology demands this; they are committed to punishment of the self whether at their own hands or at the behest of society. Again, the degree of destructiveness with which they are involved can be quite serious.

The counterphobic defense is the fourth major mental mechanism. The presence that demands warding off is the imminence of being flooded by anxiety. From early in the lives of these youngsters they have had to cope with separation fears. Later, when gender identity issues come to the fore, they are ill prepared to master castration anxiety; after all, life has already taught them that important presences come and go, that one can be left bereft. Now it is the wholeness of their bodies that can come and go. Vital organs like the genitals are here and not there, on this child's body and not on that one's. The terrifying possibility of losing what is vital, be it narcissistic support, object relatedness, or body part, is excruciating and omnipresent. Again, the child with a potential for acting out seeks an action-oriented means for relieving the pain, for coping with the anxiety. The way that is repeatedly found is to seek out the phobic area and to thrust oneself into it or, going even further, to eroticize the anxiety itself, to make the dangerous pleasurable. Then one can get one's "kicks" in that way—by being daring, bold, adventuresome, thrill-seeking in just those realms that have heretofore been the scariest and the most stressful. The child fearful of being left becomes the chronic runaway; the child most concerned about loss of dependency gratification drops out of school early and is most resistant to parental authority; the child terrified of castration becomes sexually promiscuous and is constantly thrusting at life—if not with the genitals, then by picking fights, exposure to accidents, or involvement with weapons. Whatever was once traumatically frightening is now sought out for repeated reliving; one must demonstrate to oneself and to one's world that one is not afraid, not worried, not cowardly—that, on the contrary, one loves this kind of thing and will seek it anywhere, anytime.

A complex interplay of individual endowments, familial vectors, group pressures, socioeconomic factors, and a host of health, educational, and chance events, then, produces the pattern of the delinquent personality. The individual may come from any socioeconomic level and may present a uniquely individual set of etiological factors. The term "delinquency" is at best nonspecific; it speaks more for the bitter taste the activities of these youngsters leave in the mouths of those who encounter them than it does for any unitary syndrome. Interventional modes, as various as prolonged protective incarceration and psychoanalysis, have been employed with highly unpredictable degrees of success and failure. This is a prime area for future research.

Psychotic Reactions

Of the conditions that can produce psychotic reactions at puberty, the most common today is acute drug intoxication. Methedrine (or other amphetamines) in large quantities are the most frequently encountered psychotogens, but lysergic acid diethylamide (LSD), phencyclidine (angel dust), and other hallucinogens can be all too effective. (In a number of rare instances, marijuana has been implicated.) Glue sniffing subjects the brain to the dubious consequence of certain volatile organic solvents that can have a powerful toxic impact on a vulnerable subject.

The second most frequent variety of psychotic reaction is the acute confusional state of adolescence. This stormy syndrome generally comes on abruptly with a host of frightening behaviors that resemble major psychosis. Youngsters so afflicted are terrified, confused, and depersonalized, and feel totally lost.

They may transiently fail to recognize familiar people, assert that they no longer know who they are, break up furniture, and act drunk without in fact being so. Moments of perfect lucidity alternate with this wild, confused behavior. However, there is no real thought disorder, nor are true delusions or hallucinations present, and the reaction may clear up as abruptly as it appeared. Although frightening, such a reaction does not ordinarily lead to prolonged illness. Major tranquilizers are said to be contraindicated, as they interfere with the coping mechanisms necessary for recovery. In general, the syndrome responds well to various supportive measures. Etiology is not specific. It seems to come on as a consequence of massive developmental stresses; in effect, it represents a transient overwhelming of the defenses by the tide of impulse that comes with puberty. Existing ego structures simply cannot support the load, and for a while the whole apparatus is shaken. But the ego does not fragment; it is able to recoup, control is reestablished, and, as a rule, the youngster seems to come out of it well—frightened but not otherwise damaged. The panicky agitation that accompanies the syndrome represents the fear of loss of control over forbidden impulses as well as of the threat to the ego's basic integrity.

Schizophrenic Psychosis

This condition usually tends to appear in later adolescence. Current thinking sees it as the response of an inherently predisposed ego to normal developmental stress. The usual picture is for developmental factors to combine with external demands so that the vulnerable ego begins to fail to cope, a situation leading to behavioral maladjustment which begets negative social responses and hence more stress. A downward spiral ends with the appearance of psychosis.

There are varying modes of onset, the most common of which is the acute outbreak of symptoms. There is also a type of gradual onset with a slow, progressive slipping away from reality into a more and more withdrawn lifestyle. Not infrequently, the onset appears as a turning toward aggressive acting out, and the patient is considered to be, and is all too often managed as, a delinquent. In any case, there is a loss of boundaries, a cloudiness about body outlines, a loosening of the ego's perimeter, and a sense of withdrawal from people and external reality. Things slide and slip; thoughts and daydreams become as real or more real than external perception. The distinction between the two is lost, and the patient responds to the mind's creations and the distortions they introduce into the perceptual world. Fragile ego boundaries are experienced as open and vulnerable; sights, sounds, and meanings intrude on the youth with enormous force; sounds reverberate strangely with hints of inner dread; visual images are too sharp; boundaries are less a defensive perimeter than a ravaged no-man's-land.

Initially, there is some awareness that the real world is slipping away. Such youngsters seek to cope by sharpening their sensibilities; they hear more clearly, see more brightly, feel all keyed up. Affects come in gusts. There are intense rushes of emotion; sexual fantasies dance before their eyes. They feel curiously alive. At the same time, there is a diminished capacity for sleep; a sense of dread or imminence hovers over them; something is about to happen. Then thoughts begin to gain ever greater autonomy, marching alone and in unusual forms. Strange phenomena (ideas of reference) begin to be noted. People are signaling or laughing about them, and trying to influence them. Menaced, insulted, threatened, and hounded they become frightened. All sorts of restitutive attempts are made to overcome this situation. One kind of youth begins to flail out at the environment and becomes the delinquent mentioned above. In other cases, thinking may take a mystical, philosophical, or religious turn; there is a sense of moving into another plane. Great forces are at work in the world, and evidence for this begins to be sought and found.

As these youngsters sense the crumbling of the basic structure of the ego and the loss of its boundaries, they attempt to construct an alternative arrangement, a logical explanation for what is happening based on delusional formations. Now it all makes sense; they understand. Through pseudologic of magical thinking they regain a measure of coherence and some lessening of the overwhelming anxiety. In effect, regroupment has occurred at an infantile level of ego development and object relations where self and others flow into one another, and the distinction between what is inside the self and what is outside is in large measure lost. Distancing devices come into play, separating these subjects from their own affective life. Now, as the integrity of the ego is lost, islands of function, isolated identifications, voices from the superego, memories, and fantasies may each become tangible; they speak or appear visually. It is hard to put thoughts together because things either are blocked or are running too fast and out of control.

In the face of this enormous influx of threat these youngsters fall silent or become incoherent. With more intellectual youths, where the level of ego fragmentation is less, there is a constant pressure to reorganize a sense of self and self-in-the-world. They may turn to vast generalizations about religion, philosophy, or political ideology and seek to make sense out of what is happening by addressing the forces implicit in the particular system. They are one with God, or are possessed by the devil; are persecuted by communists or are losing themselves in the great proletarian movement, the third world mystique, mystical union with unearthly forces, or some other high-order abstraction. The combinations and permutations are endless, but the loss of a coherent distinction between inner and outer experience and between magical and rational thinking is universal.

The acute state may resolve rapidly. Feinstein and Miller (1979) consider the more transient condition to be a separate entity, an acute psychotic reaction of adolescence and not properly a schizophrenic syndrome. The characteristic chronic reaction may initially look like a borderline state, an acute adjustment reaction, or a deteriorating character disorder (Masterson, 1967). Ultimately, it involves thought disorder, anhedonia, intense dependency, impaired competency, and an injured sense of self (Holzman and Grinker, 1977).

The duration of the condition is highly variable, but after the initial surge of symptoms, there is usually a gradual reintegration so that the florid psychotic manifestations presently disappear. Feinstein and Miller speak of a postpsychotic phase characterized by progressive lessening of the vestiges of the illness, heightened vulnerability to stress, and particular fragility in the face of separation. These residual disabilities may make it difficult for the youngster to work in school. Thus, after the overt psychosis clears there is a slow process of consolidation which may take as long as a year. It is a time for continued active treatment, often for continuing hospitalization, and it demands the most careful attention if adequate emergence from the pathological state is to occur.

Much work has been done on the family structure of such patients, and concepts such as double bind, pseudomutuality, and mystification have been invoked to describe the child rearing styles and the patterns of communication that typify their operation.

An almost passionate quest has been conducted to determine the nature of the biological events accompanying these conditions. Endocrine research, genetic explorations, neurotransmitter studies, and the creation of experimental psychoses by means of various psychoactive agents have all been pursued in depth. Thus far the results are powerfully suggestive but not finally conclusive. It does appear, however, that extensive twin studies have demonstrated beyond reasonable doubt that a genetic factor is present.

References

Blos, P. (1958), Pregenital drive organization. *J. Amer. Psychoanal. Assn.*, 6:47–56.
——— (1967), The second individuation process of adolescence. *The Psychoanalytic Study of the Child*, 22:162–186. New York: International Universities Press.
Bowlby, J. (1944), Forty-four juvenile thieves: Their characters and home life. *Internat. J. Psycho-Anal.*, 25:19–52; 107–127.
Bruch, H. (1973), *Eating Disorders: Obesity, Anorexia Nervosa and the Person Within*. New York: Basic Books.
——— (1978), *The Golden Cage: The Enigma of Anorexia Nervosa*. Cambridge: Harvard University Press.
Burgess, E. W., Lohman, J. D., & Shaw, C. R. (1937), The Chicago Area Project. In: *Coping with Crime: The Yearbook of the National Probation Association*. New York: National Probation Association, pp. 8–28.
Cloward, R., & Ohlin, L. (1960), *Delinquency and Opportunity*. New York: Free Press.

Cohen, A. K. (1955), *Delinquent Boys: The Culture of the Gang*. Glencoe, IL.: Free Press of Glencoe.

Coleman, M. (1971), Serotonin concentrations in whole blood of hyperactive children. *J. Pediat.*, 78:985.

Erikson, E. (1959), Identity and the life cycle. *Psychological Issues*, Monograph 1. New York: International Universities Press.

Feinstein, S. C., & Miller, D. (1979), Psychoses of adolescence. In: *Basic Handbook of Child Psychiatry: Vol. 2. Disturbances in Development*, ed. J. Noshpitz. New York: Basic Books.

Freud, A. (1936), *The Ego and the Mechanisms of Defense*. Rev. ed. New York: International Universities Press, 1966.

——— (1958), Adolescence. *The Psychoanalytic Study of the Child*, 13:279–295. New York: International Universities Press.

Freud, S. (1916), Some character types met with in psycho-analytic work. *Standard Edition*, 14:311–333. London: Hogarth Press, 1957.

GAP (1968), *Normal Adolescence: Its Dynamics and Impact*. Report No. 68. New York: Group for the Advancement of Psychiatry.

Holzman, P., & Grinker, R. R., Sr. (1977), Schizophrenia in adolescence. In: *Adolescent Psychiatry*, Vol. 5, ed. S. C. Feinstein & P. I. Giovacchini. New York: Aronson, pp. 276–290.

Inhelder, B., & Piaget, J. (1958), *The Growth of Logical Thinking from Childhood to Adolescence*. New York: Basic Books.

Johnson, A. M. (1949), Sanctions for superego lacunae of adolescents. In: *Searchlights on Delinquency*, ed. K. Eissler. New York: International Universities Press.

Kohut, H. (1971), *The Analysis of the Self*. New York: International Universities Press.

Martin, J., & Fitzpatrick, J. (1964), *Delinquent Behavior*. New York: Random House.

Masterson, J. F., Jr. (1967), *The Psychotic Dilemma of Adolescence*. Boston: Little, Brown.

Menkes, M. L., Rowe, J. S., & Menkes, J. H. (1967), Twenty-four year follow-up study on the hyperkinetic child with MBD. *Pediatrics*, 39:393–400.

Miller, W. B. (1958), Lower class culture as a generating milieu of gang delinquency. *J. Social Issues*, 14:15–19.

Millichap, J. (1973), Drugs in the management of minimal brain dysfunction. *Annals N.Y. Acad. Sci.*, 205:321.

Offer, D., & Offer, J. (1975), Three developmental routes through normal male adolescence. In: *Adolescent Psychiatry*, Vol. 4, ed. S. C. Feinstein & P. Giovacchini. New York: Aronson, pp. 121–141.

Rapaport, J. L., Quinn, P., & Lamprecht, F. (1974), Minor physical anomalies and plasma dopamine-beta-hydroxylase activity in hyperactive boys. *Amer. J. Psychiat.*, 131:386–391.

——— Lott, I. T., Alexander, D. F., & Abramson, A. U. (1970), Urinary noradrenaline and playroom behavior in hyperactive boys. *Lancet*, 2:1141.

Rotnem, D., Genel, M., Hintz, R. L., & Cohen, D. J. (1977), Personality development in children with growth hormone deficiency. *J. Amer. Acad. Child Psychiat.*, 16:412–426.

Sandler, J. (1960), On the concept of the superego. *The Psychoanalytic Study of the Child*, 15:153–154. New York: International Universities Press.

Satterfield, J. (1973), EEG issues in children with minimal brain dysfunction. *Seminars in Psychiatry*, Vol. 5. Los Angeles: Gateway House, pp. 35–46.

——— Cantwell, D., & Satterfield, B. (1974), The pathophysiology of the hyperkinetic syndrome. *Arch. Gen. Psychiat.*, 31:839–846.

Sours, J. (1969), The anorexia nervosa syndrome: Phenomenologic and psychodynamic components. *Psychiat. Quart.*, 45:240–256.

Sutherland, E. (1947), *Principles of Criminology*. 4th ed. New York: Lippincott.

Sylvester, E. (1945), Analysis of psychogenic anorexia and vomiting in a four year old child. *The Psychoanalytic Study of the Child*, 1:167–187. New York: International Universities Press.

Tanner, J. M. (1962), *Growth at Adolescence*. 2nd ed. New York: Lippincott.

Waldrop, M., & Halverson, C. (1971), Minor physical anomalies and hyperactive behavior in young children. In: *The Exceptional Infant*, Vol. 2, ed. J. Hellmuth. New York: Brunner/Mazel, pp. 343–389.

Wender, P. (1969), Platelet serotonin level in children with "MBD." *Lancet*, 2:1012.

Werry, J. S., Minde, K., Guzman, A., Weiss, G., Dogan, K., & Hoy, E. (1972), Studies on the hyperactive child: VII. Neurological status compared with neurotic and normal children. *Amer. J. Orthopsychiat.*, 15:441–452.

Wood, D., Reimherr, F., & Wender, P. (1976), Diagnosis and treatment of MBD in adults: A preliminary report. *Arch. Gen. Psychiat.*, 33:1453.

6

Adolescent Development: A Normative Perspective

DANIEL OFFER, M.D.

Ernest Jones (quoted in Birnbach, 1961) stated that "psychopathology opened a route to psychology in general, perhaps the most practical route" (p. 7). This thought is based on Freud's earlier comment (1937) that "a normal ego is like normality in general, an ideal fiction" (p. 209). This is reminiscent of the philosopher Kaplan's concept (1967) of "trained incapacity." Trained to recognize the abnormal (defenses, conflicts, and the six metapsychological points of view), the psychoanalyst and his teacher (in the office via the couch, or in the training institutes via supervision) have difficulty in recognizing, let alone conceptualizing, the normal.

The purpose of this chapter is to stimulate interest in the various concepts of normal development and to share what we consider the four basic perspectives on normality (Offer and Sabshin, 1974). In the process we mention briefly some of the highlights of a ten-year study of normal male adolescents.[1] Finally, we make some comments concerning the knotty problem of the relationship between clinical research and normal development.

[1] The longitudinal research program has been supported by the following USPHS grants: Mental Health Career Investigators Grant #4870 of the NIMH (1961–1964); Grant #08714 of the NIMH (1964–1966); and Grant #02571 of the NICHHD (1966–1969). The major findings have been reported in Offer (1969) and Offer and Offer (1975).

181

Four Basic Perspectives on Normality

A review of the psychoanalytic, social, and behavioral science literature on normality leads to a categorization of views on normality as falling within four functional perspectives (Offer and Sabshin, 1974). Although each perspective is unique and has its own definition and description, the perspectives complement each other and together represent the total behavioral, psychological, and social science approach to normality.

Normality as health. The first perspective is basically the traditional medical approach to health and illness. Most physicians equate normality with health and view health as an almost universal phenomenon. As a result, behavior is assumed to fall within normal limits when no manifest psychopathology is present; the vast majority of behavior is placed on a continuum, abnormality accounting for a small remainder. This definition of normality correlates with the traditional model of the doctor who attempts to free his patient from grossly observable signs of illness. To this physician, the lack of pathological signs or symptoms indicates health. Health in this context refers to a reasonable rather than an optimal state of functioning. In its simplest form, this perspective is illustrated by Romano (1950), who maintained that a healthy person is one who is reasonably free of undue pain, discomfort, or disability.

Normality as utopia. The second perspective conceives of normality as that harmonious and optimal blending of the diverse elements of the mental apparatus that culminates in optimal functioning. Such a definition emerges clearly when psychiatrists or psychoanalysts talk about the ideal person or when they grapple with a complex problem, such as the criteria of successful treatment. This approach is characteristic of a significant segment of psychoanalysts but is by no means unique to them. It can be found also among psychotherapists of quite different persuasions, for example, Rogers (1959).

Normality as average. The third perspective is commonly used in normative studies of behavior and is based on the mathematical principle of the bell-shaped curve. This approach conceives of the middle range as normal and both extremes as deviant. The normative approach based on this statistical principle describes each person in terms of general assessment and total score. Variability is described only within the context of groups and not within the context of a single person. Although this approach is more commonly used in psychology and biology than in psychiatry, psychiatrists have recently been using pencil-and-paper tests to a much greater extent than in the past. Psychiatrists use not only IQ, Rorschach, and Thematic Apperception tests, but also tests and questionnaires of their own devising. In developing model personalities of different societies, one assumes that typologies of character can be statistically measured.

Normality as Transactional Systems. The fourth perspective stresses that normal behavior is the end result of interacting systems. Temporal changes are essential to a complete definition of normality. This perspective stresses changes or processes rather than a cross-sectional definition of normality. Investigators who subscribe to this approach can be found in all behavioral and social sciences. Most typical are Erikson (1968) and Grinker (1956), whose thesis of a unified theory of behavior encompasses polarities within a wide range of integration. General systems theory (von Bertalanffy, 1968; Gray, Duhl, and Rizzo, 1969) has stressed the applicability of this approach in psychiatry. Normality as the outcome of transactions systems encompasses variables from the biological, psychological, and social fields, all contributing to the functioning of a viable system over time. The integration of these variables into the system and the significance of each remain to be more thoroughly explored.

Research in the Field of Normal Development

Research on normal or nonpatient populations is not exclusively of recent provenance. Anthropologists have been observing cultures other than their own for more than seventy years. Social psychologists and child psychologists have worked with people in experimental and testing situations ever since psychology became a scientific discipline. Psychoanalysts, though primarily studying patients who come to them for therapy, have extended their theories to include concepts applicable to the personality development of normal children and adults. Psychiatric and clinical studies on normal populations have increasingly been undertaken during the past decade. What has been lacking, however, are systematic longitudinal or follow-up investigations of normal populations. The clinician's experience and abilities need to be integrated with the researcher's tools and methods (Offer, Freedman, and Offer, 1972).

Almost by definition we cannot do in-depth psychoanalytic research on normal subjects; they would not have the motivation, among other things, and resistance would be too high (see, for example, Gitelson, 1954; Eissler, 1960). To assume, however, that normal functioning of feelings and behavior is simply the antonym of neurosis can be misleading. As cursory and superficial (from a psychoanalytic point of view) as studies of normal people are, they are surely better than no studies at all. Let me briefly summarize our ten-year study of normal adolescent males (Offer and Offer, 1975). Although there are very few longitudinal studies on normal populations, it is striking how similar their findings are (see, for example, Symonds and Jensen, 1961; Kagen and Moss, 1962; Cox, 1970; Block, 1971; Holmstrom, 1972; Vaillant, 1977). The most intriguing finding is that no one developmental route typifies our subject population. Three distinct subgroups, all under the general rubric of normal development could be distinguished (Offer and Offer, 1975); (1) continuous growth (23 percent of the total group); (2) surgent growth (35 percent); and (3) tumultuous growth (21 percent). Twenty-one percent of the subjects could not be classified; they had mixed scores and did not fit into any of the subgroups, statistically or clinically. They also did not make for a fourth group. Clinically they can be best described as closer to the first two groups. The psychodynamics of the three groups were as follows.

Continuous growth. The subjects in this grouping progressed throughout adolescence and young manhood with a smoothness of purpose and a self-assurance of their progression toward a meaningful and fulfilling adult life. These subjects were favored by circumstances. Their psychogenetic and environmental backgrounds were excellent. Their childhood had been unmarked by death or serious illness of a parent or sibling. The nuclear family remained a stable unit throughout their childhood and adolescence. The continuous growth subjects had mastered previous developmental stages without serious set-backs. They were able to cope with internal and external stimuli through an adaptive general cultural combination of reason and emotional expression. These subjects accepted general cultural and societal norms and felt comfortable within this context. They had a capacity to integrate experiences and use them as a stimulus for growth.

The parents were able to encourage their children's independence; the parents themselves grew and changed with their children. Throughout the ten years of the study mutual respect, trust, and affection were evident between the generations. The parents' ability to allow their sons independence in many areas was undoubtedly facilitated by the sons' behavior patterns. Since the young men were not behaving in a manner clearly divergent from that of the parents, the parents received continued gratifications through their sons. The sense of gratification was reciprocal, with the sons gaining both from their parents' good feelings toward them and the parental willingness to allow them to create their lives outside the household. The value system of the subjects in this group dovetailed with that of the parents. In many ways the young men were functioning as continuations of their parents, living out not so much lives the parents had wished for, but not attained, as lives similar to those of their parents.

In their interpersonal relationships the subjects showed a capacity for good object relationships, as measured in the clinical interview, rating scales, and psychological testing. They had close male friends in whom they could confide. Their relationships with the opposite sex became increasingly important as they reached the post–high school years. By the subjects' fourth year after high school, intimacy in the Eriksonian sense was being developed and was a goal toward which these subjects strove.

Subjects evincing the continuous growth pattern acted in accordance with their consciences, manifesting little evidence of superego problems and developing meaningful ego ideals, often identifying with persons they knew and admired within the larger family or school communities. These subjects were able to identify feelings of shame and guilt and proceeded to explain not only how the experiences provoking these responses had affected them, but also how these uncomfortable situations were mastered. A similar experience might be described by these young men, but one they had been prepared to handle better; this earlier upsetting experience was placed in a past time frame of immaturity conquered.

The young men's fantasy lives were relatively active; they were almost always able to translate their fantasy into reality and action. They could dream about being the best in their class academically, sexually, or athletically, though their actions would be guided by a pragmatic and realistic appraisal of their own abilities and of external circumstance. Thus, they were prevented from meeting with repeated disappointments.

The subjects were able to cope with external trauma, usually through an adaptive action-orientation. When difficulties arose, they used the defenses of denial and isolation to protect their ego from being bombarded with affect. They could postpone immediate gratification and work in a sustained manner for a future goal. Their delay mechanisms worked well, and, together with temporary suppression rather than repression of affect, they were generally successful in responding to their aggressive and sexual impulses without being overwhelmed or acting out in a self-destructive manner. They did not experience prolonged periods of anxiety or depression, two of the most common affects described by the entire subject population, including this subgroup.

Many of the qualities common to members of this group are included in the ideal or utopian definition of mental health. None of these subjects would portray all of these qualities, of course, but would have difficulties in one or another area. What was most distinctive about members of the continuous growth group was their overall contentment with themselves and their place in life. Compared to the other two groupings, this group was composed of relatively happy human beings. They generally had an order to their lives which could be interrupted but which would not yield to states of symptomatology or chaotic behavior as these young men progressed through the adolescent years and matured cognitively and emotionally.

None of the subjects in this group had received psychotherapy or was thought by the researchers to need treatment. The significance of the data, that these subjects were not seen by psychotherapists or counselors from the health services of schools or communities, lies in the fact that they are least likely to be the young adults from whom members of the helping professions build their studies or make their generalizations about youth populations.

Surgent growth. The surgent growth group, although functioning as adaptively as the first group, was characterized by important enough differences in ego structure, in background, and in family environment to be defined as a distinct subgroup. Developmental spurts characterized the growth pattern of this group. These subjects differed in the amount of emotional conflict they experienced and in patterns of resolving conflict. More concentrated energy was directed toward mastering developmental tasks than was obvious in members of the continuous growth group. At times these subjects would be adjusting very well, integrating their experiences and moving ahead, and at other times they seemed to be stuck at an almost premature closure and unable to move forward. A cycle of progression and regression is typical of this group. The defenses used, anger and projection, manifest a greater degree of psychopathology than do the defenses used by the first group.

One of the major differences between the surgent growth subjects and those in the continuous growth group was that their genetic or environmental backgrounds were not as free of problems and traumas; the nuclear families in the surgent growth group were more likely to have been affected by separation, death, or severe illness.

Although subjects in this category were able to cope successfully with their "average expectable environment" (Hartmann, 1939), their ego development was not adequate for coping with unanticipated sources of anxiety. Affects which usually were flexible and available would at a time of crisis, such as the death of a close relative, become stringently controlled. This, together with the fact that the subjects were not as action-oriented as those in the first group, made them slightly more prone to depression. The depression would accompany or openly follow the highly controlled behavior. On other occasions, when defense mechanisms faltered, they experienced moderate anxiety and a short period of turmoil. When disappointed in themselves or others, they tended to use projection and anger.

These groups were not as confident as were the young men in the continuous growth group; their self-esteem wavered. They relied on positive reinforcement from the opinions of important others, such as parents or peers. When this was not forthcoming, they often became discouraged about themselves and their abilities. As a group, they were able to form meaningful interpersonal relationships similar to those of individuals in the continuous growth group. The relationships, though, would be maintained with a greater degree of effort.

For subjects in the surgent growth category, relationships with parents were marked by conflicts of opinions and values. There were areas of disagreement between father and mother concerning such basic issues as the importance of discipline, academic attainments, or religious beliefs. In several cases the parents came from different backgrounds. The mothers of some of these subjects had difficulty in letting their children grow and in separating from them.

The subjects might work toward their vocational goals sporadically or with a lack of enthusiasm, but they would be able to keep their long-range behavior in line with their general expectations for themselves.

There were subjects in this group who were afraid of emerging sexual feelings and impulses. For these young adults, meaningful relationships with the opposite sex began relatively late, except for a small subgroup who started experimenting with sexuality early in high school, possibly owing to a counterphobic defense. These early sexual relationships were not lasting, though they could be helpful in overcoming anxiety concerning sexuality.

The group as a whole was less introspective than either the first or the third group. Overall adjustment of these subjects was often just as adaptive and successful as that of the first group. The adjustment was achieved, though, with less self-examination and a more controlled drive or surge toward development. Suppression of emotionality was characteristic of subjects in the surgent growth group.

Tumultuous growth. This group is similar to the adolescents so often described in the psychiatric, psychoanalytic, and social science literature. These are the students who go through adolescence with internal turmoil manifested in overt behavioral problems in school and in the home. These adolescents have been observed to have recurrent self-doubts (often unsuccessfully masked by braggadocio), escalating conflicts with their parents, and debilitating inhibitions, and often respond inconsistently to their social and academic environments.

Subjects characterized by a tumultuous growth pattern were those who experienced growing up from 14 to 22 as a period of discordance, as a transitional period for which their defenses needed mobilizing, and ego adaptations needed strengthening.

These subjects came from less stable backgrounds than did subjects in the other two groups. Some of the parents in this group had overt marital conflicts, and others had a history of mental illness in the family. In brief, the genetic and environmental backgrounds of the subjects in the tumultuous growth group were decidedly different from those of the other two groups. Also present was a social class difference. Our study population was primarily middle class, but this group contained many subjects who belonged to the lower middle class. For them, functioning in a middle and upper middle class environment might have been the occasion for additional stress.

The tumultuous growth group experienced more major psychological traumas. The difficulties in their life situation were greater than their satisfactions, and defenses were not well developed for handling emotionally trying situations. A relatively high percentage of this group had overt clinical problems and had received psychotherapy.

Separation was painful to the parents and became a source of continuing conflict for the subjects. The parent-son relationships characterizing this group were similar to those of many of the neurotic adolescents seen in outpatient psychotherapy. Further, parent-son communication of a system of values was poorly defined or contradictory.

Strong family bonds, however, were present within the tumultuous growth subjects, as they were within each of the three groups. We used the revealed difference technique to evaluate the strength and the openness of family communication. This method clearly differentiated the families of delinquent adolescents and those of our modal subjects. The method also differentiated the family of our modal sample along the three developmental routes. Best understanding between the generations was observed among the continuous growth group and least in the tumultuous growth group, with the surgent group in between (Offer, Marohn, and Ostrov, 1979).

The ability of this group to test reality and act accordingly was relatively strong in contrast to patient populations, but disappointment in others and in themselves was prevalent when contrasted to other nonpatient populations. Action was accompanied by more anxiety and depression in this group than in the other two. Emotional turmoil was part of their separation-individuation process. Without the tumult, growth toward independence and meaningful interpersonal relationship was in doubt. Wide mood swings indicated a search for who they were as separate individuals and concern about whether their activities were worthwhile. Feelings of mistrust about the adult world were often expressed in this group. Affect was readily available and created both intensely pleasurable and painful experiences. Changes in self-concept could precipitate moderately severe anxiety reactions. These subjects were considerably more dependent on peer culture than were their age-mates in the other groups, possibly because they received fewer gratifications from their relationships within the family. When they experienced a personal loss, such as the ending of a relationship with a good friend, their depression was deeper, though only very rarely associated with suicidal feelings and impulses.

The tumultuous growth subjects had begun dating activities at a younger age than had their peers described in the first two groups. In early adolescence their relationship with females was that of dependency, with the female a substitute for a mothering figure. In late adolescence, for some, heterosexual relationships gained meaning, and they were able to appreciate the personal characteristics of their female friends.

Many subjects in the tumultuous growth group were highly sensitive and introspective individuals. They were usually aware of their emotional needs. Academically, they were less interested in science, engineering, law, and medicine. They preferred the arts, the humanities, or the social and psychological sciences. However, business and engineering careers remained the most usual choice for this group as well as for the first two groups.

As a group these subjects did not do as well academically during their high school years as subjects from the first two groups, although it is possible that in the long run they will do just as well as subjects in the other groups. As with other variables, academic success differentiated the groups, but honor students and average students or workers could be found within each group. The academic or work failures were more likely to be found in the tumultuous group, as they would find the tasks upon which they had embarked to be incompatible with their needs or abilities only after having assayed them.

Adolescents in this group experienced more psychological pain than did the others, but as a result were no less well adjusted as a group in terms of their overall functioning within their respective environmental settings than were those in the continuous and surgent growth groups. They were less happy with themselves, more critical of their social environment, but just as successful academically and vocationally.[2]

Data Gathering with a Psychoanalytic Bent

The question will undoubtedly be raised by many: This is interesting phenomenological-descriptive work, but how were psychoanalytic technique and theory useful in this research? What do we really know about the internal world of these adolescents and their development through the eight years we studied them? We can best compare our work to that of an anthropologist doing field research (including depth inter-

[2] For a parallel study on the psychological development of adolescent girls see Petersen, Offer, Solomon, and Gitelson, 1978.

views) in a strange culture. The subjects with whom we worked were seen but not studied or treated by mental health professionals. They would not seek psychoanalytic therapy. They were not the type to be studied by social scientists because they were deviant. And yet they were there, all ready to be studied and to help us understand the process of adolescence.

We believe that our knowledge of depth psychology helped us to better understand these subjects because we listen to psychological material with a psychoanalytic perspective, taking into account resistance, defenses, unconscious communication, and the fantasy life of the individual. But how? First, we developed an "alliance" with our subjects which made it easier for us to make interpretations concerning resistance of an episode in each subject's life, without promising too much in the psychotherapeutic sense or shying away from asking probing questions when this was indicated (Offer, 1973). And second, we used the psychoanalytic tools of empathy and introspection to both facilitate and comprehend the subjects (Kohut, 1971, 1977).

A few examples will show how we used the interpretive road with our group of subjects. Why, for example, were some students, who impressed us as immature, resistant to the project, while others were almost too cooperative? Robert, for example, was worried about losing his parents and seemed afraid of what we might "force" him to reveal, so he talked little to us. He was the one who most often refused to answer our questions. He did not, for instance, want to tell us what he felt were the problems of adolescents, what his wishes were, or what he would do with a million dollars. Whom would he like to be with on a desert island? "I'd like to have my parents with me because then it would be safe and secure." Was he aware of his immaturity and afraid to join in a research alliance with us because of what his direct answers might reveal? He did frequently volunteer the subject of his mother's working for a particular firm. He liked neither the firm nor the idea of his mother's working. Robert himself was worried about not being able to succeed in carrying out his wishes. This fear he showed us in other ways throughout the interviews and also, perhaps, by his refusal to mention the wishes. We can make this interpretation of his refusal to cooperate on the basis of a series of other responses. He wanted to go to a particular university with high admission standards, but he did not think he could be accepted because, as he regretfully reported, he had only a C average. If rejected by the university, maybe he would become a pilot. He felt shame when he had bragged. He could not really achieve what he had claimed to have done. Robert's guilt was aroused when he did not study enough and then did poorly on an exam. We can gain insight into Robert's problems by the answers he did give and also into at least one of his ways of handling them—camouflage, his refusal to answer several questions. Robert formed the beginning of a research alliance by attending; but by refusing full cooperation, he was protecting himself.

There was another boy, Gerald, who came but refused to discuss several issues with us. He had difficulty forming the research alliance in the beginning. He seemed to have problems with forming most meaningful relationships. He refused to tell us his wishes. "What would you do with a million dollars?" "That is part of wishes, so I won't discuss it. Besides, I can't think of anything." "Whom would you like to have with you on a desert island?" "I'd like to be alone because alone, under pressure, I think better." By the third interview we were able to involve this boy. He said he was glad to see the interviewer, and he was answering all the questions. He closed the fourth interview saying, "I'd like to see you more often." Was this a mood shift, a heightened self-confidence, or the development of an alliance? Although the former two may also be true, his plea for more sessions tended to support the hypothesis of a growth in the alliance.

Phillip read a story in the newspapers that it is dangerous to poke around people's feelings, and especially their heads. He added very quickly after he made this critical statement, "I didn't mean any offense, mind you. People who don't know much about psychology should not go around asking people questions. Psychology is really very similar to philosophy and isn't a science at all." In a later interview, Phillip was quite cooperative and said he had enjoyed the interview. He wanted to know how many had dropped out and why. After much probing, he admitted that he had considered dropping out, but because the interviewer had become personable, and because he was curious each time before he came to see us, he was staying on.

Thomas gives us an example of an alliance that failed, not in the sense of its strength to provide cooperation, but in that it became more of a therapeutic alliance than a research alliance. Thomas caused us to feel slightly uneasy about our explicit intention not to do psychotherapy. This subject, who had been particularly uncooperative during the first two sessions, settled down and developed a meaningful research alliance with us. There was a seven-month interval between the fourth and fifth interviews. When the subject came to the fifth interview, in his senior year of high school, he told us that during the preceding fall he had developed a strong urge to scream out in church. He had the urge almost every Sunday. At times he had it in school, too. He also felt like running away from home. He had done neither, but the urges continued to bother him. During Christmas vacation he received a letter from us, as did every subject, thanking him for his past cooperation, stating that we would see him in the spring, and wishing him a Merry Christmas and a Happy New Year. The subject told us that he was very pleased to receive the letter and planned to tell us about his special feeling; but amazingly the urge had disappeared since his receipt of the letter.

Naturally, there were degrees in which we were used as therapists. Some subjects had difficulty breaking away from their families. In forming outside relationships, they reacted not by fear of us but by leaning on us and on the alliance. Some of these subjects, who we felt were immature, formed such a strong relationship with us that they had difficulty leaving at the end of an interview. One such boy, Kenneth, who was having problems of control, came to see us on a day when he had cut classes in order to go to the movies with a couple of girls from a different town. He told us that he enjoyed coming to see us. "I get a lot of things off my chest when I come here."

Eugene began to develop his research alliance or trust in us at the first interview. After answering many questions, he remarked, just before leaving, "I thought you might want to know that my parents have been separated for the past two years." He must have felt defensive about this, because he had not mentioned it when asked questions about his family. Can we credit the alliance we formed with having made him comfortable enough to add this "afterthought"?

Not all were anywhere near so cooperative; more usually they would cooperate only with hesitation. "Your questions are probably important," was a not infrequent commentary on the project. These subjects were not too sure. Jack wondered if people were really telling us what they felt. He felt that he was, but he wondered if the others would. Certainly we, as psychoanalysts, cannot view "cooperation" as a routine issue in interviewing but rather as a significant form of resistance that only the "interpretive road" can help us understand.

Michael thought that by now, the junior year of high school, we had lost at least one-half of our subjects. He said he came out of curiosity. When told that only a few had dropped out, he was surprised but said, "I guess they have nothing better to do. I will probably drop later." This boy continued. This conversation came after he had said that his father scared him. He seemed a little afraid that we would repeat this to his parents. In the opening interview Michael had said that he was bigger than both his parents, but two years later he still felt that his father could beat him. As with so many of the subjects, his resistance to the project was a part of his general pattern of functioning. He proceeded with fear, but he proceeded nonetheless and responded to our questions.

Timothy said he objected to the project only when it took him away from athletic practice. When we pointed out that the interviews had never conflicted with his sports activities, he responded: "Oh, yeah. I guess, then, I like it." Another subject said, "I think other people might be sensitive about this interview, but I didn't mind it. I think maybe I can learn something from the interviews."

The nonchalant attitude was best epitomized by John. "Would you like to participate, John?" "Not emphatically." "Drop out?" "Not exactly." "Continue?" "Probably." This boy proved to be open and talkative. His commitment to the project, despite the unconcerned surface, was sufficient to motivate him to continue even after he later changed high schools. Here again, this boy's verbalized attitude toward the project was indicative of his attitude toward many things. There was a combination of an "I don't care" attitude with a "But I really do." He thought school and vacations were boring, but he liked hunting and fishing and wanted to be a better student.

Several of the examples presented are illustrative of only the individuals cited. Each example shows part of an individual pattern and also indicates just why we enjoyed seeing the teenagers. Although psychological patterns of statistical clusters might make "normal students" sound uninteresting, the individual was not. As may sometimes be forgotten, the statistically "typical" student is not to be found.

These examples were not the mode; however, they will suffice to convey our use of object relations, transference, and the unconscious meanings of behavior. It is in the latter area that psychoanalytic theory was extremely helpful in enriching our understanding of these subjects. In addition, we were confident of the validity of our data once we understood the subjects in terms of their relationship with us. The subjects' responses, on a minor scale, were really not different from patients we see in therapy. The main difference is that there was a group whom we, as psychoanalysts, would by definition never have been able to study.

Creativity: A Comment

Can creative people be normal? It is essential that psychological conflict precede a creative outpouring. Is depression a necessary precondition for originality? And how about regression in the service of the ego in artists? These psychological issues have been discussed extensively in the literature. Here I will simply comment on the nature of the Rorschach in the three groups described above.

We wondered whether our continuous growth group varied in relation to the other groups in terms of adolescent fantasy life as depicted in projective tests. Subjects from the first group, who went through adolescence relatively easily, shifted to adulthood with values similar to those of their parents, and were action-oriented, had a rich fantasy life and showed great flexibility in their defenses. They in no way shied away from their own internal aggressive impulses.

We collected Rorschach data twice on our subjects. First at age 15 and later at age 21 (see Offer, 1969; Offer and Offer, 1975). We have found that the three groups differed significantly along lines usually associated with creativity.

The continuous growth had the highest Movement responses. That means they had the greatest ability to depart from the strict form quality of the card and to bring a sense of feeling and loneliness to the responses. The surgent growth group was the most accurate in its perception of Form. This shows greater intolerance for departure from a strict interpretation of reality. The tumultuous growth group was lowest in both Movement and Form responses but were highest in Shading responses. The latter means that they could depart from reality, but this was associated with considerable emotional turmoil and was less in the service of their age-appropriate developmental needs.

These findings are of interest in that they challenge the common conception that psychological conflict is *necessarily* related to creativity.

Conclusion

Is a profile emerging that reliably describes the normal man or woman? Definitely not. The more one studies normal populations, the more one becomes aware that healthy functioning is as complex, and coping behavior as varied, as the psychopathological entities. Normality and health cannot be understood in the abstract. Rather, they depend on cultural norms, societal expectations and values, professional biases, individual differences, and the political climate that sets the tolerance for deviance.

The four perspectives on normality make it possible to differentiate between different kinds of normality. There are different typologies of normality. During the past decade, increased studies of normal populations, using a variety of psychological methods, show that we have taken an important step in the right direction. Continued empirical investigations will lead to a better understanding of the complexity of healthy development. Psychiatrists and psychoanalysts are presently shifting from deduction and theorizing about normal development to empirical investigations of the relationships among the multiplicity of variables that contribute to the healthy or normal development of people. The study of normal populations has taken a very healthy turn in recent years.

It is particularly important to integrate clinical observations with developmental research. Only by understanding normal development can we understand its deviations. For example, by comparing factors involved in normal development with those in delinquency or psychopathology we may learn how problems develop and hence be better able to plan effective interventions. Similarly, the study of psychopathology or delinquency will point to problem areas and greatly enhance our understanding of the significant aspects of normal development.

References

Bertalanffy, L. von (1968), *General Systems Theory*. New York: Braziller.

Birnbach, M. (1961), *Neo-Freudian Social Philosophy*. Stanford: Stanford University Press.

Block, J. (1971), *Lives Through Time*. Berkeley, CA.: Bancroft.

Cox, R. D. (1970), *Youth into Maturity*. New York: Mental Health Materials Center.

Eissler, K. R. (1960), The efficient soldier. In: *The Psychoanalytic Study of Society*, 1:39–97. New York: International Universities Press.

Erikson, E. H. (1968), Identity, psychosocial. In: *International Encyclopedia of the Social Sciences*, Vol. 7. New York: Crowell, Collier, & Macmillan, p. 61.

Freud, S. (1937), Analysis terminable and interminable. *Standard Edition*, 23:209–253. London: Hogarth Press, 1964.

Gitelson, M. (1954), The analysis of the 'normal' candidate. *Internat. J. Psycho-Anal.*, 35:174–183.

Gray, W., Duhl, F. J., & Rizzo, N. D. (1969), *General Systems Theory and Psychiatry*. Boston: Little, Brown.

Grinker, R. R., Sr. (1956), *Towards a Unified Theory of Human Behavior*. New York: Basic Books.

Hartmann, H. (1939), Psychoanalysis and the concept of health. *Internat. J. Psycho-Anal.*, 20:308–321.

Holmstrom, R. (1972), On the picture of mental health. *Acta Psychiatrica Scandinavia*, 231:1–260.

Kagen, J., & Moss, H. (1962), *Birth to Maturity*. New York: Wiley.

Kaplan, A. (1967), A philosophical discussion of normality. *Arch. Gen. Psychiat.*, 17:325–330.

Kohut, H. (1971), *The Analysis of the Self*. New York: International Universities Press.

———— (1977), *The Restoration of the Self*. New York: International Universities Press.

Offer, D. (1969), *The Psychological World of the Teenager: A Study of Normal Adolescent Boys*. New York: Basic Books.

———— (1973), The adolescent sexual revolution. In: *Adolescent Psychiatry*, Vol. 2, ed. S. C. Feinstein & P. Giovacchini. New York: Basic Books, pp. 165–171.

———— Offer, J. B. (1975), *From Teenage to Young Manhood*. New York: Basic Books.

———— Sabshin, M. (1974), *Normality: Theoretical and Clinical Concepts of Mental Health*. New York: Basic Books.

———— Freedman, D. X., & Offer, J. B., eds. (1972), *The Psychiatrist and Clinical Research*. New York: Basic Books.

———— Marohn, R. C., & Ostrov, E. (1979), *Psychological World of the Juvenile Delinquent*. New York: Basic Books.

Petersen, A. L., Offer, D., Solomon, B., & Gitelson, I. (1978), A Study of Normal Adolescent Girls. Unpublished paper.

Rogers, C. R. (1959), A theory of therapy, personality and interpersonal relationships as developed in the client-centered framework. In: *Psychology: A Study of a Science*, Vol. 3, ed. S. Koch. New York: McGraw-Hill, pp. 184–256.

Romano, J. (1950), Basic orientation and education of the medical student. *J. Amer. Med. Assn.*, 143:409–412.

Symonds, P. M., & Jensen, A. R. (1961), *From Adolescent to Adult*. New York: Columbia University Press.

Vaillant, G. E. (1977), *Adaptation to Life*. Boston: Little, Brown.

7

Adolescents, Age Fifteen to Eighteen:
A Psychoanalytic Developmental View

EUGENE H. KAPLAN, M.D.

Among the variables influencing theoretical controversies regarding adolescence are the populations studied, the methods of observation, and the observer's theoretical orientation. Barglow and Schaefer (1976) note that analysts disagree on the value for psychoanalytic theory of data derived from outside the psychoanalytic situation by neighboring disciplines. They doubt that psychological tests, questionnaires, and limited interviews can meaningfully identify motivations, character traits, and conflicts.

Criteria for analyzability exclude the sickest as well as the healthiest patients. Moreover, Levenson, Feiner, and Stockhauer (1976) characterize the adolescent patients seen in private practice as children of permissive middle or upper class parents who can afford therapy and approve of it, and who are willing to relinquish their authority to an expert. A danger in psychoanalytic theorizing about adolescence is that the data base is often restricted to an unrepresentative sampling of analyses and the inferences drawn are then regarded as universally applicable. This pitfall must be avoided.

Relevant data may escape through the coarser net of nonanalytic studies, and the workings of psychic structure and interpersonal relationships are more difficult to discern in healthier individuals. Conditions of crisis, conflict, and pathology render structures and functions more detectable.

The rational response is integration along the lines of Barglow and Schaefer's conclusions—that nonanalytic research can

201

provide critical evaluation or validation of some psychoanalytic hypotheses, provided the studies are reproducible, utilize controls, and have demonstrable validity. Longitudinal studies are especially useful (Cramer, 1976).

In the evolution of the psychoanalytic study of adolescence, the focus has shifted from the drives to the structural viewpoint, with an emphasis on the ego and its defense mechanisms, and more recently to the developmental point of view (Neubauer, 1976). Contemporary psychoanalytic opinion disagrees with Spiegel's position (1958) that it is impossible to ascertain way stations over the course of adolescent development; rather, the adolescent subphases with their specific developmental conflicts and tasks can be distinguished in a recognizable, orderly sequence (Blos, 1962).

The adolescent process involves the developmental tasks of adapting to physical and sexual maturation, attaining independence from parents, achieving heterosexual love relationships, and planning and committing oneself to a future. These require intrapsychic restructuring and growth in a combination of regression and progression accompanied by anxiety and mourning. These intrapsychic events occur with varying degrees of overtly manifest behavioral and emotional stress, or with none at all.

Psychopathology should not be confused with the adolescent process. What Geleerd (1961) mistakenly viewed as paradigmatic for normal adolescence, Masterson (1967) has demonstrated to hold for the borderline adolescent alone.

Based on their longitudinal studies, Offer and Offer (1975) have described three developmental routes through normal male adolescence. The "continuous growth" group went from 14 to 22 smoothly and with self-assurance. Their genetic and environmental backgrounds were excellent, their families stable, and they had suffered no serious illness or object loss in childhood. Their parents encouraged independence and seemed to grow themselves with their adolescent's growth, with a reciprocal sense of gratification.

The second, "the surgent growth" group, was characterized by developmental spurts. More concentrated energy was directed to mastering developmental tasks than in the first group.

Their backgrounds were not as free of problems and trauma; their families were more likely to have experienced separations, deaths, or severe illnesses. Though they could cope with average expected emotional challenges, the surgent group's ego development was not equal to major challenges, e.g., the death of a close relative. This group was more prone to depression, anxiety, and self-esteem problems, with greater reliance on parents or peers. There were conflicts between these adolescents and their parents, and between the parents themselves, over values.

The third group, with a tumultuous psychological growth pattern, went through adolescence with an inner turmoil that was often manifested in overt behavioral problems at home and at school. Backgrounds were less stable, and the group contained more lower middle class members than did the other groups. Their strong family bonds, however, distinguished them from delinquent adolescents. They had recurrent self-doubts, escalating conflicts with parents, and debilitating inhibitions. Their separation-individuation process was accompanied by emotional turmoil.

The Offers' "tumultuous growth" group seems to correspond with the psychoanalytic models of adolescent development adumbrated by Anna Freud (1958), Blos (1962), and Deutsch (1967). Going beyond the refutation of turmoil as a requisite of healthy adolescent development, the Offers' follow-up findings suggest that in fact it is the least desirable route. At age 22, the continuous growth group showed optimal functioning and an absence of clinical psychiatric syndromes, the surgent growth group showed such syndromes in the numbers that would be expected given their rate of incidence in the adolescent population generally, and the tumultuous growth group showed twice as many as would be expected.

Ideally, the adolescent process simultaneously embraces transformation and continuity. The obligatory loosening, disruption, and reorganizing of psychic structure are not inevitably accompanied by significant emotional and behavioral disruption. Crucial here is earlier structuralization based on successful negotiation of the phase-specific tasks of previous developmental stages. While inner stress is unavoidable in this progression, an empathic, synchronous, collaborative family and sociocultural context minimizes stress without thwarting development. The principle of appropriate dosage of stress, anxiety, and frustration holds not only for childhood but for all developmental stages.

Gratification devoid of parental expectations deprives the child of pleasure in achievement and mastery, and of the related sense of competence and ability in dealing with stress. Insufficient exposure to frustration and delay interferes with the development of the sublimatory mechanisms, with failure in impulse control and self-esteem regulation (Solnit, Settlage, Goodman, and Blos, 1969). On the other hand, our emphasis on the developmental task of freeing oneself from the infantile tie to the original objects should not obscure our appreciation of the adolescent's need for stable, reliable parents. Lidz, Lidz, and Rubenstein (1976) suggest that latency peer involvement and adolescent essays in independent action also be considered "practicing periods" during which the parents continue to provide a delimiting influence and a source of shelter and security for moments of anxiety and failure.

Subphases of Adolescence

Freud drew an analogy between analysis and chess, contrasting the ease of describing their beginning and end games with the difficulty encountered in conceptualizing the middle. So it is with adolescence. Most authors identify the biological event of puberty as its beginning while the literature has focused increasingly on the end game, late adolescence, with attempts to clarify and more precisely define in metapsychological terms the vicissitudes, modifications, transformations, and consolidations occurring within the psyche at that time.

In the West, successive generations have been getting taller and attaining puberty at progressively earlier ages. In Norway, where records have been kept since 1840, the age at menarche has dropped 4 months per decade, from 17 to 13. This secular trend seems to have ended in the past ten to thirty years (Khatchadourian, 1977). Although this biological shift may have halted, there is a social tendency to lower the age at which various milestones are passed, in part a diffusion of lower class practices upward to the middle and upper classes (Stone and Church, 1957).

It is commonplace to contrast the biological initiation of adolescence with its socially defined termination. The end seems to be getting progressively later and increasingly blurred, at least for Western middle class youth. The prolongation of education postpones entry into one's vocation; among more recent social trends, cohabitation without marriage and delay or abjuration of parenthood have rendered the delineation between adolescent and adult increasingly indistinct.

Stone and Church (1957) hold that the psychological events of adolescence in our society are not a necessary counterpart of the physical changes of puberty but rather are a "cultural invention," a product of the increasing delay in the assumption of adult responsibilities. In support of this position, Trent and Medsker (1968) found that early marriage and full-time employment after high school (combined with full-time homemaking for the young wife) were associated with early identity closure, constriction of flexibility and autonomy, lowered intellectual curiosity, low tolerance for ambiguity, and a relative disinterest in new experiences. However, early closure does not invariably result in these sequelae. Healthy and outstanding adolescents may make definitive object and career choices that are chronologically precocious but psychologically appropriate.

Acknowledgment of the great importance of social factors should not cause neglect of the biological. Psychological growth is as rooted in biology as physical growth is. Spruiell (1971) proposes the achievement of physical maturity as the biological demarcator of late adolescence, initiating psychological events which together bring about a rapid restructuring within the ego of a new and more unified body image, more mature self- and object representations, and a more or less stable drive and defense hierarchy. Kestenberg (1968) believes that hormonal increases in adolescence are paralleled by an upsurge of clearly genital drives, increased depth of feeling, and augmented creativity. The most rapid increase in plasma testosterone levels occurs between 12 and 16 in boys, correlating statistically with the onset of nocturnal emission, masturbation, dating, and first infatuation (Khatchadourian, 1977).

Piaget and Inhelder (1958) have demonstrated a significant developmental advance from concrete to abstract thinking between 12 and 16, which they believe to depend on central nervous system maturation. The brain attains 95 percent of its adult weight by age 10, and whether concomitant generalized or localized cephalic growth accompanies the advance in thinking is unknown. It is established, however, that children physically advanced for their age score higher in mental tests than do those of the same age who are less mature physically (Tanner, 1962). Another neuropsychological finding supporting neural maturation is that the critical period of retaining the ability to perceive certain phonetic contrasts may range up to age 16. Kolata (1975) cites Eimas's finding that Japanese exposed before age 16 to a language (English) which distinguishes (ra) and (la) could later hear this phonetic contrast.

The years from 12 to 15, 15 to 18, and 18 to 22 are convenient subdivisions of the adolescent years, corresponding to junior high school, senior high school, and college or work, but these helpful, socially defined landmarks are of themselves inadequate in classifying adolescents as early, middle, or late. Blos (1976b) states that, developmentally speaking, it is the degree of coordination and integration of ego functions, old and new, that spells out the completion of any developmental stage. Physical, sexual, and social status and cognitive level are unreliable indices.

In this developmental context we have noted Spruiell's thesis that the attainment of adult stature and procreative capacity initiates psychological changes in the ego characterized by synthesis, with a rather abrupt transition from middle to late adolescence. Prior to this inference, he notes the agreement of most psychoanalytic authors that therapeutic work in late adolescence, explicitly or implicitly assumed to date from about age 16, is different from that undertaken in earlier stages. In contrast to the action language of the early adolescent, who barely tolerates his "instinctual anxiety" and whose feelings remain inchoate, middle and late adolescents can express themselves in language and may even ask for help directly, with words rather than action.

In support of his proposition that integration of ego operations occurs around the age of 16, Spruiell cites Wolfenstein (1966) and Piaget and Inhelder (1958). Wolfenstein found that a true state of mourning, implying a new capacity to both relate to and separate from objects, does not develop until at least midadolescence. Spruiell claims that Piaget and Inhelder showed that fully operational thinking develops only at the age of 16 or 17; they actually date its onset from age 12.

Thinking

According to Piaget, the child from 8 to 12, in the stage of concrete operations, can deal with classes and relations as long as the objects are present. Semantic conceptions, though present, are more or less stimulus-bound, dependent on sensory input. As Wolfenstein (1958) put it, the child before 12 has difficulty understanding the figurative sense of words, adhering to a concrete visual image evoked by words, which precludes a shift of meaning. Therefore proverbs cannot be understood. Riddles are enjoyable because the answer involves word play, while the original question remains unanswered and is forgotten.

In the stage of formal operations from age 12 on, the child no longer depends on perceived data. Freed from the here and now, he deals with timeless, spaceless information. He can think of the possible, the potential, and is ready to try to re-form data. Further, he can think about propositions. In addition to ideas of negation originating in the previous stage of concrete operations, he now has ideas of reciprocity—i.e., how one cause acting upon a thing can nullify another cause. He can think in terms of variables and multiple determination of events. A puzzling phenomenon will touch off numerous hypotheses. Generating abstract hypotheses involves the cognition and production of implications. The adolescent in the stage of formal operations exhibits four kinds of transformations of propositions: identity, negation, reciprocity, and correlation. These transformations are necessary for dealing with proportionality and analogies and imply an increasing ability for dealing with complexity (Guilford, 1967).

To recapitulate, this developmental advance in thinking between 12 and 16 is from the more concrete, present-oriented, simplistic right-good vs. wrong-bad to the general, formal, logical, and abstract. Dulit (1972) points out that Piaget's genetic epistemology focuses on cognition (problem solving, directed thinking) and not on a broader definition of thinking which encompasses motivations, affects, or fantasy. In the broader view, by middle adolescence the capacity to think about thinking, to work with ideas not immediately tied to concrete examples, leads to a greater appreciation of cause and effect. Thus the historical view appears—a sense of the causal significance of the past in viewing the present.

Meeks (1971) believes that developmental advance in the cognitive area reinforces the predisposition to narcissism during adolescence. "The omnipotent, messianic preoccupations in the thought of the adolescent may be determined not only by his narcissistic withdrawal from the real world and internal objects, but also by the parallel developments in the unfolding of the cognitive apparatus" (p. 18).

Dulit (1972) replicated two of the formal stage experiments of Piaget and Inhelder with groups of average and gifted adolescents, ages 14 and 16–17. He found, contrary to the impression given by the Piaget-Inhelder work, that fully developed formal stage thinking is not at all commonplace among normal or average adolescents. Dulit concludes that a unitary model of cognitive development is inadequate beyond the stage of concrete operations. He conceptualizes formal stage thinking as a potentiality only partially attained by most and fully attained only by some.

Blos (1962) cites Spiegel's view (1958) that aesthetic conceptualization develops at this time and refers to Bernfeld's observations of adolescent achievements in thought and artistic creativity (1924). He adds that the striking decline of creativity at the end of adolescence indicates it to be a function of the adolescent process. On the other hand, Grinker, Grinker, and Tumberlake's group of healthy "homoclites" (1971) did not use fantasy as a defense against anxiety, manifested no marked capacity for abstraction, and were not very creative.

Physical Maturational Landmarks

The data on adolescent physical development compiled by Khatchadourian (1977) is as follows. Average age of puberty onset is 10 to 11 for girls, 11 to 12 for boys. The average girl of 14 and boy of 16 have attained 98 percent of their adult heights. Continuing with the average, menarche at 12.8 years will be followed by the capacity for normal pregnancy by 14 to 15; 90 percent of boys experience the first ejaculation between 11 and 15, approximately 1 year after rapid testicular growth; mature sperm is in evidence between 15 and 16. Plasma testosterone levels in boys increase twentyfold between 10 and 17, the most rapid increase occurring between 12 and 16.

Spiegel (1958) located ages 16–17 as the midpoint of adolescence, the period of the transition from homosexual to heterosexual object choice. Blos (1962) links "adolescence proper" (middle adolescence) with revival of the Oedipus complex, emotional detachment from family love objects, and emergence of a nonincestuous, nonambivalent heterosexual object. In distinguishing this subphase from early adolescence, he follows Deutsch's division (1944) of "early puberty" and "advanced puberty."

Another ego psychological correlation with ages 16–17 is the beginning of resolution of omnipotentiality, which Pumpian-Mindlin (1969) considers an essential element in the maturation of certain aspects of ego development, particularly those relating to the self-concept. Extending Spruiell's argument, is it coincidental that the omnipotentiality theme starts to ebb just as physical growth is essentially completed? While the adolescent is now accustomed to his/her physical transformation and no longer very anxious about it, the very finality of "the limits of growth" poses a reality challenge to omnipotent and omnipotential fantasies. Childhood daydreams anticipating the growth to young man/womanhood are confronted by the reality of the grownup face and body. Plastic surgery to "correct" noses and ears may be a response to narcissistic disappointment.

Two to three years are required after the onset of puberty for adolescents to make their peace with the ensuing physical transformations. Waning of a profound and secret apprehension about the body is one criterion of the entrance into middle adolescence. Increasingly, bodily changes are integrated as aspects of the self. Losing their strangeness, they may come to be taken for granted. Adding two to three years to the average age for puberty onset, middle adolescence begins between 12 and 14 in girls, 13 and 15 in boys. If, however, the onset of mid-adolescence is dated from the virtual completion of physical growth and the attainment of reproductive maturity, the girl enters this subphase at about 14 or 15, the boy around 15 or 16.

In the further discussion of the subphases of adolescence, the following propositions, avowedly overschematized, may be useful for orientation. The early adolescent must redefine himself and his relationship to his parents in the wake of his momentous physical transformation. The middle adolescent must venture from the protective scaffolding of the peer group into one-to-one heterosexual love relationships; sexual identity is further delineated in this intimacy. The late adolescent must define his spiritual and worldly standards and goals, while initiating their implementation. To summarize, these successive redefinitions involve (1) his body and his parents; (2) sexual identity and the relationship to the opposite sex; (3) goals, standards, and the relationship to society.

Psychological midadolescence begins as biological adolescence, or more precisely, puberty, comes to an end. Lidz, Lidz, and Rubenstein (1976) list the midadolescent phase-specific tasks as separation from the family, assuming control of one's life; and achieving a firm ego identity and the capacity for intimacy with a heterosexual extrafamilial love object, while tolerating the inevitable anxieties and feelings of loneliness. Each of these tasks requires extensive intrapsychic restructuring and modification.

Laufer (1976) notes three major aspects of the tasks of adolescence: changing the relationship (1) with parents and (2) with contemporaries and (3) changing the attitude to one's body. Mandatory change in the relation to internal objects would normally result in the adolescent's acceptance of the fact that he alone is responsible for his sexually mature body (Laufer, 1968). Separation from the family requires the relinquishment of both external and intrapsychic childhood dependent ties, while assuming control of one's own life implies the reestablishment of self-esteem regulation on a more autonomous level, effectively divorced from parental figures. The capacity for heterosexual intimacy, fusing sexual genital strivings and tenderness, devolves upon the resolution of the Oedipus complex. Accompanying intrapsychic transformations include the shift to a more realistic inner representation of the parents, incorporating acknowledgment of their sexual lives, and changes in the superego which now entitle the adolescent to have his own sexual life, including coitus. These modifications have a reciprocal reverberating influence, e.g., the adolescent's identification with the revised, more realistic image of the parents in their adult role helps shift power to the superego, simultaneously attenuating its archaic demands (Ritvo, 1971).

Heterosexual relationships at the beginning of the middle subphase are more narcissistic, with one eye on oneself and the other on the peer group. At the end, adolescents are paired off, and they should manifest considerable capacity for empathy, tenderness, and responsibility. During midadolescence, the sense of personal identity, of being one's own self and owning one's own body rather than being defined solely as the child of one's parents, is worked out much more clearly in the peer group relationship, which ideally offers support, confidence, and distancing from the original objects (Solnit, 1976). During early adolescence the peer group lacks cohesiveness because of a minimal tolerance for group situations at that age. Group formations at this time are unstable agglomerations of individuals. By midadolescence an abatement in narcissistic body preoccupation permits a turn to peers. This investment is not a simple shift from the self to objects but is heavily laden with narcissism initially, insofar as the peer group takes over from the parents in serving as ideal standard, self-esteem regulator, and controller of impulses.

The peer group serves as the mirror for defining the body image and sense of identity. Greenacre (1975) points out that the sense of identity involves a feeling both of uniqueness and of similarity and that the individual needs at least one other similar person to preserve a sense of identity. Identifications, which in early adolescence have a holistic, imitative quality, become more selective and partial by the middle phase, as the adolescent continually borrows and experiments in the reshaping of the self.

By the end of midadolescence the individual should be more or less at ease in his sense of self and identity, self-esteem, self-regulation, independence from parents, and heterosexual love relationships. Yet the adolescent process is far from complete. The restructuring and synthesis of late adolescence, a period of consolidation and implementation, involve further changes in superego and ego ideal, with the coalescing of the hierarchy of defenses and character. The midadolescent's unfinished quality is reflected in mood swings and open emotional display. He is still incapable of sharing his emotions with intimates and hiding them from public display without feeling divided; he still lacks a life plan, a purposive striving toward reasonable goals, an obligatory feature of adolescent closure (Blos, 1976b). Identity does not incorporate definitively the sense of where he belongs in his particular society. The move to college or a job at around age 18 is the beginning of the period of implementation (Gould, 1972). With the move out of the parental home, the adolescent's self-reliance will be tested. He must be able to stand alone in a secure and adaptive relationship to his new environment.

With this review of the years from 15 to 18, roughly equivalent to midadolescence, the period after the end of puberty and before consolidation and implementation, let us consider some of the features of this subphase in greater detail.

Family

As the adolescent distances and defines himself in opposition to his parents, his denial of a continuing need for the limits and support of the family matrix may obscure our appreciation of its essential role. Solnit, Settlage, Goodman, and Blos (1969) view psychological growth as a consequence of the innate maturational developmental thrust plus the interaction between the less developed, less integrated psychic structure of the child and the more developed psyche of the adult. The adolescent still requires this interaction with adults.

The family itself must change, gradually relinquishing control of the young person while maintaining a veto against excess and danger. This relinquishment causes intrapsychic reverberations in the parent. Ravenscroft (1974) posits a temporary normal family regression during early adolescence, providing an empathic framework that reciprocally facilitates the development of both the adolescent and his family. Stierlin (1974) conceptualizes the ideal form of their conflict as a "loving fight" in which the protagonists mutually affirm the other's entitlement to existence and differentiation.

Parental narcissism is affronted by the loss of their idealized status in the eyes of the preadolescent, by the contrast between the waxing of the adolescent's sexuality and strength as their own is on the wane, by the gap between their grandiose expectations of their child as a narcissistic extension of themselves, and by the challenge to their values and ideals which earlier held their child's unquestioning adherence. Further, the child's passage through the successive phases of development revives in the parents their unresolved conflicts specific to each phase (Kaplan, 1979). These assaults on parental self-esteem cause mourning for the latency child lost to adolescence and for the exalted status lost in its train. If parental depression or hostility is too great, one of a number of pathological outcomes in the relationship with the adolescent will ensue: attempts to thwart or abort the growth process, abdication, or extrusion.

Winnicott (1972) holds that many adolescent difficulties for which professional help is sought derive from environmental failure. Miller (1973) believes that the usual cause of failure of psychological maturation is isolation from extraparental adults. Without adult support, middle and late adolescents who are psychologically disturbed find it increasingly difficult to surmount regressive dependency needs and to free themselves from the childish component of the tie to the original objects. While a stable network of extraparental adults will protect healthy adolescents from current disturbances in the parental relationship, it is a much less effective counter to earlier effects.

In a related field, life events research indicates that the availability of "social support systems" (enduring interpersonal ties providing emotional sustenance, assistance, and resources when needed, with shared values and standards) significantly reduces adult susceptibility to physical illness in the wake of stressful life changes (Rabkin and Struening, 1976). Unfortunately, the deterioration of social networks has reduced the availability of suitable adults for individual adolescents. The lack of valid authority figures makes some adolescents excessively anxious about impulse control, thereby fostering rigid defenses and a punitive superego. As adults, they may find it difficult to exercise authority at work and at home (Smarr and Escoll, 1973).

Stable, healthy families deal with problems and conflicts without damaging the adolescent or the family equilibrium, by dint of sensitivity, empathy, tenderness, and self-confidence. The marital relationship is a critical factor. When parents were mutually secure and gratifying, the adolescents were healthier, even if the parents evidenced some psychopathology (King, 1971). King's observations agree with those of Offer and Offer (1975), previously cited, on different routes through adolescence. Healthy parents respond to the adolescent with their self-esteem intact. Their own realistically muted narcissism is reflected in the sense of competence with which they view themselves and their adolescing child. They can take pride in his developmental advances, empathize with his labors to achieve those advances, and challenge him without fear of losing his affiliation or guilt about thwarting his growth.

The function of the older generation is to provide continuity. In response to the individuating midadolescent's contesting the values of his parents and society, the most important strand of parental continuity is the maintenance of standards of value and morality (Ritvo, 1971). The parents are not devalued in toto but continue to be important identificatory models. The adolescent's questioning of the validity and sincerity of the older generation's beliefs must be taken seriously. The forced reexamination of values in the face of challenge is stressful but ultimately rewarding for both sides. In Offer's study (1969), rebellion was manifested mostly in early adolescence, between 12 and 14, and almost never concerned significant differences in values or standards. Rebellious teenagers broke rules at school and at home but were not delinquent or blatantly antisocial. This behavior gradually abated with increasing involvement in social activities later in high school. Offer sees the rebellion as part of the emancipatory process, accomplished without loss of love or respect for the parents. Katz (1968) was impressed by the extent to which a sampling of late adolescent college students felt and behaved in conformity with their families as to values, occupational choice, and social expectations.

Thus, the teenager's equation of his repudiation of parental values with differentiation and independence should not uncritically be elevated to the status of a criterion for successful passage through adolescence. Here the theoretician's values and experience of his own adolescence may introduce a bias. If his adolescence involved a successful overthrow of his parents' values in leaving a traditionalist group of origin behind, the theorist may tend to view the lack of such repudiation as indicative of failure in the adolescent process. Acceptance based on submission and repudiation based on defiance are equally clear indicators that genuine autonomy has not been achieved. However, parental values, when adopted, worked over, and integrated as the adolescent's own in the course of emotional disengagement and conflict resolution, may represent a synthesis of individuation and continuity. "If you are to possess what you inherited from your forefathers, you must first earn it" (Goethe, quoted by Mitscherlisch, 1963).

In agreement with Winnicott and Miller regarding the effects of environmental failure, King's typology of adolescent development differentiates a sensitive and vulnerable subgroup under the healthy category. This subgroup goes through adolescence with significantly greater distress than the other two healthy subgroups (modal-average and highly competent) but differs from the pathological categories in several important respects, including the time-limited nature of distress. This is a true adolescent phase upheaval. Despite their clear capabilities for meaningful object relationships, they tend to be loners. Their complaints about lack of parental understanding struck the observers as valid. Provided with an extraparental adult relationship through mental health services or other sources, these college students responded well to emotional support and advice, which enabled them to continue their developmental advance.

The erosion of cohesiveness in neighborhoods and the extended family has unquestionably limited the possibilities for relationships with adults outside the family nucleus. In viewing this loss, we may tend to neglect an important channel open to the midadolescent—through his peer group to their parents. The move to the peer group also opens the door to their homes and families. This exposure to other parents provides the teenager an opportunity to compare their attitudes and relationships with his own. These observations alone may give enough confirmation to the adolescent challenging the idiosyncratic world views of his family to strengthen his sense of conviction and resolve. While the upper limits of development of ego function prior to adolescence are determined by the level attained by the family caretakers, reality testing is especially open to modification by extrafamilial influences, peer and adult, during adolescence.

Beyond this point, relationships with the parents of friends may thicken so that they become parent surrogates. Where the adolescent's relationship with his own parents is especially troubled, the mantle of idealization may be transferred to a friend's mother or father, with effects like those noted by King in his sensitive-vulnerable groups. For others, on better terms with their own parents, the friend's family is an enriching supplement, an additional source of identifications promoting ego interests; the split between good and bad parent images is not as marked in this instance. Both cases require a capacity for object relationship, implying a significant degree of earlier closeness to one or both of the parents. While this effectively eliminates a large number, it is surprising how many individuals who attain relatively healthy adult functioning despite psychotic parents had been able to enlist friends' parents as surrogates during adolescence.

In sum, the ideal phase-specific parental response to the midadolescent is a gradual ceding of control and power with a self-confident maintenance of one's own standards and values, with pride in their child's growth, and with empathy for his struggle to achieve it, based on the realization that the advance to maturity requires emotional disengagement and the resolution of inner conflicts (Blos, 1972a). The ultimate parental wisdom is the understanding that the adolescent's defensive opposition and withdrawal do not obviate a continuing need for the parental framework during restructuring; the parent must understand that the adolescent does not want to be understood (Winnicott, 1972).

Peer Relations

The psychological predicament of the early adolescent, burdened with the consequences of withdrawal from parents and rejection of comforting parental introjects, physical maturation, and the surgence of frightening and unacceptable impulses, prepares the way for a phase-specific shift to the peer group. Blos (1962) notes the "uniformism" of American middle class youth, who in contrast to European youth show a much diminished tendency to seek out and identify with extraparental adults. At this point, the adolescent's needs are primarily narcissistic, with a touchy need for total approval from peers suitable for idealization in order to shore up fallen self-esteem. These peer involvements are quasi-relationships in a self-created social milieu, used intrapsychically to modulate and synthesize the tenuously integrated split parental images; by thus overcoming the sense of divisiveness and disharmony, a sense of basic inner unity is attained (Blos, 1976a). Identification with the idealized peer or peer group at this stage is a regressive substitute for a libidinal object tie; when disillusionment sets in, the once idealized object is dropped without a backward glance or a trace of mourning (Freud, 1921), lending group formation at this stage its fickle, unstable character.

In the train of the inevitable devaluation of idealized figures, allegiance is transferred to another group or even back to the family temporarily. Youth with more psychopathology either are unable to make the initial peer involvement or quickly withdraw for good. Alternately, such a disturbed youngster may attach himself to a "pseudogroup," in which some clearly defined stereotyped behavior—e.g., drug abuse, delinquency, or fighting with other gangs—confers a sense of belonging and identity, while intimacy is avoided (Meeks, 1974).

The shift to contemporaries is a phase-specific accompaniment of a developmental progression; the normative adolescent launches himself outward from the stable empathic family. By contrast, when supports are removed by death, divorce, parental pathology, or social upheaval, the youngster abandons the sinking ship and turns to age mates as a substitute family. Precocious peer group formation is an outgrowth of deprivation and family disorganization (Bronfenbrenner, 1974) typical of the impoverished families of the inner city (Minuchin, Montalvo, Guervey, Rosman, and Schumer, 1967). With the increase in separation and divorce, this phenomenon is becoming more prevalent among middle class youth as well.

As the young person feels more secure with his body and his impulses in midadolescence, peer relations tend to jell. The peer group becomes the mirror of the body image, the social monitor, and the behavioral arbiter. Midadolescents are preoccupied with living up to the group ideal of masculinity or femininity and are concerned with whether the opposite sex finds their behavior and appearance attractive (Hofmann, Becker, and Gabriel, 1976). Only gradually are peers perceived more realistically, as separate, distinct, and imperfect individuals whose friendship is valued notwithstanding; only gradually does the capacity for intimacy evolve.

Sexuality and Love

Sexuality is a central theme in the psychic reorganization of adolescence. In the past twenty-five years, sexual attitudes and behavior have changed significantly, notably among large segments of middle and upper class youth. Adolescents of both sexes in consultation or treatment speak about their sexual experiences, including menstruation, masturbation, contraception, and coitus, with much greater openness and ease today than when I began practice over thirty years ago. This does not signal the disappearance of the phase-specific need to keep optimal distance from adults, which does interfere with intimate discussions of sex (Clower, 1975). Chess, Thomas, and Cameron (1976) found that sex was a closed topic with teenagers by the age of 16 with their parents, but not with the interviewers. Homosexuality and the content of masturbation fantasies are the exceptions here, remaining too conflicted for easy discussion. The trend toward earlier sexual relationships, with or without emotional involvement, has provoked much disquietude; many authors echo Deutsch's concerns (1967) that the inner transformation of narcissism into a capacity for genuine, enduring, heterosexual love relationships might be thwarted.

The truism still holds that all behavior must be evaluated in terms of its significance for the individual. While objections to earlier coitus are based on the developmental point of view, they overlook the change and even disappearance of certain taboos. Just as younger generations use the four-letter obscenities casually and unconflictedly in contrast to their elders' twinge of discomfort at superego defiance, so also have the taboos around virginity eroded for certain youth. The superego sanctions provoked by sexual activity seem less intense than before and are no longer reinforced by harsh social condemnation. Therefore, while early coitus may well serve regressive or defensive functions, developmental interference is neither inevitable nor irrevocable. A Sicilian brought up in a tradition which sanctions death or literal castration of a seducer by the dishonored family has a different superego attitude and level of castration anxiety than has a Parisian youth who learns that his friend's parents, like his own, engage in extramarital affairs.

This changing valence of coitus strikingly influenced two young, white, middle class victims of black rapists. Both were involved in protracted intimate heterosexual relationships when raped. Despite the clear evidence of traumatization (gradually diminishing startle reactions, recurrent anxiety dreams, and anxiety in situations reminiscent of their victimization), neither girl's capacity for heterosexual object relationships or sexual responsiveness, including orgasm, suffered appreciably. The midadolescent's great concern about peer response was mitigated when her family moved, and she became involved with a new boyfriend within a couple of months. The late adolescent expressed no such concerns; her relationship evolved into engagement within six months.

In the early 1960s, a high school senior complained that

a group of junior girls were using him in common as the tool of their defloration. At first he had been flattered by this confirmation of his attractiveness and popularity, but when he realized that each girl would have intercourse with him only once and that the relationships were confined to the girl's peer group, excluding him, he cooperated no longer. Shortly thereafter, he fell in love with a girl outside of this group, amply demonstrating the fusion of tenderness and sexuality in an enduring relationship.

In the wake of changing sexual mores in the following decade, a phenomenon highlighting the girls' biopsychological maturational lead came to my attention. In three instances, a 17- or 18-year-old virginal youth was initiated into coitus in the context of a tender loving relationship by a girl his age, sexually experienced through a series of brief liaisons devoid of significant object relationship. These earlier sexual experiences had been undertaken by the girls to explore and prove their femininity. These narcissistic trends were succeeded by and integrated with the object relationship in a phase-appropriate evolution.

Chess et al. (1976) found in their longitudinal study a progression from friends of the same sex, to companions of both sexes, to dating, to steady dating, and finally to sexual intercourse, either as an affair or as casual sex. Offer's (1973) Model Adolescent Project data, from a group whose high school years spanned 1962–1966, do not reflect the adolescent sexual revolution; how widespread these changes are today is unclear. For boys, the dating experience was not a critical one for the first 2 years of high school. In the interviews, rationalizations for not dating were often followed by inferentially oedipal associations to their mothers. Their progressively increasing dating began as a sortie from the same-sex peer group, returning to the group to share the experience in detail almost immediately after bringing the girl home. Eventually, with diminishing anxiety, the relation to the girl became central. As boys became more at ease in the dating relationship, the ambivalence in their relationship to their mothers diminished significantly. Offer states that early and midadolescent boys appear less concerned than the girls about sexuality; the boys' more important preoccupation was curbing their aggression. The girls began dating much earlier, by the end of ninth grade; all in the sample were dating by eleventh. By contrast, only 30 percent of the eleventh grade boys dated actively; half of these petted heavily; only 10 percent had coitus. More than 90 percent of the boys daydreamed about girls, but only 25 percent about a girl they knew personally. Often, it was an older women the boy knew. The nondating groups' daydreams were almost never about a girl known personally.

Masturbation. According to Francis and Marcus' (1975) review, adolescent masturbation assists the forward movement of the drives (the phase-adequate function) and helps to bring the pregenital drives under the regulation of the genital function (the phase-specific function). It functions adaptively in assisting further delineation of inner and outer reality, the development of psychic structure, furthering the development of the self-concept, with integration of all body parts into the body image. The integrative function of masturbation, like that of dreams, shows the adolescent's preferential methods for the control and discharge of tension. Masturbation fantasies help further object relatedness by bringing early autoerotic experiences into opposition with objects through fantasy. Masturbation utilizing the opposite sex as an object in fantasy is reached slowly, culminating in midadolescence.

Clower (1975) states that individual patterns of masturbatory behavior do not change much from latency to adolescence in girls with normative phase-specific conflicts. What does change is the psychological basis for the behavior. Serving early on as a defense against internal genital sensations and the wish-fear of vaginal penetration, it becomes the trigger and focal point of spreading genital excitement which heralds and augments the readiness for coitus. Repeated experiencing of the body, a growing capacity for sexual gratification, and a growing sense that the body belongs to the self help complete the dissolution of symbiotic infantile ties and support autonomy against regressive fears of the symbiotic mother who won't let go, the castrating mother who left her maimed and bleeding, and the oedipal mother who brooks no rivals.

Borowitz (1973) finds that early disturbances in object relationships may lead to inadequate development of the capacity to tolerate and integrate drive discharge and an incapacity to masturbate alone in adolescence. In some cases, an external object is used to tolerate or defend against fantasy. He believes that the capacity to masturbate alone in adolescence is a developmental achievement, a way station in the transition from infantile sexuality to adult genitality and from narcissism to object relations.

Laufer (1976) posits that the central masturbation fantasy, a universal phenomenon, is fixed by the resolution of the Oedipus complex. With this resolution, the main sexual identifications become fixed and the core of the body image established. Only during adolescence, however, does the content of the sexual wishes and the oedipal identifications become integrated into an irreversible sexual identity. During adolescence, the oedipal wishes are tested in the context of the possession of mature genitalia. The function of adolescent masturbation is both a trial action experienced within one's own thought and a way of testing which sexual thoughts, feelings, or gratifications are acceptable to the superego. A compromise solution is found which defines the person's sexual identity. Late adolescence ushers in the consolidation phase, in which this irreversible sexual position should be achieved and masturbation relinquished for true object attachment.

All mating behavior originates in mother-child behavior. More specifically, Sarlin (1970) identifies the mother-child nursing dyad as the prototype of lovemaking. Ritvo (1971) reminds us that with the establishment of genital primacy the individual becomes dependent on the body of the object in a way that has not existed since infancy. This causes a shift in the balance between the reality and pleasure principles, from gratification and discharge associated with fantasy and the autoplastic activity of masturbation, to gratification in the context of the alloplastic relationship to the external object. For the late adolescent, the new object serves functions at a higher level, resembling those served by the object of infancy and early childhood, as a stabilizer of physiological and affective processes.

Adolescent love. In view of these implications of intimacy and its anxiety-laden regressive potential, falling in love is a developmental crisis. Williams (1973) draws attention to the obstacles to this phase-specific attainment in a sociocultural and familial context, emphasizing achievement and performance that foster a competitive narcissistic ego identity. Following the initial mother-child symbiosis, Williams sees little further experience with intimacy. Yet at 18 the adolescent is expected to somehow tap that early experience and apply it to love relationships.

Kernberg (1974) deals at length with the question of ego identity as the general prerequisite to falling in love. Ego identity, the overall organization of identifications and introjections under the ego's synthetic function, reflects the capacity for intimacy (Erikson, 1956), defined as a total relation with a heterosexual object, including tenderness, full genital gratification, and human depth. Ego identity is established gradually throughout infancy and childhood, as the primitive ego organization's splitting evolves into an integrated ego employing repression and related higher-level defense mechanisms. Such ego functioning, in the context of integration of total object relations, reciprocally reinforces ego identity.

In disagreement with Erikson, Kernberg's position that the establishment of ego identity is not a universal issue in normal adolescence is supported by the findings of Jacobson (1964) and the group studies of Masterson (1967), Offer (1969), and King (1971). In Kernberg's view, identity crises are normative for adolescence; identity diffusion is not. The crisis involves a loss of correspondence of the internal sense of identity with the confirmation provided by the psychosocial environment. Diffusion, characterized by mutually dissociated ego states with disintegration extending to the superego and internalized object relations, occurs in neurotics with specific narcissistic conflicts, and in borderline and psychotic patients.

The typical clinical manifestations of sexual conflict in adolescence are the dissociation of tenderness and sexual excitement, a dichotomy between asexual idealized objects and sexually devalued objects (Madonna vs. whore), and the coexistence of excessive guilt and impulsive expression of sexual urges. These symptoms, Kernberg warns, give no diagnostic clue to the severity of psychopathology. Falling in love produces an experience of transcendence in the normal adolescent.

Going beyond Frosch (1966), Kernberg agrees that reality constancy is closely interwoven with object constancy, but that the former evolves beyond the limit of love-object constancy. The capacity to experience in depth the nonhuman environment, to appreciate nature and art, and to experience the self within a historical and cultural continuum are intimately linked with the capacity for being in love.

Psychic Restructuralization

It will be helpful in our consideration of the revisions, additions, and reorganization of psychic structure in adolescence to review preceding development. Object relations theory, as explained by Kernberg (1976), provides a congenial heuristic framework which more adequately conveys the gradualistic continuity of normal development. The progressive evolution of the mind is characterized in terms of gradual reciprocal interactions and mutual influences: Through the reshaping of experiences with external objects in the light of internal object representations and of these object representations in the light of real experiences with others, ego identity (the organized processes of internalization of object relations) evolves; simultaneously the self-concept is continuously reshaped in the context of experiences with others and of experiences with the inner world of object representations. The more integrated the self-representations, the more self-perception corresponds to the reality of the interpersonal interaction; the more integrated the object representations, the greater the capacity for realistic assessment of others, and of revising the internal representations on the basis of realistic assessments. The processes of integration, depersonification, and individualization are structural outcomes of the internalization of object relations in all agencies of the mind. Individualization refers to the gradual replacement of primitive introjections and identifications with partial, sublimatory identifications compatible with the self-concept.

In Kernberg's view, the consolidation of the ego, presupposing the supersession of splitting processes by regression, probably occurs in the second and third years. With its fusion of positive and negative introjections comes the formation of the ideal self-image, representing the striving for the reparation of guilt and for the reestablishment of an ideal, positive self-object relationship; its counterpart, the ideal-object image, represents the unharmed, all-loving, all-forgiving object (Sandler, Holder, and Meers, 1963; Jacobson, 1964). Superego components form between the second and fifth years, with definite integration mainly between the fourth and sixth, followed by depersonification and abstraction between the fifth and seventh. With integration, the absolute, fantastic nature of primitive idealization (the early ego ideal, condensed from the ideal self- and ideal-object representations), and of the sadistic forerunners of the superego (extremely hostile and unrealistic object images derived from projected and reintrojected "bad" self-object representations) is mitigated, along with a decrease in the projection of such sadistic and idealized superego nuclei.

With the decrease in projective processes, internalizations of the parental demands and prohibitions of the oedipal phase can occur on a more realistic level. Kernberg cites Jacobson's theoretical clarifications and adumbrations of structural evolution repeatedly, as do Ritvo (1971) and Blos in their considerations of the ego ideal in adolescence.

The ego ideal is the goal- and aspiration-setting agency of the mind, conceptualized variously as a component of the superego or as separate from it. Originating in infantile narcissism it remains closely related to self-esteem regulation, need satisfaction, and wish fulfillment throughout life (Lampl–de Groot, 1962). Shame is the characteristic affect of disharmony between ego and ego ideal; guilt typifies the tension between ego and the prohibiting agency, the superego (Piers and Singer, 1953). Genetically, the ego ideal operates with positive libidinal strivings; aggression prevails in the superego (Bibring, 1964). While superego demands can be fulfilled with a subsequent sense of well-being, ego ideal demands for perfection can never be fulfilled (Blos, 1974).

According to Blos, the function of the early ego ideal is to eradicate narcissistic mortification through recourse to a state of illusory self-perfection. In the oedipal phase, the oedipal realization of physical immaturity is mitigated by borrowing perfection from the idealized parents and from their narcissistic overestimation of the child. The normal childhood ego ideal state of partial integration and external regulation undergoes a radical and lasting change with the second individuation process of adolescence. Then emotional disengagement from the internalized love and hate objects of early childhood leads to the heightened narcissistic state, idealizations, and rebellious self-assertion that typify adolescence.

In the final stages of adolescence Jacobson finds a hierarchical reorganization and final integration of value concepts, arising from both ego and superego into a new coherent structure and functional unit, the ego ideal. Ritvo states that the ego ideal, as a structuralized institution of the mind, is a development of adolescence. Blos holds that the structuralization of the ego ideal renders it qualitatively different from antecedent developmental stages and determines the end phase of the adolescent process. In the intersystemic reapportionment, the ego expands at the expense of the id and the superego and cedes certain value functions to the ego ideal; the superego is encroached on by both ego and ego ideal.

Qualitatively, the striving after perfection of the ego ideal becomes a partly independent, direction-giving function, relatively independent of objects and of instinctual processes (Hartmann and Loewenstein, 1962). From being dependent, personalized, and concretized, the ego ideal proceeds to become autonomous, impersonal, and abstracted. Excessive self- and object idealization are reduced to more realistic appraisals as the ego ideal loses its more primitive wish-fulfillment quality and comes under the hegemony of ego identity.

Ritvo (1971) believes that one of the main genetic roots of the ego ideal is in the passive feminine homosexual orientation of the negative Oedipus complex (Freud, 1914); that reinstinctualization of the ego ideal by predominantly homosexual libido is a normative aspect of the adolescent process; and that the ego ideal's evolution into a structuralized institution of the mind is an adolescent development.

To summarize Blos's thesis, in essential agreement with Ritvo, definitive resolution of the Oedipus complex, involving the total renunciation of infantile object ties to both parents as sexual objects (the positive and negative components), is the inherent task of adolescence. Since the bisexual position is less conflictual for the child, the negative Oedipus complex seems less stringently affected than the positive at the end of the oedipal phase. Bisexuality in women, less conflictual throughout life, is never repressed or resolved as definitively as for men. Stabilization of femininity and attainment of the mature, desexualized, impersonal ego ideal by the late adolescent girl involve supplanting the regressive incorporation of the paternal phallus as the narcissistic regulator of the sense of completeness and perfection by an enduring identification with her mother. Even if this development is achieved, the woman's ego ideal retains the potential for reenmeshment with object relations.

Blos views the boy's development as following a different course. In early adolescence, the regressive revival of the preoedipal, omnipotent phallic mother image intensifies both castration anxiety and narcissistic identification with the maternal representation. Fearing the mother and women generally, he idealizes the father, bolstering his self-esteem by identification and defending against castration anxiety by the relationship. When the sexual impulse threatens the arousal of homosexual object libido toward the father, this defensive solution is terminated. Object displacement, leading to overt homosexuality, is unacceptable; the obligatory development is the resolution of the negative Oedipus complex and the deinstinctualization of the narcissistic homosexual object tie. In the process, all ego ideal trends coalesce into final unalterable form in the terminal stage of adolescence. The male ego ideal enshrines its history, from primary narcissism to the merger with maternal omnipotence to the oedipal love for the father. This last stage is transcended in the mature ego ideal, the heir of the negative Oedipus complex just as the superego is the heir of the positive (Blos, 1965).

Blos's masterfully evocative exegesis has a number of shortcomings, including excessively heavy reliance on libido theory, a tendency to metapsychological reification, and speculative assertions about cause and effect in intrapsychic evolution. Moreover, his views on normative development, based avowedly

2

2

2

on extrapolations from psychopathology, overemphasize the punctate crisis and lurching advance of failure. The complementary neglect of linear gradualism, which I find typical of outstanding and normal development, blurs its delineation from the abnormal in Blos's conceptualization. Therefore, while joining the cumulative consensus that changes in both quality and content of ego ideal and superego occur in adolescence, I would take exception to the notion that the ego ideal is born as a structure at late adolescence or that the transition from its personalized, dependent, and concretized qualities to impersonal, autonomous, and abstracted is confined to this phase. Restructuralization is a better term.

Summary

The early adolescent must redefine himself and his relationship to his parents in the wake of his momentous physical transformation. The middle adolescent must venture from the protective scaffolding of the peer group into dyadic heterosexual love relationships. The late adolescent must define his spiritual and worldly standards and goals of achievement, while initiating their implementation. These developmental redefinitions involve, first, his body and his family; second, sexual identity and intimacy; third, standards, goals, and the relation to society.

Psychological midadolescence begins as biological growth ends. Physical growth is virtually complete and reproductive maturity attained by age 14 or 15 in the girl; 15 or 16 in the boy. Successful negotiation of the midadolescent subphase between 17 and 19 finds the young person at ease in a sense of self and identity, with relatively stable and autonomous self-esteem and self-regulation, emotionally emancipated from childish dependence on family and capable of heterosexual intimacy.

The developmental tasks of midadolescence require extensive intrapsychic reorganization. Further restructuring, notably of superego and ego ideal, and the coalescing of character and the defense hierarchy take place before the final closure at the end of late adolescence.

References

Barglow, P., & Schaefer, M. (1976), A new female psychology? *J. Amer. Psychoanal. Assn.*, 24:305–350.

Bernfeld, S. (1924), *Vom dicterischen Schaffender Jugend* (On Poetically Creative Youth). Vienna: Internationaler Psychoanalytischer Verlag.

Bibring, G. (1964), Some considerations regarding the ego ideal in the psychoanalytic process. *J. Amer. Psychoanal. Assn.*, 12:517–521.

Blos, P. (1962), *On Adolescence: A Psychoanalytic Interpretation.* New York: Free Press.

———— (1965), The initial stage of male adolescence. *The Psychoanalytic Study of the Child*, 20:145–164. New York: International Universities Press.

———— (1967), The second individuation process of adolescence. *The Psychoanalytic Study of the Child*, 22:162–186. New York: International Universities Press.

———— (1972a), The function of the ego ideal in adolescence. *The Psychoanalytic Study of the Child*, 27:93–97. New York: Quadrangle.

———— (1972b), The generation gap: Fact and fiction. In: *Adolescent Psychiatry*, Vol. 1, ed. S. C. Feinstein & P. Giovacchini. New York: Basic Books, pp. 5–13.

———— (1974), The genealogy of the ego ideal. *The Psychoanalytic Study of the Child*, 29:43–88. New Haven: Yale University Press.

———— (1976a), The split parental image in adolescent social relations: An inquiry into group psychology. *The Psychoanalytic Study of the Child*, 31:7–34. New Haven: Yale University Press.

———— (1976b), When and how does adolescence end? *J. Phila. Assn. Psychoanal.*, 3:47–58.

Borowitz, G. H. (1973), The capacity to masturbate alone in adolescence. In: *Adolescent Psychiatry*, Vol. 2, ed. S. C. Feinstein & P. Giovacchini. New York: Basic Books, pp. 130–143.

Bronfenbrenner, U. (1974), The origins of alienation. *Scientific American*, August, p. 231.

Chess, S., Thomas, A., & Cameron, M. (1976), Sexual attitudes and behavior patterns in a middle-class adolescent population. Paper presented at American Orthopsychiatric Association Annual Meeting, Atlanta, Georgia, March.

Clower, V. L. (1975), Significance of masturbation in female sexual development. In: *Masturbation from Infancy to Senescence*, ed. I. M. Marcus & S. J. Francis. New York: International Universities Press, pp. 107–143.

Cohen, R. S., & Balikov, H. (1974), On the impact of adolescence upon parents. In: *Adolescent Psychiatry*, Vol. 3, ed. S. C. Feinstein & P. Giovacchini. New York: Basic Books, pp. 217–236.

Cramer, B. (1976), Outstanding developmental progression in three boys: A longitudinal study. *The Psychoanalytic Study of the Child*, 30:15–48. New Haven: Yale University Press.

230   EUGENE H. KAPLAN

Deutsch, H. (1944), *The Psychology of Women*, Vol. 1. New York: Grune & Stratton.
———— (1967), *Selected Problems of Adolescence*. New York: International Universities Press.
Dulit, E. (1972), Adolescent thinking à la Piaget: The formal stage. *J. Youth & Adolescence*, 1:281–301.
..rikson, E. H. (1956), The problem of ego identity. *J. Amer. Psychoanal. Assn.*, 4:56–121.
Francis, S. J., & Marcus, I. M. (1975), Masturbation: A developmental view. In: *Masturbation from Infancy to Senescence*, ed. I. M. Marcus & S. J. Francis. New York: International Universities Press, pp. 9–51.
Freud, A. (1958), Adolescence. *The Psychoanalytic Study of the Child*, 13:255–278. New York: International Universities Press.
———— (1969), Adolescence as a developmental disturbance. In: *Adolescence: Psychosocial Perspectives*, ed. G. Caplan & S. Lebovici. New York: Basic Books, pp. 5–10.
Freud, S. (1914), On narcissism. *Standard Edition*, 14:73–102. London: Hogarth Press, 1957.
———— (1921), Group psychology and the analysis of the ego. *Standard Edition*, 18:69–143. London: Hogarth Press, 1955.
Frosch, J. (1966), A note on reality constancy. In: *Psychoanalysis: A General Psychology*, ed. R. M. Loewenstein, L. M. Newman, M. Schur, & A. J. Solnit. New York: International Universities Press, pp. 349–376.
Geleerd, E. (1961), Some aspects of ego vicissitudes in adolescence. *J. Amer. Psychoanal. Assn.*, 9:394–405.
Gould, R. L. (1972), The phases of adult life: A study of developmental psychology. *Amer. J. Psychiat.*, 129:521–531.
Greenacre, P. (1975), Differences between male and female adolescent development. In: *Adolescent Psychiatry*, Vol. 4, ed. S. C. Feinstein & P. Giovacchini. New York: Aronson, pp. 105–120.
Grinker, R. R., Sr., Grinker, R. R., Jr., & Timberlake, J. (1971), "Mentally healthy" young males: Homoclites. In: *Adolescent Psychiatry*, Vol. 1, ed. S. C. Feinstein & P. Giovacchini. New York: Basic Books, pp. 176–255.
Guilford, J. P. (1967), *The Nature of Human Intelligence*. New York: McGraw-Hill.
Hartmann, H., & Loewenstein, R. M. (1962), Notes on the superego. *The Psychoanalytic Study of the Child*, 17:42–81. New York: International Universities Press.
Hofmann, A. D., Becker, R. D., & Gabriel, H. P. (1976), *The Hospitalized Adolescent*. Riverside, NJ.: Free Press.
Jacobson, E. (1954), The self and the object world. *The Psychoanalytic Study of the Child*, 9:75–127. New York: International Universities Press.
———— (1964), *The Self and the Object World*. New York: International Universities Press.
Kaplan, E. H. (1979), Unfinished business: Revival of the parent's unresolved conflicts during the adolescence of his child. In: *Clinical Psychoanalysis*, Vol. 3, ed. S. Orgel & D. Fine. New York: Aronson, pp. 235–247.
Katz, J. (1968), *No Time for Youth*. San Francisco: Jossey-Bass.
Kernberg, O. (1974), Mature love: Prerequisites and characteristics. *J. Amer. Psychoanal. Assn.*, 22:743–768.

———— (1976), *Object-Relations Theory and Clinical Psychoanalysis*. New York: Aronson.

Kestenberg, J. (1968), Phases of adolescence, with suggestions for correlation of psychic and hormonal organization: Part 3. Puberty growth, differentiation and consolidation. *J. Amer. Acad. Child Psychiat.*, 7:108–151.

Khatchadourian, H. (1977), *The Biology of Adolescence*. San Francisco: Freeman.

King, S. H. (1971), Coping mechanisms in adolescents. *Psychiat. Annals*, 1:10–45.

Kolata, G. B. (1975), Behavioral development: Effects of environments. *Science*, 189:207–209.

Lampl-de Groot, J. (1962), Ego ideal and superego. *The Psychoanalytic Study of the Child*, 17:94–106. New York: International Universities Press.

Laufer, M. (1968), The body image, the function of masturbation, and adolescence: Problems of the ownership of the body. *The Psychoanalytic Study of the Child*, 23:114–137. New York: International Universities Press.

———— (1976), The central masturbation fantasy, the final sexual organization and adolescence. *The Psychoanalytic Study of the Child*, 31:297–316. New Haven: Yale University Press.

Levenson, E. A., Feiner, A. H., & Stockhauer, N. N. (1976), The politics of adolescent psychiatry. In: *Adolescent Psychiatry*, Vol. 4, ed. S. C. Feinstein & P. Giovacchini. New York: Aronson, pp. 84–100.

Lidz, T., Lidz, R. W., & Rubenstein, R. (1976), An anaclitic syndrome in adolescent amphetamine addicts. *The Psychoanalytic Study of the Child*, 31:317–348. New Haven: Yale University Press.

Masterson, J. F., Jr. (1967), *The Psychiatric Dilemma of Adolescence*. Boston: Little, Brown.

Meeks, J. T. (1971), *The Fragile Alliance*. Baltimore: Williams & Wilkins.

———— (1974), Adolescent development and group cohesion. In: *Adolescent Psychiatry*, Vol. 3, ed. S. C. Feinstein & P. Giovacchini. New York: Basic Books, pp. 289–297.

Miller, D. H. (1973), The drug-dependent adolescent. In: *Adolescent Psychiatry*, Vol. 2, ed. S. C. Feinstein & P. Giovacchini. New York: Basic Books, pp. 70–97.

Minuchin, S., Montalvo, B., Guervey, B. C., Jr., Rosman, B. L., & Schumer, T. (1967), *Families of the Slums: An Exploration of their Structure and Treatment*. New York: Basic Books.

Mitscherlisch, A. (1963), *Society Without the Father*, trans. E. Mosbacher. New York: Schocken, 1970.

Moore, W. T. (1975), Some economic functions of genital masturbation during adolescent development. In: *Masturbation from Infancy to Senescence*, ed. I. M. Marcus & S. J. Francis. New York: International Universities Press, pp. 231–276.

Neubauer, P. (1976), *The Process of Child Development*. New York: New American Library.

Offer, D. (1969), *The Psychological World of the Teenager*. New York: Basic Books.

———— (1973), The adolescent sexual revolution. In: *Adolescent Psychiatry*, Vol. 2, ed. S. C. Feinstein & P. Giovacchini. New York: Basic Books, pp. 165–171.

———— Offer, J. (1975), Three developmental routes through normal male adolescence. In: *Adolescent Psychiatry*, Vol. 4, ed. S. C. Feinstein & P. Giovacchini. New York: Aronson, pp. 121–141.

Piaget, J., & Inhelder, B. (1958), *The Growth of Logical Thinking from Childhood to Adolescence*. New York: Basic Books.

Piers, G., & Singer, M. B. (1953), *Shame and Guilt*. New York: Norton.

Pumpian-Mindlin, E. (1965), Omnipotentiality, youth and commitment. *J. Amer. Acad. Child Psychiat.*, 4:1–18.

——— (1969), Vicissitudes of infantile omnipotence. *The Psychoanalytic Study of the Child*, 23:213–226. New York: International Universities Press.

Rabkin, J. G., & Struening, E. L. (1976), Life events, stress and illness. *Science*, 194:1013–1020.

Ravenscroft, K., Jr. (1974), Normal family regression at adolescence. *Amer. J. Psychiat.*, 131:31–35.

Ritvo, S. A. (1969), A psychoanalytic view of the family. A study of family member interactions. *Psychoanal. Forum*, 3:13–27.

——— (1971), Late adolescence: Developmental and clinical considerations. *The Psychoanalytic Study of the Child*, 26:241–263. New York: Quadrangle.

——— (1976), Adolescent to woman. *J. Amer. Psychoanal. Assn.*, 24:127–138.

Sandler, J., Holder, A., & Meers, D. (1963), The ego ideal and the ideal self. *The Psychoanalytic Study of the Child*, 18:139–158. New York: International Universities Press.

Sarlin, C. N. (1970), The current status of the concept of genital primacy. *J. Amer. Psychoanal. Assn.*, 18:282–299.

Smarr, E. R., & Escoll, P. J. (1973), The youth culture, future adulthood, and societal change. In: *Adolescent Psychiatry*, Vol. 2, ed. S. C. Feinstein & P. Giovacchini. New York: Basic Books, pp. 113–126.

Solnit, A. J. (1971), Adolescence and the changing reality. In: *Currents in Psychoanalysis*, ed. I. M. Marcus. New York: International Universities Press, pp. 98–110.

——— (1976), Inner and outer changes in adolescence. *J. Phila. Assn. Psychoanal.*, 3:43–46.

——— Settlage, C. F., Goodman, S., & Blos, P. (1969), Youth unrest: A symposium. *Amer. J. Psychiat.*, 125:1145–1159.

Spiegel, L. A. (1958), Comments on the psychoanalytic psychology of adolescence. *The Psychoanalytic Study of the Child*, 13:296–308. New York: International Universities Press.

Spruiell, V. (1971), The transition of the body image between middle and late adolescence. In: *Currents in Psychoanalysis*, ed. I. M. Marcus. New York: International Universities Press, pp. 111–132.

Stierlin, H. (1974), *Separating Parents and Adolescents*. New York: Quadrangle.

Stone, L. J., & Church, J. (1957), *Childhood and Adolescence*. New York: Random House.

Tanner, J. M. (1962), *Growth at Adolescence*. 2nd ed. Oxford: Blackwell.

Trent, J. W., & Medsker, L. L. (1968), *Beyond High School*. San Francisco: Jossey-Bass.

Williams, F. S. (1973), The adolescent sexual revolution. In: *Adolescent Psychiatry*, Vol. 2, ed. S. C. Feinstein & P. Giovacchini. New York: Basic Books, pp. 162–165.

Winnicott, D. W. (1972), Adolescence: Struggling through the doldrums. In:

Adolescent Psychiatry, Vol. 1, ed. S. C. Feinstein & P. Giovacchini. New York: Basic Books, pp. 40–50.

Wolfenstein, M. (1958), Children's understanding of jokes. *The Psychoanalytic Study of the Child*, 13:296–308. New York: International Universities Press.

——— (1966), How is mourning possible? *The Psychoanalytic Study of the Child*, 21:93–123. New York: International Universities Press.

8

The Tides of Change in Adolescence

HENRY P. COPPOLILLO, M.D.

The integration, organization, and regulation of ego functions during adolescence are topics that have received relatively little attention.

Integration may be conceptualized as the fusion of two or more functions of lesser complexity to produce a number of functions of greater complexity. The repertoire of behavior or the number of functions available to the individual after integration is greater than the sum of the individual functions prior to integration.

For our purposes, the organization of the ego is the manner in which ego functions are deployed or grouped at any given period to meet the requisites of the individual and of the environment or to relieve the strain between environmental constraints and individual wishes.

Regulation may be considered the process of first perceiving the need for a change in the deployment of ego functions (or the need to maintain them unchanged) and then undertaking these changes or stabilizing maneuvers.

With these definitions we may construct a model that demonstrates the processes of integration, organization, and regulation.

Where better to begin to look at adolescence than Shakespeare's great ode to youth in *Romeo and Juliet*? Romeo, after crashing the Capulet party, goes to his confidant and teacher Friar Laurence to exult about his love for Juliet. The friar is astounded, as only the day before Romeo had been desperately in love with Rosaline. Romeo breezily states that his passion for Rosaline has passed and that he now loves another. The friar continues to be amazed that so desperate a love could have passed so quickly. Romeo is irritated by this reasonable perplexity and reminds the good friar that he had chided Romeo for loving Rosaline so intensely and that while Juliet returns his love, Rosaline had never done so. The friar, with wisdom and insight, explains Rosaline's reticence with the lines, "O, she knew well / Thy love did read by rote, and could not spell."

Apparently the adolescent's tendency to assume an attitude, experience a feeling, or immerse himself in a state for the sake of the state, attitude, or feeling was well known as far back as we care to look. In addition, adult perplexity and amazement at adolescents' turbulent emotions and apparently quixotic behavior are not new. Despite the fact that it has been described and redescribed by such master observers of the human condition as Shakespeare, it would be difficult to find today an adult who has not been charmed, seduced, perplexed, and even victimized by the storms of emotion and the vagaries of behavior that characterize young people who are traversing that brief but critically important span of life called adolescence.

To pass from the romantic to the commonplace, imagine the father of an adolescent boy settling into his chair in front of the television after a grueling day with the conviction that he has earned his preprandial drink and a half hour's peace. His son, with whom he has been on surprisingly good terms for several days, slouches into the room and in response to his father's greetings mutters something that might have been equally well understood as "Hello" or "Hell No!" Ten minutes or so go by in silence when in response to the news commentator's remark on the energy crisis, the son begins to mutter angrily. The father, thinking that the boy's vocalizations are an invitation to conversation, says something so viciously provocative as, "It looks as if we'll be facing some pretty tough problems in the next few years." In response the boy begins with a condemnation of his father's entire generation. As he warms to the task, he becomes more pointed and specific, reminding his father that if he were only willing to walk or bicycle the seven or eight miles to work instead of driving the gas-guzzling Volkswagen, the energy shortage would be resolved. But no! The hedonistic, materialistic, and self-indulgent orientation displayed by his father and all his contemporaries is robbing the boy's generation of any hope of physical warmth, mobility, and perhaps even survival.

To emphasize his disgust with the situation, the boy announces he is going to go find his mother. If dinner isn't ready, he plans to raise hell. If it is ready, he won't eat. The father once more is left feeling that whenever he interacts with his son he misses some crucial point that would explain the whole interchange. The son is indeed not at dinner, and rather than face another crisis the father decides to let the boy maintain his posture of righteous asceticism. An hour or two later the father is startled by a cheerful "Hey, Dad" voiced by his persecutor of a short time before. The greeting is followed by a request to use the family car to take his girl to a pizza parlor across town. The father points out that there is a pizza house within two very walkable blocks of his girlfriend's house and if he really wants to save gas for posterity, he can walk. No! That just won't do! The pizza across town is just what he has a taste for at that moment. All other considerations are unimportant. He must have that particular pizza with his girl at this moment. He needs the car and nothing else will do. The father is not quite sure what appetite his son is driven to indulge, but he is sure that in the space of a few short hours the boy has passed from a trappist-like asceticism to a hedonism that would make Henry VIII seem inhibited by comparison. He cannot understand how the boy can reconcile his position two hours earlier with the request he has just heard. The father concludes that adolescence is indeed a period of "normal psychosis" through which all human beings must pass and turns to something infinitely more predictable than his son, like the stock market, and puts the event out of mind.

From his point of view, the son simply cannot understand what the problem with his father is. What does wanting to take your girl to a pizza parlor have to do with what went on before? Life seems complicated enough when he contemplates girls and dating without the added burden of being held responsible for what occurred in a different time and under other circumstances. He is sure that his father's demand for such ridiculous consistency is only a ploy to deny him the car.

Stories of these quick emotional changes, contradictory attitudes standing side by side, and behaviors that belie verbal communications are legion when adults describe their exchanges with adolescents. Gradually, however, we are beginning to understand some of the phenomena that are responsible for these paradoxes. I would like to present a model—a way of conceptualizing adolescence—that may help us to explain a little bit, and allow us to ask questions about a good deal more, regarding these developmental three-ring circuses.

My interest in this topic evolved from a curiosity about psychological functions that could be used by individuals to raise their thresholds to certain stimuli. In the course of attempting to understand threshold phenomena, I found two papers by David Rapaport (1951, 1958) particularly helpful. In discussing the ego's autonomies, Rapaport emphasized that the ego is neither totally vulnerable to intrusions (or stimuli) from the outside world nor completely at the mercy of the instinctual drives. If one kicks a stone (i.e., applies stimuli from outside its structure), the stone has no choice but to react according to the laws of physics. In contrast, stimuli which impinge on living matter can be reacted to in a variety of ways. This capacity for alternative responses to stimuli impinging from without Rapaport called "the autonomy of the ego from the environment." He held that the drives are primary guarantess that the ego will not, like the stone, be a slave to external stimuli. But neither is the ego at the mercy of the drives. A drive can be deflected, inhibited, ignored, or partially indulged. This capacity Rapaport termed "the autonomy of the ego from the id." He postulated that the capacity to perceive the external world, to take action, to think, to reevoke memory traces, to synthesize perceptions, etc.—in a word, to use the primary autonomous functions of the ego—is the guarantor of the ego's autonomy from the id. Finally in what is perhaps the most elegant part of this conceptualization, he argued that these autonomies of the ego stand in reciprocal, inverse relation to each other.

Thus the ego can be thought to have two areas of sensitivity. One faces and is sensitive to stimuli from the external world; the other sensitivity is to stimuli that impinge on it from the internal environment. By virtue of their reciprocal relationship,

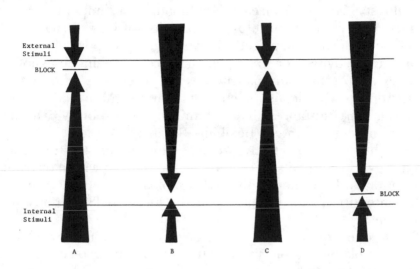

FIGURE 1. Graphic representation of the reciprocal "autonomies" of the ego.

any change in one area of sensitivity is accompanied by an
inverse change in the other. If, for example, the ego is forced
into a state of autonomy or insensitivity to the external environment by sensory deprivation, it quickly becomes extremely
permeable to wishes and impulses from within (Figure 1A). In
a matter of a few hours or a few days, depending on the individual, the subject begins hallucinating gratifying or terrifying
internal states or wishes and may become delusional. Conversely, if environmental stimuli become so compelling that they
cannot be ignored, as in brainwashing techniques, the individual becomes virtually incapable of attending to internal states
and wishes (Figure 1B).

Clinically, what we see more frequenty is the opposite of what has just been described. Increased drive impetus, due to adolescence, climacterium, or pathology (Figure 1C), is accompanied by reduced sensitivity to the environment. An example of this state, drawn from early childhood, is the temper tantrum, during which attendance or responsivity to the external environment is grossly impaired. Conversely, self-imposed blocking of drive activity—for example, that occurring in obsessional states or in schizophrenia—may result in endless, ruminative attention to the details of environmental stimuli, or even, in extreme circumstances, in an inanimate-like responsivity to the environment, as in waxy flexibility (Figure 1D).

Thus the ego actively processes and adapts to stimuli by raising or lowering its thresholds to stimuli from within or from without, and the state of these thresholds will often determine the intensity if not the nature of the individual's response to stimuli.

If one ponders Rapaport's elegant ideas and formulates some explanations of clinical situations in these terms, it becomes evident that while he focused on two areas of sensitivity and responsivity in the ego, clinical observation forces us to acknowledge that there are at least three such areas. These include the two that Rapaport described (namely, the ego's sensitivity to external and internal stimuli) and the ego's capacity to observe and be sensitive to itself and to that totality of wishes, capabilities, convictions, identifications, values, ideals, prohibitions, liabilities, sensitivities, and talents that are called the "self."

With these three areas of sensitivity in mind we can now describe events that happen in the phase of human development that we call adolescence. This treatment of the topic of adolescence is, of course, focal and makes no pretense at being exhaustive. But its focus may allow us to scrutinize certain phenomena in a more microscopic way.

In many discussions the period of adolescence is described as a period of transition. There then follows a description of different states at the beginning and at the end of adolescence; or in some instances the description may be of an early, a middle, and a late adolescent state. The process by which the youngster moves from one state to another may be ignored or left to be inferred. While the description of various states is legitimate and necessary, it may deflect our attention from an equally important and legitimate scrutiny of the *process* by which one state merges into another. Below, adolescence is first described by comparing certain aspects of ego organization at puberty with these same aspects as maturity. In addition, some ideas are discussed regarding the process by which the adolescent proceeds from one state to another. To begin, we must explore some antecedents of adolescence.

In prepuberty, the child has lived through a period in which the external world has been invested with a tremendous amount of authority and attention. By establishing a workable equilibrium between the push of individual strivings and wishes and the immovable rigidities of the external and internal realities that oppose them, the child has achieved enough internal serenity to begin attending, between the ages of about 2 and 12, to all manner of issues in the external world. During this time, the amount of substantive information the child absorbs from the external world is enormous. The child's orientation to this information is, however, relatively indiscriminate and uncritical. There seems to be no capacity to recognize the possible significance of this information to the child's state or situation. About the time of puberty, relevant information is just beginning to be turned into usable knowledge, and the child must await further development before this knowledge can become wisdom. Note, for example, that one of the most frequently found books in the latency child's home is the *Guinness Book of World Records*. More recently the *Book of Lists* has been popular with the younger set. When the school age child is not intrigued by the disconnected facts contained in these books, he can always turn to the batting averages of major league players or to the vital statistics of Hollywood stars.

This capacity to absorb and process information and stimuli from the external world is not matched in the child by equal sensitivity to the inner world of wishes, impulses, appetites, and strivings. Following their brush with sexual and aggressive impulses during the oedipal period, postoedipal children find evidence for the existence of these impulses in the external world and perceives them only dimly in themselves.

The child's sense of self is even more discontinuous and inconsistent. While it may seem at times that the child may have a relatively well-developed sense of self, closer scrutiny reveals that in most instances the identity and the traits ascribed by the child to himself are *assigned* by the environment rather than developed or evolved by self-awareness. One can hear at any time from the prepubertal child phrases like "I am Daddy's son"; "I am Mrs. Jones's third grade student"; or "The gym teacher says I am the best runner in the class." It is a time for self-images that children perceive as assigned to them by the environments in which they live.

Due to the relatively indiscriminate and uncritical manner in which the child absorbs information, the clinician can on occasion see the destructiveness wrought by the depreciated identities assigned children by ignorant, prejudiced, or mischievous environments.

Graphically, the ego of the child may be depicted as having a relatively well-developed system for perceiving and organizing external events (Figure 2A), a poorly developed and relatively thin capacity to perceive internal strivings and states (Figure 2B), and a set of spotty, inconsistent glimpses of the self (Figure 2C). Both of these latter percepts the child frequently feels are elicited or evoked by the environment.

Continuing with this model, one may say that the child moves in adolescence from an ego organization as depicted in Figure 2 to a more evenly balanced and adaptively more efficient configuration such as that depicted in Figure 3. Here we may conceive of a person with excellent sensitivity to environmental stimuli, experienced as objective phenomena, as in A_2; or as potential recipients of drive investment, as in A_3; or as an amalgam of the interactions between the self and the object world, as in A_1. Internal states may in turn be perceived relatively comfortably, in relation with environmental percepts, as in B_1; as pure internal states or wishes, as in B_2; or as part of the self-system, as in B_3. Similarly, the self-system can be experienced in relation to one's surroundings (C_1); in relatively isolated self-contemplation (C_2); and in relation to aspirations,

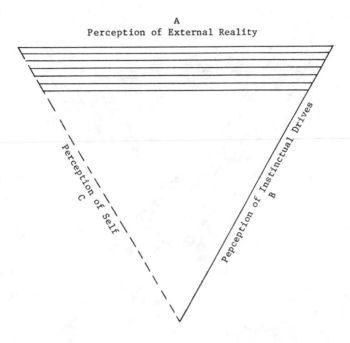

FIGURE 2. Deployment of ego functions in the prepubertal child.

wishes, and drives (C_3). Integrations have occurred that place the mental images of the individual's drives and derivative appetites in the context of a self-system that interacts with an environment that is perceived both in its own right and for its potentially gratifying objects. As our adolescents might say, the individual has "gotten it all together."

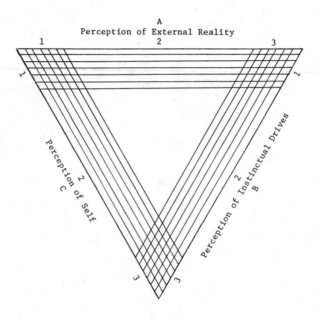

FIGURE 3. Deployment of ego functions in the adult.

In this context I would like to address the manner in which the ego develops into the full and balanced agency of the adult from the incompletely integrated and unevenly developed configuration presented in childhood. Clinical evidence presented by adolescents suggests that the development of the various clusters of ego functions (i.e., those that perceive and regulate external reality; those that experience and integrate impulse life; and those that monitor the self) appears to be discontinuous. Now one component, now another, occupies center stage, appearing to develop independently and perhaps even at the expense of the other two. This, of course, is more apparent than real, since any change in one group of ego functions will alter other groups. But it appears that the adolescent is at one moment invested in relating to a particular aspect of the environment, ignoring consideration of the self or of the drives. At another moment, the adolescent seems captivated almost entirely by drives, wishes, or appetites, ignoring the external environment or self-representations. At still another time, the youngster seems lost in contemplation of the self, oblivious to drives or wishes and to the stimuli or reactions of the external world.

In addition, clinical observation suggests that when the development of one component of the ego reaches a certain level of competence, this newfound competence acts as a trigger for a new phase of development of ego functions in another of the ego's components.

Thus, the process of change is ushered in by the well-known need of the early adolescent to leave the shelter of his family. Compelling and dimly perceived sexual and aggressive stirrings as well as changed environmental expectations demand that the youngster venture out into the world of peers. Blos (1967) describes this time as the second separation-individuation phase. Behaviorally this thrust is manifested as a quest for more freedom and independence than the family usually affords and as a rejection by the adolescent of some of the family standards and values. This desire to overthrow strict regulation is more apparent than real, however. If one looks closely, children disavow parental regulation and their values, often in a truculent manner, at the same time declaring their autonomy and independence as they move into their peer group. They are going to dress as they like, talk about what they like, and think as they like. A look at an adolescent peer group, however, reveals that the freedom it affords is in part illusory. The group prescribes standards of dress and behavior that often are more intransigent than any the parents ever dreamed of enforcing. In many instances, the child finds comfort in this rigidity, having come into the group well equipped to perceive and understand its ground rules by processing external cues. The regulatory function of the early teenage group uses equipment that children have already developed to protect and buffer them from the intrusion of sexual and aggressive impulses with which they have had only limited experience.

Gradually, however, this new adaptation is in its turn disrupted. Johnny, who has used the peer group to make new adjustments, one day cannot help noticing that Mary fills out her jeans and T-shirts in a manner disturbingly different from the way he and his male friends fill out theirs. Despite his attempts to distract himself and others through horseplay, pseudo–male chauvinism, and other ploys, thoughts of Mary's curves and contours intrude at the most inopportune times and occasion embarrassing and perplexing reactions.

Looking at this sequence of events reveals how the organization of the ego in prepuberty (Figure 2) was helpful in allowing our young man to adapt to his group. Yet, as this ego state (or this profile of the deployment of ego functions) became more sensitive to the external environment filled with Mary's curves and was also catalyzed by hormonal changes in Johnny, he was catapulted by the stimulation into a situation in which he could not escape the perception of wishes and stirrings that came from within him (Figure 4A). A number of children experience these stirrings and impulses as if they were imposed on them from the external world (Spiegel, 1961). Time and repeated experience, however, convince the youngster that the impetus for sexual strivings come from within him.

Let us suppose then that young Johnny struggles with his sexual arousal for a time. Old prohibitions against sexual expression, prohibitions which had acquired mental representation during the days of oedipal strife, as well as new ones in the image of a coach[1] who promises instant brain rot to the boy

---

[1] I am not suggesting that our coaches and teachers are insensitive and psychologically punitive regarding adolescent striving. I am suggesting that transference of past prohibitions occurs during this period, and adults in the adolescent's current world are often the reluctant recipients of these transferences.

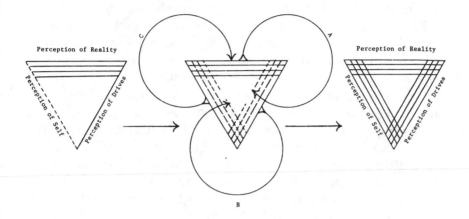

FIGURE 4. Depiction of shifting investments in the process of moving from a prepubertal ego organization through adolescent organization, to the organization of adulthood: the shift from attention to external stimuli to attention to instinctual drives; the shift from perceiving instinctual drives to perception of self; and the shift from perceiving the self to perception of external reality.

who masturbates, vie against sexual feelings. In adolescence, however, sexual strivings are not readily stifled by repression, as they are during the oedipal phase (Lidz, 1968). They are bolstered by a physiologically generated impetus and sooner or later must be integrated. And so Johnny may toss and turn in bed for a while and finally decide that a bit of brain rot would never be detected by the coach. With each subsequent experience with sexual or aggressive strivings and their derivatives, the ego deploys functions which perceive and understand sexual and aggressive wishes and attempt to integrate these strivings on the one hand with external reality and, on the other, with a sense of self.

Before moving on, we must consider the state of the young person who indulges sexual wishes with a fantasy or in masturbation. The mentation and activity involved in indulging sexual striving in such a psychologically undisguised manner are new and reevoke the reactions of shame and guilt that belong both to a past era and to the values and standards of the adolescent's current life. These evocations are enough to precipitate a more contemplative state of personality organization in which the child begins to scrutinize the self and its values (Figure 4B). In part because of shame and humiliation at having fantasized or masturbated, and perhaps because of the exuberance and excitement of the sexual wish itself, the adolescent begins to ponder such questions as "Who am I?"; "What do I stand for?"; and "Do normal kids do what I do?" These are common preoccupations during this phase. Other preoccupations include comparisons of one's size with others, assessment of talents and liabilities, and often painful reviews of past identifications.

Even if the prepubertal child came into adolescence with some stable sense of self, changes in body image occasioned by the growth spurt, as well as other physiological changes that accompany puberty, disrupt these islands of self-awareness and make this phase of the adolescent process important and poignant. The adolescent, struggling with questions and issues pertinent to the self, eventually turns to the environment to check percepts and to put a stop to painful ruminations. As adolescents move back into the peer group (Figure 4C) to compare themselves and to be comforted by their friends, one cycle follows another, perhaps in different sequences but always shifting from one mode to another in the continual scrutiny of self, the drives, or external reality. It would appear from clinical observations that this process of shuttling between these modes allows the adolescent to accomplish the important task of leavening the harsh, prohibitive cast of the superego of the oedipal phase and of latency. As Lidz points out (1968), the superego now becomes an agency that channels the drives and helps shape their appropriate expression rather than simply prohibiting them and threatening the child with guilt. And so the ego functions organize themselves now into one state, now into another, and we who observe see Narcissus at the pond one moment, Don Juan the next, and a modern-day Saint Thomas Aquinas at still another time.

To return to the young man we described at the outset, one could say that while upbraiding his father he was almost totally oriented toward resonance and sensitivity vis-à-vis the external environment. In this majestically ascetic state his own drives and appetites became unimportant, even to the extent of going hungry to make his point. Later in the evening, however, his outwardly directed focus, aided by a grumbling stomach, made him think of his girlfriend and triggered the shift to more hedonistic pursuits. Once the shift took place, he, like most people of his age, committed himself to it with a vengeance. It would not be at all surprising if, after being satiated by the pizza and by his girlfriend, our young man might make still another shift in his attention and begin to wonder what he really stands for and who he is or wants to be.

Children are ripe for these processes in adolescence. Buffeted as they are by the storms of change, young people have no choice but to readapt. Not only are there compelling physical changes taking place within them, but, as Benedek and Rubinstein (1942) have observed, their endocrinological state occasions new thoughts and fantasies. Both the inchoate feelings engendered by the altered anatomy and physiology, as well as the structured mental representations of new wishes and desires, are experienced by pubertal children as something thrust upon them over which they have little or no control or regulatory mastery. Shifting ego states are necessary to attend to the perception of these wishes and to master the effects of these percepts.

In addition, new cognitive capacities begin to make their appearance during this phase. Piaget (1957) calls this new ability to think in abstract terms and to make logical deductions from hypothetical propositions the stage of formal operations. These new cognitive tools permit youngsters to take an image of the self and place it in the context of the world of their reality. In the comparative safety of private thoughts, rehearsals for living or trial actions may be undertaken. And so, pushed by physical and emotional changes and pulled by newfound capacities, our adolescents move to implement new levels and methods of integration, adaptation, and self-regulation. Gradually, using propositional thought as well as direct experience, the youngster next begins to experience control of these cycles as existing to some extent within the ego rather than being totally dependent on external events. One may imagine that the first time Johnny sees Mary watching him play football, his attention feels drawn irresistibly to her. As he commits himself to doing his best to impress her, he finds that he must learn to concentrate on the game if he is to be effective and win her admiration. This involves barring certain external stimuli from reaching awareness so that he may more effectively attend to certain other stimuli regarding the ball game. Looking at the same phenomenon from Mary's point of view, she may be distracted from her studies by her reactions to Johnny's presence in the classroom, but gradually she finds that she can impose concentration on herself for an hour and organize her mental apparatus in a way that will permit her to attend to the external issues presented by whatever she is studying. When the hour is over, she can voluntarily turn her attention inward to enjoy or struggle with her reactions. This passage of the regulatory functions from their being perceived as externally imposed to being perceived as an internal process is once again an important developmental step and requires that the adolescent be more aware of drives and wishes, as well as noninstinctual aspects of the self, than ever before.

This internalization is important "once again" because it is not the first time the child has used this psychological mechanism to help develop a regulatory mechanism for mastering the inner world. Let us consider the vignette of a toddler who has been admonished not to touch or pluck the leaves from his mother's favorite fern. One day he finds himself in the vicinity of the fern, and the little fingers are already on their way to the leaves before he can evoke the concrete image of his mother to help him control his disastrous though delightful intentions. In a voice that has an almost uncanny similarity to that of his mother, we may hear him say, "No! No! Johnny!" If the internal plea for help is successful, he swells with pride at being a good, big boy. If the evoked image and voice of the mother came too late, Johnny may go on to spank his own hand. In so doing he has externalized the deed but internalized the regulatory quality of his mother. It is not surprising to see Johnny become, in only a few weeks, the plant's primary defender and protector. This mechanism of internalizing standards and values from the external world to help manage internal strivings and form self images is an old friend by the time one is an adolescent. The issues that are being struggled with are different, of course, and they come into awareness in a different form, but the nature of the struggle is not new.

Awareness is, of course, necessary to perceive change or the need for change or sameness in any system. Without this perception it would be difficult to imagine adaptive shifts of state or organization in the personality. In a personal communication Sander (1978) suggested that a compelling need in our field is to develop ways of studying the ontogenesis of awareness. Perhaps as neonatologists view the phenomenon during infancy, other researchers may look at it during other phases of the life cycle to see how it is integrated with other functions of the mental apparatus.

Introspection and clinical evidence suggest that as the regulatory functions become internalized, the self-system begins functioning in two ways. One portion of it represents the subjective sensor. The other portion groups together traits, values, beliefs, and experiences to serve as the composite mental representation of the self as the person interacts with the external world or seeks to regulate the drives and their derivatives. Thus, the subjective "I" of the self-system observes and evaluates the particular objectified qualities, traits, and equipment that are marshaled to achieve a task and that represent at that time and in those circumstances the composite "me." The composite "me" is a constantly changing melange of qualities and traits that present themselves to the subject.

In conclusion, this model of adolescent development may be scrutinized from the point of view of its utility. While the Eriksonian model and the classical developmental concepts of adolescence give an important overview of the changes that occur during this phase, they use as a time reference the period that begins with puberty and ends with adulthood. The changes thus are described over a number of years, whereas this model attempts to supplement that broad sweep by scrutinizing the changes that occur on a day-to-day and hour-to-hour basis. It attempts to examine what has variously been called the normal turbulence of adolescence or the natural lability of the period.

The use of such a model permits us to ask questions that would be more difficult to ask without it, questions for instance regarding the relation of ego functions fostering self-awareness to those sensitizing the individual to the environment. Another question is whether an ego function that may be deficient when employed in one area, as for example perception in reading subtle cues in a social situation, is deficient also in the perception of internal strivings or in self-evaluation.

Finally, this model enables a more accurate assessment of the child's position on the road from puberty to adulthood. Remembering how uneven the process of development can be, we may easily conceive of a child who has made great strides in experiencing the external world and sexual desires in a sophisticated way, but is quite slow in the development of an internally generated sense of self. By meticulous description of the organization and flexibility of the child's capabilities, we can more closely approximate the richness, the variety, and the wonder of adolescence.

References

Benedek, T., & Rubinstein, B. (1942), The sexual cycle in women: The relation between ovarian function and psychodynamic processes. *Psychosomatic Medicine*, Monograph 3. Washington, DC: National Research Council.

Blos, P. (1967), The second individuation process of adolescence. *The Psychoanalytic Study of the Child*, 22:162–168. New York: International Universities Press.

Lidz, T. (1968), *The Person*. New York: Basic Books.

Piaget, J. (1957), *Logic and Psychology*. New York: Basic Books.

Rapaport, D. (1951), The autonomy of the ego. *Bull. Menn. Clin.*, 15:113–123.

———— (1958), The theory of ego autonomy. *Bull. Menn. Clin.*, 22:13–35.

Spiegel, L. (1961), Identity and adolescence. In: *Adolescents*, ed. S. Lorand & H. Schneer. New York: Hoeber.

9

The Influence of Family Dynamics on Adolescent Learning Disorders

IRWIN M. MARCUS, M.D.

We all agree that the interdependence of individual endowment, growth, maturation, and learning is indeed complex during the active years of development in children and adolescents. Except for purposes of discussion, we cannot isolate these multidetermined factors. Growth factors are measured against time. We can describe changes in the structure of physiology of various components of the body over a given period. With these growth changes occurs a change in the capacity to perform or behave; thus the unfolding of newer functions expands the concept of growth into one of maturation. The modification of behavior based on experience and use represents learning. The many experiences offered by the environment are intended, it is hoped, to enhance the child's development. However, if there are limiting factors in any of several spheres, the individual may fail to learn and perform a given task successfully. His reactions to the failure and the reactions of the environment to his failure may reverberate into a new series of problems that make further learning more difficult or even impossible.

The education and rearing of children and adolescents must therefore be adapted to their capacity to master the situation. Assessing the capacity and potential for learning is not an easy task for anyone, let alone a teacher confronted with a classroom full of students, each developing in a unique manner. Pediatric studies clearly demonstrate that a young adolescent may vary in growth and maturation from the level of an older

253

child to that of a young adult. It is essential that we view each person as he is, then, and to evaluate his resources and current potential rather than compare him to others his age. Thus, maturity is not a final product of any age but, rather, a characteristic of function relative to one's own capacity at a particular time.

Learning is not merely a process of adaptation to environmental influences and stimulation, but a process of inner organization of the personality. Intellectual and motor skills are only part of the issue; the developing individual must also learn to manage his emotional life. This influences attitudes, attentiveness, and the entire integrative function so essential in learning. Emotional responses may aid or interfere with learning, and in turn alter self-awareness, interpersonal responses, identifications, and identity. Problems in learning may be due primarily to personal, interpersonal, or pedagogical factors, or to varying admixtures of these ingredients. Regardless of the essential factors producing the problem in learning, there are usually secondary reactions to the learning failure. These dependent variables must not mislead one into confusing the effect with the cause.

The child who is consistently failing in school, regardless of the cause, has a disturbing effect on his parents if they value education. The parents become anxious and depressed or angry. They may punish and reject the child because he diminishes their self-image as successful parents. One parent may blame the other, depending on their marital relationship and their view of the other's relationship with the child, or blame may be directed at the teachers and the school. Parental anxiety and feelings of failure undermine confidence in their role and lead toward confusion in how to remedy their child's problem in learning. If the parental reaction causes deterioration in the marital relationship, the adolescent is confronted not only with personal problems but with complex interpersonal family issues as well.

Personal reactions attend a learning problem, of course, with its failure to provide pleasure from mastery and success, painful criticisms and rejection from parents and teachers, self-hatred and a lowering of self-esteem. Anger born of frustration, confusion, and a sense of helplessness may burst forth in a variety of ways. If it is expressed directly, the adolescent may physically attack a parent, the teacher, or even the school. Newspapers carry such stories, of varying degrees of violence. Through group action the adolescent may become involved in gang warfare or attacks on strangers of any age. If the anger is controlled and defended by unconscious processes, he may become depressed and withdrawn or even suicidal. When the anger is contained more consciously, he may stubbornly refuse to do homework or cooperate in the classroom. He may develop behavior in the classroom or home that is annoying and disturbing to others, and thus gain some attention. A desire to escape from the unpleasantness altogether may lead to running away, playing hooky, regressing into infantile behavior, daydreaming of simple pleasures, masturbating excessively, or engaging in other sexual experiences. The adolescent who is athletic and has maintained his peer group relations can direct all of his energies to sports and seek in this way to neutralize the failure he feels in academic life. Granted that we see a number of patterns that may be the result rather than the cause of learning problems, we can recognize that all causes may have complicating secondary manifestations.

One important category of disturbance has been designated Primary Neurotic Learning Inhibitions (PNLI) by Grunebaum, Horwitz, Prentice, and Sperry (1962). Pearson (1954) described a similar condition in which the learning process is involved in neurotic conflict, but did not specify the criteria for poor performance. Grunebaum et al. limit their category to students whose academic difficulties are present from the very beginning of school. Internal conflict in the student has been displaced directly onto the schoolwork. The term PNLI was reserved for students or at least normal intelligence, free of neurological or physical impairment, and from homes without gross social pathology. They were "at least two years behind their chronological age in one major skill such as reading, spelling or arithmetic and at least one year behind in another, as measured by the Metropolitan Achievement Tests" (p. 463). Their resistance to therapeutic efforts led the Grunebaum group to conclude that this symptom was "deeply embedded in the total family organization" (p. 462). Unconscious conflicts in the child, such as unresolved oedipal struggles and fears of abandonment, are present at the time the child starts school and allow the latter to become a target for projections. The teacher may come to represent a mother or even a derogating, ambivalent father with deep personal problems in the area of expected performance by the child. The child's defensive struggle against these unconscious conflicts eventually depletes his available energy, causing him to appear apathetic and restless.

Pearson (1954) used digestive activity as a model for learning. The basis for his analogy was provided by Freud's impression that the psychic function of the ego has its precursor in the ego's role in the physical sphere. Thus, the learning process is viewed in terms of intake, correlation (digestion), output, and contribution to successful overall functioning. Early childhood conflicts and disturbing experiences in the oral sphere contribute to problems in the first area. Severe intrapsychic conflicts, involving both intake and output, are considered sources for a disturbance in correlation. Conflicts around the excretory function are associated with output (the expression of what one has learned), and inhibition in the use of knowledge is seen as the result of fears of sibling rivalry or anxiety, guilt, and the dread of castration. Switching metaphors, Pearson viewed these disturbances as resembling sexual impotence and referred to them as "learning impotence," a term later set aside as a separate category by Rubinstein, Farlik, and Eckstein (1959). One can see the similarity between the picture drawn by Pearson and that of the apathetic child presented by Grunebaum et al. Severe regressions, which may disorganize logical thinking or disturb the orientation to reality, would also produce disturbances in learning.

Liss (1940) pointed out that where the subject matter and its use are heavily loaded with hostile impulses, guilt and anxiety may become a deterrent to successful learning. Bettelheim (1950) has discussed examples of hostile, competitive feelings in boys toward their fathers resulting in the avoidance of learning. I have collected similar data during psychoanalytic work with male adults who had had severe learning problems in their school years. Learning problems in these cases revealed an unconscious association of knowledge with power, and power with the ability to destroy their fathers. The stronger muscle development in boys and their innate aggressive drive, encouraged by society, become identified with masculinity. However, the learning situation requires the control and inhibition of the motility outlet and the sublimation of this drive. Perhaps this contributes to the fact, generally reported, that learning problems occur approximately four time more often in boys than in girls. Other factors that probably affect this differential include the greater vulnerability of males to stress, and the fact that boys' maturational readiness at the age for starting school lags behind that of girls.

Schizophrenia is still an illness of unknown origin or, perhaps, a variety of illnesses with similar manifestations. There are a great number of theories, and some individuals even claim to have the cure. Is a disturbance as severe as schizophrenia to be considered an organic condition, an emotional disorder secondarily producing a learning problem, or a disorder completely involving the learning process? De Hirsch (1963) described a primarily disturbed group of adolescents with ego impairment, who did rather well in their earlier schooling because of their high intelligence. She found them highly articulate, with good competence in abstract thinking; many were avid readers. When they reached the upper grades, however, they began to do poorly in most subjects. Her description of this group, mostly boys, emphasized their lack of ego strength, their physiological immaturity and passivity, and their relative lack of psychic energy to invest in areas that might otherwise have interested them.

Yet it seems to me that these differences in the development of learning disturbances may not necessarily represent separate processes. Perhaps the difference is, in part, one of degree. Early disturbances involving the learning process may vary from severe to mild, from acute to chronic, and the capacity to adapt to the disability may vary as well. Thus, a learning disorder that may appear acute at a later period in development may be either reactive to stress not involving the learning process as such or the result of decompensation in a chronic problem that did involve the learning process. Basic to a complete

evaluation of a learning problem are a thorough history of the
child's development; physical evaluation and extensive psychological testing; skillful clinical studies of the child and his family;
and evaluations from the school.

Secondary or reactive disorders are easier to treat if acute
but may be quite difficult if chronic and complicated by a weak
background in major subject matter. Fear or guilt over competitive, hostile, or sexual feelings can lead to avoidance reactions to learning, from inhibited curiosity to the avoidance of
school altogether. Many school phobias involve marked conflicts
around separation from the mother, often entailing an intense
sadomasochistic relationship. Unpleasant experiences in school
or with the teacher may lead to similar avoidance reactions.
Conversely, many individuals for years respond favorably to
learning because of their relationship with the teacher and their
wish to be approved of and, in a sense, loved by the authority.
Maturation to the level of "love of learning" is an ideal goal,
many individuals unfortunately never achieve. Both the relationship with the teacher, which influences identification, and
the manner in which the subject matter is presented affect the
child's response. Mastering material is pleasurable and fosters
the child's eagerness to learn. However, if these associations are
engulfed in painful experiences, the child may hate the subject,
the teacher, or even learning in general. Insecurity in the child's
life or strong, emotionally laden preoccupations can lead to
inattentiveness, daydreaming, and secondary learning problems.

One group of primary causative factors may be classified
as organic, either structural or physiological. The individual's
difficulty may be due to lower intellectual endowment, lack of
development of the associative pathways, or disease or injury
to the central nervous system. The ramifications of the deficiency extend into difficulties in identifying with parents and
in dealing with anxiety, as well as trauma to parental narcissism
and a consequent rejection of the child. Such children thereby
develop a combination of organic and psychological factors,
further weakening their learning ability. Sensorimotor disturbances, cerebral dysfunction, and minimal brain damage are included in this category. I feel that neurophysiological disturbances

producing a maturational lag should be given separate consideration.

The maturation of visual-motor patterns is usually sufficiently advanced by 6 years of age to overcome tendencies toward letter reversal. Those with problems in this area may continue to invert material, to confuse similar words, or to omit words and phrases when reading. Persistent reading disabilities must be evaluated by experts to arrive at a definitive corrective approach. It is unfortunate when those with persistent perceptual difficulties are labeled careless or defiant. Either visual or auditory perception problems will seriously handicap reading, which is fundamental to school achievement and progress. Perceptual disorders will alter and inhibit concept formation. The recognition of relationships, configurations, and quantity concepts are all impaired by this defect in a developing child. In addition, the child may have difficulty dealing with abstract ideas and so tend to cling to literal and concrete thought patterns.

More easily seen in the organic type of disorders is lack of impulse control, easy distractibility, and short attention span. When hyperactive motor behavior is not present, one can see a tendency toward disorganized thinking, uninhibited speech, or both. Pressure from randomly associated ideas or from stimuli in the external environment interferes with the organization of thoughts so necessary in classroom assignments. Emotional lability and occasional outbursts when confronted with new and more difficult tasks lead to very erratic and unpredictable performance. Such children may be considered inept, lazy, or uncooperative or may at times be mistaken for withdrawn daydreamers. Perceptual disorders represent only one factor in the overall problem of reading and learning disabilities. These serious organic causes of learning difficulties have been the subject of much study and experimentation. Hand-eye coordination exercises and classrooms structured to reduce external stimuli are among the many corrective measures undertaken in such situations.

This category of immature children should be considered separately, as they are usually pushed into learning before they are emotionally and physiologically ready. When evaluated early in their schooling because of restlessness, hyperactivity, or inattentiveness, this group shows signs of visual-motor immaturity. They may be slow in learning to read or may in their frustration actively reject reading altogether. In time they do learn to read, sometimes quite well, but may in adolescence continue to show signs of a language disability. Their spelling and vocabulary may remain poor, although the bright youngsters among them can do well in math or science. Their handwriting may continue to be messy, and their written assignments are often quite poorly organized and inferior. Learning a foreign language can be a tremendous chore for them, because their auditory discrimination may not have adequately developed. Frustrations in the learning experience produce unhappiness, insecurity, and painful situations when parents and teachers are critical and confused by the student's poor performance. Withdrawal from academic interest, in one way or another, is often the inevitable result. The maturational lag here occurs independently of environmental experiences and cannot be accounted for by intrapsychic dynamics. These children may well come from family backgrounds that are basically healthy and secure, and their childhood development may not have been traumatizing. It is important that we distinguish between children who have been indulged and are emotionally immature from lack of discipline, and those with a specific, neurophysiologically caused maturational lag. The former may fail to learn because they are pleasure bound and unable to tolerate tension and frustration. They lack an interest in learning because it requires effort, self-discipline, and the postponement of gratification. Their drives are not sublimated or channeled into learning pursuits but remain in the original pleasure context. These children need a therapeutic teaching environment that slowly helps them tolerate tension and redirects their energies and attention to learning. Their parents need therapeutic guidance to help them understand and then correct the influence of their permissiveness on the child's personality structure. Both groups of children may do well in sports, hobbies, and social life. Their anger and defiance are directly mainly at the idea of schoolwork, at those who insist that it be done, or at siblings whom the parents praise for academic achievement.

In studies of PNLI, evidence has been found that the child's emotional disorder is typically enmeshed in family conflicts. I have conducted intensive studies (Marcus, 1966) of a small group of families whose adolescent children had chronic learning disturbances. The students were between the ages of 12 and 14 and were all in good physical health and above average in intelligence. The families showed unrealistic and conflicting expectations and images of their children. Their earlier views of them as superior in potential had altered to a very pessimistic attitude. All the families attempted a variety of techniques, including punishment, to cope with the learning disturbance, and finally ended in an absence of response toward their child. A considerable amount of marital conflict and unhappiness was present and of long standing in all the families, but was not always overtly manifest. Mutual concern over the learning problem increased communication in the marriage, but in certain instances one parent would deny the problem. Whereas some couples were brought closer by their shared anxiety, hostility, and guilt, others used the situation to intensify and rationalize their conflicts. Although none of the mothers acknowledged school problems of their own, most of the fathers reported to having had them, and each appraised the child's problem differently. Most of the parents had gone to college for a varying number of years; the fathers tended to be better educated than their wives. One or both parents had low self-esteem, aggravated by the marriage relationship and their child's failure.

The children expressed a feeling of distance or isolation from their parents, and denied any awareness of conflict or unhappiness between their parents, although some acknowledged conflict during more intensive work with them. They frequently rationalized their failure as being within their own control, and avoided blaming parents or teachers. They did feel hostile and anxious about the demands made on them for grades, some showing depressive reactions and withdrawal from family and teacher relationships and, in certain instances, from peers who were more successful. Most of the children avoided seeking help from the teacher and expressed a preference for their father, who they felt helped them. They frequently denied sexual tension or sexual feelings, and revealed a lack of desire for maturation and variability in their passive or aggressive patterns. They showed low self-esteem, but occasionally this was concealed beneath a defensive grandiosity or pseudomaturity. All showed a lack of motivation in their schoolwork, but those with a more evident immaturity maintained an interest in athletics. I will present a few contrasting cases to demonstrate these impressions.

Case Presentations

Family A

Mrs. A underwent psychoanalytic therapy several years before this study for severe chronic depression. At that time her son was about 2½ years old and her daughter 5. There was a lack of satisfactory communication in her marriage and a lack in her sexual responsiveness. Mrs. A also had severe feelings of inadequacy and inferiority, but covered them over with a friendly manner and active community interests. She needed and received continuous reassurance of her acceptability from associates in organizations where her work was respected and admired, but she did not feel satisfaction in her home life, and the children were frequently in the care of trusted domestic help.

Mrs. A was a bright, attractive person capable of warmth and had many friends. Her husband was proud of her activities but resented her not spending her time with household duties or remunerative work. Her basic fears were of abandonment and rejection. She also had severe oral and dependency conflicts. She struggled with periodic gains in weight and defended against dependency needs by appearing self-sufficient, assertive, and controlling. She was envious and competitive in areas of social or community status. Her mother and father worked in a small neighborhood business, but she associated with a group of higher socioeconomic status. She felt deprived of her own mother, had unresolved oedipal conflicts concealed beneath depreciation and disdain for her father, and was envious and competitive with her brother.

Her daughter, Ann, developed severe compulsions that were successfully treated. At 6 years of age her son Jim presented character traits of considerable passivity—finger sucking, encopresis, and fearfulness. During the course of his therapy he showed a preoccupation with killing and death. In play therapy he initiated war games that included choking, shooting, and bombing both parents and children, as well as the therapist and others. He went through a period of hiding his feces, but eventually became symptom-free and developed more healthy aggressive behavior in his daily life. He got along well for the next six years, until he entered adolescence. Then he began to associate with boys overtly defiant of both school and parental authority. He and this group began smoking cigarets, let down on their academic performance, and engaged in some homosexual sex play; at home Jim was lighting small fires in his room. He refused any involvement in treatment.

Mr. A was a successful businessman whose family of origin was of higher socioeconomic status than his wife's. His mother was a hard-working, compulsive woman who maintained an active interest in the family business after her husband died and her son took over the management.

Mr. A never really responded to parental controls and was more interested in partying than in academic achievement during high school and college. He accepted his son's defiance as being "normal"—just like his own. He resented his wife's attempts to enforce discipline or to push him into doing so. He felt that her involvement in community activities and her absence from the home during the day was the cause of Jim's difficulty. She felt she was expected to rear the children herself, because her husband usually avoided disciplining the children or even supporting her when she was faced with the problem. Her depressive tendencies were revived by feeling abandoned and unappreciated both by her children and by her husband.

Mr. and Mrs. A were seen together in family sessions on a weekly basis for almost a year. Their rejection and blaming of each other had reached an intense level. Sporadic outbursts of rage against Jim alternated with the avoidance of involve-

ment either with him or with each other. As therapist, my efforts
were directed at reestablishing meaningful communication between them. The usual therapeutic techniques were used in
elucidating their conflicts and offering some understanding of
their son's conflicts and defenses. Jim's oedipal struggles, his
defenses against dependency, his sexual conflicts in adolescence, his techniques for playing off one parent against the
other in his power struggle—all these were included in our
discussions. There was a gradual improvement in the parents'
relationship, and for a brief period a great improvement in
their sexual relations.

Jim's WISC testing showed a verbal of 144, performance
of 124, and a full-scale IQ of 138. On the Stanford Achievement
Tests, the only low areas were in spelling and study skills. Rorschach testing indicated his ego strength only fair and a tendency to act impulsively under pressure. Anxiety in the areas of
male identifications and accepting female figures was predominant. His overt preference was for his father. Jim showed erratic performance in school: he had high intelligence but was
difficult to reach through adult relationships or in private tutoring by a young college male. His ego structure showed residual infantile characteristics, and his early passive traits were
now well covered by hostile aggressive behavior. He showed a
lack of investment of interest in academic, athletic, or hobby
areas. On the surface he can now maintain an amiable front,
but he avoids real investment of feelings in object relations in
order to avoid anxiety, rage, disappointment, and other feelings.

The foregoing is an example of family therapy being necessary but of itself insufficient to alter the ego function toward
renewed learning for the adolescent. Direct help for Jim will
be necessary. How to bridge the avoidance reactions involving
identification and object relations and to develop an aggressiveness toward learning will be crucial issues.

Family B

Mrs. B was always a timid, withdrawn woman who remained close to home and was loving, kind, soft-spoken, and
indulgent of her only child, Bob. Mr. B was a successful, com-

pulsive, vociferous, and aggressive man who dominated his family. Bob was close with his mother and fearful of his father.

Bob's grades were F's and D's, and he had done poorly since the fourth grade. He was overtly passive, quiet, and well-behaved. Though he communicated quite well, he daydreamed both at school and at home, especially when he tried to do his homework. He had practically no peer group relations.

Mr. and Mrs. B refused therapeutic help unless they were "in it together." They were seen weekly in family therapy for almost a year, during which time they began to establish real communication. Throughout their marriage, Mrs. B had been the listener to her husband's orders and criticism, but at times she was passively defiant. Their sex life diminished to the point of chronic frustration after about six months of early marital satisfaction. Mr. B developed a peptic ulcer, felt deprived of being loved, and in the sessions lamented his undeserved rejection by both wife and son. He claimed to be quite confused. Mrs. B's fears and hostility toward her husband were brought into the open; he was amazed to hear the effect he had on her and exposed his long-held fantasies of a divorce. Husband and wife improved not only their marital relationship but also their understanding of their role in Bob's problems.

Here it was necessary to alter the parental interaction in order to avoid Bob's being forced back into his original position in the family conflict. The therapeutic response was good.

Family C

Whereas Jim and Bob were not overtly hostile to teachers, Jean felt hatred toward her teachers for several years, and her repeated failures required summer school and, later, a change in school. Her mother was ambitious, compulsive, and domineering in relation to her children, but submissive in relation to her husband, who was strong, firm, and silent. Mrs. C felt quite alone in rearing the children and was held responsible for any failure on the part of Jean or her younger brother; she was terrified of her husband's criticism and therefore of Jean's failure. The interaction between Jean and her mother was continuously hostile, although Jean did not feel close to her father, either. The therapy consisted of individual sessions with Jean, occasional mother-daughter joint sessions, and individual guidance work with Mrs. C. Since Mr. C would not come near the treatment situation, the interaction had to focus on Mrs. C and her daughter. Jean had shown signs of relative immaturity throughout her development, in personality as well as in mastering language and reading skills. She clung to oral-dependent patterns and had a weight problem. She was explosive, demanding, and hostile, though concealed beneath this was a good deal of anxiety. Her tolerance of frustration was low, and she expressed a complete lack of interest in school.

Discussion

Psychoanalytic studies have shown that a positive object relationship is requisite to the development of the mechanisms of identification and incorporation, and that learning is dependent on these basic mechanisms. The children under study showed disturbances in the child-parent relationship and in certain instances avoided the risk of investing positive feelings in the relationship with a teacher or private tutor. They all seemed to be blocked on this early level and did not show much movement toward either phallic or genital object relationship. We saw in the case examples the pregenital impulses that demanded direct gratification, with substitute methods of discharge only weakly consolidated.

In family A, Jim, under the care of household help, did not receive much of the necessary gentle stimulation of an attentive and loving mother. His ego development suffered, as the sensual stimulation from his environment was less than optimal. He showed signs of inability to tolerate much instinctual tension, and continued finger sucking and soiling into the latency period. His attention remained more focused on his inner world, and early signs of learning disturbance were evident. He became fearful of the environment, and inhibited aggressiveness in exchange for the pleasure of a passive-dependent existence. His usual play was with his sister; identifications were directed to her because contact with his father were minimal. In therapy during this latency period, Jim's need for instinctual release through motor activity was encouraged, and warlike games allowed for a release of hostile and fearful feelings about his parents, as well as gradual improvement in his perceptions of reality. However, over a period of six years he continued to be exposed to two narcissistic parents who had never allowed adequate sublimation of their own instincts and showed impulsive characteristics. Jim incorporated these characteristics and, with the upheaval of adolescence, resorted to direct instinctual gratifications, including smoking, homosexual play, and the excitement of fire setting; a collapse of previously developed learning patterns also ensued. Mrs. A had a brother transference toward both her son and her husband, and struggled with both repressed incestuous feelings and hostile competitive wishes in order to be superior and thereby castrate them. Her guilt was intense and revived depressive feelings and the strategy of withdrawal, which, alternating with outbursts of rage, served to coerce better performance by Jim and support from her husband. Mr. A wanted to win Jim over to his side in order to justify his own patterns of behavior; through identification, he found Jim's patterns acceptable. He also enjoyed proving to his wife that her absence from the home led to failure. Beneath this, Mr. A's hostility toward his mother and his wife, for their failure to satisfy his needs, was evident. He saw Jim's actions as evidence of manliness and found this reassuring in the presence of unconscious homosexual anxiety. Jim, however, not only had a learning problem based on ego impairment, as described above, but also rejected academic work because he associated it with his mother. His defense against oedipal conflicts—hostility toward a frustrating mother—and awareness of his father as a newfound ally reinforced his learning disturbance.

Whereas Jim avoided a trusting relationship with adults and peers, Bob was very accepting of therapy and was interested in overcoming his problems. Mrs. B gave Bob too much gratification, which impeded adequate development of his ego. She used him as an extension of herself, a phallic symbol that gave her magical security that protected her from a hostile, over-aggressive, and demanding husband. Mr. B was furious with her for depriving him of his sexual needs and separating him from his son; she had, in effect, castrated him. Bob's passivity reflected his identification with his mother, his disdain for his father, and a high level of anxiety about the dangers of retaliation, from both parents, for any aggressiveness he might express or even silently harbor. Bob could do nothing but accept unpleasant tasks when his father stood over him and forced the issue; otherwise, he turned to the gratifications of daydreaming as a means of avoiding the unpleasant family environment. Unfortunately, this outlet was used in the classroom and during homework time. His reality testing began to suffer, and there was further evidence of a chronic depressive reaction associated with feelings of fatigue. Other aspects of his inhibited aggressiveness and competitiveness were related to unresolved oedipal conflicts. His wish to be accepted by peers increased his learning difficulty, because he feared good grades and denied his wish for approval by teachers. His classmates, however, rejected him for his passive-feminine traits and lack of participation in sports or rough play. Academic learning then became associated with hostile impulses, and was rejected because of guilt and anxiety. Bob's parents, like Jim's, used their son's failure to demonstrate each other's inadequacy as parents.

In the C family, Jean's developmental immaturity caused her to build a backlog of academic weakness, and she withdrew from learning to avoid the pain of failure. She lashed out at anyone who tried to pressure her into doing her schoolwork. She rejected learning and dreaded promotion as a sign of increased responsibility and maturation, a phenomenon reported over thirty years ago by Liss (1937). The family directed their hostility at Jean in response to her failures, and the home environment became disturbed and confused.

Children have a tendency to rely on certain defense mechanisms to the exclusion of others. The use of denial with regard to the disturbed family environment and their conflicted feelings about school, teachers, and sexuality is a striking and serious hindrance to solving their problems. Denial is a primitive mechanism which used to excess can seriously interfere with adaptation to reality. The families in the study appeared to participate in denial mechanisms and thereby encouraged this defense in their children. Avoidance of the painful reality of unhappy and frustrating home relationships appears to be stronger than avoidance of the pain attending criticism by parents or teachers for poor grades. The children appeared to cling to the pleasure principle of their childhood, seeking outlets in direct gratification through food, play, and daydreaming. They seemed much more concerned with maintaining contact with the internal reality of their needs than with the external reality of adjustment to school. Unfulfilled assignments and forgetting to bring books for homework were frequent occurrences. Denial of unpleasant reality is a natural step in development, but mastery of the problem by the ego requires further denying of the denial. The children studied had lost confidence in themselves and the adult environment. This may account for their need to cling to the denial, since they felt an inability to deal with the frustrating and unpleasant features of their real world.

The relative emotional immaturity of the adolescent, and of one or both parents, was an easily recognizable quality consistent with the foregoing discussion. The family histories of child care indicate a tendency for the families to indulge and even foster the prolongation of pregenital development, which is then punctuated by efforts at sudden termination. Adequate sublimation of early needs, an important requisite for learning, seems deficient.

Therapeutic measures for organic learning disorders, whether structural or physiological, are best applied early. Correct diagnosis is essential, or the secondary psychological damage will soon proliferate into a complexity of factors that may permanently damage the child's self-image. When teachers and parents are correctly oriented to the child's disability, their attitudes will change from critical and rejecting to appropriately supportive. Tutoring or proper academic placement, when brought to bear sufficiently early, can often preclude an irreversible gap in the child's schooling. Such punishments as deprivation of athletic participation or social life will only close the child's few remaining avenues for building self-esteem. Students whose emotional immaturity is based on family factors rather than a neurophysiological lag require similar guidance. In such cases, however, both family and child require additional therapeutic guidance to correct the effects of overindulgence and overpermissiveness and to remove them as pathogenic factors. Prentice and Sperry (1965) advocate therapeutic tutoring for individuals with primary learning inhibitions when insight therapy is either impossible or inadvisable. The tutor in such instances must be oriented in psychotherapy but must gear his efforts to the learning process. He learns to recognize the child's neurotic mechanisms and employs techniques that circumvent unresolved problems. He avoids arousing unconscious, anxiety-laden material that might foster regression. When unfavorable situations do occur, the child's attention is shifted to reality, and reassurance is given. Other possible approaches include collaboration between a therapist and a tutor, and therapy with occasional tutoring intervention. My own experience has been mostly with the collaborative approach, but I feel that therapeutic tutoring has considerable potential. The tutor will have to be creative, talented, sensitive, and flexible, in addition to having a background both in education and in dynamic psychology.

For each of the past few decades, several million students have been high school dropouts. The United States Office of Education estimated that more than half of these students will have the ability for further education and training. Drugs, emotional problems, mental limitations, family failures, and social issues are among the many factors that contribute to these continuing high rates. The emotional disturbances are often interwoven with primary learning problems. These youths may be unhappy and depressed, aggressive, rebellious, and suspicious. When students act upon paranoid feelings, direct physical attacks on their teachers and administrators may occur. Others are withdrawn, insecure, and anxious. In various high schools throughout our country, there are some students carrrying weapons into the classroom. It is extremely difficult for an educator to offer empathy and guidance when intimidated by those in the hostile category. We know that every potential dropout cannot be kept in school, but there is a real need to understand as much as possible about the various causes for learning disturbances and the varying degrees of underachievement. Both primary and secondary emotional reactions can be severe for the individual, his family, and the community. A more versatile and psychologically oriented educational system, with an active, effective guidance service to coordinate early corrective action, is essential. These programs must be assisted by cooperation from the family and from various societal institutions. They cannot succeed by themselves.

References

Ackerman, N. (1958), *The Psychodynamics of Family Life*. New York: Basic Books.

Bettelheim, B. (1950), *Love Is Not Enough*. Glencoe, IL.: Free Press.

Blos, P. (1962), *On Adolescence: A Psychoanalytic Interpretation*. New York: Free Press.

Coleman, J. S. (1965), *Adolescents and the Schools*. New York: Basic Books.

de Hirsch, K. (1963), Two categories of learning difficulties in adolescents, *Amer. J. Orthopsychiat.*, 33:87–91.

Freud, S. (1905), Three essays on sexuality. *Standard Edition*, 7:130–243. London: Hogarth Press, 1953.

Grunebaum, M. G., Horwitz, J., Prentice, N., & Sperry, B. (1962), Fathers of sons with primary neurotic learning inhibitions. *Amer. J. Orthopsychiat.*, 32:462–472.

Harley, M., ed. (1974), *The Analyst and the Adolescent at Work*. New York: Quadrangle.

Keill, N. (1964), *The Universal Experience of Adolescence*. New York: International Universities Press.

Liss, E. (1937), Emotional and biological factors involved in learning processes. *Amer. J. Orthopsychiat.*, 7:483–488.

——— (1940), Learning: Its sadistic and masochistic manifestations. *Amer. J. Orthopsychiat.*, 10:123–128.

Marcus, I. M. (1956), Psychoanalytic group psychotherapy with fathers of emotionally disturbed preschool age children. *Internat. J. Group Psychother.*, 6:61–67.

——— (1966), Family interaction in adolescents with learning difficulties. *Adolescence*, 1:261–271.

——— (1969), School to work: Certain aspects of psycho-social interaction. In: *Adolescence: Psychological Perspective*, ed. G. Caplan. New York: Basic Books.

——— (1971), The influence of teacher-child interaction on the learning process. *J. Amer. Acad. Child Psychiat.*, 3:481–500.

——— (1977), The psychoanalysis of adolescence: Interpretation, working through, and dreams. In: *International Encyclopedia of Neurology, Psychiatry, Psychoanalysis and Psychology*, Vol. 1. New York: Van Nostrand Reinhold, 1977, pp. 260–265.

Pearson, G. H. (1954), *Psychoanalysis and the Education of the Child*. New York: Norton.

Prentice, N. M., & Sperry, B. M. (1965), Therapeutically oriented tutoring of children with primary neurotic learning inhibitions. *Amer. J. Ortho-psychiat.*, 35:521–530.

Rubinstein, B. O., Farlik, M. L., & Eckstein, R. (1959), Learning impotence: A suggested diagnostic category. *Amer. J. Orthopsychiat.*, 29:315–323.

10

The Influence of Development on Career Achievement

IRWIN M. MARCUS, M.D.

It may be of value to our understanding of late adolescence and early adulthood to examine the vicissitudes of personality development, fantasy, and conflicts of significance to career achievement.

Even in Anna Freud's systematic and unique studies of normality (1965), the concept of developmental sequences is limited to particular, circumscribed parts of the child's evolving personality. The basic interactions between intrapsychic phenomena at various developmental levels and environmental influences appear to be far more complex than some behaviorists would admit. The variables are myriad as the young child evolves from an egocentric view of life and autoerotic play, through games, hobbies, and school activities, to arrival at a career.

Available evidence indicates that prior to puberty the child's concept of work is in terms of adult activities and that whatever vocational interests are expressed are linked to wishes to grow up. Ginzberg, Ginsburg, Axelrad, and Herma (1951) hold that the young child's ideas of work are in the realm of fantasy and are unrelated to actual interests or abilities. Males and females have characteristically different developmental lines in their life histories, so that the understanding of factors in the transition from academic activities to a career necessarily involves concepts that are not equally relevant to both genders.

Tiedeman, O'Hara, and Baruch (1963) have shown that sex role and family status are no less significant than self-concept in influencing occupational choice. Their studies indicate that interest and personality inventories are more effective predictors of choice of work than are aptitude tests and confirmed the impression of Ginzberg et al. (1951) that self-concept in boys is in the process of consolidation during the high school years. The interests stage during the sophomore year of high school is followed by the development of work values by the senior year. Rather than attempting to predict vocational choice, many of the serious researchers in this field are turning their attention to studying the vicissitudes of personality-environment interaction crystallizing into vocational or career identity.

Searching out the components that constitute a self-concept can be thorny and much too complex for practical counseling. Note the variation even in conceptualizing self-concept (e.g., Freud, 1914; Hartman, Kris, and Loewenstein, 1946; Fenichel, 1953; Sullivan, 1953; Josselyn, 1954; Eissler, 1958; Greenacre, 1958; Wheelis, 1958; Erikson, 1959; Spiegel, 1959; Jacobson, 1964; Kohut, 1966; and Levin, 1969). The transition to a career commitment may be viewed as a multifaceted form of behavior which evolves over eight to ten years, passing through a series of stages. This process has a degree of irreversibility in that earlier decisions limit the options for later decisions. Compromise is also a prominent feature. To a large degree, personal attributes are in interaction with environmental circumstances, and the work direction during maturation is channeled by the total situation, not just by the self-concept. The transition from school to career seems to go through an initial fantasy phase between 10 and 12 years of age, followed by a tentative period from puberty into middle adolescence to about 17 years of age, and is finalized by the realistic stage extending into early adulthood. The fantasy phase is self-explanatory. In the tentative period, the adolescent begins to consider personal abilities and interests more seriously. Those who have done poorly in mathematics and science are less prone to speak of careers requiring facility in these areas; however, the subjective approach is still predominant. The adolescent's preoccupation gradually shifts from individual interests to a rough impression of the capacities required for various jobs and to values such as those vested in job status. The realistic stage goes a step further and includes the necessary compromises with environmental opportunities and the actual awareness of skills, abilities, and other factors. In late adolescence, exploratory activity varies with the initiative, curiosity, and aggressiveness of the individual. I have had children in this age group call me to discuss the field of psychiatry specifically, as well as medicine in general. Others have asked me about social work as a career.

The significant issue in the sequential phases is the irreversibility feature—namely, the fact that academic choices along the way increasingly limit the available options. Thus, the time factor during this transition period is such that the later the decision, the less freedom for a change in direction. The "identity crisis" described by Erikson is complex in dynamics derived from both intrapsychic and environmental factors. Progress throughout schooling becomes a key issue in the vocational goals and identity that can be established by an individual. Where "work identity" becomes a pillar in the self-esteem structure, positions providing less gratification and lower status, as well as later retirement, can—and often do—trigger a depressive reaction or some other form of mental disturbance. Therapists and counselors should therefore understand these work-identity interactions and related problems.

Neff (1968) views the "work personality" as having a "semi-autonomous" function. This is consistent with my own observations (Marcus, 1971) that individuals with severe character problems can continue to function effectively in skilled and complex occupations. The transition toward a career occurs within the matrix of total personality development. It is academic to argue that sexual and aggressive needs and feelings are the primary drives and that the vicissitudes of these "instincts" lead to interest and pleasure in mastery, or rather that mastery is a separate basic drive (Hendrick, 1943; Hartmann, 1958). Motor patterns and associated pleasure are seen by Mittelmann (1954) as independent urges intimately connected with almost all other functions of the individual. Lantos (1943) identifies the latency period as the time when the transition from pleasure in motor activity to pleasure in mastery occurs. Erikson (1959) similarly places the shift in stages at this period when the child wants to learn to do things and to enjoy accomplishment. He associates this phase with a "sense of industry" whereby the child enjoys recognition and prestige from "producing things." During this stage the child may feel inadequate and inferior when confronted with unresolved conflicts and in comparison to adults and more effective children.

Perhaps the concept of the superego or of conscience may be expanded to include the internalization not only of parental prohibitions but of other social and cultural demands as well. Thus, the compulsion to work, as seen in the "workaholic," may be viewed not only as a superego demand, but also as a drive influenced by the ego ideal and its images of the strived-for level of achievement.

One man in his late twenties was having great difficulty maintaining a consistent work level. He was about to lose his position because he often acted out his rage toward authorities. His hostility to his parents was rooted in considerable parental neglect throughout his childhood. The treatment uncovered his association of knowledge with power, an association which apparently had contributed to his long history of a partial learning disability. This serious symptom was related to his guilt-ridden defenses. He wished to avoid integrating knowledge and thus prevent the destructive revengeful fantasies he harbored and feared would emerge if he approached any degree of successful achievement. He was in constant fear that he would be unable to answer pertinent questions by superiors regarding his work activities. He had a history of changing schools and an urge frequently to change his place of residence. If this pattern had continued during his education and into his career, his record of being an unreliable, transient, and unstable worker would have fulfilled his father's dreaded prophecy that he would end up "a bum."

This example emphasizes the importance of unconscious conflictual factors which may influence career achievements adversely. Obviously, to arrive at a successful level of work ability, individuals must be capable of cooperative relationships with superiors and peers and not be blocked by intrapsychic conflicts in achieving competence.

The following is a brief example, in the area of work compulsions, of the complex interaction between personality factors and vocational attitudes. A man in his mid-thirties worked from about 7:00 A.M. to about 10:00 or 10:30 P.M. weekdays, with another five or six hours on Saturday and Sunday. This work style was similar to that of many physicians, attorneys, and businessmen I have treated. Some of these patients were single; others were married. The avoidance of a wife or children at home did not appear to be a determining feature of their pattern. With specific individual variations, each of the men in this category felt deprivations in reaction to the type of mothering he experienced in childhood. In one instance, the patient's mother was depressed, withdrawn, and bedridden; in another, the mother died early in the man's childhood; in a third case, the mother was depressed, worked outside the home, and ultimately remarried following the father's death (the patient felt rejected by his mother's attention to her new husband). The deprivations were experienced as oral needs and threats to survival. All of these patients were overweight from overeating or had difficulty controlling their alcohol consumption.

The patient in this example had learning problems all the way through his schooling and into his college education. He flunked out of one college and held on marginally in another. He was superior intellectually and ingested considerable information but refused to give it back when confronted with examinations. His toilet training had been traumatic; he was subjected to enemas and had to show his feces before being allowed to flush the toilet. The therapy revealed the association in his mind of academic examinations and having his bowel irrigated and his product checked over. Further, in his compulsive work pattern he unconsciously associated his vocational exertions with his mother's demands and the financial compensation with her feeding him. He felt close to his mother and happy and secure while working, but he felt depressed and anxious when away from the job. This patient was not an example of the "Sunday neurosis" described by Ferenczi (1919) or the sublimation of aggression and hostility through work suggested by Menninger (1942). Anxiety is aroused when the person is faced with inactivity, and defense mechanisms are utilized to contain the anxiety, with resulting symptom formation.

The developmental transition toward a career involves much more than a mere change of environment. It is also a change from supportive, friendly relationships with parental and school authorities to those with often impersonal work authorities—the institution, company, or corporation. There is a change in living style and often in community environment. The necessary reorganization of personality orientation to one's self and others may produce a postadolescent identity crisis or a self-image crisis, to use Wittenberg's concept (1968). The anxiety level may be sufficient to create a variety of symptoms, including transient depersonalization. This may occur not only in borderline character pathology but also in the neurotic and even so-called normal or healthy personality. The feeling is one of confusion about one's self-image; the familiar continuity of one's personality seems lost, and the ability to feel comfortable and oriented toward the environment is similarly changed. I have seen this phenomenon in people going from high school to college, in others who changed jobs in the same city or who changed cities in the same corporation, and in a number of immigrants from such varied places as Europe, South America, and Asia. Many of these disturbances may be treated without drugs or hospitalization. I explore the patients' memories of their previous, more secure environment and foster reintegration from that point forward. So far, this brief psychotherapeutic technique has been successful.

The adolescent's revolt against the superego, which is identified with restrictions by parents and other authorities, allows the individual to feel more independent in the reorganization of the personality. However, in the transition to the occupational world, which in the young adult may be characterized as the postadolescent phase, the conflict is somewhat different. The need to establish an equilibrium between ego ideals and superego is precipitated by the necessity of making serious decisions for adult life. Space does not permit a theoretical discussion of whether superego and ego ideal concepts are to be viewed as a single functional unit or as separate concepts (Erikson, 1959; Arlow and Brenner, 1964; Jacobson, 1964).

Conflicts between ego ideals and superego stir the self-image crisis. If one distinguishes the pseudo-ideal from the true ego ideal, the former would be linked with the grandiose, omnipotent fantasies of childhood. Learning problems in the college years in certain instances may be a result of impossible expectations and of a rigid, cruel superego demand for these "superman" achievements. The ensuing feelings of discontent, failure, severe self-hatred, and projected or real perception of disappointment in the parents have led some students to drop out of school and run away. It has led others to suicide, serious drug or alcohol abuse, or other "copouts." Understandably, psychiatric work with young men and women during their self-image dilemmas is difficult and must be done with thoughtfulness, kindness, and as much understanding as one can muster from training and experience. A rigid, harsh superego that demands fulfillment of unrealistic ego ideals can be a constant source of conflict and symptom formation, particularly depression. For example, to be a good parent and spend time at home with one's children and spouse may run counter to the wish to be dedicated to one's career and achieve success. The conscience can lash out at the self-image either way, producing a continuous state of discontent, irritability, and sense of failure. One defensive maneuver which emerges as a solution to a superego/ego ideal or superego/pseudo-ideal conflict is to attack the representatives of the superego. A 19-year-old girl who dropped her educational pursuits to live in a "free-spirited" style was intent on humiliating her parents and thus downgrading their values and diminishing their influence on her. However, when the superego is projected against a society or government, hostility is vented in that direction. Provocations are brought to a point where attacks from those sources are unconsciously welcomed to rationalize the conclusion that authorities are indeed bad or stupid and that the "system" must be totally revised. The desperate effort to cling to waning youth in the transition from adolescence to adulthood is revived when people have delayed consolidation of their personalities. I have seen an incomplete transition lay dormant for many years and suddenly disrupt many years of a seemingly happy marriage and career. People in this situation attempt to look, act, and think young. The reality of the "adult world" appears boring, and they seek the "last chance" to live an exciting life and recapture or develop a sense of individuality and identity. Both groups—young people in transition and older ones who try to return to a new transition—have in common an aggressive, firm, and anxious desire to return to living by the pleasure principle. There is a wish for fulfillment of their self-images and an underlying depressive longing for freedom and happiness without the burden of responsibility to anyone but themselves.

Adolescents in transition are alert to the effect of their behavior, achievements, and goals on their parents' self-image. They have difficulty at times deciding whether they are gratifying themselves or their parents when they are progressing in an acceptable direction. Similarly, if hostility and parental conflict are high, they feel mingled pleasure and guilt when their parents are embarrassed or enraged at unacceptable directions. I reported a study of learning problems in adolescents in whom these conflicts unconsciously influenced the school failures (Marcus, 1967). In another study, involving 110 student nurses, I found that the autonomy need—to "handle their own problems" and make their own decisions regarding the pursuit of nursing as a career or to drop out and explore other work goals—prevented many girls from consulting others about their problems. They avoided not only the available student advisors but also their own peer group. The fear of outside influence on their identity struggles, combined with sensitivity regarding their self-images, led to impulsive decisions to drop out of a nursing career. The student nurses presented false excuses to the director of their school to rationalize their actions. As a result, the school did not know how to approach or solve the real problem of their relatively high dropout rate. My study of this group of late adolescents led to an approach which favorably influenced the problem (Marcus, 1969).

In conclusion, the developmental influence on career achievement involves unconscious processes in interaction with academic, social, and economic factors. Personality factors can enhance or disturb the development of career performance. However, the crystallization of a work personality allows for semiautonomous functioning. Thus, upheavals in nonwork areas of the personality may not necessarily influence work patterns. On the other hand, developmental disorders influencing the transition from academic life to the adult world cannot be solved by simply guiding the person toward a new commitment. Psychotherapeutic work, brief or long-term as indicated, can be crucial to the futures of those presenting serious transition problems.

References

Arlow, J., & Brenner, C. (1964), *Psychoanalytic Concepts and the Structural Theory*. New York: International Universities Press.

Eissler, K. R. (1958), Reports in Panel on problems of identity, rep. D. L. Rubinfine. *J. Amer. Psychoanal. Assn.*, 6:131–142.

Erikson, E. H. (1959), Identity and the life cycle. *Psychological Issues*, Monograph 1. New York: International Universities Press.

Fenichel, O. (1953), Identification. In: *The Collected Papers of Otto Fenichel*, Vol. 1. New York: Norton, pp. 97–112.

Ferenczi, S. (1919), Sunday neurosis. In: *Further Contributions to Psycho-Analysis*. 2nd ed. London: Hogarth Press, 1950, pp. 174–176.

Freud, A. (1965), *Normality and Pathology in Childhood*. New York: International Universities Press.

Freud, S. (1914), On narcissism. *Standard Edition*, 4:30–59. London: Hogarth Press, 1953.

Ginzberg, E., Ginsburg, S. W., Axelrad, S., & Herma, J. L. (1951), *Occupational Choice: An Approach to a General Theory*. New York: Columbia University Press.

Greenacre, P. (1958), Early physical determinants in the development of the sense of identity. *J. Amer. Psychoanal. Assn.*, 6:612–627.

Hartmann, H. (1958), *Ego Psychology and the Problem of Adaptation*. New York: International Universities Press.

——— Kris, E., & Loewenstein, R. M. (1946), Comments on the formation of psychic structure. *The Psychoanalytic Study of the Child*, 2:11–38. New York: International Universities Press.

Hendrick, I. (1943), Work and the pleasure principle. *Psychoanal. Quart.*, 12:311–329.

Jacobson, E. (1964), *The Self and the Object World*. New York: International Universities Press.

Josselyn, I. (1954), Ego in adolescence. *Amer. J. Orthopsychiat.*, 24:223–237.

Kohut, H. (1966), Forms and transformations of narcissism. *J. Amer. Psychoanal. Assn.*, 14:243–272.

Lantos, B. (1943), Work and instincts. *Internat. J. Psycho-Anal.*, 24:114–119.

Levin, D. C. (1969), The self: A contribution to its place in theory and technique. *Internat. J. Psycho-Anal.*, 50:41–51.

Marcus, I. M. (1967), Learning problems. In: *Adolescence*, ed. G. Usdin. Philadelphia: Lippincott, pp. 94–110.

———— (1969), From school to work: Certain aspects of psychosocial inter-action. In: *Adolescence: Psychosocial Perspectives*, ed. G. Caplan & S. Le-bovici. New York: Basic Books, pp. 157–164.

———— (1971), The marriage-separation pendulum: A character disorder as-sociated with early object loss. In: *Currents in Psychoanalysis*, ed. I. M. Marcus. New York: International Universities Press, pp. 361–383.

Menninger, K. (1942), Work as sublimation. *Bull. Menn. Clin.*, 6:170–182.

Mittelmann, B. (1954), Motility in infants, children, and adults. *The Psychoan-alytic Study of the Child*, 9:142–177. New York: International Universities Press.

Neff, W. S. (1968), *Work and Human Behavior*. New York: Atherton.

Spiegel, L. (1959), The self, the sense of self, and perception. *The Psychoanalytic Study of the Child*, 14:81–109. New York: International Universities Press.

Sullivan, H. S. (1953), *Conceptions of Modern Psychiatry*. 2nd ed. New York: Norton.

Tiedeman, D. V., O'Hara, R. P., & Baruch, R. W. (1963), *Career Development: Choice and Adjustment*. Princeton, NJ: College Entrance Examination Board.

Wheelis, A. B. (1958), *The Quest for Identity*. New York: Norton.

Wittenberg, R. (1968), *Postadolescence*. New York: Grune & Stratton.

11

Mid-Adolescence: Foundations for Later Psychopathology

AARON H. ESMAN, M.D.

Adolescence is by definition a transitional phase of human psychological development. Whether its duration is brief, as in traditional and "primitive" societies (Muensterberger, 1961) or unnaturally extended, as in ours, it looks Janus-like, back to the childhood past and forward to the adult future. To the extent that it carries the seeds of future pathology, these derive in part from its phase-specific conflicts and developmental issues, and in part from the unresolved problems of early childhood and latency and the shadows they cast on the adolescent process.

To understand the foundations and precursors of future psychopathology inherent in the mid-adolescent period, it is desirable to reconsider the salient issues (or, to speak teleologically, "tasks") of this phase as they occur in industrialized societies. The adolescent between 15 and 18 has in most cases already experienced the major impact of the physiological changes of puberty. He (or she) has experienced the rebelliousness and turmoil which Offer (1969) acknowledges are characteristic of most early adolescents and which Anna Freud (1958) maintains are a necessary aspect of the adolescent experience. He is well into the throes of "object removal" and has, in his first postpubertal forays, begun to shift his major object investments to peers and idealized "crush" figures, typically from the world of sports or show business. In his early gropings toward sexual objects he may have enjoyed some experimental homosexual play but is by now reaching out to heterosexual partners, however tentatively. These heterosexual objects are, however, perceived largely along narcissistic lines—"I love what I would like to be," as Blos (1962) has formulated it. Life is lived locally and for the moment, though the growth of formal operational thought (Piaget, 1969) is preparing the way for experimentation with abstract concepts and for a wider view of life and its possibilities.

The passage into mid-adolescence is in many ways analogous to that from Mahler's "hatching" subphase of separation-individuation to the "practicing" period. The 15- to 18-year-old has acquired an impressive array of new capacities and resources, both biological and psychological, which he is now ready to deploy in his inner world as well. Erikson (1956) has subsumed much of the work of this subphase under the process of "identity formation." This includes such matters as the establishment of a sexual identity as masculine or feminine (as opposed to gender identity as male or female, which is settled in early childhood) and of a capacity for mutuality in relations with others, particularly with heterosexual partners.

A further component of this process is the development of an orientation to the future—in particular, toward vocational opportunities and choices. This may involve the trying out—either mentally or physically—of alternatives, an aspect of the critical tendency of mid-adolescents to test the possibilities that the world offers them. Not the least important among these is the range of possible value orientations; both the aspirations and aims of the ego ideal and the prohibitions of the superego are subject to review and reorganization during adolescence (Esman, 1972).

All of these phenomena occur in the context of the major task of adolescent development—the process of "object removal." Made urgent by the reactivation of oedipal wishes and fears, made possible by growing cognitive maturation and physical powers, this process entails the ultimate resolution of dependence-independence conflicts as well as of the incestuous longings and castration anxieties that inhere in the oedipal triangle. In a large sense, it is in the arena of this struggle that many of the aforementioned concerns are settled. By age 18 most of this work will normally have been done; it is left to the stages of late adolescence and (that artifact of our times) "youth" to consolidate the advances that have occurred during the high school years. And it should not be forgotten that, even today, for many young people, perhaps most, high school graduation marks the end of adolescence and the initiation of adult life.

Unfortunately, as Winnicott (1962) has said, "some individuals are too ill (with psychoneurosis or depression or schizophrenia) to reach a stage of emotional development that could be called adolescence or they can reach it only in a highly distorted way" (p. 86). For these, the roots of future psychopathology lie in the unresolved conflicts and developmental deviations of earlier periods. For others, the normative developmental events of adolescence itself offer the potential for faulty resolution and maladaptive solutions. It is these situations we shall examine here, seeking to delineate some of the intrinsic, familial, and social factors that contribute to deviant outcomes. It must be understood, however, that development is a continuous process; the seams in its web are imposed by the observer who seeks to order the data into conceptual segments.

Maturational Delays and the Body Image Problem

By age 15 most adolescents will, as mentioned earlier, have passed through puberty as a physiological process. Especially is this true of girls; some boys on the descending side of the bell-shaped curve may still experience pubertal changes in their sixteenth year. For them, however, as for that small number whose puberty is delayed beyond the norm, substantial problems arise, with both short-term and long-term consequences.

Schoenfeld (1969) has set forth in detail the bodily changes in adolescence and the immediate consequences for body image formation of deviations from the norm. He stresses the fact that, for adolescents, "to be different is to be inferior." The 15-year-old boy who is forced into invidious dressing-room comparisons of genital size and pubic hair development with more biologically favored peers is likely, in order to protect his self-esteem, to withdraw from such situations; he thus risks further stigmatization as a "faggot" or a "bookworm." At least a measure of social awkwardness, at most a pattern of detachment and discomfort in social intercourse, may be the psychological consequence of such physiological disparity.

The problem of body image disturbance is even greater among adolescent girls. This can be accounted for by a variety of factors, both sociocultural and intrapsychic. Ours is a culture that imposes on young women, through the mass media, demands for conformity to thoroughly unrealistic standards of bodily form—long-legged, pencil-thin, large-bosomed—that are the despair of most adolescent girls and the delight of the magazines they devour to advise them in their desperate efforts to achieve the unachievable. (The prevailing ethos is manifest in the slogan, "There are two things it's impossible to be—too rich or too thin.") Peer pressure toward the achievement of ultimate thinness is frequently intense, and even moderate obesity is often the occasion for ridicule and social discrimination (Johnson and Maadi, 1986). At the same time, the normal secondary sexual characteristics are consciously or unconsciously associated with burgeoning sexuality, which may in certain family and social contexts be a source of intense shame or guilt.

Such conditions may pave the way for conditions that are among the most flamboyant afflictions of young women —anorexia nervosa and bulimia. Often setting in during the mid-adolescent phase, these disorders occur with equal frequency in late adolescence or young adulthood. Bruch (1973) has defined the multiple determinants of this complex and baffling group of disorders; prominent among them are disturbances of body image and self-perception (often related to earlier traumata as well as to adolescent irregularities). The role of sexual conflicts has been less stressed in recent studies (Bruch, 1973; Minuchin, Rosman, and Baker, 1978) than in earlier discussions (Waller, Kaufman, and Deutsch, 1940) but should not be overlooked. Oral impregnation fantasies and the unconscious equation of "fat" and "pregnant" are common findings in such cases (Risen, 1982; Wilson, 1986) and interdigitate with the separation-individuation and body image issues emphasized by Bruch, Sours (1969), and others.

The counterpart of such conflictual disturbances in body image is the overinvestment characteristic of certain hysterical and narcissistic character types. Here, although crucial predispositions may be laid down in earlier phases, adolescence may be the point of crystallization. The adolescent girl requires affirmation of the femininity which is an aspect of her total personality development. In particular, she requires acceptance and encouragement from the primary male figures in her life—especially a father who can respond to her growing sexuality with neither defensive withdrawal nor seductive acting out (Tessman, 1982). The integration of sexuality as but one element in a total self-system allows for the enlargement of self-esteem from a variety of intellectual, interpersonal, and conflict-free sources. Where such alternative sources are lacking, the adolescent girl may seek reassurance from excessive (at times monolithic) attention to her appearance and in the development of styles of seductive exhibitionism. Should this be consolidated by parental support or peer approval, the nucleus for later character pathology will be well formed by the end of high school.

Depression and Its Analogues

If the central theme in mid-adolescence is the pursuit of object removal, it follows that at certain points a state of relative objectlessness will prevail in the adolescent's mental life. Detaching his primary emotional engagement from ("decathecting") the mental representations of his parents, he has not yet succeeded in replacing them with stable alternative figures. Much of his activity during these years is devoted to the quest for such attachment-objects; for some, this process is fraught with difficulty and frustration. For the adolescent who is shy or temperamentally slow to warm up (Chess, Thomas, and Birch, 1967) or for whom early oral disappointments have led to impairment in "basic trust" (Erikson, 1950), or whose characterological style is passive rather than active (Rapaport, 1953), the restoration of abandoned object ties may prove an insuperable task. Chronic and lifelong feelings of loneliness and isolation may ensue, along with a depressive orientation toward life. The fragility of the attachments that are established and their overinvestment as sources of refuge from feelings of loneliness may lead, in especially vulnerable adolescents, to major depression and suicidal acts when and if they are disrupted by circumstances or by active disengagement by the partner.

The more or less ubiquitous dysphoric potential in adolescence is normally warded off in a variety of ways. Among these are frenetic hypermotility and social hunger, with overtones of hypomanic denial and the use of chemical agents—alcohol and drugs. For most adolescents these activities are transitory, experimental, and self-limited. For the most vulnerable, however, the use of alcohol and drugs may serve as permanent anodynes against the pains of object hunger. Addiction or drug abuse is therefore among the pathologies that may arise from the miscarried process of object removal (Wieder and Kaplan, 1969; Paton, Kessler, and Kandel, 1977).

Sexual Identity

Although gender identity appears to be laid down in the preoedipal years, a clear sense of self as masculine or feminine and of one's mode of function in one's sexual life is a product of the adolescent process. Several currents contribute to the ultimate emergence of this configuration. Important among these is the fortification of earlier identifications by new ones, especially with peer group members and idealized parent surrogates (not least, those supplied by the mass media). In the resolution of recrudescent oedipal conflicts, such fortifying identifications are crucial, both in promoting the movement toward nonincestuous objects and in buttressing the oedipal identification with the same-sex parent.

A crucial aspect of sexual development and of the formation of sexual identity is masturbation. Masturbation is the primary sexual experience of most adolescents in our culture, even in this period of "sexual revolution" (Esman, 1977a). It is a vital resource in aiding the adolescent in organizing his sexual fantasies, and in permitting experimentation with the pregenital and perverse wishes that ultimately can be integrated into the foreplay of genital heterosexuality. The capacity to masturbate alone and with relative freedom from guilt is, as

Borowitz (1973) has pointed out, an essential acquisition in the adolescent's progress toward maturity (see the case of Mike, later in this chapter).

The possibilities for deviant outcome abound, of course, in so complex a process. As with other aspects discussed here, earlier predispositions play a critical role in determining the outcome of the phase-specific conflicts. Deviant early identifications, particularly those involving intense bisexual ties, will tend to skew the picture, and leave the adolescent open to current influences that may have critical shaping force.

Don F. had emerged from latency with a clear male identity but with a complex pattern of identifications with a powerful and overbearing "phallic" mother and a remote and critical father who offered little protection or support. Don's longing for an internalized sense of masculine power could be gratified only by oral incorporation. Seduced in early adolescence by an older male friend of the family into fellatio, he came to use this means to seduce his peers, from whom he sought not sexual gratification per se, but friendship and acceptance. This pattern became consolidated during his high school years so that by 17 he was a confirmed though highly conflicted homosexual. Fantasies of biting off the penis represented not only his wish to incorporate the phallus and gain its power, but a persistent identification with the mother, whom he experienced as devouring and castrating.

Leslie T. was a depressed, somewhat bewildered 21-year-old girl, fresh out of a prestigious college for women and uncertain about her direction in life. Her sadness was a reaction to the departure for Europe of a young woman who had been her homosexual lover through three college years. Leslie's family situation was bizarre. Her father lived and worked in a midwestern city. Her mother had taken Leslie and her 2-year-old brother to live in Florida when Leslie was 12, and the father came for occasional visits and vacations. Mrs. T. was a vain, narcissistic woman who was completely idle and emotionally detached from her children. Leslie grew up an unhappy, object-hungry girl who at 15 formed a homosexual liaison with a classmate, an arrangement that did not preclude heterosexual friendships and dates. In this relationship, as in the subsequent one in college, her aim was clearly to be cared for and mothered by a warm, dominant lover.

By contrast, Blos (1957) described the type of adolescent girl who takes flight into precocious and promiscuous hetero- sexuality from the unconscious pull toward an erotized tie to the preoedipal mother. In her eagerness to disavow such long- ings, tinged as they are with homosexual and infantile depend- ent meanings, such a girl becomes, as Blos puts it, a "Diana" intent on pursuing her masculine prey with pseudosexual se- ductions. Others, with conflicts and motives similar to Leslie's, will turn their erotic attention to males as well, seeking from them maternal care rather than mature heterosexual mutuality. In adult life such women are likely to experience repeated fail- ures in their love lives or to immerse themselves, out of their terror of abandonment and loneliness, in masochistic depend- ence on men to whom they remain attached despite repeated disappointments or sadistic manipulation. Beating fantasies may appear in such women; behind the sadistic male figure in such fantasies is the rejecting angry mother of preoedipal times.

Future Orientation and Work Goals

Prior to mid-adolescence, children are essentially present- oriented—at first because of their dependence on adults and immaturity of their cognitive organization and then, in early adolescence, because of their intense narcissism and primary preoccupation with puberty and its consequences. In the high school years this begins to change. The cognitive development described by Piaget (1969) permits a broader awareness of the nature of the world and the possibilities it affords, and of the realities of adult life. Emergence from pubertal narcissism in the direction of more substantial object attachments serves fur- ther to promote the anticipation of adult social role require- ments. In addition, growing consolidation of identifications, positive or negative, engenders vocational interests attuned to them as well as to intrinsic interests and talents that are emerging.

Here, too, there is a potential for problems. For the middle class adolescent, at least, the range of vocational possibilities is broad and allows for the accommodation of individual tastes, interests, and special capacities. Premature closure and unreflective decisions based on defensive identifications or avoidance intended to obviate anxiety, or due to ideological commitments attendant on ego ideal reshaping (Erikson's "absolutism") or submissive conformity to parental demands and pressures, may lead to lifelong dissatisfaction or to repeated changes of vocation in later life. The adolescent who is too closely tied to his primary objects, who fears detaching himself and establishing his own identity, or who, due to parental overindulgence is unwilling to relinquish the infantile dependent position may avoid experimentation and exploration with regard to work possibilities. Locked into a passive posture, he may either defer such choices endlessly and assume the position of "prolonged adolescence" described by Bernfeld (1938) or settle submissively into a predetermined situation unrelated to his gifts.

It must be acknowledged that forces exist in the contemporary world that promote such prolongation of adolescence. What Erikson has called the "psychosocial moratorium"—that period during which society allows for experimentation and deferral of commitment—has been further and further extended in recent decades, with the prolongation of the period of education demanded by young people and with the need to keep them out of the labor force as long as feasible. For some, the absence of external pressure to end this moratorium and/or the absence of opportunity to do so resonate with inner passivity and dependency wishes to produce a type of prolonged adolescence characterized by the "hippies" of the 1960s, the marginal street youth, the peripatetic remittance man, and the perpetual student. If to this is added a failure to resolve renascent oedipal conflicts, potency difficulties or flight from commitment to sexual objects will complete the syndrome.

Ego Synthesis and the Management of Regression

The traditional picture of normal adolescent development would have it that puberty initiates a prolonged period of instability and turmoil, marked by multiple and shifting regressions and progressions in drive and ego organization, until sometime in late adolescence a process of synthesis and coalescence takes place that engenders the stable ego and character organization of adult life. Only in recent years have workers such as Masterson (1968) and Offer (1969) challenged this view, setting forth evidence suggesting that the turmoil-ridden adolescent is a disturbed adolescent and that most young people negotiate the high school years with no major disruption of personality.

That this is the case does not, of course, minimize the stresses of the mid-adolescent period; it suggests, rather, that most young people have at their disposal a system of defenses and coping capacities that enable them to weather these stresses. It is well known, however, that a significant number cannot do so. For those who bring to this phase a fragile ego, the burdens of individuation on the one hand (Masterson, 1973) and the establishment of intimate object ties on the other (Erikson, 1989) may prove insuperable.

The vulnerable adolescent faced with such threats may break down completely, evidencing an acute psychotic disorder which may, or in rare cases may not, be the prelude to long-term schizophrenic illness. In order to maintain a semblance of integrity, however, he will more frequently protect his tenuous psychic structure by withdrawing into a schizoid isolation, communing in dereistic fantasies with the introjected—and at times, projected—figures of his infantile objects.

Jim R., 16 years old, was referred to me after he had just dropped out of college during the Christmas vacation of his freshman year. For a month before the break he had been avoiding classes, sleeping during the day and awake at night, preoccupied with ideas about precognition and psychokinesis.

Mathematically gifted, he was determined that he could find a way to forecast the vagaries of the stock market and predict the winners of horse races—indeed, to determine these events by the power of his own thoughts. By the time he came to see me he had some awareness of the irrationality of these ideas but was still occupied with them and oscillated between belief and skepticism.

Jim was the only child of relatively elderly parents who doted on him and were gratified by his intellectual precocity. He had been overprotected in early childhood and his earliest memory was of his acute anxiety and tearfulness when put on a bus to go to day camp at age 5 or 6. Academically, school had posed no problems for him and he coasted through quickly with little or no effort; his grades declined in his last year in high school but not enough to preclude his admission to a prestigious college. His matriculation there marked the first time he had ever been away from home for any extended period. He had always "hung out" with peer groups in the neighborhood, but had no intimate friends. Though fascinated by girls and involved in ruminations about social and sexual triumphs, he had never really dated a girl before he left for college.

Thus Jim was confronted by a succession of stressful circumstances on entering college. Not only did he have to cope with separation from his overinvolved parents, but he was thrust into dormitory life, which imposed on him demands for closeness with peers and simultaneously threatened his shaky sexual identity. Further, his somewhat grandiose narcissism felt the shock of more stringent academic pressures, and his rapid realization that he was no longer the boy wonder he had been in high school.

The result was breakdown and regression in several areas of ego function; his emergency defense was largely that of intellectualization and a reinforcement of other obsessive-compulsive defenses—a desperate effort to control his world by means of thought. Removal from the traumatic situation and return home provided rapid relief, but it was only after several months of intensive therapy that his thinking became more reality-bound and that he was able to take a job until enrolling at a local university the next year. He lost one job because of persistent lateness and lack of commitment, and his initial return to college was similarly unsuccessful. The second time he set up an easy schedule and seemed able to function at an adequate but marginal level. He continued in therapy until he was almost 19. Although there was no indication of further psychotic thinking or behavior, his character became consolidated into a rather shallow, narcissistic one with a focus on the quick solution and the "easy buck."

Ego Ideal and Superego Development

As Blos (1974) and I (Esman, 1972) have pointed out, adolescence affords an opportunity for the reshaping of the ego ideal and a readjustment of the superego. The former—more closely attuned to current reality, closer to consciousness, and normally less peremptory in nature—is likely to undergo more extensive reorganization on the basis of new identifications. Much of the psychological activity of adolescence is related to the revamping of the value system; the constant experimentation of adolescents with values alternative to or in conflict with those of their parents or of the dominant ethos reflects not merely "rebellion" but a genuine effort to find and formulate a self-syntonic system of values. The oft-described decline in the credibility of traditional sources of values (Esman, 1977b) makes this process all the more urgent and all the more difficult.

The superego (in the restricted sense of a store of prohibitive and self-critical values) also undergoes modification. Certainly, it loses its categorical, all-or-none quality, as the evolving cognitive system allows for more shading and concessions to reality (Nass, 1966). The earlier absolute prohibitions against sexual activity, for instance, are adjusted to the adolescent's new needs and capacities. Normally the incest taboo is not only maintained but fortified, although incestuous fantasies are not unusual, even in consciousness.

It is precisely with regard to this adaptation to current and future reality that the potential for later pathology resides. Although the ultimate consolidation of the ego ideal and the superego are the work of late adolescence, the way is paved during the mid-adolescent period. Preservation of archaic value-centered introjects (Sandler, 1960) threatens the maintenance of self-esteem under conditions of stress, with both shame and guilt as irrational and potentially self-damaging consequences. Thus the failure to adjust narcissistically tinged introjections of overvalued parent figures may induce totally unrealizable goals of a grandiose or omnipotent nature. The college student who fails to achieve in conformity with such goals (or, even worse, who fails in the course of his desperate efforts to do so) may react with acute depression, feelings of hopelessness, and even suicide. Similarly, adolescents who fail to resolve sexual prohibitions, including those against masturbation, may emerge with lifelong sexual conflicts which may lead to the acting out of perverse or deviant fantasies in ostensibly nonsexual ways.

Mike, a 19-year-old college junior, came to treatment because of chronic feelings of self-doubt and inferiority and intense social and sexual anxieties. Born to a rich family, reared in an exclusive suburb, educated in expensive private schools, he appeared slovenly and unkempt, with holes in his trousers, long shaggy hair, and a droopy blond mustache. He was an ex–drug user, having had three or four years regular experience with marijuana and LSD and the values attending them before abruptly abandoning them completely after a "bad trip" during which he had almost jumped out of a window.

Mike's sexual inhibitions were profound. He was extremely shy with women, constantly concerned about sexual performance, and generally experienced premature ejaculation in coitus. He elaborated complex, compensatory fantasies of sexual triumph associated with situations in which, as a radical political leader, he would be jailed or hospitalized, achieving through his martyrdom reconciliation with his conservative parents and amatory successes with beautiful young women devoted to his political cause.

For a long period during his analysis Mike insisted that he had never masturbated before he was 17. Gradually, however, it became clear that he was referring to manual masturbation. In fact, from age 14 he had masturbated by rubbing his genitals against his bed sheet while in a prone position. This, however, he did not consider masturbation; i.e., he was able to carry on this activity while at the same time denying what he was doing because of profound feelings of guilt and shame, related in part to conscious incestuous fantasies about his sister. The inhibitions implicit in this pattern were clearly expressed in his sexual symptoms. His fantasies, however, with their passive, masochistic character similarly served as continuing expressions of the masturbatory fantasies of his early and mid-adolescent years.

By contrast, Johnson (1949) described situations in which parental sanction or complicity generated superego defects or "lacunae" that may portend long-lasting character pathology: "The child's superego lacunae correspond to similar defects of the parents' superegos which in turn were derived from the conscious or unconscious permissiveness of their own parents" (p. 225). Such persons will demonstrate focal deviation, with no intrapsychic conflict, from culturally shared norms of behavior.

It is apparent, then, that the mid-adolescent period is of crucial significance in the evolution of adult personality. As Giovacchini (1973) puts it, "the adult personality is psychopathologically constructed insofar as it is the outcome of reactions against what has been *experienced* as a traumatic adolescence" (p. 279; italics in original). The person's experience of adolescence will reflect, not only the observable realities of a life situation, but also the personality structure and characteristics he brings to them. It is, of course, commonplace for patients—and nonpatients, as well—to ascribe the "traumatic" or stressful quality of their adolescence, whether current or remembered, to external circumstances—not least to parents, teachers, and other adults. It is well to recall that the picture one receives is filtered through the veil of retrospective distortion and influenced by the persistence of primitive object representations and of introjective-projective defenses that make the reconstruction of adolescent experience particularly difficult in adult analysis. "We fail," wrote Anna Freud (1958), "to recover . . . the atmosphere in which the adolescent lives . . ." (p. 260). What remains for most adults is a profound sense that adolescence was a period they would not want to live through again. "Experience tells us," says Blos (1977), "that unresolved psychological issues are always bound to remain; it is, however, their stable integration into the adult personality that gives these persistent issues a patterned and rather irreversible structure" (p. 16). For some, unfortunately, this pattern, this irreversibility, takes a pathological form.

References

Bernfeld, S. (1938), Types of adolescents. *Psychoanal. Quart.*, 7:243–253.

Blos, P. (1957), Preoedipal factors in the etiology of female delinquency. *The Psychoanalytic Study of the Child*, 12:229–249. New York: International Universities Press.

———— (1962), *On Adolescence: A Psychoanalytic Interpretation.* New York: Free Press.

———— (1974), The genealogy of the ego ideal. *The Psychoanalytic Study of the Child*, 29:43–88. New Haven: Yale University Press.

———— (1977), When and how does adolescence end? *Adolescent Psychiat.*, 5:5–17.

Borowitz, G. (1973), The capacity to masturbate alone. *Adolescent Psychiat.*, 2:130–143.

Bruch, H. (1973), *Eating Disorders: Obesity, Anorexia, and the Person Within.* New York: Basic Books.

Chess, S., Thomas, A., & Birch, H. (1967), Behavior problems revisited: Findings of an anterospective study. *J. Amer. Acad. Child Psychiat.*, 6:321–331.

Erikson, E. H. (1950), Growth and crises of the healthy personality. In: *Symposium on the Healthy Personality, Suppl. II. Transactions of the 4th Annual Conference on Problems of Infancy and Childhood*, ed. M. J. E. Senn. New York: Josiah Macy Foundation.

———— (1956), The problem of ego identity. *J. Amer. Psychoanal. Assn.*, 4:56–121.

———— (1989), Elements of a psychoanalytic theory of psychosocial development. In: *The Course of Life*, Vol. I, ed. S. I. Greenspan & G. H. Pollock. Madison, CT: International Universities Press, pp. 15–83.

Esman, A. H. (1972), Adolescence and the consolidation of values. In: *Moral Values and the Superego Concept in Psychoanalysis*, ed. S. C. Post. New York: International Universities Press, pp. 87–100.

———— (1977a), Adolescence and "the new sexuality." In: *On Sexuality: Psychoanalytic Observations*, ed. T. Karasu & C. Socarides. New York: International Universities Press, pp. 19–28.

———— (1977b), Changing values: Their implications for adolescent development and psychoanalytic ideas. *Adolescent Psychiat.*, 5:18–34.

Freud, A. (1958), Adolescence. *The Psychoanalytic Study of the Child*, 13:255–278. New York: International Universities Press.

Giovacchini, P. (1973), The adolescent process and character formation: Clinical aspects. *Adolescent Psychiat.*, 2:269–285.

Johnson, A. (1949), Sanctions for superego lacunae of adolescence. In: *Search-lights on Delinquency*, ed. K. R. Eissler. New York: International Universities Press, pp. 225–245.

Johnson, C., & Maadi, K. (1986), The etiology of bulimia: Biopsychosocial perspectives. *Adolescent Psychiat.*, 13:253–273.

Masterson, J. (1968), The psychiatric significance of adolescent turmoil. *Amer. J. Psychiat.*, 124:1549–1554.

——— (1973), The borderline adolescent. *Adolescent Psychiat.*, 2:240–268.

Minuchin, S., Rosman, B., & Baker, L. (1978), *Psychosomatic Families: Anorexia Nervosa in Context.* Cambridge: Harvard University Press.

Muensterberger, W. (1961), The adolescent in society. In: *Adolesence*, ed. S. Lorand & H. Schneer. New York: Hoeber, pp. 344–368.

Nass, M. (1966), The superego and moral development in the theories of Freud and Piaget. *The Psychoanalytic Study of the Child*, 21:51–68. New York: International Universities Press.

Offer, D. (1969), *The Psychological World of the Teenager.* New York: Basic Books.

Paton, S., Kessler, R., & Kandel, D. (1977), Depressive mood and illegal drug use: A longitudinal analysis. *J. Genet. Psychol.*, 131:267–289.

Piaget, J. (1969), The intellectual development of the adolescent. In: *Adolescence: Psychosocial Perspectives*, ed. G. Caplan & S. Lebovici. New York: Basic Books, pp. 22–26.

Rapaport, D. (1953), Some metapsychological considerations concerning activity and passivity. In: *Collected Papers of David Rapaport*, ed. M. M. Gill. New York: Basic Books, pp. 530–568.

Risen, S. (1982), The psychoanalytic treatment of an adolescent with anorexia nervosa. *The Psychoanalytic Study of the Child*, 37:433–460. New Haven, CT: Yale University Press.

Sandler, J. (1960), On the concept of superego. *The Psychoanalytic Study of the Child*, 15:128–162. New York: International Universities Press.

Schoenfeld, W. (1969), The body and the body image. In: *Adolescence: Psychosocial Perspectives*, ed. G. Caplan & S. Lebovici. New York: Basic Books, pp. 27–53.

Sours, J. (1969), Anorexia nervosa: Nosology, diagnosis, developmental patterns and power-control mechanisms. In: *Adolescence: Psychosocial Perspectives*, ed. G. Caplan & S. Lebovici. New York: Basic Books, pp. 185–212.

Tessman, L. H. (1982), A note on the father's contribution to the daughter's ways of loving and working. In: *Father and Child: Developmental and Clinical Perspectives*, ed. S. Cath, A. Gurwitt, & J. M. Ross. Boston: Little Brown, pp. 219–242.

Waller, J. V., Kaufman, M. R., & Deutsch, F. (1940), Anorexia nervosa: A psychosomatic entity. *Psychosom. Med.*, 2:3–16.

Wieder, H., & Kaplan E. (1969), Drug use in adolescents: Psychodynamic meaning and pharmacogenic effect. *The Psychoanalytic Study of the Child*, 14:399–451. New York: International Universities Press.

Wilson, C. P. (1986), The psychoanalytic psychotherapy of bulimic anorexia nervosa. *Adolescent Psychiat.*, 13:274–314.
Winnicott, D. (1962), Adolescence: Struggling through the doldrums. In: *The Family and Individual Development.* New York: Basic Books, 1965, pp. 79–87.

12

Vulnerability of Adolescents and Young Adults to "Cult" Phenomena

HEIMAN VAN DAM, M.D.

Cults continue to draw the attention of the public and the news media. Although the term "cult" is often used in a pejorative sense, especially by the news media, this is not the intent here. As will become clear, the line where cults end and other kinds of group phenomena begin cannot always easily be discerned. As a matter of fact, individuals may cross that border in either direction without there being any signs or signals to indicate to them what is going on. What distinguishes cults from other groups is the degree of involvement on the part of both leaders and members. As a result of this greater degree of involvement, certain personality changes may come about. This fact is acknowledged both by those who see cults as a danger to society and by those who defend or belong to so-called cults. Within a given cult some members may be less involved than others. As a result, some of the changes associated with cults may not be seen in all members. It must also be recognized that some people have such an inner need to be involved with a group that for them the degree of involvement can become cultlike even though the group they are involved with is not a cult.

An example is to be found in the workplace, where individuals can be observed who are totally devoted to their work, to the complete exclusion of other interests and other human involvements. One of the main motives here is devotion to the employer (or to the labor union leader). These inner needs may involve an unconscious wish to be the favorite child, i.e., the

301

favorite employee, consequent on certain childhood experiences. If the employer has a complementary unconscious wish—i.e., to be seen as the perfect parent—a vicious cycle can be set up between employer and employee. Increased devotion on the part of the employee is rewarded with increased status as favorite by the employer. Of course, when the employer plays little or no actual part in this deep involvement, the increased status may be purely psychological, or even imaginary on the part of the employee. One can see the same phenomenon occurring in the classroom between student and instructor. Here deep involvement may again be either one-sided or mutual. It is to be distinguished from the ordinary concern that student and teacher have for each other. Once again, these are relative matters and the borders are not all that distinct, especially early on in the involvement.

The phenomenon of deep involvement must be distinguished as well from the compulsive phenomenon seen popularly in the figure of the workaholic. This work compulsion, which does not primarily involve a leader (a teacher or employer), allows relationships with people other than the employer or instructor to remain intact. The compulsion serves to ward off anxiety, the cause of which is not clear to the compulsive, or is based on a conscious fear of displeasing an authority figure. In the cult phenomenon, by contrast, there is a conscious need to *please* the authority figure, as well as an identification with the aggressor. The work compulsive is devoted to work; the cult member to an individual, who may have a "cause." This cause can be religious, political, occupational, psychological, etc.; its nature is not decisive as to whether cult phenomena may be said to occur. The same cause can be taken up in both cult and noncult situations. For instance, in the same classroom may be found one A student who is very bright and hard working, and who shares an esprit de corps regarding his alma mater; another A student who is very compulsive; and a third who in reality or fantasy is too involved with the instructor. This example may help to explain why such contradictory claims are made about what constitutes a cult. What distinguishes a cult from a noncult is the degree of involvement required by the group. For instance, the Catholic Church in

America is not a cult, because 80 percent of American Catholics do not agree with or follow the church's teaching on birth control. One might object by stating that the church requires obedience to this rule. The criterion, however, is the degree of coercion used by the leadership to enforce the acceptance of a belief, as well as the tolerance toward those who do not accept the belief. In a cult there is near total compliance with all the requirements of the group. Members who make individual choices in areas prescribed by the cult are not fully involved. In what follows, the psychological changes that make it possible to give up individual choice will be described. To the individuals involved this seems a desirable state, to the point that they have never felt so free. The situation is identical to that of an individual who lives under a dictatorship but happens to agree with everything the dictator stands for. Only from the viewpoint of the outsider or "dissident" does the dictatorship appear oppressive. In addition, it will be demonstrated why adolescents and young adults are especially prone to seek solutions to their problems via groups of one kind or another. It should be emphasized, however, that groups constantly attract individuals of all ages, and examples will be included of other age groups as well.

Group Psychology

In 1921 Freud published "Group Psychology and the Analysis of the Ego." Prompted by Freud's observations on nationalism during World War I, by the postwar upheaval in Germany and Austria, and by his earlier experiences with hypnosis, it gave Freud the opportunity to explore further his structural hypothesis of the psychic apparatus. In it he described groups, not cults. The reason is obvious: the term "cult" does not have scientific status. As mentioned before, the phenomena one sees in so-called cults are more pronounced than those seen in groups generally. In this paper Freud noted the similarity of groups such as the Catholic Church or an army on the one hand and the hypnotic situation on the other. In both there is a leader and one or more followers. The follower obeys the leader and allows the leader's judgments to become his own. The follower has given up his own superego and ego ideal. The leader has become the superego and ego ideal for the follower. In more modern terminology, the superego contents have become reexternalized.

Developmentally, the small child feared the object's disapproval. Gradually the child made the wishes and prohibitions of the parent his own. This process of internalization takes place over a number of years, but is especially pronounced between the ages of 4 and 6, converting a preschooler who constantly needs to be watched into a reliable school child. The process receives its impetus from the oedipal struggle the child undergoes during this period. The fact that the superego has in large part come about through the internalization of external demands makes it possible for the reverse to occur. What is internalized can be externalized again. This is a weakness, a predisposition of the superego which, however, has its positive value.

As Harold Blum noted in a recent panel of the American Psychoanalytic Association (Tyson, 1985), "the superego is subject to modification and new identifications with objects and groups throughout life" (p. 221); "the adolescent superego reorganization, . . . because the superego is highly susceptible to environmental influences, . . . may represent varying degrees of discontinuity with the infantile past" (p. 224). This is in rather sharp contrast to older views according to which the superego is seen as a rather fixed and autonomous structure throughout life, reflecting the vicissitudes only of the infantile neurosis (Hartmann and Loewenstein, 1962). In both "normal" and disturbed individuals, then, the superego (including the ego ideal) is changeable throughout life. And groups are often a major factor in bringing about such changes. Freud's observation that groups can profoundly affect superego structure and functioning is amply confirmed by current observation. Several years ago, for instance, the Reverend Jones successfully ordered about 700 of his followers in Jonestown, Guyana, to not only commit suicide but to kill their 200 children as well. A second example is the Watergate phenomenon so well described by Rangell (1980). Charles W. Colson, he notes, had the reputation of being so devoted to the President that "He would walk over his grandmother to help reelect Nixon." Colson testified in court under oath:

> I had one rule . . . to get done that which the President wanted done. While I thought I was serving him well and faithfully, I now recognize I was not . . . at least in the sense that I never questioned whether what he wanted done was right and proper. . . . I rarely questioned a Presidential order. Infrequently did I question the President's judgment.
>
> These two things, unquestioned loyalty on the one hand and a feeling of self-sacrifice on the other, caused me to lose sight of some very fundamental precepts. . . . I lost my perspective to a point where I instinctively reacted to any criticism or interference with what I was doing or what the President was doing as unfair and as something to be retaliated against [p. 103].

In addition to changes in superego structure and function, this testimony reveals a number of other aspects of intensive group involvement. Colson's reality resting was impaired in the sense that he stopped questioning the President's judgments. Yet at the same time he continued to function well in other areas. One sees this always in group involvement—ego functions that interfere with group functioning have to be abandoned, whereas those that are not conflictual remain intact. Criticism of the leader is defended against by denial and arouses anger and withdrawal rather than evaluation. Decision making, another ego function, is interfered with in areas that are surrendered to the group.

Sometimes ego functions that are not conflictual vis-à-vis the group become impaired as well, partly because so much of the ego's energy goes into group activities and into defense mechanisms set up by the group involvement. For instance, a student may give up his studies either because the group demands he become involved in recruiting, fund raising, etc., or because he finds he has lost interest in his studies, preoccupied as he is with the group and what it stands for. Groups may control sexual activities. In certain religions sexual relations with menstruating women are forbidden. Sexual activities are to be abstained from on certain holidays. On other holidays a Mardi Gras type of sexual license is permitted in other religious or cultural settings. In some cults, sexual activities (including orgies), mass weddings, or partial to total sexual abstinence may be part of the belief system, and are rigidly adhered to. Object relationships are affected profoundly by intense group involvement. Leaders are often referred to as Father or Mother, as the case may be, and group members are experienced as siblings; often one experiences the feeling of being reborn into a new family. Ties with the "old" family are often discouraged or prohibited in order to intensify the attachment to the group and to the leader. Part of basic military training is restriction to the base; this serves to loosen ties with family, girlfriends, etc., and to create bonds within the military structure. Many groups with a religious purpose discourage all contact with the outside world, which they see as living in sin. Reading newspapers or listening to radio or television is discouraged for the same reason. The new object ties in such groups have archaic features, regressing on occasion to symbiotic ties with the leader and fellow members. This regressive clinging to the new family group is satisfying and so reinforces the need to surrender individual judgment and actions. The leader, omniscient and omnipotent, knows best. Freud compared the psychological changes occurring in group members to those attendant on falling in love. Love is blind for the same reason: a bond is maintained at the expense of ego and sometimes even superego functioning. Freud (1921) notes Shaw's "malicious aphorism to the effect that being in love means greatly exaggerating the difference between one woman and another" (p. 140).

Group involvement, then, may affect the channeling of the libidinal drive; it may also have the effect of redirecting aggression. Colson testified that criticism was responded to with retaliation. Aggression is directed away from the leader and fellow group members, and is directed instead to the outside world. Examples of this abound. One sees it in terrorist groups, and soldiers in combat will at times sacrifice their own lives to save a fellow soldier, while in the process of killing the enemy. Much of the aggression in cults becomes directed at family members, while love is reserved for those within the group. The world is divided into insiders and outsiders, good people and bad. Friendships and even marriages are given up for the sake of the group. This regressive evaluation of the world as divided into all-good and all-bad parts is a reactivation of a world view from earliest childhood. Blos (1976) has drawn attention to this phenomenon.

Because everyone is born into a group—the family—group involvement later on is very hard to resist. Parents functon not only as drive objects, but as the earliest group leaders. In order not to lose the drive object or its love the infant and the child obey—i.e., they become followers. As part of human development the individual moves from one group to the next—from the family to the school. During latency an imaginary group figures in the youngster's world: the child imagines he belongs to another family (the "family romance" phenomenon), an anticipation of what will happen in adulthood. In adolescence the opportunities expand for participation in groups. In adulthood, new groups are added: falling in love, the work place, the country club, the labor union, marriage, parenthood, Parents without Partners, and so forth.

The ubiquity of groups in human experience prompted Freud (1921) to a startling remark: "Each individual therefore has a share in numerous group minds—those of his race, of his class, of his creed, of his nationality, etc. . . . he can also raise himself above them to the extent of having a scrap of independence and originality" (p. 129). Generally, psychoanalysts tend to think of themselves as specializing in individual psychology. However, it should by now be clear that individual psychology cannot be understood in isolation from group psychology. As already indicated, it is often via groups that individuals change their superego contents. Group involvement is part of progressive development but can at times lead to regression and fixation. Erikson (1959) has drawn attention to how young people sometimes use groups to effect a "moratorium." The Army or the Peace Corps has been used for this purpose by individuals who did not feel ready for their next forward step—e.g., college or graduate school. According to Eckland and Henderson (1981), 81 percent of the college entrants in 1972 had left college by 1976. One third of these eventually returned. What percentage join groups of one kind or another during this period is unknown, but very likely it is quite high. Some students who drop out join cults and may not always be able to extricate themselves. The deeper the involvement, the stronger the tie with the group becomes and the less cathexis remains available for objects and interests outside the group.

The Adolescent Process as It Relates to Group Psychology

What distinguishes the adolescent's group involvement from that occurring earlier and later is its intensity and degree of involvement. Latency children participate in groups—the school, Little League, scouts, etc.—but usually there is no problem connected with this; as a result, little attention is paid in the analytic literature to group phenomena during this period. Often the parent has selected the school, the Brownie troop, etc., for the child. Group participation becomes a problem only if the child's involvement becomes too great. A child who loses interest in schoolwork and is interested only in after-school drama lessons arouses anxiety in the parent. In latency the tie to the parent is sufficiently strong that this creates a conflict for the child, but in adolescence this tie is sufficiently loosened that parental concern over the group involvement can easily be brushed aside: "It's my life, isn't it?" As a matter of fact, it is precisely in order to loosen this tie that the adolescent needs to find activities, including participation in groups, that are different from what the parents might want. Some upheaval with parents—the generation gap—is a healthy and normal sign during this period. The only question of concern is whether the group is helpful in the long run as well as the short run. Upon joining a cult, many people report signs of improvement—drug habits are given up, depression and anxiety are diminished, sexual conflicts disappear, etc. What is most striking and tragic about a film depicting life in Jonestown a few months before the mass suicide is that so many of the cultists reported how happy they were. Perhaps they were ordered or "brainwashed" to say this, but the matter goes deeper. Intrapsychic changes brought about by group involvement eventuate in structural change. The result may be a relief of tension.

What one needs to determine is the degree of involvement with the new group. Does involvement go to the point where independent judgment is surrendered in some areas? Do the new object ties lead not only to a decathexis of the ties to one's parents and siblings, but also of those to friends and "worldly pursuits"? Has the adolescent substituted group addiction for drug addiction, speaking in tongues for psychedelic experience? In other words, what price relief?

The need for new groups is very strong in adolescence, because the need to distance oneself from one's parents and siblings is much greater then than at any other time. Sexual feelings and fantasies about family members were acceptable during prelatency and repressed during latency. But the increased intensity of the sexual drive in adolescence requires defenses and new solutions. One solution is the reversal of affect. Instead of feeling closer to the parents, the child now treats them like strangers. As a result the adolescent is lonely and in need of companionship. In early adolescence heterosexual companionship is unpredictable and unreliable at best—for a variety of reasons, including the fact that adolescents may seek pregenital outlets for their drives (e.g., overeating). Such adolescents have yet to develop the ego skills to cope with a newly intensified genital drive. The adolescent ego is threatened also by the awareness that many of its defenses are identifications with parental figures. As such, these defenses become too conflictual during this period. Before new ego skills are developed, regression in ego functioning may occur. New groups offer not only a new family, but also help the ego cope with the increased strength of the libidinal and aggressive drives. A similar crisis occurs also in the superego. As children enter adolescence, much of their superego is derived from the parents. In order to differentiate themselves from the parents and the family, adolescents and young adults need to find new values and new prohibitions. In addition, much of the superego's content has outgrown its usefulness. For instance, the superego of the latency child helps in the repression of oedipal wishes, masturbation, and interest in the opposite sex. In adolescence all this changes. Via new groups the superego changes—masturbation becomes acceptable; interest in the opposite sex is a matter of shame no longer, but a matter of pride. In short, the adolescent needs groups because of changes in the drives, the ego, and the superego. The need to distance oneself from the family in the attempt to become an individual contributes also to this search for new groups. What makes the adolescent vulnerable to groups with a regressive appeal is the fact that in adolescence changes going on within the individual occasion reactions marked by temporary regression. Well attuned to this, such groups often approach adolescents by first inviting them to a rap session and a free meal. This appeals to their loneliness and to the pregenital oral regression of the libidinal drive. At this meeting there may be singing and dancing, as well as a presentation of a new belief system or political philosophy, one entirely different from that of the family. This often seems like an answer to the adolescent superego and ego ideal crisis, as new explanations and solutions are given for the imperfections of the world. As in hypnosis, once recruits become involved they are ordered to do certain things; for instance, they are told they cannot leave until the weekend is over. Recruits thus become dependent, the price paid for acceptance by the group and for the relief it provides from the unresolved problems of adolescence.

Nothing has been said so far about individuals with psychopathology. To join groups, it is not at all necessary for an individual to be seriously disturbed. Participation in groups is in fact a requisite of normal development. But individuals with serious pathology, who evince regressions and fixations, are more likely than others to be drawn to groups that foster regression.

References

Blos, P. (1976), The split parental imago in adolescent social relations: An inquiry into group psychology. *The Psychoanalytic Study of the Child,* 31:7–33. New Haven: Yale University Press.

Bornstein, S. (1935), A child analysis. *Psychoanal. Quart.,* 4:190–225.

Calder, K. C. (1979), Panel report: Psychoanalytic knowledge of group process. *J. Amer. Psychoanal. Assn.,* 27:145–156.

Eckland, B. K., & Henderson, L. B. (1981), College attainment for years after high school. Research Triangle Park, NC: Research Triangle Institute.

Erikson, E. H. (1959), Late adolescence. In: *A Way of Looking at Things. Selected Papers of Erik H. Erikson from 1930 to 1980,* ed. S. Schlein. New York: Norton.

Freud, A. (1963), The concept of developmental lines. *The Psychoanalytic Study of the Child,* 18:248–258. New York: International Universities Press.

Freud, S. (1921), Group psychology and the analysis of the ego. *Standard Edition,* 18:69–143. London: Hogarth Press, 1955.

Hartmann, H., & Loewenstein, R. M. (1962), Notes on the superego. *The Psychoanalytic Study of the Child,* 17:42–81. New York: International Universities Press.

Katan, A. (1951), The role of "displacement" in agoraphobia. *Internat. J. Psycho-Anal.,* 32:41–50.

McDevitt, B. (1967), A separation problem in a three-year old girl. In: *The Child Analyst at Work,* ed. E. R. Geleerd. New York: International Universities Press.

Rangell, L. (1980), *The Mind of Watergate.* New York: Norton.

Tyson, P. (1985), Panel report: Perspectives on the superego. *J. Amer. Psychoanal. Assn.,* 33:217–231.

13

The Sleeping Beauty: Escape from Change

HILDE BRUCH, M.D.

When the little princess, on her fifteenth birthday, examined the spindle of a spinning wheel, she pricked herself and began to bleed; thereupon she fell into a deep sleep. A hedge of roses grew around the castle, and she kept on sleeping until finally awakened by a prince who had cut through the hedge of thorns. The fairytale conveys the idea that adolescence and growing up have always confronted youngsters with challenges and tasks from which some would withdraw. The fairytale explains the princess's long sleep as caused by a curse at the time of her birth. We are inclined to relate such reluctance to face new tasks to developmental disturbances. The fairytale gives modern sounding information along this line. The princess was an only, late-born child, excessively loved and overvalued by her parents and everyone else, a paragon of virtue and obedience during her childhood.

Escape from adolescence takes many forms and, as Bettelheim (1976) points out, a certain passivity may be a normal reaction; the transition to abnormal states may be vague. Some, when they feel the pressures and demands are too much, may change the meaning of their experiences, create a different symbolic reality for themselves, and suffer a schizophrenic breakdown. Others use drugs or stimulants to change the way their mind experiences reality; this too may lead to withdrawal from ordinary living. Still others, in a counterphobic declaration of independence, make the social demands the scapegoat, fight them openly, break the rules and mores, and become delin-

313

quent, or they join radical political groups or strange religious
cults.

I shall focus here on adolescents who in this struggle for
specialness change their own body and thus set themselves apart
and avoid demands which to them are unacceptable. By excessive food intake they will increase their size, or they accomplish
the opposite, severe emaciation with the undoing of the biological pubescence, through rigid discipline, hyperactivity, and
severe dietary restrictions (Bruch, 1973c). Such youngsters
carry the badge of their incompetence and suffering in an externally visible way.

The conditions are referred to clinically as *developmental
obesity* (Bruch, 1957a) and *anorexia nervosa*. Though they look
like extreme opposites, they have many features in common.
The eating function is misused in an effort to solve or camouflage problems of living that appear otherwise insoluble. If
this fails or is interfered with, be it by premature reducing in
obesity or forced feeding in anorexia, the symptomatology of
borderline states of schizophrenic disorganization may become
manifest, a measure of the severity of the underlying psychological disturbance (Bruch, 1957b, 1973a).

In both conditions severe disturbances in body image and
self-concept are dominant. These youngsters do not feel identified with their bodies but look upon them as external objects
over which they must exercise rigid control (anorexia nervosa)
or in relation to which they feel helpless (obesity) (Bruch,
1973b). Though stubbornness and negativism are conspicuous
in the clinical picture, these youngsters suffer, behind this fa-
cade, from a devastating sense of ineffectiveness. They feel
powerless to control their bodies and also to direct their lives
in general. They experience themselves as empty and as controlled by others. They are helpess and ineffective in all their
functioning, neither self-directed nor truly separate from others, and they lack a sense of ownership of their own bodies.
They act and behave as if they were the misshapen and wrong
product of somebody else's action, as if their center of gravity
was not within themselves. They lack discriminating awareness
of bodily needs; specifically they are inaccurate in identifying
hunger. They also are inaccurate in recognizing other states of

bodily discomfort, such as cold or fatigue, or in discrminating bodily tensions from anxiety, depression, or other psychological stress.

These deficits in the sense of ownership and control of the body color the way these youngsters face their problems of living, their relationships to others. With approaching adolescence they are poorly equipped to become self-sufficient and to emancipate themselves from their dependency on their mothers and families. Frequently they feel deprived of the support and recognition from their peers which help normal adolescents in this process of liberation.

A number of questions offer themselves. Why are these youngsters so unprepared to meet the challenge of adolescence and to engage in relationships with their age group? What goes on in families who fail to transmit an adequate sense of competence and self-value to a child? How is it possible for a bodily function as basic as eating to develop in a way that it can be misused to camouflage other problems and lead to abnormal changes in bodily size?

Biological Aspects

The bodily deviations are so dramatic that there has been a continuous search for some constitutional or physiological explanation (Bruch, 1973a). The quest for some endocrine factor which would explain the conditions has stood in the foreground. This was pursued in the hope of discovering some substance the injection of which would cure the abnormal weight and do away with all problems. Though the methods of study have become much more refined and many neuroendocrine changes have been described, there is no evidence that endocrine factors precipitate the condition. On the other hand, the abnormal nutritional states are associated with secondary changes, including the neuroendocrine pathways and metabolic transformations. Many of the physiological abnormalities that are often cited to explain the disorders are the consequence of the abnormal nutrition. Once abnormal metabolic patterns have been developed, in particular those due to overnutrition, they have a tendency to become self-perpetuating. Obesity becomes treatment resistant, scarcely influenced by short-term diets.

Psychological Development

Psychoanalysis has played a significant role in the effort to understand the psychological development of these youngsters. It was a revolutionary step when Freud, at the turn of the century, drew attention to the importance of psychic forces within human nature. Expressed in the simplest possible language, his outstanding contribution to psychiatry and to the science of human behavior was the recognition that mental illness was related to the way an individual had functioned before he became manifestly sick.

He was biological in his basic orientation when he pointed out that human behavior and psychological development, and their neurotic or psychotic distortions, were related to the way biological need (which he called *Triebe,* a word subsequently translated as *instinct*) was met and satisfied (Freud, 1905). He traced the whole gamut of emotional development, character, and symptom formation to the instinctual drives and the more fortunate or hapless ways in which they developed.

Throughout his life Freud struggled to revise his theory, and he remained critical of all his efforts to formulate a fixed theory of instinct. He defined instinct as "a borderline concept between the mental and the physical, being both the mental representative of the stimuli emanating from within the organism and penetrating to the mind, and at the same time the measure of the demands made upon the energy of the latter in consequence of its connection with the body" (Freud, 1915).

When Freud defined his concept of libido, he did it as a parallel to hunger, which he thought of as the instinct of nutrition. "Everyday language possesses no counterpart of the word 'hunger' but science makes use of the word 'libido' for that purpose." Hunger is such a common word that it is easily overlooked as a rather complex concept with many different meanings. Hunger is used to refer to the physiological state of nutritional depletion or severe food deprivation, or to long continued starvation, namely the complex, unpleasant, and compelling sensation an individual feels when deprived of food, resulting in searching, even fighting, for food to relieve torment. In the more pleasant form of desire for a particular food it is called "appetite," and it plays an important role in our eating habits (Bruch, 1969).

There is a third way in which the word "hunger" is used, namely, as a symbolic expression of a state of need in general, as a simile for want in other areas. In analytic explorations the emphasis has been mainly on the symbolic significance of the abnormal food intake. In anorexia nervosa it had been a standard explanation that the food refusal and weight loss symbolized unconscious fear of oral impregnation (Waller, Kaufman, and Deutsch, 1940). It was felt that this explained why these youngsters shied away from adolescence. In obesity too many different symbolic meanings of the abnormal food intake were recognized. Food may symbolically stand for an insatiable desire for unobtainable love, or an expression of rage and hatred; it may substitute for sexual gratification or indicate ascetic denial; it may represent the wish to be a man and possess a penis, or the wish to be pregnant, or the fear of it (Hamburger, 1951). It may help to achieve a spurious sense of power and self-aggrandizement, or it may serve as a defense against adulthood and responsibility. This incomplete list indicates that food may carry an enormous variety of different, often contradictory, connotations.

Traditionally it had been assumed that bringing such underlying conflicts into consciousness would result in the abandonment of the abnormal symptoms. Neither in obesity nor in anorexia nervosa does insight into the various symbolic conflicts bring about improvement or affect the way these youngsters approach life and view themselves (Bruch, 1970). They may talk fluently about the unconscious meaning of their behavior. Such insight is only a thing they passively accept from their therapists, but which they are unable to assimilate for their own living. It was recognized that patients with eating disorders suffer from a basic disturbance in the way the sensation of hunger is experienced, and this is closely interrelated to the broad spectrum of their other psychological disturbances. Pursuit of this question led to the formulation that hunger, the ability to recognize nutritional need, is not an innate capacity of the organism but something that contains important elements of learning (Bruch, 1969). In patients with eating disorders something has gone wrong in the experiential and interpersonal processes surrounding the satisfaction of nutritional and other bodily needs. As a result, such individuals are incorrect and confused in recognizing "hunger," the need to eat, and in differentiating it from signals of bodily discomfort or emotional tension that have nothing to do with food deprivation and may be aroused by the greatest variety of conflicts and problems.

Once the question was formulated in this way, evidence of a deficit in hunger awareness rapidly accumulated. Anorexic patients will spontaneously declare, "I do not need to eat," and seem to mean it literally. Actually they have taught themselves to disregard the sensation or to transform it into something pleasurable (Bruch, 1978). Basically they suffer from the fear of having no control over their eating; at times they are overpowered by the urge to gorge themselves, and bulimia with vomiting become troublesome symptoms. Fat people, when questioned on this point, will answer with an immediate sense of recognition that all their lives they had suffered from an inability to know whether or not they needed food or had had enough.

Corroborative Observations

Direct observations on the ability to recognize correctly the nutritional state have given support to these theoretical considerations. Measured amounts of food were introduced into the stomachs of subjects of normal and abnormal weight. Marked individual differences were observed in the accuracy of recognizing whether or not, and how much, food had been received. Some healthy normal subjects were consistently accurate; others, though of normal weight, were less so. However, obese and anorexic patients were significantly more inaccurate (Coddington and Bruch, 1970). Stunkard (1969) reported that, during the presence of stomach contractions, fasting obese women usually failed to report awareness of hunger, or epigastric emptiness, or a desire to eat, whereas nonobese women usually would report such sensations.

Through a series of ingenious experiments in which external factors were manipulated, Schachter (1968) showed that obese subjects were affected in their eating habits by external cues, such as the sign of food, its availability, and apparent passage of time, whereas subjects of normal weight eat according to enteroceptive determinants. Physiologists have been familiar with this for some time. Hebb (1949), summarizing his experiences and those of others, concluded that the sensation of hunger was not inborn, and that the state of nutritional deprivation was apt to be disruptive of food-seeking behavior. Wolff (1966) observed in neonate infants that hunger has a disorganizing effect on goal-directed activities, after an initial augmenting phase.

Many observations on the functional deficits of animals reared in isolation point in the same direction. Monkeys raised on cloth-covered wire dummies, referred to as "mothers," but without access to other live monkeys, were grossly abnormal when fully grown, apathetic, stereotyped in their responses, suffering from abiding affectional deficiency, incapable of grooming behavior, exhibiting many bizarre mouthing habits, and inadequate in sex behavior, though having undergone physiological puberty (Harlow and Harlow, 1966).

Infancy

The older psychoanalytic vocabulary has the implication that the infant in some fairly adequate though not necessarily conscious ways knows how he feels and what he wants, and furthermore that, unless forced to repress this knowledge by specific prohibitions from the environment, he is perfectly capable of utilizing whatever opportunities the environment presents for the satisfaction of his needs. But there is no evidence that the infant knows that his actions are his own, that he had initiated them, or that they are in any way related to his finding satisfaction. It must be assumed that the human infant starts life, in his subjective experience, unable to differentiate himself from others, and his biological needs are unidentified and unidentifiable states of tension and discomfort. The achievement of the sense of separateness is the outcome of developmental experiences which are of crucial significance for the later sense of effective identity. How does a normal child learn an integrated concept of his bodily existence as separate from the outside? And how does he become aware of his having control over his own sensations and impulses and mastery in his interpersonal and social relationships? And what miscarries in the development of those who fail to achieve this?

Another tradition has it that the infant is utterly helpless, completely dependent on the environment. This model of infantile development neglects the fact that there are intraorganistic processes that need to become distinct to him. A one-sided concept of the child being a helpless receiver of the adult's administration neglects the fact that the infant, though immature, gives the cues and signals indicating his disequilibrium, wants, and needs. How they are responded to, fulfilled, or neglected appears to be the crucial point for his becoming conscious of his needs and for developing a sense of separate identity and control over his body (Bruch, 1973e).

Two basic forms of behavior, namely behavior initiated in the infant and behavior in response to stimuli from the outside, need to be differentiated from birth on. This distinction applies to both the biological and the social-emotional field and also to pleasure- or pain-provoking states. The mother's behavior in relation to the child is either responsive or stimulating. The interaction between the environment and the infant can be rated as appropriate or inappropriate depending on whether it serves the fulfillment of his factual need or whether it disregards or distorts his cues. These elemental distinctions permit the dynamic analysis, irrespective of the specific area or content of the problem, of an amazingly large variety of clinical situations.

Appropriate responses to cues coming from the infant, in the biological field as well as in the social and emotional field, are necessary for the child to organize the significant building

stones for the development of self-awareness and self-effec-
tiveness. If confirmation and reinforcement of his own initially
rather undifferentiated needs and impulses have been absent,
or have been contradictory or inaccurate, then a child will grow
up perplexed when trying to differentiate between disturbances
in his biological field and emotional and interpersonal experiences, and he will be apt to misinterpret deformities in his
self-body concept as externally induced. Thus he will become
an individual deficient in his sense of separateness, with "diffuse
ego boundaries." He will also feel helpless under the impact of
bodily urges, as if controlled from the outside, as if not owning
his own body.

The confusion in hunger awareness, the deep fear of having no inner controls from which patients with eating disorders
suffer, can be related to these early experiences. These children
were well cared for in every physical detail, but things were
done according to the mother's decisions and feelings, not according to the child's expressions of need. A mother who is
sensitively atttuned to her child offers food when he shows signs
of nutritional deprivation; gradually the child learns to recognize "hunger" as a distinct sensation. If a mother's reactions are
inappropriate or contradictory—neglectful, oversolicitous, or
inhibiting—the child fails to learn to differentiate between hunger and other sources of discomfort, and grows up without a
discriminating awareness of his bodily sensations, without the
conviction of having control over them.

If a mother's concepts are not out of line with the child's
physiological needs, everything may look normal on the surface.
When she overestimates the child's needs, or when she uses
food indiscriminately as a universal pacifier, she will produce
a fat child (Bruch, 1940). In normal-looking children with this
background, the gross deficit in initiative and active self-awareness becomes manifest only when confronted with new situations and demands. If every tension is experienced as "need to
eat" instead of arousing anxiety, anger, or other appropriate
reactions, he will become progressively obese. The anorexic
tries to compensate for these deficits in inner control in an
exaggerated way by overrigid discipline and denial of hunger.

The early feeding histories of many fat and anorexic pa-

322

HILDE BRUCH

tients have been reconstructed in great detail. Often they are
conspicuous by their blandness. The parents feel there is nothing to report: The child never gave any trouble, ate exactly
what was put before him; the mother was the envy of her friends
and neighbors because her child did not fuss about food, nor
was he difficult in other ways. Others will report with pride that
they always "anticipated" their child's needs, never permitting
him to "feel hungry."

Evidence from Studies of Child Development

It would be impossible to include in this brief discussion
any of the wealth and detailed observations of child development that bear on the problem under discussion. The model
of development as circular, reciprocal transactions between parent and child is in good agreement with other studies of infancy,
though, as far as I know, no one has expressed this in quite
such simple and general terms. Discussions of the psychological
events of the first year of life have become much more detailed
and clearly defined. They no longer focus on a particular
"trauma" during one or the other specific phases, but on the
steps necessary for progressive maturation and on the ongoing
interpersonal patterns that encourage or hinder this progress.

Piaget (1954) spoke of these reciprocal processes as "accommodation," the transformation induced in the child's perceptual schemata and behavior patterns by the environment,
and "assimilation," the incorporation of objects and characteristics of the environment into the child's patterns of perceptual
behavior, with corresponding transformation of these objects.
He thinks of the total developmental growth of biological adaptation as a dynamic equilibrium between the processes of
accommodation and assimilation. The organization of the stimuli from the infant's own biological needs into recognizable
patterns is here considered part of the mode of experience
Piaget calls assimilation.

Spitz (1945) stressed the importance of adequate maternal
care for proper physiological and mental development when
describing the poignant fate of neglected infants. The earliest

mode of experience, which he called "coenesthetic" perception, he considered to be present at birth (Spitz, 1965). Escalona (1963) speaks of the infant's experience as the matrix of his psychological growth and gives many details of the transactions between mother and child as reciprocal. She considers such experiences, with their countless and successive adaptations, essential for normal as well as disturbed development. However, she considers "hunger" an innate biological given. Mahler (1963) describes in detail the individuation-separation processes as circular, when infants were observed in the actual presence of their mothers. She considers the earliest period of infancy a "symbiotic phase," during which the mother needs to strike a balance between frustration of and intrusion on the infant's "inborn wisdom" of his needs.

An interesting example of pathogenic, nonappropriate transactional patterns between a mother and her two small children was described by Henry (1961) in his naturalistic observation of the families who had produced a hospitalized schizophrenic child. His overall summation of her attitude toward the feeding of the children was that it was "biologically markedly inappropriate." They showed a series of patterned elements, of the mother overpowering the children with food when they rejected it after they had been left to cry to a high pitch of exhaustion, or her disregarding defensive maneuvers against this forced feeding, often in terms that seemed inappropriate.

In a study aimed at defining factors involved in the development of a child's attachment to his mother, Ainsworth and Bell (1969) observed that the differentiating factors in the feeding situation during the first three months of life were not related to the technique of feeding, such as schedule versus demand, or breast versus bottle feeding, but to the relevance of the mother's responses to the signals of the child's needs. When observed at 1 year, the child's trusting attachment to the mother but also readiness to explore were related to the sensitivity and appropriateness with which the mother had interacted with her child. Some mothers would overfeed the baby, either by treating too broad a spectrum of cues as signals of hunger or in an effort to produce a baby who would demand little attention and would sleep for long periods. Such babies, who were rated "overweight" by their pediatricians at age 3 months, continued to be overweight at 1 year. Yet they differed in the security of their attachment to the mother and readiness to separate, depending on the intent of the overfeeding.

Erikson's model (1968) of the "epigenesis of identity" is that of a continuous interaction between the individual and his surroundings, with a special task at each developmental phase of the life cycle. He considers the most fundamental prerequisite of mental vitality the experience of a sense of basic trust, a pervasive attitude toward oneself and the world derived from the experiences of the first year of life, with a fundamental sense of one's own trustworthiness. He did not specifically mention one's awareness of and control over one's biological functions as part of this basic trust, nor does his formulation exclude this. His emphasis is on psychological awareness; but without the sense of "ownership of one's body," the sense of being "all right" probably cannot be experienced. Erikson postpones the development of the sense of autonomy to the next phase in development which includes toilet training. He feels that the mutual regulation between adult and child is severely tested during this phase. Actually this mutual regulation has been operative since the first day of life in the feeding situation, where one child learns to demand or reject food according to need, while another will fail to acquire this discriminating awareness, unable to reject the feeding his mother imposes on him. Lack of control over eating is associated with a devastating deficit in having an autonomous and self-directed self.

Early Childhood

The leitmotif in the reconstructed developmental histories of these youngsters is supergoodness, "never any trouble." Parents will report with gratitude and pride how easy it had been to raise this particular child, who had been clean, obedient, and considerate. Not one expressed concern about the lack of initiative and autonomy that this type of obedient behavior implies. In anorexia nervosa oppositional behavior during the classical period of resistance is conspicuously absent. Instead of testing their capacities for self-reliance and a will of their own, these children slavishly adhere to the rules and concepts laid down by their parents. The youngsters themselves describe later their relationships with their parents, particularly their mothers, as unusually close, that they always knew what the other was thinking. This mind-reading quality continues to the time of the illness. During family sessions it is often difficult to determine in whose name anyone is speaking, something I have called "confusion of pronouns."

The individuation and separation of the child from the mother that are expected to occur during late infancy and early childhood (Mahler, Pine, and Bergman, 1975) take place only to a limited extent. The one-sidedness with which care was imposed during infancy has left the child deficient in self-trust and capacity for self-assertion. Efforts at separation will be weak at best. A mother who needs this child to feel complete or as proof of her own perfection might show displeasure when the child makes attempts to move away and will not encourage expressions of individual initiative. Overconformity remains the pattern of childhood behavior. In the few instances where there had been a psychiatric consultation before the manifest illness, the reason was a change away from overcompliance, as if that were the norm; efforts at self-assertion were treated as disturbances. The outcome is a serious deficit in the sense of self, of being a self-directed, unified person. They take all cues and rules from the outside, continuously worrying how they look in the eyes of others, with strained efforts at outguessing what the grownups expect them to do or to be (Bruch, 1977).

Early disturbances in inner representation of the self and objects interfere not only with emotional but also with overall conceptual development. We have learned from Inhelder and Piaget (1955) that conceptual development goes through definite phases which though partly innate require, for appropriate development, interactions with an encouraging environment. Potentially anorexic youngsters cling to the style of thinking of early childhood, the period of egocentricity, of preconceptual and concrete operations. The next steps culminating in the capacity for formal operations, the ability to perform new abstract thinking and evaluations that are characteristic of adolescent development, are deficient in them or completely absent.

The discovery of real defects in conceptualization came as a surprise since anorexic patients usually excel in their school performance, and this has been interpreted as indicating great ability and intelligence. Not uncommonly, the excellent academic achievements are the result of great effort which becomes even greater after they become ill. Sometimes it comes as a shocking surprise that performance on college aptitude tests or other evaluations of general ability fall short of what the excellent school grades had suggested. As a group, these patients are what one might call academic overachievers.

A much more serious indication of a disharmonious development is found in their everyday thinking, in their rigid interpretation of human relationships, and in their defective self-evaluation and self-concept. A symptom that has been puzzling for a long time is a nearly delusional disturbance in "body image"; they are unable to "see" themselves and their severe emaciation or obesity realistically (Bruch, 1973c; Garner and Garfinkel, 1977). This distortion must be viewed as part of a much wider pattern of misperceptions.

They continue to function with the morality of a young child, remaining convinced of the absolute rightness of the grownups and of their own obligation to be obedient. Following their own inclinations or expressing desires of their own has never occurred to them. This overcompliance extends to minute details in everyday living. They accept presents of their parents' choosing, what they are "supposed" to get, and dare not express wishes of their own, either because they do not have independent wishes or because they do not want to disappoint the giver by expressing a wish for something different.

Prepuberty

The excessive closeness with the parents persists or increases throughout childhood. Not uncommonly each parent seeks affection and confirmation from this, their perfect child, who may function as a go-between and compensate them for their deep dissatisfaction with each other (Selvini, 1974). A child's feelings of worth and importance may derive from being needed by each parent, and the recognition they get outside the home seems less rewarding. With all efforts going into satisfying the parents, little energy is left for personal development. With the new demands of puberty and adolescence, their inner emptiness is laid bare (Bruch, 1971).

Distortions in self-concept are also expressed in behavior outside the home. They usually are hard-working students who are praised for their devotion to work and for being helpful with less advantaged students. School is the place where they receive measurable acknowledgment of their efforts, and this may be a positive and sustaining experience. Others, even when praised for excellent work, are not satisfied. They may compare themselves to a sibling or friend who is more gifted in a certain field, or belittle what they themselves achieve because it comes easy. As times goes on the demands they make on themselves become more and more unrealistic; only the most exhausting work is adequate. Some are in competition with themselves, living in fear of performing less well when they continue with work in which they have been successful, sometimes giving it up as a result.

Friendship patterns reveal the same overcompliant adaptation to others that characterizes their whole life. They may have a series of friendships, only one friend at a time. With each new friend they will develop different interests and a different personality. They conceive of themselves as blanks who just go along with what the friend wants and enjoys, as if having nothing of their own to contribute. One such anorexic girl, who later in college became quite popular, was disturbed by not feeling like her own person in relation to others. She described one episode: "I was sitting with these three people but I felt a terrible fragmentation of myself. There wasn't a person inside at all. I tried with whoever I was with to reflect the image they had of me, to do what they expected me to do. There were three different people and I had to be a different person to each, and I had to balance that. It was the same when I was a child and had friends. It was always in response to what they wanted."

Some take care of the newcomers in school or of others who are in some way handicapped and do not belong to any particular group. Over and over they repeat the painful experience that these lame duck friends gain a position in some group and leave them behind. If they have one particular friend, they are invariably in the role of follower. Even a seemingly active social life may be an expression of overcompliance with continuous concern: "What do they say about me? Do they like me, do they think I'm right?"

Social isolation is part of the picture of adolescent obesity and anorexia and is usually explained as being due to the abnormal state. Actually they have begun to isolate themselves much earlier. Some will explain that they withdrew from their friends, others that they felt they were being excluded. Some are critical of the social activities of the others, particularly of the girls who are interested in dating and parties, and express their disagreement with the values of their peers in rather condescending and judgmental terms. They complain that the others are too childish, too superficial, too much interested in boys, or in other ways do not live up to the ideal of perfection according to which they themselves function and adherence to which they also demand of others. These youngsters cling with superstitious fervor to the rules of living they had accepted for themselves when they were quite young. The new ways of acting and thinking of normal adolescents are strange and frightening to them. Increasingly they grow out of step with their age group and the illness becomes manifest.

Adolescence

Puberty signals the end of childhood and is associated with marked changes in appearance and bodily functions, in psychological awareness and social demands. A childhood of compliant accommodation and of fulfilling other people's expectations has left these youngsters ill prepared for positive self-assertion, which becomes unavoidable with adolescence, when an attitude of "fitting in" is no longer appropriate. They are least prepared for the bodily changes of pubescence, which they consider alarming and unacceptable. The rapid growth, the new body configuration, the onset of menstruation, and most of all the increase in weight are frightening experiences. The increased appetite that accompanies the growth spurt convinces them that their body is out of control.

All adolescents, particularly girls, are preoccupied with the attractiveness of their appearance, specifically their weight. Those with early deficits in hunger awareness become obsessed with the problem of size and seem unable to solve it realistically. They do not feel identified with their body, but consider it an ugly thing which they are condemned to carry through life. Deeply dissatisfied with their appearance, they are hypercritical about any flaw in perfection and ashamed of their appetite, which they condemn as greediness. Those who become obese give in to the desire to eat, without self-regulation and inner control; and by misinterpreting any dissatisfaction and mood disturbance as "need to eat," they become progressively heavier, feel despised for being fat, and withdraw from the activities of their age group. Anorexics exercise discipline and control in an exaggerated way, but however low a weight they reach, they still feel "too fat" and become withdrawn and socially isolated. Whether fat or thin, they do not "see" themselves realistically and suffer serious disturbances in body image and body concept. Their obsessive concern with their appearance reflects their conviction of inner inadequacy and ugliness. At the same time they indulge in dreams of unheard-of achievement and superspecialness. These dreams include the hope that one day they will be magically released from their isolation, inner ugliness, and despised body. This point needs to be clarified before they will be ready to engage in meaningful therapy.

References

Ainsworth, M. D. S., & Bell, S. M. (1969), Some contemporary patterns of mother-infant interaction in the feeding situation. In: *Stimulation in Early Infancy*, ed. A. Ambrose. New York: Academic Press.

Bettelheim, B. (1976), *The Uses of Enchantment: The Meaning and Importance of Fairy Tales.* New York: Knopf.

Bruch, H. (1940), Obesity in childhood: III. Physiologic and psychologic aspects of the food intake of obese children. *Amer. J. Dis. Child.*, 58:738–781.

—————— (1957a), Developmental obesity. In: *The Importance of Overweight.* New York: Norton, pp. 227–243.

—————— (1957b), Weight and psychosis. In: *The Importance of Overweight.* New York: Norton, pp. 267–297.

—————— (1969), Hunger and instinct. *J. Nerv. & Ment. Dis.*, 149:91–114.

—————— (1970), Psychotherapy in eating disorders. *Internat. Psychiat. Clin.*, 7:335–351.

—————— (1971), Family transactions in eating disorders. *Comprehensive Psychiat.*, 12:238–248.

—————— (1973a), Biological basis of eating disorders. In: *Eating Disorders: Obesity, Anorexia Nervosa and the Person Within.* New York: Basic Books.

—————— (1973b), Body image and self-awareness. In: *Eating Disorders: Obesity, Anorexia Nervosa and the Person Within.* New York: Basic Books.

—————— (1973c), *Eating Disorders: Obesity, Anorexia Nervosa and the Person Within.* New York: Basic Books.

—————— (1973d), Evolution of a psychotherapeutic approach. In: *Eating Disorders: Obesity, Anorexia Nervosa and the Person Within.* New York: Basic Books.

—————— (1973e), Hunger awareness and individuation. In: *Eating Disorders: Obesity, Anorexia Nervosa and the Person Within.* New York: Basic Books.

—————— (1973f), Obesity and schizophrenia. In: *Eating Disorders: Obesity, Anorexia Nervosa and the Person Within.* New York: Basic Books.

—————— (1977), Psychological antecedents of anorexia nervosa. In: *Anorexia Nervosa*, ed. R. Vigersky. New York: Raven Press, p. 1–10.

—————— (1978), *The Golden Cage: The Enigma of Anorexia Nervosa.* Cambridge: Harvard University Press.

Coddington, R. D., & Bruch, H. (1970), Gastric perceptivity in normal, obese and schizophrenic subjects. *Psychosomatics*, 11:571–579.

Erikson, E. H. (1968), *Identity, Youth and Crisis.* New York: Norton.

Escalona, S. K. (1963), Patterns of infantile experience and the developmental process. *The Psychoanalytic Study of the Child*, 18:197–244. New York: International Universities Press.

Freud, S. (1905), Three essays on the theory of sexuality. *Standard Edition*, 7:130–243. London: Hogarth Press, 1953.

—————— (1915), Instincts and their vicissitudes. *Standard Edition*, 14:111–140. London: Hogarth Press, 1957.

Garner, D. M., & Garfinkel, P. E. (1977), Measurement of body image in anorexia nervosa. In: *Anorexia Nervosa*, ed. R. Vigersky. New York: Raven Press, pp. 27–30.

Hamburger, W. W. (1951), Emotional aspects of obesity. *Med. Clin. No. Amer.*, 33:483–491.

Harlow, H. F., & Harlow, M. (1966), Learning to love. *American Scientist*, 52:244–272.

Hebb, D. O. (1949), *Organization of Behavior.* New York: Wiley.

Henry, J. (1961), The naturalistic observation of the families of psychotic children. In: *Recent Research Looking Toward Preventive Intervention*, ed. R. H. Ojemann. Iowa City: State University of Iowa, pp. 119–137.

Inhelder, B., & Piaget, J. (1955), *The Growth of Logical Thinking from Childhood to Adolescence: An Essay on the Construction of Formal Operational Structures*. New York: Basic Books.

Mahler, M. (1963), Thoughts about development and individuation. *The Psychoanalytic Study of the Child*, 18:307–327. New York: International Universities Press.

——— Pine, F., & Bergman, A. (1975), *The Psychological Birth of the Human Infant*. New York: Basic Books.

Piaget, J. (1954), *The Construction of Reality in the Child*. New York: Basic Books.

Schachter, S. (1968), Obesity and eating. *Science*, 161:751–756.

Selvini, M. P. (1974), *Self-Starvation: From the Intraphysic to the Transpersonal Approach to Anorexia Nervosa*. London: Chaucer.

Spitz, R. A. (1945), Hospitalism: An inquiry into the genesis of psychiatric conditions in early childhood. *The Psychoanalytic Study of the Child*, 1:53–74. New York: International Universities Press.

——— (1965), *The First Year of Life*. New York: International Universities Press.

Stunkard, A. (1969), Obesity and the denial of hunger. *Psychosom. Med.*, 21:281–290.

Waller, J. V., Kaufman, M. R., & Deutsch, F. (1940), Anorexia nervosa: A psychosomatic entity. *Psychosom. Med.*, 2:3–16.

Wolff, P. H. (1966), The causes, controls, and organization of behavior in the neonate. *Psychological Issues*, Monograph 17. New York: International Universities Press.

14

Contributions of an Innovative Psychoanalytic Therapeutic Program with Adolescent Delinquents to Developmental Psychology

MILTON F. SHORE, PH.D.
JOSEPH L. MASSIMO, ED.D.

In the United States the major concern with adolescence as a specific biopsychosocial developmental phase distinct from childhood and adulthood can probably be traced to the well-known work of G. Stanley Hall in 1904. The breadth and scope of Hall's interests can be seen in the title of his classic work: *Adolescence: Its Psychology and Its Relation to Physiology, Anthropology, Sociology, Sex, Crime, Religion and Education* (1904). In addition to this magnum opus, one of Hall's most significant contributions can be considered to be the link he forged between his own work on the psychology of adolescence and that of psychoanalysis, for it was Hall who was instrumental in bringing Freud to the United States in 1909 to lecture at Clark University.

Since that early contact between developmental psychology and psychoanalysis there have been a number of significant psychoanalytic contributions to the understanding of adolescent development. Anna Freud (1958) and Peter Blos (1962) have published basic works in the area. In this chapter we shall not review the unique characteristics of psychoanalytic theory or the ways in which it offers a creative, in-depth understanding of adolescent behavior. Rather, what we will attempt to do is to apply certain psychoanalytic concepts to the planning and implementation of a special clinical program for chronic delinquent adolescents, who traditionally have been hard to reach, and to describe how the evaluation of this program, using psychoanalytic concepts, has contributed to our knowledge about adolescent development in general, and characterologically disturbed, acting-out youth in particular.

A number of psychoanalysts have made theoretical and clinical contributions to the understanding of antisocial disorders in adolescence. Schmideberg (1935), Friedlander (1945), and Eissler (1950) have written detailed clinical studies. Johnson and Szurek (1952) have identified and described what they call superego lacuna in antisocial adolescents. Erikson and Erikson (1957) have formulated and refined the concept of negative identity. Redl and Wineman (1951, 1952) have vividly detailed the ego maneuverings of antisocial youth.

One of the pioneers in the psychoanalytic treatment of delinquent youth was August Aichorn, whose highly original work is still extremely relevant. Aichhorn (1935) developed a combined clinical and educational approach for characterologically disturbed antisocial youth in a residential setting based on psychoanalytic principles.[1]

One of the major themes of the psychoanalytic literature on adolescence has been the new opportunity the psychosocial stage offers for working out early developmental problems. The intense maturational pressures resulting in part from pubescent development (often described as a "developmental crisis") are believed to create major disequilibria offering a unique opportunity for personality change. Psychoanalytic theory has stressed how any given developmental phase has its own special features forming an arena around which various earlier unresolved conflicts are played out and, given certain corrective opportunities, resolved.[2] For the adolescent, issues of indivi-

[1] Unfortunately, the close ties between the disciplines of psychoanalysis and education, exemplified by such notable figures as Aichhorn and Anna Freud, have often been ignored or underplayed in recent psychoanalytic work, while the ties to medicine, particularly in the United States, have been emphasized and fostered.

[2] In Shore and Massimo (1968), theories of adolescent development were classified in two categories: those that focus on the repetition of earlier developmental issues during the adolescent phase (recapitulative theories); and

duation are, for the first time in life, expressed in attempts to separate psychologically from the family unit and to relate more closely to the broader context of society. One of the most vivid descriptions of this task is presented by Erikson (1968), who expanded and broadened psychoanalytic theory by showing how intrapsychic forces in the adolescent combine with social and cultural forces to result in the final formation of a true ego identity. The significance of Erikson's views for undertaking new strategies of psychoanalytic intervention for certain groups of adolescents has not been adequately recognized. Some psychoanalysts, such as Laufer (1973) in a drop-in clinic in London, have attempted to adapt psychoanalytic techniques in a creative way to reach adolescents who have not been reached by the more traditional psychoanalytic techniques. This chapter will deal with another adaptation of psychoanalytic ideas for treating characterologically disturbed adolescent delinquents in the community.

As mentioned earlier, one area of great importance for adolescents is the beginning of their adaptation to the broader sociocultural world, and to its values and expectations. One way this adaptation can take place in young people is through employment and work experiences. The implications of such experiences have yet to be explored in theory, research, and practice.

Although Freud recognized work as a major area of functioning in adults, little has been written in psychoanalysis about the profound significance of employment for adolescents. In many ways, work experience in modern society can be viewed increasingly as an important avenue for working through a number of psychological developmental problems of adolescence. Clinicians who have had professional or personal contact with adolescents employed in human service organizations (crisis centers, homes for the aged, medical hospitals, educational institutions, etc.) have frequently seen remarkable growth in these young people. Dropouts from high school, after a meaningful experience on a job, have often decided to return to

---

those that stress the emerging elements of the period (emergent theories). This theoretical dimension, the authors believe, is most important for determining how an intervention program is planned and implemented.

school with clear direction as to career choice and some resolution of the relationships with their families, other adults, and peers. Unlike adults, whose work can often be isolated from other areas of their daily lives, with compensatory satisfactions sometimes gained from other activities, employment for the adolescent appears to be extremely important as a door to the world of adulthood and the development of social and personal responsibilities, both major factors in the formation of identity. It seems that concrete job experiences allow the skills gained during the latency period to be consolidated and broadened in such a way as to prepare the youth for dealing with issues tied to functioning within the historical context of the society. The opportunity to interact with adults outside the family, the need to develop and expand effective skills valued and rewarded by society through payment, and the necessity to interact successfully with peers in a team situation are some of the areas that play a significant role in defining oneself and one's social and personal boundaries. In some ways, the role of work in an adolescent's life may be seen as equivalent to that of the role of play in the life of a child. While the value of play has been recognized by society as appropriate, even necessary for adequate psychological development, the importance of work, for a number of reasons, has tended to be valued less. Thus, in our society jobs often are not available for youth, rewards are few, and those jobs that are available are frequently meaningless in terms of assisting in personal growth.

Although jobs may in themselves offer positive, constructive experiences, there is a second contribution they can make. Specific job experiences provide the opportunity for specially planned corrective, educational, and emotional experiences. Via employment one can add therapeutic learning and psychotherapy so that previous areas of major psychological difficulty may be worked out and clarified. Aichhorn (1935) was well aware of the value of work within a treatment setting, as is evident in the following case description:

> If a change could be brought about in his relationship to
> his mother and sisters, and if he could find suitable work,
> it seemed likely that great improvement would result.

Mother was easily dissuaded from her plan to force the boy out of the house to seek work as a laborer. I was able to arrange that he be given credit for his first year of apprenticeship and go on with learning carpentry. He began work two weeks after our first meeting and did well. He gave no indication of laziness [p. 65].

Although some psychoanalysts have recognized how work experiences can gratify, sublimate, and assist in working out conflicts, the use of employment as an intervention in psychoanalytic therapy has not been given the consideration it merits. For many groups of young people, work in itself cannot resolve problems. Rather, it is through the work experience that one can identify the academic difficulties and ego deficiencies which, in the context of the concrete work experience, can become targets of a comprehensive psychotherapeutic intervention program. How work was used in this way to assist antisocial youth will be illustrated below.[3]

Selection Procedures and Principles of Intervention

The features of the ego functioning of characterologically disturbed, delinquent adolescents are well described in the literature: low frustration tolerance, excessive narcissism, minimal expression of anxiety and guilt, stress on action with little use of verbal symbolization, high impulsivity with the goal of immediate gratification, concrete thinking, little or no long-term planning, minimal impairment of perception and reality testing, and extreme manipulation of others in service of self-satisfaction.

[3] This view of the importance of work in personality development has been seen by some as reflecting the Protestant ethic whereby it was believed, simplistically, that work of any kind inherently built character. Such is not the case. Little attention was given years ago to the psychological needs of the individual at a given developmental phase and the kind of meaningful work experience that was necessary for personality development to take place. Instead, the needs of the marketplace were considered paramount rather than those of the individual. It is for that reason that child labor laws were instituted so as to protect young people from the exploitation that inhibited rather than fostered their growth.

Since the project we planned aimed at studying the treatment of a specific disorder, it was important that the group selected for participation be homogeneous. For a number of reasons it was not appropriate to do the usual careful individual and family diagnostic workups. These youths were extremely resistant and were neither available nor motivated for diagnostic study. Therefore, a homogeneous group had to be obtained by using information from school files and from those in the school who knew the youths (usually they were quite well known to school personnel because of their provocative acting out). The information gathered from these two sources, when evaluated, insured relative homogeneity. The criteria used for selection were as follows. The youth had to be 15 to 17 years of age, so that employment would be possible in accordance with state and Federal laws. Intellectual functioning on a standard intelligence scale should be above 85 (to eliminate mental retardation or severe organic impairment). There should be evidence of a long history of antisocial behavior, with repeated truancies from school (the youth had to have been on probation at least once). The youth also had to have longstanding problems in school adjustment and severe academic performance difficulties not diagnosed as caused by neurological dysfunctioning. The youth also had to have been suspended or expelled from school or to have voluntarily dropped out because of a combination of poor school performance and antisocial behavior. There should also have been no observable psychotic behavior. In addition, there should have been no previous psychotherapy for the boy or members of his family that lasted longer than a month. It was on the basis of these criteria that these youths were called character-disordered delinquents.

The twenty boys in this study lived in a Boston suburb and were selected according to the criteria by the attendance officer at the school. By random assignment ten were placed in the treatment program, the other ten being left to the sources available in the community. The program, called "Comprehensive Vocationally Oriented Psychotherapy" (Massimo and Shore, 1967), lasted ten months, and each youth was aware of its duration.

Once the group was selected, a treatment plan was developed consonant with psychoanalytic theory and with previous experience in the outpatient treatment of characterologically disordered adolescent delinquents. The plan was, of course, adapted to individual needs, and the strategies varied with the specific clinical issues being dealt with at a given time. Nevertheless, certain general principles formed the basis for intervention.

Principle 1. These antisocial young people by definition are characteristically resistant to help. A major initial task, therefore, is to arouse anxiety and, hence, motivation. Could there be a time, we asked, when they might be particularly amenable to help? Although it may not be considered a crisis of major proportions, we felt that when any youth either left school or was expelled from school permanently, it was necessary for him to reevaluate himself, rethink his direction, and develop new patterns of behavior. The need for these new adaptations to a life without school, we believed, might be considered a situation producing some anxiety. Contact was made within twenty-four hours after the boy had left school. This immediate contact was meant to avoid the possibility that he might resolve the discomfort and harden his characterological defenses. The use of "crisis" in this way is not what is called "crisis intervention." Most crisis intervention work is of short duration and aims at alleviating an immediate disequilibrium. Here, by contrast, the crisis was used to make contact with the youth in the hope that he could be involved in intensive, relatively long-term therapeutic contact. At the conclusion of the therapeutic program, many youths reflected on this first contact. They remembered that they were indeed in a state of discomfort, needed to reevaluate their lives and were vulnerable to therapeutic contact.[4]

Principle 2. These disturbed youths had experienced a number of unsuccessful contacts with community agencies. It was therefore important that the therapist separate himself from school, police, courts, social agencies, or other authorities. Although many of these youths soon asked, "Who the hell do

---

[4] Such immediate contact at vulnerable times has been compared to the manner in which adult criminals are often able to "capture" young people and direct them to criminal activity (e.g., drug use, prostitution). Mental health people have characteristically missed such opportunities.

you work for?" the program, which was independently fi-
nanced, could honestly be described as not connected with any
organized community agency or group. The absence of the
usual organizational restraints of a formal agency base permitted a great deal of flexibility and autonomy, a major element
in implementing the program.

Principle 3. Outreach into the community offered an opportunity for these youths, who were nonverbal, to show the
therapist their world rather than be forced prematurely to verbalize about their lives. Therefore, initial contact was made away
from an office and took place in the community—in a car, at
a restaurant, or on a streetcorner—depending on the youth's
preference. These youths were comfortable having the therapist "on their own turf" rather than having to come to the
therapist's office. Sometimes they chose to have friends with
them as "protection."

Principle 4. Initial contact was made in terms of opportunities to look for a job, with other "help" available, if needed.
These youths appeared particularly attracted by the notion of
a job. In line with adolescent expectations, as well as with their
fantasies of wealth and power, they were often eager at least
to take a chance in exploring the possibilities of employment.
The wish for a job offered an avenue for discussion of many
other activities, as well as background. Their very severe limitations in learning and interpersonal skills were manifested
early in the contact. At the beginning, efforts were made to
encourage acceptance of any type of work that offered financial
compensation and was in line with the boys' dynamics and desires. They could then move to other jobs as skills and opportunities increased. In order to sustain motivation, the jobs could
not be dead-end positions. Throughout treatment there was
discussion about moving up.

Principle 5. From previous clinical experience we had
learned that these young people, once we made contact, typically indulged in detailed descriptions of sadomasochistic orgies, some of which were real and some fantasy. Given the
primitive ego structure of these young people and their focus
on manipulation, we soon learned that permitting them to indulge in these descriptions too soon in the contact was anti-

therapeutic. We knew from experience that they could be overwhelmed by the material and never return. Therefore, although some information was obtained in the first interview, the emphasis was on the goal of exploring concrete tasks—job interests, job possibilities, job skills, and the fears that might be related to taking some clear initiative with the therapist toward finding employment. This task orientation seemed to bind the desire to indulge in omnipotent fantasy and turned out to be a major factor in keeping these youths in treatment.

Principle 6. The therapist was available for contact at any time of day or night. Each youth was given the therapist's telephone number to call if he wished.[5] To test the availability of the therapist, calls at first were made at three or four in the morning. The therapist made clear that his role was not to rescue young people who might be in trouble, but instead to help figure out, over the telephone, ways in which the youth could handle a situation. The therapist would help in considering the realities of the situation, the choices that were made, what had happened, why, and the consequences; the youth would himself have to make the decisions. In some ways, the approach could be compared to the life-space interview of Redl and Wineman (1952). Sometimes a young person was seen for three or four hours at a time, sometimes for a much shorter period. Characteristically, contacts took place in the community, at home, or in the car.

Principle 7. Where possible, the jobs were selected in terms of a youth's particular needs. Thus, an extremely uncontrolled, aggressive youth was able to find a job on a housewrecking crew. A boy who wished to control his weight was found a job in a frozen food factory where he could see the food but not eat it immediately. None of the jobs was preselected. In fact, part of the therapeutic contact was for the therapist and the youth to explore together what was available in terms of the

---

[5] The importance of diagnosis is highlighted in determining when to give someone a telephone number. Facetiously, it has been said that one offers one's telephone number to those least likely to call. Highly dependent individuals would misuse the opportunity and call frequently. In this group, where dependency was constantly denied, any call to the therapist would be an acknowledgment of the need for help and thus be a sign of progress.

youth's interests, his limited skills, and the job market. This was done through such activities as looking at newspaper ads and visiting various business establishments. It was clearly understood that any jobs had to be meaningful and rewarding, personally and financially. Following the preparation for seeking a first job, the therapist went with the youth to the job interviews. After a job was found, the focus of therapy switched to on-the-job problems, both academic and personal.

Principle 8. The therapist entered all aspects of the youth's life. He went with him to court appearances and initial job interviews, and helped him shop, open a bank account, and get a driver's license. The therapist used role play to anticipate with the youth what might happen in some of these situations. A concrete, goal-directed focus was extremely important, always within the context of understanding dynamically what was going on at a given time. The youth was constantly encouraged to take his own initiative. Dependency was not fostered, although the emphasis was on working together. That is, the therapist could be counted on for support and assistance in specific ways, such as being with the youth in situations where it was clear such support would be therapeutically useful.

Principle 9. Because of these youths' poor learning skills (despite being in high school, their average reading level was third grade), an integral part of the therapeutic program was to develop and implement an individual learning program. No youth was encouraged to return to regular high school unless he chose to do so.[6] Instead, alternative learning resources were found, such as night schools, correspondence courses, and on-the-job training. Individual tutoring with the therapist was also part of the program. The therapist developed unique techniques by which the youth could improve his skills in reading, vocabulary, and arithmetic through the use of automobile

---

[6] Many school dropout programs have, as a major goal, the return to high school. Often what happens is that the person drops out of school again. What needs to be recognized is that school personnel are often relieved when an antisocial youth leaves school, as he has been a source of frustration and difficulty to them. Returning to a situation where the youth has been labeled "a troublemaker" can only result in the same kind of pressures that originally forced him out.

driver's manuals, restaurant menus, and automotive magazines. Often it was difficult for the youth to recognize his academic deficiencies, since his omnipotent fantasies were used to deny his basic feelings of inadequacy and fears of humiliation. However, on the job these deficiencies soon became evident. Instead of permitting self-pity, regression, or counterphobic acting out, the therapist used the opportunity to improve the youth's learning skills and understanding. Academic materials were always made relevant to the youth's concrete job goals and activities.

Principle 10. Dependency, homosexuality, and primitive fears related to their overt behavior were discussed openly and bluntly with these youths when appropriate. As Redl and Wineman (1952) have suggested, the ego structure of many antisocial young people makes it possible to deal with these areas directly and frankly. Unlike the borderline or psychotic individual, whose ego structures are fragile, confrontation is possible in treating these youths once some minimal trust has been established (in fact, such frankness serves to increase this trust).

Principle 11. Because of the severe manipulative tendencies in these young people, the establishment of separate, discipline-bound agency "departments" whereby different individuals are used for academic help, job counseling, and psychotherapy was rejected. A study using separate administrative units found that these youths, because of their ability for environmental manipulation, were very clever at creating staff dissension, disruption, and anger. It was felt, therefore, that all components of the program should be the responsibility of one individual, who would be responsible for all aspects of work with a youth. Thus, the therapist would be educator, job counselor, psychotherapist, and anything else that might be needed.

Although the therapist was deeply involved in all aspects of the young person's life, no efforts were made to foster a true transference neurosis, since the aims of the study were limited. The belief was that by producing certain changes at a sensitive time in life, processes of change might be mobilized that would continue when the youth was on his own. Despite the severity of the disturbances of these youths, it was felt that the forces of change in adolescence were on our side and that, given the normal disruptions of this developmental phase, effective intervention could bring about major long-lasting change.

Principle 12. Throughout treatment, motility and action were stressed. Field trips were made, and a great deal of therapeutic work was done over coffee, in automobiles while transporting a youth, and through casual, informal contacts at the job site.

Principle 13. Natural crises on the job site offered opportunities for major therapeutic interventions. The arrangement with the employer was that the youth had to meet the same standards as the other employees. If he did not, the employer could discharge him. However, the employer agreed to contact the therapist if such an event occurred so that it could be used in therapy.

Principle 14. The focus of treatment was on the individual youth. The family was not seen. It was our belief that, unlike the usual close-knit family interactions of neurotics, these youths were isolated from their parents, who were involved primarily in meeting the overwhelming economic needs common to large families of lower social class. The parents were grateful that they would not need to take a day off from work to appear at school or in court. The youth, when given an opportunity to earn money, soon began to think of ways to move out of their parents' homes.

Research Strategies and Findings

One of the major avenues of research in psychoanalysis is to generate understanding about personality development and functioning through careful study of the therapeutic intervention process. The aim of the study described here was to use that method to determine what changes, if any, occurred during the ten-month treatment period and the significance of those changes.

Three approaches were used to study the nature and degree of change resulting from treatment. The first was a multilevel analysis of change over the treatment period. Three levels were distinguished: (1) overt behavior—legal situation, employment situation, school situation, and general observable behavior; (2) academic cognitive functioning—standard achievement tests were administered in vocabulary, reading, arithmetic problems, and arithmetic fundamentals; (3) ego structure—to determine changes in specific aspects of ego functioning, a group of clinical psychologists selected TAT-type pictures they believed would elicit material in the areas of attitude toward authority, control of aggression, and self-image (it was assumed that the way the youth handled the instructions to make up a story to the stimulating conditions of the picture shown him would be a valid measure of ego functioning).

A second strategy was a follow-up study of all youths in the program. This enabled us to determine if the changes that took place were merely efforts to please the therapist or were indeed substantive alterations in personality functioning. Follow-up evaluations were done two, five, ten, and fifteen years after the program ended.

A third methodological consideration was to find a random group of suburban adolescent youths of the same social class who had no history of characterological delinquency problems. These youths were tested twice on the same measures as the twenty delinquent youths over a ten-month period in order to compare their functioning with that of the study population (both those in the program and those not). The contents of all the stories elicited from the three groups by the TAT-type pictures were analyzed for specific ego functions such as guilt, object relations, and verbalization.

General Findings

Comparisons were made between the overt behavior of the treated and the untreated groups before and after the ten-month program. Descriptive tables were used to make comparisons, as there are no adequate ways of quantifying such areas as legal difficulties or job performance. Since these acting-out youths had been identified in the community as sources of trouble, they would also be the first picked up by the police as suspects, whether or not they had actually committed an antisocial act.

To measure cognitive changes, scores on the achievement

tests were compared for the treated and untreated groups at the beginning and end of the ten months.

To measure personality changes, a special rating guide was devised based on test material taken from the files of known character-disordered delinquents who were not part of the study. Criteria were developed to determine what should be considered a sign of positive or negative change in the handling of the stimulus situation, i.e., the request for stories to certain pictures of known stimulus value. The stories told before and after treatment were paired, and a highly experienced clinical psychologist was asked to make judgments of improvement or deterioration on the basis of criteria described in the rating guide. As his global judgments of change showed 90 percent agreement with those of two other psychologists who were asked independently to rate a randomly selected group of story pairs, the results of his ratings were considered reliable.

In all areas (overt behavior, cognition, and ego function-ing), highly significant positive changes were found in the treated group; that is, although the treated and untreated de-linquent groups (who had been selected randomly) showed no differences prior to treatment, at the end of treatment in every area (other than attitude toward authority) the treated group had significantly improved.[7] Thus, comprehensive, vocationally oriented psychotherapy was effective in bringing about signif-icant improvement in this group of hard-to-reach antisocial youth (Massimo and Shore, 1963).

The information and test material collected on the treated and untreated delinquent groups and on the group of non-delinquents offered an opportunity to explore further signifi-cant dimensions of personality functioning, particularly in light of psychoanalytic theory. Some of these issues will now be dis-cussed.

Object Relations

The concept of object relations in psychoanalytic theory is an extraordinarily difficult one, not only to define, but also to

[7] The finding that attitude toward authority was the area that changed the least adds to the internal validity of the study, since adolescence, by its very nature, is a time when opposition to authority is not only common but expected.

quantify. Nevertheless, it remains an extremely important theoretical concept. Object relations might be defined as "the inner world of a person's feelings to others which determines in a fundamental way the individual's relationship to people in the external world" (Phillipson, 1955, p. 7). Building on the work of Phillipson at the Tavistock Clinic in London, we analyzed the stories given to the selected picture cards using the Leary Scale of Interpersonal Analysis (Leary, 1957). The scale divides all interactions along two dimensions: affect and activity. Four interpersonal categories are obtained: positive active (leading, teaching, directing); negative active (aggression, destruction, criticism, attack); positive passive (joining, agreeing, accepting), and negative passive (hesitating, delaying, and passively resisting). Using this scale to analyze the preconscious fantasy material obtained from the stories, we felt, would be one way of measuring object relations. The Leary scores on these stories before and after treatment were then correlated with the other tests (achievement and IQ). The results were remarkably consistent with expectations from psychoanalytic theory (Shore, Massimo, Kisielewski, and Moran, 1966; Shore, Massimo, Moran, and Malasky, 1968).

In successfully treated adolescent delinquents there was a significant improvement in object relations from negative to positive. No change was found in the active-passive dimension; that is, the youth continued to focus on action and activity. Thus, the *quality* of the activity was changing rather than the *degree*. What appeared to be taking place was socialization, with interactions with others perceived as more gratifying, satisfying, accepting, and constructive. Open defiance, opposition, and resistance were no longer necessary. Positive, active interactions took their place.

It should be remembered that this program did not foster passivity but rather focused on the individualized aspects of a youth's ability to make independent decisions and take the consequences. The changes found, therefore, were consistent with the nature of the program. However, one may wonder how much passivity should be encouraged in mental health treatment of adolescents. Could we, in our therapeutic approaches, perhaps be focusing too much around the acceptance or rejection of passivity, rather than encouraging adolescents to become more constructively active?

Correlations with the achievement tests showed highly significant association between the quality of object relations and academic performance in all areas (arithmetic, vocabulary, and reading). Learning was highly correlated with increased socialization. Consistent with psychoanalytic theory, the learning difficulty in this group was not associated with symbolic meanings and the problems one often sees in neurotics, nor with the difficulties in processing information found in brain-damaged or intellectually limited individuals. Rather, learning difficulty resulted from a rejection of school and school-associated material as a socializing force. Once this rejection of socialization is altered through appropriate therapeutic intervention, major learning can then take place.[8]

Guilt

Kohlberg (1964) has written a great deal about the developmental stages of guilt, expanding and elaborating the work of Piaget (1932). Concurrently, psychoanalytic theory has focused on the development and growth of the superego. As noted by Johnson and Szurek (1952), one of the major disturbances in youths with characterological acting-out difficulties occurs in the area of superego functioning. In this study, the stories given to pictures of aggressive activity were analyzed using a guilt scale constructed in line with developmental principles. Thus, stories suggesting the early stages of external control, expressed as fear of retaliation and revenge, were given very low scores, while stories dealing with remorse, concern,

---

[8] An analogy has been drawn between the therapeutic program for adolescents described here and the struggles of the toddler during the separation-individuation stage as described by Mahler (1974). The toddler, in relation to one person (the mother), has to learn to develop object constancy. Nonverbal behavior and limited symbolization predominate. As coping improves and greater individuation occurs, thought processes (abstract thinking), delay, and words all arise to deal with aggression. All this is done within the basic narcissistic orientation of the first nonautistic interpersonal object relationships (beginning with symbiosis and continuing until some individuation has taken place).

and desires for self-control and restraint were given higher scores. The results showed a significant increase in more highly developed levels of expression of guilt in the successfully treated group (Shore, Massimo, and Mack, 1964; Shore, Massimo, Mack, and Malasky, 1968). These changes were associated with independently judged changes in overt behavior (marked reduction in overt aggression) and a marked improvement in academic functioning. Thus, internalization of controls was taking place with major improvement in superego functioning.

Verbalization

One goal in therapeutic work with acting-out youths, according to psychoanalytic developmental theory, is the fostering of vicarious rather than direct ways of impulse expression. Words are a means of such vicarious expression. This study was able to offer some insight into this area. Since these youths were requested to tell stories to pictures, it was possible, for each picture stimulus, to look at the number and quality of the words used before and after treatment. Posttreatment results showed a significant increase by the treated group, as compared with the untreated delinquents, in word use in response to stimuli that aroused aggression (Shore and Massimo, 1967). This increase in the use of words was associated with reduced acting-out behavior. In fact, the number of words used was greater in the treated delinquents than in the nondelinquents tested. What seemed to be occurring was that the treated youth were overusing words as a way of controlling impulses, a common occurrence in clinical work, where one often sees overresponsiveness, overreaction, and overuse of new behavior patterns before they become well integrated and more flexibly used in personality functioning.

Cognitive Functioning in Delinquents

The cognitive structure of these characterologically disturbed delinquent adolescents was studied by comparing their test results to the group of nondelinquents of the same social class. When stories of the delinquent and nondelinquent youths scored on the Leary Interpersonal Analysis Scale were compared, many clinical impressions about the cognitive structure of antisocial youths were confirmed (Shore, Massimo, and Moran, 1967). For example, although the number of words used by delinquent youths in telling stories was almost identical to that used by nondelinquents, the number of interpersonal, action-oriented events in the stories was significantly greater. The events described by the delinquents were significantly more attuned to manipulation, action, and aggression, and significantly less to descriptions and symbolic elaborations commonly used in communication with others. The cognitive structure, therefore, reflected clinical descriptions of these youths as hyperalert and oversensitive to opportunities for manipulation within the context of a sadomasochistic orientation. Such a cognitive focus was at the expense of more elaborate and developmentally more advanced symbolic activities.

Time

A very important area of ego functioning is the personal conception of time. It is through the development of a sense of personal time that one can begin to plan, organize, and reflect. Indeed, the use of time is closely tied to reduced impulse gratification and restraint of overt behavior. Telling stories to pictures permitted the subject's perception of time to be evaluated by noting the time frame in which the stories were told. Were they told in the past or the future? If so, how far in the past or the future? This measure of ego functioning showed very significant results in the treated delinquent youth (Ricks, Umbarger, and Mack, 1964). But the findings are of still greater interest. There was no increase in the use of the past time frame after treatment. However, the treated and untreated groups significantly differed at the end of treatment in future time orientation. Two reasons might be given for this finding: (a) perhaps adolescence, by its very nature, should be seen as a developmental phase geared toward the future; and (b) the program focused on the consequences of acts rather than the origins of behavior. It was our strong belief that attempts to tie the past to current behavior would have limited success in this diagnostic group. The results on perceived time certainly indicate its relevance as a meaningful dimension of ego functioning, especially in relation to acting-out behavior.

Adolescence as a Unique Opportunity for Intervention

The follow-up studies completed two, five, ten, and fifteen years after the program ended continued to find major differences between the treated and untreated groups. These findings reinforce the importance of adolescence as an opportunity for major changes to occur (Shore and Massimo, 1966, 1969, 1973, 1979). The optimistic view that adolescence is a second chance for the basic reorganization and restructuring of the personality appears substantiated by the current study. Over a ten-year period, the twenty individuals in the study showed no reversal of direction; that is, those who showed improvement over the treatment period in adolescence continued to improve over ten years; those who dropped out continued to deteriorate. The fifteen-year follow-up showed one reversal. One of the treated youths who had done well, for reasons that could not be determined, became involved in drugs and alcohol, was no longer employed, was divorced, and was in deep legal trouble. Thus, over a fifteen-year period, only one youth reversed direction.

The findings are remarkably consistent with Erikson's theory of the importance of the formation of identity in adolescence. Adolescence seems to be a developmental period in which appropriate interventions can have major consequences. In fact, even interventions that are brief may end up having major effects. The openness to change of most young people in the throes of adolescence offers a chance to bring about some major change in a short period of time, provided we are aware of what is needed, and provided we are able to develop the flexible strategies and innovative techniques for bringing about such change.

Case Illustration

Mark, age 15, was expelled from high school in his sophomore year because of his overtly hostile destructive behavior. He was preoccupied with violence and participated in any brawls he heard about. Although considered above average in intelligence, he did not work in school and was failing all his subjects. Mark was reading at a fifth-grade level. He was in trouble with the police, having been put on informal probation for drinking, later on formal probation for car theft.

Mark's mother would probably be diagnosed as a paranoid schizophrenic. His father was a severely disturbed man. He was an outstanding draftsman who, despite his education, had not done well financially. Mark's father had left the family when Mark was 9 years old. Two years later the divorce was made final. Mark was the oldest of four children.

The initial interview revealed that Mark's destructive impulses were so overwhelming that he could talk about only his desires to destroy anything and everything. Since initially it was not possible to deal with Mark's psychological conflicts, the therapist attempted to redirect Mark's hostile behavior into more constructive channels.

In each initial interview in the study, the focus was not only on jobs that were available if the boys wanted them but that were also in some way related to psychodynamics. For example, only after much discussion did the therapist realize that Mark might be interested in working for a demolition company. The job was found by Mark and the therapist when they combed the want ads. They then visited the firm, where Mark was immediately employed as a helper in demolishing houses.

The therapist spent many hours with Mark discussing housewrecking, as Mark would relate intimate details of demolition and destruction. They attended a few stock car races. One day the firm decided to move a house that had been slated for destruction. Mark seemed angry over the change. It was this event that led to a turning point in his treatment. The therapist discussed with Mark how his life had been focused only on destruction. Exploring this further, he exposed Mark's use of aggression to hide, among other things, his own fears of attack and his use of omnipotence as a defense. Not long after, Mark began to show increased interest in cars and changed to a job with an automobile salvage company where parts from cars were saved prior to destruction of the car for scrap metal.

In this auto salvage job Mark did very well. He enjoyed going to scenes of death and destruction to obtain the wrecked cars. As his performance improved on the job, Mark was given more responsibility. This required taking phone calls, reading auto parts catalogues, and writing orders. It was at this point that remedial education became essential, and the therapist and Mark worked on spelling and reading. Because of Mark's high native ability, he was able to learn rapidly.

Following his job in salvage work, in the eighth month of treatment, Mark became interested in auto body work. This meant further involvement in terminology, catalogues, and other educational pursuits. The therapist and Mark visited auto body shops to find out about the necessary requirements for a mechanic's job. Mark even learned to handle an oxyacetylene torch.

After nine months of treatment Mark was able to talk about the origins of his rage. He began to see how his feelings of helplessness during early experiences influenced his view of life as a primitive fight for survival.

During the three years following treatment, Mark took a correspondence course and received his high school equivalency diploma. He had some minor traffic violations, but none serious enough to place him on probation.

In the two years before the five-year followup he had married and become a mechanic. Ten years later he had become a specialized diesel mechanic and had two children. He is currently the coach of a Little League team and is described as a "solid citizen." He has had no legal problems for over ten years.

Some of the treated youths who later had marital problems were able to get help from family agencies in the community. Such help would not have been sought prior to their participation in the program.

Concluding Remarks

This study shows the relevance of psychoanalytic theory to new treatments within a community context. Psychoanalytic theory need not be confined to traditional settings but can be used as the basis of social policy stressing new ways of working with hard-to-reach individuals with major social problems. The significance of psychoanalytic theory for social policy is exemplified by the work of Robertson (1958), whose psychoanalytic insights on hospitalized young children have led to a number of revolutionary changes in medical settings in Great Britain, the United States, and other parts of the world. It is indeed possible that the psychoanalytic insights derived from work on characterologically disturbed adolescent delinquents will offer us insights into the types of programs necessary for adequate development to occur in adolescence, as well as for new treatment approaches for highly distressed youth. The saddest finding in this study was how those young people who were not in comprehensive, vocationally oriented psychotherapy, but who were left to the available community resources, had great difficulty in later life, many ending up as adult criminals (Shore and Massimo, 1966, 1969, 1973, 1979).

References

Aichhorn, A. (1935), *Wayward Youth*. New York: Viking.

Blos, P. (1962), *On Adolescence: A Psychoanalytic Interpretation*. New York: Free Press.

Eissler, K. R. (1950), Ego psychological implications of the psychoanalytic treatment of delinquents. *The Psychoanalytic Study of the Child*, 5:97–121. New York: International Universities Press.

Erikson, E. H. (1968), *Identity: Youth and Crisis*. New York: Norton.

—— Erikson, K. T. (1957), The confirmation of the delinquent. *Chicago Rev.*, 10:15–23.

Friedlander, K. (1945), Formation of the antisocial character. *The Psychoanalytic Study of the Child*, 1:189–204. New York: International Universities Press.

Freud, A. (1958), Adolescence. *The Psychoanalytic Study of the Child*, 1:189–204. New York: International Universities Press.

Hall, G. S. (1904), *Adolescence: Its Psychology and Its Relation to Physiology, Anthropology, Sociology, Sex, Crime, Religion and Education*. New York: Appleton.

Johnson, A. M., & Szurek, S. (1952), The genesis of antisocial acting out in children and adults. *Psychoanal. Quart.*, 21:323–343.

Kohlberg, L. (1964), Development of moral character and moral ideology. In: *Review of Child Development Research*, Vol. 1, ed. M. L. Hoffman & L. W. Hoffman. New York: Russell Sage, pp. 383–433.

Laufer, M. (1973), Studies of psychopathology in adolescence. *Adolescent Psychiat.*, 2:7.

Leary, T. (1957), *Interpersonal Diagnosis of Personality*. New York: Ronald Press.

Mahler, M. S. (1974), Symbiosis and individuation. *The Psychoanalytic Study of the Child*, 29:89–106. New Haven: Yale University Press.

Massimo, J. L., & Shore, M. F. (1963), The effectiveness of a vocationally oriented psychotherapy program for adolescent delinquent boys. *Amer. J. Orthopsychiat.*, 33:634–643.

——— ——— (1967), Comprehensive vocationally oriented psychotherapy: A new treatment technique for lower class adolescent youth. *Psychiat.*, 30:229–236.

Phillipson, H. (1955), *The Object Relations Technique*. Glencoe, IL.: Free Press.

Piaget, J. (1932), *The Moral Judgment of the Child*. Glencoe, IL.: Free Press, 1948.

Redl, F., & Wineman, D. (1951), *Children Who Hate: The Disorganization and Breakdown of Behavioral Controls*. Glencoe, IL.: Free Press.

——— ——— (1952), *Controls from Within: Techniques for the Treatment of the Aggressive Child*. Glencoe, IL.: Free Press.

Ricks, D., Umbarger, C., & Mack, R. (1964), A measure of increased temporal perspective in successfully treated adolescent delinquent boys. *J. Abnormal & Social Psychol.*, 69:685–689.

Robertson, J. (1958), *Young Children in Hospitals*. New York: Basic Books.

Schmideberg, M. (1935), The psychoanalysis of asocial children and adolescents. *Internat. J. Psycho-Anal.*, 16:22–48.

Shore, M. F., & Massimo, J. L. (1966), Comprehensive vocationally oriented psychotherapy for adolescent delinquent boys: A follow-up study. *Amer. J. Orthopsychiat.*, 36:609–616.

——— ——— (1967), Verbalization, stimulus relevance, and personality change. *J. Consulting Psychol.*, 31:423–424.

——— ——— (1968), The chronic delinquent during adolescence: A new opportunity for intervention. In: *Adolescence: Psychosocial Perspectives*, ed. G. Caplan. New York: Basic Books, pp. 335–343.

——— ——— (1969), Five years later: A follow-up study of comprehensive vocationally oriented psychotherapy. *Amer. J. Orthopsychiat.*, 39:769–774.

——— ——— (1973), After ten years: A follow-up study of comprehensive vocationally oriented psychotherapy. *Amer. J. Orthopsychiat.*, 43:128–132.

——— ——— (1979), Fifteen years after treatment: A follow-up study of comprehensive vocationally oriented psychotherapy. *Amer. J. Orthopsychiat.*, 49:240–245.

——— ——— Kisielewski, J., & Moran, J. K. (1966), Object relations changes resulting from successful psychotherapy with adolescent delinquents and their relationship to academic performance. *J. Amer. Acad. Child Psychiat.*, 5:93–104.

——— ——— & Mack, R. (1964), The relationship between levels of guilt in thematic stories and unsocialized behavior. *J. Projective Techniques*, 28:346–349.

——— ——— ——— (1965), Changes in the perception of interpersonal relations in successfully treated adolescent delinquent boys. *J. Consulting Psychol.*, 29:213–217.

——— ——— ——— & Malasky, C. (1968), Studies of psychotherapeutic change in adolescent delinquent boys: The role of guilt. *Psychother.*, 5:85–89.

——— ——— & Moran, J. K. (1967), Some cognitive dimensions of interpersonal behavior in adolescent delinquent boys. *J. Research in Crime & Delinquency*, 4:243–248.

———— ———— Moran, J. K., & Malasky, C. (1968), Object relations changes and psychotherapeutic intervention: A follow-up study. *J. Amer. Acad. Child Psychiat.*, 7:59–68.

15

Late Adolescence to Early Adulthood

CARL P. ADATTO, M.D.

Late adolescence and early adulthood are characterized by restructuring and integration of the mind. The adolescent upheaval is brought to a close, and adult structures are laid down. This chapter will deal with the vicissitudes of the mental apparatus formed in childhood and adolesence, the metamorphosis during the period from 18 to 23, and the significance of these changes for future development.

Developmental processes can best be examined through changes in mental structures and object relationships. Id, ego, and superego undergo modifications and functional changes, finally reintegrating into adult patterns. Object relationships are the medium through which mental development is stimulated and social determinants have their effect. In the conduct of an analysis a special form of object relationship—the transference—provides a window into the derivatives of the unconscious workings of an individual's mind and also a means by which psychic development can be catalyzed. The point of view presented here comes primarily from the experience of psychoanalyzing patients in this age group; the mind is described and explained as a phenomenon observed in the analytic situation.

Developmental Concepts

Freud (1905b) introduced his concepts of puberty in a psychosexual developmental framework and in so doing brought into perspective the impact of the infantile period on structur-

357

ing the mind. Puberty was described as a time when the previously infantile life is given its final shape, centering around the primacy of the genital zone and the finding of new sexual aims and objects. Some time elapsed before adolescence was given more attention in the psychoanalytic literature (Jones, 1922; Bernfeld, 1923; Aichhorn, 1925). Not until much later were late adolescence and early adulthood designated as specific phases, even though many of the early cases which shaped analytic theory fell into this age group: Anna O., age 21; Katharina, 18; Elisabeth von R., 24 (Breuer and Freud, 1893–1895); Dora, 18 (Freud, 1905a); the Wolf-Man, 23 (Freud, 1918); and the case of homosexuality in a woman, 18 (Freud, 1920).

Jones (1922) stated that in adolescence "the individual *recapitulates and expands* in the second decennium of life the development he passed through during the first five years of life, just as he recapitulates during these first five years the experiences of thousands of years in his ancestry, and during the pre-natal period those of millions of years" (p. 398). Wittels (1949) included a second phallic and latency period in his four subdivisions of adolescence. Jones's recapitulation theory corrected the neglect of infantile sexuality in previous conceptualizations of adolescence, but it failed to delineate the qualitative changes later described by Anna Freud.

While the importance of the infantile period is central in psychoanalytic theory, its mutability and differentiation in adolescence are still actively under study. Recently the fate of the separation-individuation phase of infancy (Mahler, 1968) as it relates to adolescence and early adulthood has been a focus of interest. Blos (1967) views adolescence as a second separation-individuation period. Furman (1973) and Schafer (1973) point out the great differences between toddler and adolescent, bringing into question the limits of individuation as an explanatory concept with regard to adolescence. Spiegel (Marcus, 1973) attempts to bridge this gap by correlating early phallic and later genital drives in individuation. One can view the importance of the processes of separation and individuation in both periods of life, but the maturation of the psychic apparatus and changes in object relationships brings new forces and tasks into play.

Characteristics of Late Adolescence and Early Adulthood

Most authors place the age span for late adolescence and early adulthood between 18 and 25 years. Individual differences and socioeconomic factors influence the transition between the two phases. For instance, graduate education may prolong the transition, while early marriage or economic demands may shorten it.

By the time an individual reaches 18, most of the storm of puberty has passed, and its basic physical and physiological changes have taken place; individual physical and psychic patterns have become relatively stable. However, even physical maturation is incomplete, as evidenced by continuing epiphyseal closure in some individuals. Studies of these phases emphasize both the radical changes and the fixations that take place at this time in life. Small qualitative changes, intrapsychic and interpersonal, can realign already established psychic structures and patterns. It is erroneous, however, to view this period as definitive, for considerable change, especially following developmental crises, occurs in many individuals.

The characteristics of these phases are ill defined, and the transition from late adolescence to adulthood is by no means easily ascertained. Psychoanalysts who have described these periods use many criteria for differentiating the two. Jones (1922) uses difference in intellect, integration, egocentricity of fantasy life, dependency, and sexual maturity as distinguishing characteristics. Erikson (1968) describes the psychosocial crises in adolescence as identity vs. identity confusion; in the young adult, intimacy vs. isolation. Fountain (1961) lists five qualities of adolescence: intensity and volatility of feeling, need for frequent and immediate gratification, ineffective reality testing, failure of self-criticism, and lack of concern for worldly affairs and other people. He states that most or perhaps all of these qualities owe their existence to the oedipal struggle and that adulthood is reached when the intensity of cathexis to the oedipal figures is diminished. Blos (1976) described four developmental tasks leading into adulthood: second individuation process, ego continuity, residual trauma, and sexual identity.

Laufer (1976) considers that young adulthood (ages 22 to 25 "or so") is reached when the late adolescent (ages 18 to 21) establishes his final sexual organization. He views the distinction between the two phases to be important both clinically and theoretically.

The multiplicity of characteristics chosen by different analysts reflects the complexity of the underlying psychic process and the continuing search for more knowledge about these phases. Recently, considerable attention has been given this age group, with the result that a number of subtle but definite differences from other groups have come to light. These differences will be discussed under various headings.

Changes in Object Relationships

Late adolescence is characterized by the end phases of removal from infantile object relationships (Katan, 1937) and the beginnings of the establishment of adult love objects. By early adulthood, the instinctual aims toward parents are defused, and newly formed need-gratifying relationships offer a stability to the individual.

Anna Freud (1958) compared the reactions of adolescents in analysis to unhappy love affairs and mourning, both characterized by the mental pain involved in giving up a relationship that offers no further hope for return of love. The renunciation of parental ties in late adolescence is in many ways a welcome relief. The threat of regression to early ties and the uncertainty of commitment to new ones are characteristic of the 18- to 23-year-old youth. Considerable experience and the working through of adult relationships are necessary before constancy in relationships can be achieved.

The process of changing object relationships is different than in previous development because the emphasis is now toward permanency of a love relationship rather than gradual detachment from old ones. Individuation, in some form, has been achieved; the aim is now to secure its certitude, a prerequisite for stable adult relationships.

Intermediary objects, such as temporary love relationships

or idealizations made in late adolescence, often are important as catalysts to change in the formative period. Winnicott (1953) described the transitional object—an inanimate object such as a blanket or toy—in infancy as acting as an intermediate area of experience between the infant himself and his mother. During late adolescence the new object—a human being—though encompassing narcissism, acts as a transition between infantile and adult love objects. Ritvo (1971) suggests that a new object in late adolescence can become an organizer in a way similar to the objects of infancy and early childhood. He views the new object as helping the adolescent make the transition from narcissistic to object cathexis required for adult love relationships. Pedersen (1961) observes that the first loves of youth often provide an important impulse toward psychic transformation, while owing their fascination to a revival of some special phase of the oedipal constellation.

The revival of infantile object relationships through new objects creates a fresh opportunity for more definitive resolution of the infantile neurosis and its revisions made during adolescence. The individual now has sufficient ego capacity to deal with conflicts and to engage in the self-observation needed to reexamine and update infantile and more recent ties. New love objects act as relief from the adolescent storm; however, in addition to their benefits they also pose the problem of acting as a defense against continued resolution of infantile and adolescent conflicts.

The duality of maturation and defense was observed (Adatto, 1958) in the analyses of late adolescents whose motivation to continue analysis was diminished once sufficient resolution of the infantile neurosis was achieved to form new love relationships. The analyst, earlier sought out for gratification of unfulfilled instinctual aims as a transference object, now became a threat to regression to infantile ties. The same individuals reanalyzed as adults were able to analyze the transference, once sufficient psychic maturation was achieved to view the analyst with more detachment (Adatto, 1966).

The course and development of an individual's object relationships may be observed during analysis in the manner in which he views the analyst. The analysis of the transference to the analyst is a reliving of neurotic conflicts and thus a central aim of the analysis. The patient's use of the analyst as an intermediary object becomes a stabilizing force in the analysis and is not subject to analysis unless it becomes "conflictualized." Thus the analyst is able to observe the force of the residual conflicts connected to the infantile objects and also the progress being made toward achievement of a mature relationship. Connecting the nature of the transference with derivatives of unconscious fantasies facilitates the process of derepression of psychic conflicts. Through this route the patient is able to experience and observe the nature of the obstacles standing in the path of achieving adult relationships.

The development of a sense of self or identity and the development of object relationships are reciprocally interrelated and difficult to separate clinically. The totality of the psychic apparatus reflects the narcissism of an individual, which is vital to a person's functioning and is reflected in the kinds of object relationships formed. The adolescent's object choice invariably contains elements of narcissistic and infantile object identifications. One task of youth is to resolve these identifications so as to create a situation in which the needs of the self and the need for objects are satisfied. Sacrifice of one for the other creates an imbalance which leads to crisis or pathological formations.

Late adolescence in many ways resembles the narcissistic personality disorders described by Kohut (1971), characterized by vague feelings of emptiness and depression while struggling with feelings of grandiosity and intense object hunger. While some adolescents indeed have pathological disorders, most are working through the last vestiges of separation from infantile objects and taking stock of themselves. By contrast, young adults emerge from regressions which accompany psychic transformations and are more clearly object oriented, with narcissistic conflicts less in evidence. Pumpian-Mindlin (1965) describes the omnipotentiality of the 16- to 22-year-old—an outgrowth of earlier omnipotence, characterized by the feeling and conviction that at this age one can do anything or resolve any problem in the world. He characterizes the young adult as engaged in commitment. The differences in tasks reflect the normal developmental shift from considerable preoccupation with the self in adolescence to newly found relationships in the young adult.

Establishment of Sexual and Aggressive Organization

Integration of pubertal changes with other aspects of the personality is a significant task of this period, requiring a resolution of residual sexual and aggressive conflicts, establishment of sexual identity, the determination of gender preference, and the formation of an adult sexual pattern. Unconscious fantasies condense the past and current aim, object, and direction of the sexual and aggressive drives and act as a force directing instinctual organization.

Laufer (1976) attaches considerable importance to a central masturbatory fantasy whose contents contain the various regressive satisfactions and the main sexual identifications. He holds that a final sexual organization is established at the end of late adolesence, and that criteria for the passage from late adolesence to early adulthood are whether the libido is now object directed, whether the individual is able to integrate his physically mature genitalia, and whether thoughts and behavior show some detachment from the central masturbatory fantasy. Some patients report this type of fantasy in preparation for or during sexual activity with partners. It is not the detachment from the fantasy that is significant but the resolution of the conflictual elements embodied in the fantasy. Sexual fantasies are reported by most analysands, and often psychic transformation can be measured through changes in the fantasies.

Blos (1962) views masturbation with its accompanying fantasies as facilitating forward movement of the instinctual drives, leading to definitive consolidation of the self. The entry into adulthood, he argues, is marked by the formation of an irreversible sexual position. Moore (1975) considers the masturbatory-complex fantasy to be a significant part of psychological growth during adolescence and its successful conclusion essential to a final sexual identity and the establishment of adult relationships. Eissler (1958) maintains that orgasm is endowed with the power to create and affirm convictions and that during adolescence convictions are formed which in later life become associated with orgasm.

The choice of sexual partner reflects the vicissitudes of preferences developed from infancy through adolescence. The interaction of drive gratification (or its lack) during sexual encounters often reveals an individual's conditions for sexual gratification. Vacillation of sexual preference observed in some late adolescents often can be traced to identifications with infantile objects as well as to conflicts involving castration anxiety. During late adolescence sexual preferences are much more open to change than in early adulthood. The relative psychic stability of early adulthood includes stability in sexual organization. The fate of the oedipal conflicts and their revision during adolescence is reflected in the choice of sexual partners.

A panel on the psychology of women in late adolescence and early adulthood (Galenson, 1976) reflects the current interest in revisions of female psychology. Further clarification is much needed in order to understand the processes of becoming a man or a woman.

In contrast to sexuality, changes in the aggressive drives in youth are relatively obscure; there is a paucity of literature in this area. Studies in delinquency (Aichhorn, 1925; Eissler, 1949) have dealt with aggression primarily in the younger adolescent, while Friedman, Glasser, Laufer, Laufer, and Wohl (1972) have studied attempted suicide and self-mutilation in adolescence. Rebellion and violence in youth have been approached through the application of psychoanalytic theory to social phenomena, but few patients with overt aggressive conflicts present themselves or are suitable for psychoanalysis, perhaps accounting for the paucity of psychoanalytic data.

Ego Changes

Widening and consolidation of ego functioning characterize development into adulthood. Changes occur as the result of maturation, the freeing of the ego from defensive activities as earlier conflicts are more fully resolved, and catalytic activity prompted by new objects.

Anna Freud (1958) described adolescence as a state of disequilibrium, an interruption in peaceful growth; equilibrium and peaceful growth are restored only in early adulthood. Reliance on reality testing, self-observation, and introspection, as well as other ego functions, is necessary to do analytic work. The effectiveness of analysis often is increased as the patient reaches early adulthood and the ego reintegrates. For instance, amnesias of early childhood observed in late adolescent analyses are lifted in adulthood as the result of conflict resolution and the strengthening of memory function. Ego activity becomes more autonomous or conflict-free in early adulthood, permitting synthetic functioning to prevail. Concurrent with an increase of mutability of the ego is an increased capacity to cope with adaptational problems. Especially significant is the capacity to integrate and cope with the resurgent instinctual demands of adolescence.

What of the fate of adolescent ego defenses against infantile object ties and impulses (A. Freud, 1936, 1958)? Residues of the defenses of reversal of affect, displacement, withdrawal of libido to the self, asceticism, and uncompromising attitudes are still in evidence in late adolescence, but are considerably attenuated. Intellectualization, a common defense of puberty, has an unusual fate in many youths who engage in graduate education; the need to use the intellect in pursuing studies often increases its use defensively, thus delaying conflict resolution. Spiegel (1958) notes that toward the end of adolescence there is a greater directedness of thinking; he feels that adolescents with creative ability, such as dramatic writing, may diminish their activity because of increasing psychic consolidation. One can observe that the intellect and thinking processes, while still serving defensive purposes, also change in function.

Geleerd (1961) observed that real-life traumata in adolescence often have a serious impact and may lead to neurosis in adult life because of ego vulnerability. Trauma in late adolescence, such as the death of a parent or sibling, while less crippling than earlier traumas, may nevertheless have the effect of delaying resolution of the adolescent phase or may leave the individual in early adulthood with a new version of an old neurotic problem. Thus, while the ego is considerably more effective, gains can be tenuous.

Character formation, the result of ego activity and compromises, is shaped more definitively in late adolescence. Analysis of young adults often reveals that character traits formed during the infantile period have only recently taken their adult form. Stable ego activity, newly acquired, has the advantage of permitting the psyche to function more economically; however, this is accompanied by an economy in the defense and containment of neurotic structure. Gitelson (1948) viewed character synthesis as an essential task of adolescence. Blos (1968) associated the outcome of character in adolescence with psychic restructuring and saw character as stabilizing the newly attained personality of adulthood.

Superego and Ego Ideal

During adolescence external changes in the relationship to infantile objects are paralleled by inner changes in the superego. Revival of oedipal conflicts creates a disruption in the superego's regulatory and stabilizing functions. Not only are oedipal conflicts revived, but also preoedipal and postoedipal determinants that are modified and condensed in the current version of the superego. It is necessary to reinstinctualize the infantile objects in order for the adolescent to form adult instinctual patterns. Without this shift, adult sexuality is greatly impaired. The adolescent of either sex must work through castration anxiety and anxiety around genital mutilation in order to achieve satisfactory object relationships. Spiegel (1958) noted that during analysis one no longer has the superego as an ally and that marked castration anxiety and decreased superego anxiety frequently characterize the situation. Guilt, formerly observed, is often overtly diminished as the adolescent integrates newly found experiences.

By late adolescence the individual has revised his distorted internal version of parental objects, bringing them into harmony with the reality of what adults are like, himself included. Primitive concepts of the parents as controlling, omnipotent, and protective are modified, together with the concept of the self. As the internalized parents are updated, the individual has a sense both of freedom from restriction and of sadness over the loss of the parental presence.

Freud (1923) described the superego as a precipitate of the ego, consisting of father and mother identifications and reactions against them, and as having the task of repressing the Oedipus complex. The superego gives permanent expression to the influence of the parents and of society; as the child grows up, the parental roles are carried on by teachers and others in authority. Freud considered self-judgment, injunctions and prohibitions, moral censorship, a sense of guilt, and social feelings and identifications to be subsumed under the superego. Later Freud (1933) defined the ego ideal as a function of the superego, a vehicle "by which the ego measures itself, which it emulates, and whose demand for ever greater perfection it strives to fulfill" (p. 65). He stated that the ego ideal is a precipitate of the old picture of the parents and the child's expression of admiration of the perfection he attributed to them. Anna Freud (1936) described the repeated internalization involved in superego formation as it changes with development.

Some analysts consider the ego ideal to be a function separate from the superego. However, Hartmann and Loewenstein (1962), using a functional and genetic framework, expressed the now prevailing view that the ego ideal is part of the superego, that it originates in oedipal conflicts and differs from earlier identifications. They hold that in postadolescence both superego and ego development are prolonged and that ideally there is a workable equilibrium and tension between the two. Jacobson (1961) noted that the adolescent has no new psychic system to help him break away from his infantile love objects, but that the modification and restructuring of the superego lend him support in this endeavor. Lampl-de Groot (1960, 1962) viewed the ego ideal as an agency of wish fulfillment and the superego as a restricting agency, noting that adolescents have difficulty in coping with the narcissistic injury engendered by clinging to the superego objects, but that giving them up implies giving up part of oneself. Laufer (1964, 1965) maintained that the content of the superego does not change, but that the interrelationship of superego functions and of ego and superego change through new identifications, especially with contemporaries. Ritvo (1971) stated that the ego ideal attuned to reality is a development of late adolescence and is necessary for the adaptive tasks of adult life, and that crises of this period are marked by failures of adequate ideal formation and ego ideals insufficiently attuned to reality. Settlage (1972) argued the ego ideal compensates for infantile narcissistic losses and that early aspirations influence the later content of the ego ideal, regardless of familial or cultural influences. He considered the feasibility of superego change in late adolescence to be a potential for constructive change in both the individual and society.

The ego ideal, then, can be viewed on a developmental continuum and its functions as mutable. Clinical observations in analyses of late adolescents, when compared to those made with young adults, verify the rapidity of these structural changes and the ease with which developmental antecedents can be evoked, especially in areas of pathological conflict. When there is relative stability of the psychic apparatus, with ego, id, and superego functioning in harmony, the unconscious meanings and origins are difficult to detect.

Societal Influences

At no time in life does society have as direct an influence on personality development as it does during youth. Social values and ideals are originally transmitted through parents, and later by siblings, teachers, relatives, others in the child's world. Separation from infantile objects and the formation of new ones create a vacuum in which the individual is receptive to social forces transmitted through contemporaries and newly discovered (or rediscovered) people—teachers, religious leaders, politicians, and celebrities are among the many possible new objects chosen for emulation. These identifications, while not creative of basic psychic change, give shape and direction, especially to the superego and the ego ideal.

Aries (1962), a cultural historian, has described how adolescence had no special social recognition until the nineteenth century. The rapid redefinition of youth's role in current society has been the object of psychoanalytic study. A panel discussing the genetic, dynamic, and adaptive aspects of dissent (Gillman, 1971) seemed generally to agree that dissent was an essential feature of youth in its transition from adolescence to adulthood, and that social institutions can transcend individual motivation and help define behavioral roles and moral standards. Deutsch (1967) has described her experiences in brief contact with patients, covering both psychic and group phenomena in campus life. Lustman (1972) observed that during a year of campus confrontation two groups emerged: one engaged in caretaking of adults and children in an apolitical way, and a radical group interested primarily in the events. His study has the sobering effect of avoiding generalizations about the kinds of identifications a student might make in times of unrest. Solnit (1972) has suggested that changes in the biological timetable in the direction of more rapid and elaborate maturation intensify the conflicts and dilemmas of the adolescent in our society.

The extensive literature in this area emphasizes the interrelation between societal forces and psychic development. Erikson (1968) described the importance of a psychosocial moratorium for adolescents in their psychic restructuring and consolidation. However, there is no moratorium of the mind. Psychic activity and change are intense during this period, challenging one to understand the rapid shifts observed in a youth undergoing analysis.

Pathology

Because late adolescence is characterized by psychic upheaval together with reorganization, the separation of pathological from normal activity is a difficult task. Surgent instinctual activity, revived infantile conflicts, changes in the stability of the superego, and ego vulnerability can lead to alarming behavior. Assessment of mental activity, rather than of behavior alone, is a requirement for understanding a given individual; generalizations can easily lead to misdiagnosis.

Especially common is the difficulty in differentiating psychotic or severe neurotic states from normal disruption. Late adolescents entering analysis with the appearance of being overtly psychotic often regain their psychic equilibrium in a short time and show remarkable restoration of function. Because of the mercurial behavior changes typical of the period, the clinician must exercise caution in diagnosis and give the patient an opportunity to resume functioning in a way that is least disruptive to his life. For instance, a decision to hospitalize a patient might have the effect of reinforcing pathological defenses rather than resolving them. Decisions of this type are difficult to make, especially when symptoms, such as depression, are intense.

There is a need to take into account the special characteristics of this age group—structural and object relationship changes—and use them as diagnostic guideposts. Anna Freud (1958) notes the etiological elements characteristic of adolescence to be the danger felt not only from the id impulses and fantasies, but also from love objects of the individual's past. One observes intense reactions to parents when they are treated as archaic figures from the past rather than as present realities. New relationships in which the transference to earlier objects surfaces also become threats to be defended against. In the course of an analysis some patients seem to be besieged on three sides—by the living parents, by new love objects, and by the analyst. All three, including the parents, can become objects of transference revivals of the infantile past. Narcissistic retreat, a part of the regression necessary for progress to occur, also created anxiety in the youth and his family.

Changes in the superego, with resultant weakening or strengthening of the controlling function, can lead to delinquent or asocial behavior with a lessening of overt guilt or to masochistic symptoms accompanied by intensification of guilt. The ego ideal, instead of functioning in the service of maturation, can act as a barrier to change. The entire range of the infantile neurosis can be revived. Clinical experience reveals that intensification of pathology can be part of the process of mastering old problems, much in the manner of play, only with less pleasure in the activity.

The shift from late adolescence to early adulthood creates a stability that greatly facilitates the differentiation of pathology from normality. Blos (1972) believes that the consolidation process of early adulthood structures the adult neurosis into its definitive form. Laufer (1976) maintains that because a person's final sexual organization is established by the end of adolescence it is essential to determine if the adolescent developmental process is either seriously interfered with by internalized conflict or has stopped as a result of the breakdown of functioning. Treatment aims to restore progressive development. Laufer believes the treatment of young adults should be directed toward understanding and working through the traumata and pathological solutions of adolescence.

Because of the vulnerability to pathology during late adolescence, it becomes imperative to give the individual an opportunity for sorting out and evaluating his mental functioning. It is a time in life when considerable change can occur as a result of analytic assistance.

Technique

The psychoanalysis of late adolescents and young adults follows the basic principles of analytic technique: analysis of the transference and resistance, and resolution of the transference neurosis. The unique characteristics of youth shape the special technical interventions and act as a guide in the evaluation of psychic change.

Current interest in developmental defects and their effect on later pathology has evoked considerable discussion on the need for change in technique. Eissler (1950) dealt with differences in the kinds of technique required in the psychoanalysis and therapy of delinquents. Knowledge of deprivations in infancy and childhood and their effects on later development has called for reassessment of the efficacy of different techniques. However, such changes would alter the aim of standard analytic technique from the analysis of conflict to attempts to create psychic function that has never fully developed. Little has been written about this change of technique as it relates specifically to youth.

Analysis of the transference is essential in youth as it is in other phases. Freud (1905a) cited failure in mastery of the transference as a reason for Dora's early interruption of her analysis. A feature differentiating late adolescence and adulthood is the quality of the transference neurosis—the new edition of the infantile neurosis directed toward the analyst (Adatto, 1971; Blos, 1972; Ritvo, 1974; Sandler, Kennedy, and Tyson, 1975). The late adolescent, because of the threat of regression experienced in the relationship with the analyst and the vulnerability of the psychic apparatus, evidences an attenuated or sporadic transference neurosis as compared to its full expression in the adult. The incompleteness of the transference neurosis is reflected in the patient's inability to fully explore the infantile neurosis and its later versions during analysis. Thus, one observes that many late adolescents interrupt their analysis once satisfying love relationships are established and sufficient analysis is accomplished for them to achieve adult stability. Often as adults they resume their analytic work.

There is also a focus on the importance and difficulties of reviving the adolescent period in the analysis of adults, and especially of the attitudes toward parents during adolescence (A. Freud, 1958; Lampl-de Groot, 1960; Hurn, 1970; Feigelson, 1976). The reconstruction of childhood has always been taken as a given in adult analysis; the necessity of understanding of the adolescent phase is now recognized as well. No doubt the vagueness, secrecy, and psychic discomfort of the period contribute to the paucity of information offered by adult analysands about their adolescence. Even in the analysis of late adolescents, it is difficult to revive the earlier adolescent period, which often was crucial in determining the structure of the psyche.

References

Adatto, C. P. (1958), Ego reintegration observed in analysis of late adolescents. *Internat. J. Psycho-Anal.*, 39:172–177.

———— (1966), On the metamorphosis from adolescence into adulthood. *J. Amer. Psychoanal. Assn.,* 14:485–509.

———— (1971), Developmental aspects of the transference neurosis. In: *Currents in Psychoanalysis,* ed. I. M. Marcus. New York: International Universities Press, pp. 337–360.

Aichhorn, A. (1925), *Wayward Youth.* New York: Viking, 1948.

Aries, P. A. (1962), A social history of adolescence. In: *The Psychology of Adolescence: Essential Readings,* ed. A. H. Esman. New York: International Universities Press, 1962.

Bernfeld, S. (1923), Uber eine typsiche Form der mannlichen Pubertat (On a typical form of male puberty). *Imago,* 9:169–188.

Blos, P. (1962), *On Adolescence: A Psychoanalytic Interpretation.* New York: Free Press.

———— (1967), The second individuation process of adolescence. *The Psychoanalytic Study of the Child,* 22:162–186. New York: International Universities Press.

———— (1968), Character formation in adolescence. *The Psychoanalytic Study of the Child,* 23:245–263. New York: International Universities Press.

———— (1972), The epigenesis of the adult neurosis. *The Psychoanalytic Study of the Child,* 27:106–135. New York: Quadrangle.

———— (1976), When and how does adolescence end? Structural criteria for adolescent closure. *J. Phila. Assn. Psychoanal.,* 3:47–58.

Breuer, J., & Freud, S. (1893–1895), Studies on hysteria. *Standard Edition,* 2. London: Hogarth Press, 1955.

Deutsch, H. (1967), *Selected Problems of Adolescence: With Special Emphasis on Group Formation.* New York: International Universities Press.

Eissler, K. R. (1949), Some problems of delinquency. In: *Searchlights on Delinquency: New Psychoanalytic Studies,* ed. K. R. Eissler. New York: International Universities Press, pp. 3–25.

———— (1950), Ego-psychological implications of the psychoanalytic treatment of delinquents. *The Psychoanalytic Study of the Child,* 5:97–121. New York: International Universities Press.

———— (1958), Notes on problems of technique in the psychoanalytic treatment of adolescents: With some remarks on perversions. *The Psychoanalytic Study of the Child,* 13:223–254. New York: International Universities Press.

Erikson, E. H. (1959), Identity and the life cycle. *Psychological Issues,* Monograph 1. New York: International Universities Press.

———— (1968), *Identity: Youth and Crisis.* New York: Norton.

Feigelson, C. I. (1976), Reconstruction of adolescence (and early latency) in the analysis of an adult woman. *The Psychoanalytic Study of the Child,* 31:225–236. New Haven: Yale University Press.

Fountain, G. (1961), Adolescent into adult: An inquiry. *J. Amer. Psychoanal. Assn.,* 9:417–433.

Freud, A. (1936), *The Ego and the Mechanisms of Defense.* Rev. ed. New York: International Universities Press, 1966.

———— (1958), Adolescence. *The Psychoanalytic Study of the Child,* 13:255–278. New York: International Universities Press.

Freud, S. (1905a), Fragment of an analysis of a case of hysteria. *Standard Edition,* 7:7–122. London: Hogarth Press, 1953.

———— (1905b), Three essays on the theory of sexuality. *Standard Edition,* 7:130–243. London: Hogarth Press, 1953.

———— (1918), From the history of an infantile neurosis. *Standard Edition,* 17:7–120. London: Hogarth Press, 1955.

———— (1920), The psychogenesis of a case of homosexuality in a woman. *Standard Edition,* 18:147–172. London: Hogarth Press, 1955.

———— (1923), The ego and the id. *Standard Edition,* 19:12–66. London: Hogarth Press, 1961.

———— (1933), New introductory lectures on psycho-analysis. *Standard Edition,* 22:5–182. London: Hogarth Press, 1964.

Friedman, M., Glasser, M., Laufer, E., Laufer, M., & Wohl, M. (1972), Attempted suicide and self-mutilation in adolescence: Some observations from a psychoanalytic research project. *Internat. J. Psycho-Anal.,* 53:179–183.

Furman, E. (1973), A contribution to assessing the role of infantile separation-individuation in adolescent development. *The Psychoanalytic Study of the Child,* 28:193–207. New Haven: Yale University Press.

Galenson, E. (1976), Panel report: Psychology of women: Late adolescence and early adulthood. *J. Amer. Psychoanal. Assn.,* 24:631–645.

Geleerd, E. R. (1961), Some aspects of ego vicissitudes in adolescence. *J. Amer. Psychoanal. Assn.,* 9:395–405.

Gillman, R. D. (1971), Panel report: Genetic, dynamic and adaptive aspects of dissent. *J. Amer. Psychoanal. Assn.,* 29:122–130.

Gitelson, M. (1948), Character synthesis: The psychotherapeutic problem in adolescence. *Amer. J. Orthopsychiat.,* 18:422–431.

Hartmann, H., & Loewenstein, R. M. (1962), Notes on the superego. *The Psychoanalytic Study of the Child,* 17:7–122. New York: International Universities Press.

Hurn, H. T. (1970), Adolescent transference: A problem in the terminal phase of analysis. *J. Amer. Psychoanal. Assn.,* 18:342–357.

Jacobson, E. (1961), Adolescent moods and the remodelling of psychic structures in adolescence. *The Psychoanalytic Study of the Child,* 16:164–183. New York: International Universities Press.

Jones, E. (1922), Some problems of adolescence. In: *Papers on Psycho-Analysis,* 5th ed. London: Bailliere, Tindall & Cox, 1948, pp. 389–406.

Katan, A. (1937), The role of displacement in agoraphobia. *Internat. J. Psycho-Anal.,* 32:41–50, 1951.

Kohut, H. (1971), *The Analysis of the Self.* New York: International Universities Press.

Lampl-de Groot, J. (1960), On adolescence. *The Psychoanalytic Study of the Child,* 15:95–103. New York: International Universities Press.

———— (1962), Ego ideal and superego. *The Psychoanalytic Study of the Child,* 17:94–106. New York: International Universities Press.

Laufer, M. (1964), Ego ideal and pseudo ego ideal in adolescence. *The Psychoanalytic Study of the Child,* 19:196–221. New York: International Universities Press.

———— (1965), Assessment of adolescent disturbances: The application of Anna Freud's diagnostic profile. *The Psychoanalytic Study of the Child,* 20:99–123. New York: International Universities Press.

———— (1976), The central masturbation fantasy, the final sexual organization, and adolescence. *The Psychoanalytic Study of the Child*, 31:297–316. New Haven: Yale University Press.

Lustman, S. L. (1972), Yale's year of confrontation: A view from the Master's house. *The Psychoanalytic Study of the Child*, 27:57–73. New York: Quadrangle.

Mahler, M. (1968), *On Human Symbiosis and the Vicissitudes of Individuation: Vol. I. Infantile Psychosis.* New York: International Universities Press.

Marcus, I. M. (1973), Panel Report: The experience of separation-individuation in infancy and its reverberations through the course of life. *J. Amer. Psychoanal. Assn.*, 21:155–167.

Moore, W. T. (1975), Some economic functions of genital masturbation during adolescent development. In: *Masturbation: From Infancy to Senescence*, ed. I. M. Marcus & J. J. Francis. New York: International Universities Press, pp. 231–276.

Pedersen, S. (1961), Personality formation in adolescence and its impact upon the psycho-analytical treatment of adults. *Internat. J. Psycho-Anal.*, 42:381–388.

Pumpian-Mindlin, E. (1965), Omnipotentiality, youth and commitment. *J. Amer. Acad. Child Psychiat.*, 4:1–18.

Ritvo, S. (1971), Late adolescence: Developmental and clinical considerations. *The Psychoanalytic Study of the Child*, 26:241–263. New York: Quadrangle.

——— (1974), Current status of the concept of infantile neurosis: Implications for diagnosis and technique. *The Psychoanalytic Study of the Child*, 29:159–181. New Haven: Yale University Press.

Sandler, J., Kennedy, H., & Tyson, R. L. (1975), Discussions on transference: The treatment situation and technique in child psychoanalysis. *The Psychoanalytic Study of the Child*, 30:409–441. New Haven: Yale University Press.

Schafer, R. (1973), Concepts of self and identity and the experience of separation-individuation in adolescence. *Psychoanal. Quart.*, 42:42–59.

Settlage, C. F. (1972), Cultural values and the superego in late adolescence. *The Psychoanalytic Study of the Child*, 27:74–92. New York: Quadrangle.

Solnit, A. J. (1972), Youth and the campus: The search for social conscience. *The Psychoanalytic Study of the Child*, 27:98–105. New York: Quadrangle.

Spiegel, L. A. (1958), Comments on the psychoanalytic psychology of adolescence. *The Psychoanalytic Study of the Child*, 13:296–308. New York: International Universities Press.

Winnicott, D. W. (1953), Transitional objects and transitional phenomena. *Internat. J. Psycho-Anal.*, 34:89–97.

Wittels, F. (1949), The ego of the adolescent. In: *Searchlights on Delinquency: New Psychoanalytic Studies*, ed. K. R. Eissler. New York: International Universities Press, pp. 256–262.

16

Passages from Late Adolescence to Early Adulthood

STUART T. HAUSER, M.D., PH.D.

WENDY M. GREENE, ED.M.

The passage from adolescence to young adulthood represents a major psychosocial transition. During this transition, formerly held beliefs are often reevaluated, adjusted, or even relinquished. The loss of old values and the concomitant assumption of new ones entails a dual process of learning and adjustment. In order to achieve satisfaction in new roles, emotional investment in previous roles must be abandoned. Acute discomfort and confusion can be aspects of the strain of learning a new role (Riley and Waring, 1976). Levinson, Darrow, Klein, Levinson, and McKee (1978) comment that transitional periods function as links or "bridges" between two more stable life stages. Transitional periods are characterized as times of reflection, self-evaluation, and possibly upheaval, for primary tasks are to reassess current values and goals and to explore options for growth in the self and the world. As individuals pass through periods of transition, they essentially terminate past modes of life and commence new ones. The end of a transitional period is signified by a commitment to new choices, values, and life goals. The emotional concomitant of personal and social transitions is described by Haan (1981) as involving anxiety regarding future risks and uncertainties. Individuals may also mourn the loss of their current ways of being in the world, and anxiously anticipate the changes that inevitably accompany developmental transitions (Levinson, 1986).

Late adolescents encounter these aspects of transitions, as

well as others that are more specifically tied to the passage from adolescence to adulthood. With the advent of adulthood, relationships and institutions that once supplied coherence and stability no longer serve these functions as fully. As an adult, one is expected to become a "self-propelling" individual who can attain goals through successful manipulation of the environment (Neugarten, 1969). Potential benefits of this developmental transition include greater life options and more freedom than ever before. But late adolescents can experience the responsibility of adult choice and independence as an encumbrance; in fact, the weight of these new choices and expectations can make the losses or costs of growing up seem much more intense or "real" than the possible benefits (Levinson, 1986). Late adolescents often respond to the developmental tasks of this period with feelings of alienation, vulnerability, and uncertainty regarding their abilities to function successfully in the adult world (Cox, 1970). Havighurst (1953) sees this phenomenon as so pervasive that he characterizes the young adult period as a time of "storm and stress." Neugarten (1969) notes that individuals often evaluate their success or maturity through determining how they measure up to age norms and societally defined expectations. Comparisons with friends and classmates, as well as one's internalized vision of what is socially expected, can become the basis for determining self-worth. During the transition to young adulthood, this type of self-evaluation can be painful; for in late adolescence, individuals are often particularly invested in being socially effective and appropriate (Haan, 1981).

Understanding the development from late adolescence to young adulthood becomes an especially intriguing and important enterprise when we consider the implications of this stage of life. It is during this transitional phase that individuals will attempt to leave a world where they lived as children and adolescents, and enter a world where they will be considered adults (Levinson et al., 1978). Primary tasks of the passage to adulthood include finding a preliminary adult identity, making interpersonal and occupational commitments, and deciding upon a value system that is compatible with both self and society. Levinson characterizes this stage of the life cycle as rich in

energy and potential, yet fraught with external pressures. Indeed, he suggests that early adulthood may be the most dramatic period of the life span.

The study of late adolescence, early adulthood, and the
transition between these developmental phases is truly inter-
disciplinary. As the volume *Themes of Love and Work in Adulthood*
(Smelser and Erikson, 1980) exemplifies, this complex area is
now the province of social science (life span developmental
psychology, social psychology, sociology, anthropology) and
clinical observation (psychiatry, clinical psychology). Relevant
theoretical and empirical contributions from these perspectives
provide the basis for our detailed consideration of the passage
from the late adolescent to the young adult years.

Basic Domains in the Transition to Young Adulthood

Four themes persistently surface in discussions of this transition: separation-individuation, consolidation of identity, establishment of intimate relationships, and the launching of a
career. In the following sections, we explore each of these
themes independently, and consider how they interpenetrate
one another.

Separation-Individuation

In his seminal work on the second individuation process
of adolescence, Blos (1979) argues that the adolescent must
abandon infantile ties to parents as a prerequisite to joining the
adult world. This perspective is echoed by Adatto (see chapter
15), who characterizes late adolescence as a time when individuals disengage from parents to the extent that they are free to
pursue nonfamilial heterosexual love relationships. Ausubel
and Kirk (1977) concur that one of the most important aspects
of the transition to young adulthood is the late adolescents'
separation from parents. This disengagement precedes the establishment of an autonomous identity.

These theoretical formulations are supported by the results
of various empirical investigations. For example, Gould (1972)
investigated phase-specific concerns of patients in various stages

of the life span. The patients were assigned to homogeneous age therapy groups (16–18, 18–22, 22–28) and observed continuously by one of the study group staff. Each member of the research team was asked to describe the group in the simplest, most obvious terms. Patterns identified in the first observations of these groups were again observed by new members of the research team six months later, as well as by medical students who listened to tapes of the group therapy sessions. Moreover, questionnaires administered to a nonpatient population revealed similar age-specific concerns. The results of these studies indicated that key issues for these late adolescents and young adults involved establishment of autonomy through separation from parents. In the oldest group, 22 to 28 years old, a primary concern was the reestablishment of a connection with the parents, together with the need to prove their ability to function as adults.

More recently, Hoffman (1984) studied the relationship between the psychological separation of late adolescents from their parents and subsequent personal adjustment. Extrapolating from descriptions of the separation-individuation phase during infancy and early childhood, Hoffman conceptualized four separate aspects of the process of psychological separation during adolescence: functional independence, attitudinal independence, conflictual independence, and emotional independence. One hundred fifty college students (18 to 22 years old) responded to a variety of self-report measures, including an inventory assessing psychological separation and a checklist assessing personal adjustment. Overall, greater emotional independence was associated with better personal adjustment. There were also gender-specific results. For female students, greater conflictual independence was associated with better overall personal adjustment, while for males this type of independence was correlated with greater satisfaction in intimate relationships.

Lasser and Snarey (1989) investigated relationships between late adolescent girls' levels of ego development and their ability to accomplish the developmental task of psychologically separating from the family. One hundred thirty-one white middle class girls (16 to 17 years old) from intact families were studied in terms of ego development and their perceptions of parental behavior. Twelve subjects were randomly chosen from this group to participate in more intensive interviews; these included four from each of three broad ego development groupings (preconformist, conformist, and postconformist).[1] Girls functioning at the earliest stages (preconformist) had the most difficulty achieving autonomy. These girls presented as insecure, dependent, and prone to mood swings. They portrayed their mothers as needy and their fathers as uncommunicative and uninvolved with them. Mothers and daughters within this group exhibited a degree of emotional closeness that was so intense it appeared to impede the daughter's ability to separate from the family.

Girls intermediate in development (conformist) expressed ambivalence over becoming more autonomous. Presenting as relatively subdued and restrained, they appeared uncertain of their ability to function independently in the adult world. These girls characterized their mothers as concerned and involved, but also overly invested in how their daughters should conduct their lives. In contrast, their fathers were described as critical and uncommunicative. Nonetheless, their fathers were depicted as more involved than those of the preconformist girls.

Girls functioning at the highest ego development stage (postconformist) expressed the least difficulty in achieving autonomy. They appeared self-confident, friendly, and warm. They seemed able to integrate both positive and negative emotions regarding themselves and their parents. Their mothers were characterized as independent, caring, and supportive of

---

[1] Individuals functioning at preconformist stages of ego development are generally impulsive, wary, and manipulative. Their interpersonal style is dependent or exploitive, with an emphasis on receiving. Those functioning at conformist stages are typically preoccupied with personal appearance, social acceptability, and banal feelings. They attempt to be helpful to others and are concerned wth belonging, but their interactions are superficial. Their cognitive style is characterized by conceptual simplicity and cliches. Finally, individuals at postconformist stages are aware of differentiated feelings and motives. They are concerned with self-respect and achievements. Their cognitive style is characterized as conceptually complex. They demonstrate an increased toleration for ambiguity, and an understanding of psychological causation. Interpersonally, they are responsible and concerned with communication.

their daughters' efforts to become more independent. Fathers were seen as consistent and actively concerned with their lives. The authors conclude that the adolescent girl's level of ego development and her ability to separate from her family are directly related to the dynamics of the mother-daughter, the father-daughter, and the joint parenting relationship.

These studies suggest a connection between psychological separation from parents in late adolescence and an increase in psychosocial competence. However, the developmental paradigm which emphasizes separation and independence from parents as key tasks of late adolescence is not unequivocally accepted by all observers. Kaplan, Klein, and Gleason (1985) comment that this model focuses on issues that are salient for men in this stage of the life span. They question the adequacy of this developmental framework in addressing the experiences of late adolescent women. More specifically, they argue that attainment of greater levels of independence, autonomy, and separation may not characterize women's development. As an alternative, these researchers conceptualize development as "fluid" and continuous, suggesting that women's continued engagement in primary relationships may enhance rather than impede growth.

Kaplan, Klein, and Gleason critique Blos's theoretical notion of a second separation-individuation phase in adolescence (1979), and argue instead that continued close engagement and identification between mothers and daughters are aspects of healthy development. Also challenging the "discontinuity perspective" is Galatzer-Levy (1984), who observes that in the prevailing psychoanalytic view, normal adolescence ends when individuals renounce primary object ties. He suggests that the concept of completely separating from parents is indigenous to European and American culture, where the goal of development is "psychological individualism." This model is contradicted by observations of normal growth which indicate that maintaining relationships with parents and grandparents actually fosters development. Consistent with this vantage point is the work of Offer, Ostrov, and Howard (1981), who investigated the self-images of thousands of adolescents through a questionnaire tapping functioning in multiple areas. Their findings indicate that normal adolescents characterize their family interactions as enjoyable, fulfilling, and generally free of intergenerational conflicts surrounding issues of separation.

Grotevant and Cooper (1986) highlight some important problems in investigations emphasizing "continuity." The techniques utilized in such studies are often large-scale surveys or highly structured interviews. These instruments may not tap areas that are conflictual for the adolescent. For example, the technique relied on in the investigation of Offer, Ostrov, and Howard (1981) calls for the adolescent to respond numerically to statements along a continuum of "describes me very well" to "doesn't describe me at all." This format may not capture subtle nuances and less obvious feelings embedded in parent-adolescent relationships. Other methodological constraints may bias results in the clinical and sociological studies which claim to support the separation perspective. Sociological studies which emphasize "separation" usually examine how families negotiate power. This dynamic is typically assessed through a group decision-making task in which only one person can win. As a result, patterns of conflict and dominance rather than more egalitarian interactions emerge (Grotevant and Cooper, 1986). Likewise, clinicians who equate separation and autonomy with growth and psychological maturity base these conclusions on clinical experiences with troubled adolescents. Investigations of family interactions indicate that troubled adolescents and their families may not successfully renegotiate the parent-adolescent relationship to one in which there is increased equality and mutual respect between family members. In these families, the division of power remains similar to that characterizing the families of young children. This can lead to distant, angry, and mistrustful relationships between parents and their adolescent children (Hill, 1980).

Suggesting that the parent-child relationship is characterized by *both* continuity and change, Grotevant and Cooper (1986) offer a third perspective, which holds that the parent-child relationship undergoes transformations as the individual traverses adolescence. From this vantage point, there is continued engagement between parents and children, but the terms of the relationship are renegotiated to accommodate each member's changing needs. This perspective is consistent with Murphy, Silber, Coelho, Hamburg, and Greenberg's (1963) investigation of late adolescents' development of autonomy and the maintenance of parental relationships, which focused on patterns of parent-child interaction that took place around the transition from high school to college. Through a series of interviews, college bound high school seniors were rated on dimensions of autonomy and relatedness. Autonomy was defined as the ability to make responsible choices independently, to accept responsibility for one's decisions, and to view oneself as separate from parents. Relatedness was defined as satisfaction in a primarily positive relationship with parents.

Subjects who were rated highly on both autonomy and relatedness were engaged in parental relationships characterized by both continuity and change. Parents of these subjects encouraged their offspring's efforts to achieve greater autonomy and independence. Regarding separation and the college experience as necessary for normal development, they nonetheless remained available should their adolescent request help or guidance. Adolescents in this group were able to separate emotionally from parents, while reporting increased satisfaction with parental relationships characterized as egalitarian and mutually respectful. In a discussion of transformations in family relationships during adolescence, Hill (1980) observes that during the high school years there is an increase in subjective feelings of autonomy that is positively associated with a sense of closeness to parents.

The theme of continuity and change in the parental relationship as the adolescent approaches adulthood also appears in the work of Levinson et al. (1978). These researchers suggest that as individuals enter young adulthood a key developmental task is to maintain engagement with parents while changing aspects of the relationship which are no longer adaptive. For example, young adults may find that adolescent behaviors, such as acting out in rebellious or excessively compliant ways, no longer serve any purpose for them. As immature features of the parent-child relationship are abandoned, they are replaced with increased levels of mutual respect and a growing awareness and appreciation of each other's unique and separate identity.

McGoldrick (1982) considers renegotiation of the adolescent-parent relationship the critical developmental task of late adolescence. In McGoldrick's model, relationships between parents and their late adolescent children become increasingly symmetrical. One aspect of this process of change is that late adolescents become more appreciative of their parents for who they are, accepting their limitations and viewing them more realistically and empathically.

Staples and Smarr (see chapter 17) cite the 1968 Group for Advancement of Psychiatry Report on Normal Adolescence. Among the developmental markers listed there as indicating the passing of adolescence are the adolescent's separation from parents in order to develop more autonomously. Once the adolescent has attained some degree of independence and a sense of separateness, the task is to return to the parents but to relate in a new, more equal way. This entails the resolution of ambivalent feelings toward parents to the extent that parent-adolescent interactions become more mutually respectful and tolerant.

The theme of evolution toward mutuality in the parent-adolescent relationship is discussed also by White, Speisman, and Costos (1983). According to them, parent-child relationships go through a series of transformations as children mature from adolescence into young adulthood. An early signal of change in the parent-adolescent relationship is the adolescent's effort to separate from parents and function more independently. Subsequently, adolescents demonstrate an increased ability to empathize with parents and to see them as separate, unique individuals. Longitudinal observations of 156 young adult men and women provide some support for this model. Findings based on ego development and self-report measures indicate that separation from parents, greater ability to see parents' perspective, and growing equality in the parent-child relationship are successive steps in the achievement of fully mature relationships between adults and their parents.

In an investigation of parent-adolescent relationships in 121 white middle class two-parent families, Grotevant and Cooper (1986) observed that these relationships change considerably as individuals progress from early adolescence through young adulthood. A family interaction task, in which family members were instructed to discuss plans for a hypothetical vacation, was assessed in terms of communication patterns that signal independence and autonomous functioning as well as connection and engagement between family members. The findings portray parent-child relationships as evolving from childhood into early adulthood toward increased mutuality of influence, with family relations characterized by qualities of individuality *and* connectedness.

Several of these studies converge in their emphasis on the complexity of late adolescents' relationships to parents. Changes in these relationships may show how late adolescents resolve several related tasks: consolidating an identity, launching a career, and establishing new intimate relationships. If late adolescents can differentiate from parents without severing parental ties or seeking substitutes or replacements for parents in their intimate relationships, they will be better able to decide on personal life goals and commitments. Without the attainment of some degree of independence from parents, late adolescents will have difficulty with the developmental tasks appropriate to this stage of the life cycle (McGoldrick, 1982).

Consolidation of Identity

Blos (1979) posits that the termination of any phase of development is indicated by increased stabilization and coordination of ego functions. He describes late adolescence as a "consolidation phase" during which the individual becomes progressively more consistent in both motivation and behavior. More specifically, within this phase one begins to formulate realistic plans and goals for the future and demonstrates an increasingly clear value system. In Blos's view, the late adolescent's progressive stabilization of identity is associated with a process of introspection whereby the individual attempts to organize or gain insight into his or her personal life history. This period of reflection results in adolescents' formulating their *own* perspective on their past, present, and future. Gains in emotional, physical, and moral independence are also associated with this process, and signal that adolescence is passing.

Staples and Smarr (chapter 17) similarly characterize late

adolescence as a time when individuals must organize their various identifications into a cohesive sense of self. The "self" or identity that emerges must satisfy both internal needs and external demands. The psychological process of consolidation is complex and multifaceted. It encompasses the resolution of oedipal issues that have assumed renewed importance in adolescence, development of an autonomous self in relation to parents, assumption of a realistic view of one's capabilities, and the establishment of a firm sexual identity (Jacobs, 1984b). Another aspect of the consolidation process is that late adolescents often successfully resolve conflicts from earlier developmental periods. Along with facilitating greater levels of autonomy, this helps to free the ego from former defensive activities (see Adatto, chapter 15). Subsequently, individuals become increasingly adept at integrating and coping with the renewed instinctual demands of adolescence. Fountain (1961) describes adolescence as a psychologically turbulent time. He considers the gradual reestablishment of psychic equilibrium to indicate passage into adulthood. Late adolescents can achieve psychic stability through utilizing their newly expanded range of opportunities to test which defenses work most effectively and how to apply them. This process leads to a decrease in the mood swings and impulsive actions so characteristic of adolescents. Jacobs (1984b) comments that other manifestations of the stabilization and integration of ego functions include young adults' greater tolerance for conflict and frustration, as well as their increased energy to invest in new interests and activities.

White's observations (1952) of the natural developmental process of late adolescence and young adulthood also indicate a trend toward stability and consistency of identity. Maturation in the direction of stabilization represents late adolescents' growing awareness of their abilities to influence the world around them, as well as increased confidence in their potential for personal growth. White states that the new circumstances and interpersonal interactions that late adolescents encounter are instrumental in helping them develop more organized and stable self-perceptions. Over time and with ample experience, individuals begin to respond to new events in ways consistent with their value systems and self-identifications. Summarizing much recent literature on adolescent development, Petersen and Craighead (1986) detail a spectrum of personality dimensions that display gradual maturation throughout adolescence and adulthood. Most relevant to our considerations is their discussion of progression in moral and ego development, self-esteem, and the establishment of a stable identity.

The association between family variables and various forms of "identity status"[2] was investigated by Waterman (1982). He found that late adolescents in the identity foreclosure status described relationships with parents as very close and involved; late adolescents in the identity diffusion status reported that relationships with parents were "distant"; and late adolescents in the moratorium and identity achievement statuses spoke critically of parents, describing relationships with families as conflictual. Waterman hypothesized that in these latter groups intrafamilial tension may have been associated with the ambivalence of both parents and offspring over the adolescents' attempts to separate from the family. He suggested that once adolescents resolved their identity crises, family relationships would become more harmonious.

The correlation between identity foreclosure and close relationships between late adolescents and their parents may reflect the inability of these late adolescents to differentiate between their own values and commitments and those of their parents. Staples and Smarr (chapter 17) suggest that when individuals choose identifications which are uncritical, wholesale imitations of parents, without the self-examination and exploration of options that mature identity requires, the consequence may be premature foreclosure. They posit that adolescents typ-

[2] In Erikson's model (1950), the major task of adolescence is consolidation of ego identity. Based on Erikson's work, Marcia (1966) derived and operationalized four types of "identity status." The status of *identity achievement* describes individuals who have explored various possibilities before committing to an identity. Individuals who settle on an identity before exploring various possibilities are considered to be in the *identity foreclosure* status. The *moratorium* status describes individuals who are exploring various possibilities but have not yet committed to an identity. The status of *identity diffusion* refers to individuals who have neither explored identity possibilities nor committed themselves to an identity.

ically need to experiment with a variety of identifications before deciding on an enduring system of values and goals.

The longitudinal findings of Block (1971) are consistent with the perspective that as adolescents develop into young adults they demonstrate increased coherence and stability of ego identity. In addition, as Block's subjects progressed from late adolescence to their early thirties, they manifested growth in important interpersonal areas. For example, they seemed able to give more fully of themselves when interacting with others and appeared more adept at taking responsibility for themselves and others. Staples and Smarr (chapter 17) also delineate connections between consolidation of identity and increased capacity for mutually satisfying interpersonal relationships. They contend that achievement of fulfilling love relationships is critical to considering oneself connected to the outside world in a positive way. Once this occurs, young adults experience a reduction in emotional conflict and an increase in energy to invest in educational pursuits, career exploration, and learning the ways of the world.

Intimacy

The developmental relationship between identity achievement and the establishment of intimate relationships has not yet been established in the psychological literature. On the one hand, Staples and Smarr (chapter 17) adopt Sullivan's perspective (1953) that an intimate relationship is critical to the formation of an identity. In contrast, Erikson (1950) views the achievement of an identity as *preceding* the establishment of intimate relations, considering genuine intimacy to both indicate and test the strength of boundaries between self and others. He observes that if attempts to establish intimate relationships fail, the impact can be devastating for some young adults. Difficulties arising during this developmental stage often signal unresolved issues from the previous developmental task of identity formation. Once identity issues are worked through, the young adult is better equipped to truly engage with another person.

In Erikson's model, the developmental task of late adolescence and early adulthood is the establishment of reciprocal intimate heterosexual relationships. Intimacy is defined as the willingness and ability to commit oneself to relationships which may engender compromise and sacrifice (Erikson, 1982). The mutual devotion that characterizes intimate relationships imbues the lives of young adults with vitality, strength, and cohesiveness (Erikson, 1968). Fischer (1981) posits that the establishment of an intimate style of relating is one of the most important aspects of the transition to young adulthood. Expanding Erikson's definition of intimacy to include friendship, she characterizes intimate relationships as mutually supportive, open, nonegocentric, and friendly.

Fischer studied developmental change in relationship style from adolescence to young adulthood through questioning college and high school students about same-sex and cross-sex relationships. Each subject responded to a questionnaire about his or her closest extrafamilial relationship. These responses were then assessed in terms of such dimensions as friendship and intimacy, and were grouped into four categories. Subjects who were above the median on both the friendship and intimacy variables were characterized as "integrated" in their style of relating. Subjects below the median on both dimensions were classified as "uninvolved"; those above the median on intimacy and below the median on friendship were labeled "intimate"; and those below the median on intimacy and above the median on friendship were termed "friendly."

When compared to the males in this study, young women were more frequently found to relate in an "intimate" fashion. This led Fischer to observe that if an intimate style of interacting is indeed characteristic of adulthood, the young women in this study appeared more mature than their male counterparts. There were no significant differences in the interaction styles of the high school and college men. Both cohorts described their relationships as typically same-sex and uninvolved. Fischer notes that in Erikson's framework lack of engagement between men may not impede resolution of the developmental task of intimacy, as Erikson explicitly characterizes intimate relationships as heterosexual. However, if men do not utilize their same-sex relationships as forums where they can practice more intimate styles of relating, they may feel uncomfortable or unprepared in subsequent attempts to form intimate relationships with women. In fact, men's lack of experience with intimate styles of relating may impair their abilities to form satisfying cross-sex intimate relationships.

The relationship between identity achievement and the establishment of intimate relationships has been the subject of several empirical investigations. Yufit (1956) systematically studied individuals who were engaged in intimate relationships and individuals who were unable to achieve intimacy. He found that successful resolution of the intimacy versus isolation crisis was most dependent on the successful resolution of previous psychosocial crises: trust, autonomy, and identity. In terms of identity, the subjects who had difficulty establishing intimate relationships were less certain of their occupational identities than were subjects who had achieved intimacy.

Orlofsky, Marcia, and Lesser (1973) considered the relationship between identity status and intimacy in a group of 53 male college students. Based on structured and semistructured interview data, their analyses indicated that the quality of interpersonal relationships is significantly associated with identity status. In their study, many of the identity achievement subjects had attained gratifying and mature intimate relationships. The moratorium subjects generally had intimate relationships with same-sex friends, but very few were engaged in lasting heterosexual love relationships. The interactions of the foreclosure subjects appeared superficial, lacking the intensity and genuine caring characteristic of the achievement subjects' relationships. Patterns of interaction in the identity diffusion group were similar to those characteristic of the foreclosure subjects. Their relationships were devoid of true and genuine engagement, or else they were isolated, with no close same-sex or cross-sex friends.

Although an association was found between identity status and resolution of the intimacy crisis, the sample for this study was all male, and thus the results may not be applicable to women. Tesch and Whitbourne (1982) note that Erikson (1950) considers a woman's identity incomplete until she establishes an intimate relationship. This suggests that the sequence of identity formation and intimacy characterizing female development may be the reverse of that representative of male development. In their study of 92 young adult men and women, Tesch and Whitbourne report that many subjects could be classified either as intimate or preintimate. The authors posit that this pattern may be associated with the subjects' ages, as they were five to six years older than the college-age participants of previous investigations. This finding provides support for Erikson's view that the developmental task of intimacy is negotiated during the early adult years. Contrary to what was expected, significant gender-specific patterns did not emerge. The identity and intimacy data of most female subjects were similar to that of the men, where high intimacy was associated with identity achievement. In addition, there were instances where women were successful at achieving an identity despite the absence of an intimate relationship. Likewise, there were examples of men and women who were engaged in intimate relationships even though they had not yet successfully resolved the identity crisis. However, in general, the findings from this investigation support the premise that resolution of identity issues facilitates the attainment of intimacy.

Renegotiation of the adolescent-parent relationship in late adolescence also plays a critical role in the adolescent's ability to become intimately involved in heterosexual relationships. With sufficient disengagement from parents, late adolescents have greater energy to invest in extrafamilial love interests (see chapter 15). There is a subsequent "freeing of personal relationships" (White, 1952), as late adolescents are better able to realistically assess current relationships, without burdening these new ties with inappropriate past reactions. White observes that as individuals negotiate the transition into young adulthood their repertoire of coping strategies expands considerably. This leads to greater flexibility, ease, and enjoyment when interacting with others.

Difficulties emerge during this transitional period when individuals have not yet resolved earlier developmental issues, especially those related to separation from parents and identity formation (Golan, 1981). Incomplete resolution of these developmental tasks interferes with their efforts to achieve gratifying relationships with others. For example, Winch (1950) found that males who were psychologically dependent on their mothers had problems establishing intimate heterosexual relationships. In contrast, girls who were able to emotionally separate from fathers had better adjustment in love relationships (Hoffman, 1984). Hoffman concludes from these findings that when young adults have unresolved conflictual feelings toward parents they may approach intimate relationships from an insecure and mistrustful vantage point.

Work and Socialization

A basic premise of Neugarten's approach to adult development (1969) is that people use societal norms and age expectations to measure their performance in the adult world. Through evaluating one's position on a continuum of socially defined expectations, one determines whether one is "off-time" in relation to achievements associated with particular developmental stages.

In young adulthood, work assumes a more important and complex role in this process of self-evaluation. Kohn (1980) states that work exerts a profound influence on people's self-concepts, values, intellectual development, and orientation to society. Induction into the labor force is often the young person's first direct encounter with societal values and institutions. This can be an alienating experience, for social mandates may be experienced as incompatible with the individual's present value system and life style. Keniston (1970) observes that tension between late adolescents or "youth" and society is often a theme during this stage of the life span. Successful resolution of this issue involves the integration of one's own needs and values with those of society, to the extent that both self and society are affirmed.

Exposure to societal norms may lead to internal and external conflict, but the opportunities provided by work for socialization and the assumption of responsibility are key dimensions of the transition to adulthood. The Panel on Youth Report (Heyneman, 1976) emphasizes involvement and exposure vis-à-vis work as the most important facets of the transition to young adulthood. The workplace provides a setting where late adolescents can assume various "real world roles." As employees, late adolescents are encouraged and expected to manage their own affairs, take initiative, and act responsibly and reliably. In addition, work plays a critical role in the socialization of late adolescents, since the interpersonal demands of the work environment are often different from those previously encountered by the adolescent (Steinberg, Greenberger, Jacobi, and Garduque, 1981). Work relationships entail extensive role adjustment and offer adolescents exposure to more heterogeneous populations than are usually encountered in school. These experiences are often instrumental in helping adolescents to become less self-centered and more aware of individual differences.

Piaget (1977) characterizes work as signaling the passage from adolescence to adulthood. From this vantage point, occupational roles play a critical role in orienting late adolescents to reality, for as individuals confront real world economic and social demands they are forced to reassess their dreams of changing society through ideology. This process of reassessment involves a continual refocusing of perspective, which Piaget calls "decentering." The decentering process enables adolescents to integrate their dreams with the social reality and indicates the beginning of adulthood:

> But the focal point of the decentering process is the entrance into the occupational world or the beginning of serious professional training. The adolescent becomes an adult when he undertakes a real job. It is then that he is transformed from an idealistic reformer into an achiever. In other words, the job leads thinking away from the dangers of formalism back into reality [p. 441].

The passage to young adulthood depends to a large extent on the ability of adolescents to reevaluate and abandon grandiose fantasies and dreams. These are replaced with more realistic assessments of capabilities and opportunities. This "decentering" process enables late adolescents to more objectively determine how to implement the developmental tasks that are expected at this stage of the life span. The late adolescent's work identity plays a central role in this process of reassessment. One redefines dreams for the future on the basis of what seems possible, given one's educational level and job options. It is then through job-related opportunities and compensation that these dreams are pursued (Levinson et al., 1978).

The establishment of an occupational identity helps late adolescents become more autonomous and independent. Placement in a work setting provides adolescents with a foothold in the adult world outside the parental home (Gould, 1980). As members of the labor force, late adolescents feel they can more legitimately consider themselves adults, and expect the world to accord them greater levels of respect and responsibility. In the workplace there are increased opportunities to interact with adults, both as peers and supervisors, and to identify with these new role models. More concretely, the money obtained from jobs helps adolescents disengage from parents and develop more autonomously (Shore, 1972). In addition, work plays an integral role in identity formation (Erikson, 1982). In fact, Erikson asserts that until one explores, tests, and commits to an occupational identity one has not successfully resolved the identity crisis. Placement in an occupational position is also accompanied by social recognition that one is a member of a particular profession—for example, that one *is* a teacher. This affords late adolescents and young adults a way of further defining who they are. Through performing the duties of a given profession, one has increased opportunities to develop a clearer and more stable sense of self (White, 1952).

In his discussion of development and career achievement, Marcus (see chapter 10) describes transformations that take place during the transition from school to career. From the ages of 10 to 12 there is a "fantasy phase" during which the child imagines a wide range of job options, considering only the enjoyment and excitement a particular occupation provides. This is followed by a "tentative period" lasting from puberty into mid-adolescence, in which the child more carefully and realistically assesses job options relative to his or her own capabilities and opportunities. A "realistic stage" follows the tentative period and lasts into early adulthood. This stage is characterized by compromise, as one recognizes that career options are heavily dependent on the skills one has acquired thus far. Along with this realization comes the understanding that professional choice is no longer limitless. This process culminates in the emergence of a work direction that reflects one's own capabilities and talents interacting with one's options and circumstances.

The developmental transition toward a career entails transformations in the interpersonal realm as well. Individuals must shift from nurturant relationships with parental and school authorities to work relationships which may be more impersonal (see chapter 10). In order to negotiate these changes successfully, late adolescents must reevaluate and adjust their orientation to themselves and others. Marcus (chapter 10) observes that this can be a disconcerting experience leading to confusion regarding identity or self-image. The familiar continuity of one's self-perceptions may seem jeopardized, and the ability to feel safe and anchored to the environment is temporarily lost.

At this stage of development, individuals are particularly vulnerable to societal mandates. Adatto (chapter 15) and Jacobs (1984a) note that in adolescence and young adulthood societal and cultural forces have an unusually strong influence on life choices and goals. One reason for this may be that the developmental task of separating from parents creates a void in the lives of late adolescents and young adults. Individuals may attempt to fill this void through absorbing societal values and rules.

In her longitudinal analyses, Haan (1981) reports that as late adolescents approach adulthood, they demonstrate an increased commitment to social values and institutions. They strive to develop qualities that will serve them well in the adult world, such as reliability, consistency, achievement motivation, and single-mindedness. These qualities often replace spontaneity and unpredictability. Haan notes that some life stages, such as young adulthood, seem characterized by accommodation. Other periods of the life cycle, such as adolescence, are characterized by assimilation.[3] The emphasis on accommoda-

---

[3] In assimilatory periods, the focus is on integrating new information; in accommodatory ones, on determining ways to incorporate potentially desirable possibilities, or to change what seems undesirable in the self. Haan (1981) considers adolescence to be an "assimilative" phase of life, while young adulthood is characteristically "accommodative."

tion in young adulthood is adaptive, for there are many concrete tasks that are expected at this stage of development (e.g., launching a career, establishing an intimate relationship, deciding on a life style). In order to successfully function in the world, young adults must learn to live and work within the framework of societal values and norms.

Jessor's findings (1983) indicate that one psychological aspect of the transition from adolescence to young adulthood is increased investment in living according to the rules of society. In a longitudinal investigation of psychosocial change from adolescence to young adulthood in 596 male and female subjects, there was a significant increase in conventional values and behaviors. Specifically, these subjects placed greater value on achievement and appeared more intolerant of deviance. They were less likely to criticize the status quo and seemed less invested in independence. A particularly interesting finding was that as they progressed through adolescence these subjects appeared to become increasingly tolerant of deviance. However, when assessed in young adulthood, they portrayed themselves as less tolerant of deviance than ever before. The subjects were also divided into low, medium, and high conformist groups according to their responses as adolescents, to determine where the greatest movement toward conformity took place. All three groups maintained their relative positions over the course of the study, with the low and medium conformist groups both becoming significantly more conventional, converging on the high conformist group, which remained static.

Accommodation to the environment and the return to conventionality suggest that social institutions and values play important roles in the transition to young adulthood. Haan (1981) observes that late adolescents must learn the rules of their communities in order to function successfully as adults. Yet rather than blindly accept societal norms, young adults ideally come to an understanding of environmental rules while maintaining their own values, self-identifications, and integrity. Finding this balance can be difficult, and young adults often overaccommodate to the environment (Haan, 1981). A consequence of this sacrifice may be frustration or anger, for the cost of adulthood then seems very high. Gould (1980) notes that young adults often view the world from a narrow perspective, where there is only one right way to do things. They may set up arbitrary internal standards by which to evaluate themselves, and desperately attempt to adhere to the rules "out there." This external focus on appearance and socioeconomic necessities takes place at the expense of introspection. Young adults may thereby spend much of their energy attempting to prove to others that they are competent adults who can master the environment. By mid-life, as individuals are more confident of their adult status, they may reexamine these self-imposed limits. This can result in an increase in introspection, as interest in personal growth and development increases.

Directions for Future Research

The changes which signal the passage from late adolescence into young adulthood take place slowly, and are often almost imperceptible (Fountain, 1961). Thus, it is difficult to determine the exact timing of this developmental transition. In this respect, the termination of adolescence differs significantly from its onset, for there are clear biological markers to signal the beginning of adolescence. Blos (1979) comments that the simultaneity of physiological and psychological changes that is characteristic of early adolescence fades as adolescence comes to a close. In terms of physical development, it is relatively easy to discern when changes referred to as "pubertal" come to an end. However, measuring the psychological component of the termination of adolescence is far more elusive (Blos, 1979).

Difficulties in identifying the beginning and end of this transitional period render investigations particularly problematic. There is great variability among researchers in the criteria used to distinguish adolescents from young adults. For example, in his discussion of the termination of adolescence, Fountain (1961) considers four qualities that distinguish adolescents from adults: adolescents are subject to great mood swings, displaying an intensity of emotion that appears attenuated by young adulthood; the impulsive need-gratifying behaviors characteristic of adolescents seems to wane by young adulthood; reality testing skills, which often are faulty in adolescence, improve by young adulthood; and, finally, young adults have a far more encompassing world view than adolescents do, appearing less egocentric and thus able to care about aspects of the world that do not directly affect them.

Another set of criteria used to distinguish adolescence from adulthood involves developmental tasks. Arguing that the termination of adolescence can be understood only through a consideration of psychological variables, Blos (1979) identifies four developmental tasks whose resolution signals the onset of adulthood: the integration of one's personal history to the extent that one has a clear and coherent sense of one's past, present, and future; the establishment of a clear sexual identity; separation and independence from parents; and the working through of traumas from earlier stages of development. Other investigators employ an age-grading strategy to determine where adolescence ends and adulthood begins. Levinson et al. (1978) suggest that the years 17 to 22 encompass the transitional period from adolescence to young adulthood, with the young adult phase occurring between the ages of 22 and 45. Havighurst (1953) considers early adulthood to span the ages of 18 to 30. In an extensive review of the literature on the late adolescent passage, Arnstein (1984) observes that while some researchers consider adolescence to end at age 25, others see age 17 as signaling the onset of adulthood. He concludes that the expressions "late adolescence" and "adulthood" are ambiguous and calls for a clearer terminology. In addition, chronological age is not unequivocally accepted as a variable that can distinguish developmental phases. Haan (1981) observes that the age at which major life events occur differs considerably among individuals and cultures. She therefore cautions against relying on chronological age as an index of development.

This lack of a clear conceptual framework to distinguish adolescents and young adults has led to inconsistencies in terminology. Blos (1979) refers to the period before adulthood as "late adolescence" or "postadolescence." In Levinson's framework, this phase of development is the "early adult transition," lasting from ages 17 to 22. Hoffman (1984) investigated subjects aged 18 to 22 and referred to them as "late adolescents." Observing that neither "late adolescence" nor "young adulthood" accurately captures this transitional period, Keniston (1970) offers the term "youth." Investigations of the late adolescent–young adult period are hindered by these inconsistencies. A key direction for future research is the establishment of clear conceptual and operational definitions of the adolescent-adult transition.

Levinson (1980) emphasizes the importance of considering both the individual and the individual's engagement with society in the study of adulthood. Adults affect the world around them and are in turn responsive to the life circumstances and social organizations they encounter (Pearlin, 1980). Identifying specific elements of the social structure that affect people's lives will greatly facilitate our understanding of adolescent and adult development. Blos (1979) succinctly illustrates this point when he states that successful consolidation of identity in late adolescence will be maintained over time only if relatively benign circumstances prevail.

Environmental circumstances such as the availability of employment and the sociopolitical climate are among the dimensions that deserve consideration. In his discussion of development and career achievement, Marcus (chapter 10) notes that "work identity" can become an important factor in self-esteem. Positions which provide few opportunities for improvement and little gratification can lead to feelings of dissatisfaction, depression, and diminished self-worth. Petersen and Craighead (1986) observe that high rates of unemployment and fierce job competition lead many adolescents and young adults to fear they will not find any work at all, much less meaningful employment. This may result in ambivalent feelings about entering adulthood. The prevailing social values and norms for particular historical periods also color what it means to be an adult. For example, Jessor (1983) stresses that the return to conventionality in the subjects he investigated might reflect the societal trend at that time in history, rather than signify an invariant stage of development.

As late adolescents and young adults are better understood within their social contexts, so are important life events better understood within their contexts. Levinson (1980) presents the idea of identifying "marker events" when considering the adult life course. "Marker events" are major life events which represent the culmination of relatively long, often subtle processes of change. Levinson observes that the deeper processes of change that precede major life events are important sources of information on development in adulthood. Investigations of these more subtle aspects of growth will contribute in important ways to the current literature on the transition to young adulthood. For example, the launching of a career is considered essential to this transition, yet there is a sparse literature on the intrapsychic dynamics leading to resolution of this task. The establishment of intimate relationships is a key aspect of this transition, yet there are large gaps in our understanding of this complex domain. To address these issues adequately, detailed, process-oriented investigations of developmental tasks within the individual's psychological and social contexts are needed.

Systematically studying the impact of individual differences on the transition from adolescence to young adulthood is yet another direction for future research. Neugarten (1969) observes that people change as the result of accumulated experiences. As individuals grow older, they have increasingly long life histories and greater reserves of past experience. The circumstances which adults encounter are far more complex and varied than those to which children are exposed. The intricacies of adult commitments and interpersonal relationships render the lives of adults more complicated than those of children, and more different in relation to one another. Haan (1981) asserts that the constant fluctuations which characterize adult lives and circumstances indicate that only relatively abstract and general conceptualizations can accurately describe the life span.

Conclusions

The passage from late adolescence to early adulthood is complex and multifaceted. The late adolescent must renegotiate relationships with parents as a prerequisite to establishing an autonomous self. Another aspect of the maturation process is the development of integrated and consistent self-identifications. Emotional independence from parents and consolidation of identity enable late adolescents to pursue intimate extrafamilial love relationships. Exploration of and commitment to a career offer late adolescents an anchor in the adult world, while providing them the means to live independently as adults.

Resolution of these developmental tasks can present a formidable challenge. Environmental factors, such as intense competition for jobs and high unemployment rates, can render the transition from school to career particularly difficult. In addition, there is little social assistance for late adolescents as they attempt to join the adult world. Havighurst (1953) posits that the passage from adolescence to adulthood signals the transition from an "age-graded" to a "social status graded" society. For adults, attaining goals no longer entails simply "growing into them"; rather, it becomes a matter of how successfully one manipulates the environment. Late adolescents can find their first exposures to the rules of adult society confusing and alienating, and there are often no social supports to ease this transition. In fact, Havighurst (1953) characterizes the years from 18 to 30 as the loneliest, most disorganized period of the life span.

In addition, the passage to adulthood is often characterized by ambivalence. Late adolescents may eagerly anticipate the new freedoms that accompany adult status, but may also mourn the many losses that this transition entails. Separation from parents can leave a temporary vacuum in their lives. Adult choices and commitments by definition entail the modification or even abandonment of some options and dreams. Haan (1981) observes that late adolescents are understandably reluctant to narrow their range of choices and commit to one spouse. Swindler (1980) notes that our culture views adult commitments as representative of the defeat rather than the culmination of the search for identity. The conflictual aspects of the transition to adulthood are thus exacerbated by our society's fascination with youth culture and the concomitant repudiation of adulthood.

Passages from late adolescence to young adulthood can be facilitated if late adolescents have an understanding of environmental circumstances and societal options. Clear and consistent cultural messages regarding what is expected of individuals at this stage of the life span can take some of the confusion and mystery out of this transition (see Blaine and Farnsworth, chapter 18). Additional social supports and increased opportunities for employment are other factors that will ease the passage into adulthood. These environmental conditions, in conjunction with the individual's ability to resolve phase-specific developmental tasks, will allow late adolescents to focus on the possibilities, rather than the limitations, of the passage to adulthood.

References

Arnstein, R. (1984), Young adulthood: Stages of maturity. In: *Normality and the Life Cycle*, ed. D. Offer & M. Sabshin. New York: Basic Books, pp. 108–145.

Ausubel, D., & Kirk, D. (1977), *Ego Psychology and Mental Disorder: A Developmental Approach to Psychopathology*. New York: Grune & Stratton.

Block, J. (1971), *Lives Through Time*. Berkeley: Bancroft Books.

Blos, P. (1979), *The Adolescent Passage*. New York: International Universities Press.

Cox, R. D. (1970), *Youth into Maturity*. New York: Mental Health Materials Center.

Erikson, E. H. (1950), *Childhood and Society*. Rev. ed. New York: Norton, 1963.

——— (1968), *Identity: Youth and Crisis*. New York: Norton.

——— (1982), *The Life Cycle Completed*. New York: Norton.

Fischer, J. L. (1981), Transitions in relationship style from adolescence to young adulthood. *J. Youth & Adolescence*, 10:11–23.

Fountain, G. (1961), Adolescent into adult: An inquiry. *J. Amer. Psychoanal. Assn.*, 9:417–433.

Galatzer-Levy, R. M. (1984), Adolescent breakdown and middle-age crises. In: *Late Adolescence: Psychoanalytic Studies*, ed. D. Brockman. New York: International Universities Press, p. 29–51.

Golan, N. (1981), *Passing Through Transitions: A Guide for Practitioners*. New York: Free Press.

Gould, R. L. (1972), The phases of adult life: A study in developmental psychology. *Amer. J. Psychiat.*, 129:521–531.

——— (1978), *Transformations: Growth & Change in Adult Life*. New York: Simon & Schuster.

——— (1980), Transformations during early and middle adult years. In: *Themes of Work and Love in Adulthood*, ed. N. Smelser & E. Erikson. Cambridge: Harvard University Press, pp. 213–238.

Grotevant, H., & Cooper, C. (1986), Individuation in family relationships: A perspective on individual differences in the development of identity and role-taking skills in adolescence. *Human Devel.*, 29:82–100.

Haan, N. (1981), Adolescents and young adults as producers of their development. In: *Individuals as Producers of Their Development: A Life Span Per-*

spective, ed. R. M. Lerner & N. A. Busch-Rossnagel. New York: Academic Press, pp. 155–182.

Havighurst, R. J. (1953), *Human Development and Education.* London: Longmans, Green.

Heyneman, S. P. (1976), Continuing issues in adolescence: A summary of current transition to adulthood debates. *J. Youth & Adolescence,* 5:309–323.

Hill, J. P. (1980), The family. In: *Toward Adolescence: The Middle School Years,* ed. M. Johnson. Chicago: University of Chicago Press, pp. 32–55.

Hoffman, J. A. (1984), Psychological separation of late adolescents from their parents. *J. Counseling Psychol.,* 3:170–178.

Jacobs, T. J. (1984a), The psychoanalysis of the young adult: Theory and technique: An introduction. Paper presented at the December meeting of the American Psychoanalytic Association, New York.

——— (1984b), Psychoanalytic treatment of the young adult: Technical and theoretical considerations. In: *Late Adolescence: Psychoanalytic Studies,* ed. D. Brockman. New York: International Universities Press, pp. 273–292.

Jessor, R. (1983), The stability of change: Psychosocial development from adolescence to young adulthood. In: *Human Development: An Interactional Perspective,* ed. D. Magnusson & V. L. Allen. New York: Academic Press, pp. 321–341.

Kaplan, A., Klein, R., & Gleason, N. (1985), Women's self-development in late adolescence. Unpublished manuscript.

Keniston, K. (1970), Youth as a stage of life. In: *Human Life Cycle,* ed. W. Sze. New York: Aronson, 1975, pp. 631–654.

Kohn, M. L. (1980), Job complexity and adult personality. In: *Themes of Love and Work in Adulthood,* ed. N. J. Smelser & E. H. Erikson. Cambridge: Harvard University Press, pp. 193–210.

Lasser, V., & Snarey, J. (1989), Ego development and perceptions of parental behavior in adolescent girls. *J. Adolescent Res.,* 4:319–355.

Levinson, D. J. (1980), Toward a conception of the adult life course. In: *Themes of Love and Work in Adulthood,* ed. N. J. Smelser & E. H. Erikson. Cambridge: Harvard University Press, pp. 265–290.

——— (1986), Development in the novice phase of adulthood. In: *Suicide and Depression Among Adolescents and Young Adults,* ed. G. Klerman. Washington: American Psychiatric Press, pp. 1–17.

——— Darrow, D. N., Klein, E. B., Levinson, M. H., & McKee, B. (1978), *Seasons of a Man's Life.* New York: Knopf.

Marcia, J. E. (1966), Development and validation of ego identity status. *J. Personality & Soc. Psychol.,* 3:551–558.

McGoldrick, M. (1982), Normal families: An ethnic perspective. In: *Normal Family Processes,* ed. F. Walsh. New York: Guilford Press, pp. 399–424.

Murphy, E. B., Silber, E., Coelho, G. V., Hamburg, D. A., & Greenberg, I. (1963), Development of autonomy and parent-child interaction in late adolescence. *Amer. J. Orthopsychiat.,* 33:643–652.

Neugarten, B. L. (1969), Continuities and discontinuities of psychological issues into adult life. *Human Devel.,* 12:121–130.

Offer, D., Ostrov, E., & Howard, K. (1981), *The Adolescent: A Psychological Self Portrait.* New York: Basic Books.

Orlofsky, J. L., Marcia, J. E., & Lesser, I. M. (1973), Ego identity status and the intimacy versus isolation crisis of young adulthood. *J. Personality & Soc. Psychol.*, 27:211–219.

Pearlin, L. I. (1980), Life strains and psychological distress among adults. In: *Themes of Love and Work in Adulthood*, ed. N. J. Smelser & E. H. Erikson. Cambridge: Harvard University Press, pp. 174–192.

Petersen, A., & Craighead, W. (1986), Emotional and personality development in normal adolescents and young adults. In: *Suicide and Depression Among Adolescents and Young Adults*, ed. G. Klerman. Washington: American Psychiatric Press, pp. 17–53.

Piaget, J. (1977), The growth of logical thinking from childhood to adolescence. In: *The Essential Piaget: An Interpretive Reference and Guide*, ed. H. E. Gruber & J. J. Voneche. New York: Basic Books, pp. 405–444.

Riley, M., & Waring, J. (1976), Age and aging. In: *Contemporary Social Problems*, ed. R. Merton & R. Nisbet. New York: Harcourt Brace Jovanovich, pp. 355–410.

Shore, M. F. (1972), Youth and jobs: Educational, vocational, and mental health aspects. *J. Youth & Adolescence*, 1:315–323.

Smelser, N. J., & Erikson, E. H. (1980), *Themes of Love and Work in Adulthood.* Cambridge: Harvard University Press.

Steinberg, L. D., Greenberger, E., Jacobi, M., & Garduque, L. (1981), Early work experience: A partial antidote for adolescent egocentrism. *J. Youth & Adolescence*, 10:141–157.

Sullivan, H. S. (1953), The interpersonal theory of psychiatry. In: *The Collected Works of Harry Stack Sullivan*, vol. 1, ed. H. S. Perry & M. L. Gawel. New York: Norton, pp. 3–393.

Swindler, A. (1980), Love and adulthood in American culture. In: *Themes of Love and Work in Adulthood*, ed. N. J. Smelser & E. H. Erikson. Cambridge: Harvard University Press, pp. 120–147.

Tesch, S. A. & Whitbourne, S. K. (1982), Intimacy and identity status in young adults. *J. Personality & Social Psychol.*, 43:1041–1051.

Waterman, A. S. (1982), Identity development from adolescence to adulthood: An extension of theory and a review of research. *Devel. Psychol.*, 18:341–358.

White, K. M., Speisman, J. C., & Costos, D. (1983), Young adults and their parents: Individuation to maturity. In: *Adolescent Development in the Family*, ed. H. D. Grotevant & C. R. Cooper. San Francisco: Jossey-Bass, pp. 61–76.

White, R. W. (1952), *Lives in Progress: A Study of the Natural Growth of Personality.* New York: Holt, Rinehart & Winston.

Winch, R. F. (1950), Some data bearing on the Oedipus hypothesis. *J. Abnorm. & Soc. Psychol.*, 15:481–489.

Yufit, R. (1956), Intimacy and isolation: Some behavioral and psychodynamic correlates. Doctoral dissertation, University of Chicago. Ann Arbor, MI.: University Microfilms, BF698, 9 S6V8.

17

Bridge to Adulthood: The Years from Eighteen to Twenty-Three

HERMAN D. STAPLES, M.D.
ERWIN R. SMARR, M.D.

The years between 18 and 23 may properly be claimed by both late adolescence and young adulthood; likewise, they may be considered a bridge between these two developmental stages. Interest in late adolescence and the early adult years has been stimulated recently by several factors, among them the ascendancy of the psychoanalytic developmental perspective to its present central position as regards the life span of the individual. The contributions of many authors, most notably Erikson and Blos, have expanded our understanding of the phases of adolescence. On the basis of intrapsychic forces, Blos (1962) demarcated five subphases of adolescence: preadolescence, early adolescence, adolescence proper, late adolescence, and postadolescence. The last two of these are especially pertinent to our topic.

It has often been said that the end of a developmental stage is harder to recognize than is its beginning. Since our task is to examine both the resolution of adolescence as well as the transition to adulthood, we have a dual problem. No discrete physiological or hormonal event characterizes the end of adolescence (in contrast to the advent of puberty, which is signaled by menarche or the first seminal ejaculation). By 18 or 20 years of age, the individual's physical growth potential has been reached, and all the physiological equipment is present for the remainder of life's journey. Young adulthood is then more a psychocultural status than a distinct physiological stage.

In the realm of cognitive development, so brilliantly elaborated by Piaget, the changes to formal operations and abstract thinking that are characteristic of adolescence have normally occurred in early and middle adolescence. No further change has been noted that is specifically associated with late adolescence or early adulthood. It is more a matter of the uses to which cognition is put; much greater attention is paid to both external and internal reality and to the modifying of values. These tasks depend on the progressive development of ego functions, assisted by developments in the ego ideal and in the area of object relations. This survey of the intrapsychic development of this phase in the life cycle will center around these events.

From Adolescence to Adulthood

Three basic approaches have been used to delineate the interpersonal and intrapsychic factors involved in the development from adolescence to adulthood. These approaches overlap in many respects and are by no means mutually exclusive. Each way of looking at developmental changes can contribute to our total understanding. The three approaches are (1) outlining the main psychological characteristics of the adolescent and showing how these characteristics are transformed in the adult; (2) enumerating the tasks that are expected to be completed by an adolescent before he or she may be considered an adult; and (3) tracing the changes in psychic structures, defensive operations, adaptive functions, object relations, etc., that accompany advancement into adult life.

Transformations of Adolescent into Adult Characteristics

Fountain (1961) selected five qualities which are found in most adolescents but which most adults do not show.

Emotional volatility. The well-known intensity and volatility of emotion and the strong urge to experience a variety of feelings in adolescence are reduced in adulthood.

A need for immediate gratification. The adolescent's intolerance of anxiety, frustration, and postponement of gratification gives way to the adult's greater tolerance and patience.

Impaired reality testing. In contrast to the adult, the adolescent is more likely to be less aware of the consequences of his actions and of the feelings of others.

The failure of self-criticism. The adolescent is less able than the adult to see himself as others see him, to judge the impact on others of his behavior, or to consider another person's point of view.

Indifference to the world at large. Having lived through the activistic late 1960s and early 1970s, one might question this so-called characteristic of the adolescent, although here Fountain was really referring to the adolescent's greater propensity to be preoccupied with his personal needs and urges, whereas the world of public events belongs to adults.

Conversely, adulthood may be said to be characterized by emotional stability, tolerance and patience, impulse delay, fairly reasonable reality testing and sense of reality, insight, an objective viewpoint on oneself, tolerance of criticism, and a chosen stance in relation to the public world.

Completion of the Tasks of Adolescence

The GAP report, *Normal Adolescence* (GAP, 1968), lists six tasks the completion of which ideally characterizes the "resolution" of adolescence. The list is representative of many of its genre and would probably be acceptable to most observers. The tasks enumerated are (a) the attainment of separation and independence from the parents; (b) the establishment of sexual identity; (c) the commitment to work; (d) the development of a personal moral value system; (e) the capacity for lasting relationships and for both tender and genital sexual love in heterosexual relationships; and (f) a return to the parents in a new relationship based on a relative equality. Attainment of each of these capacities is influenced simultaneously by intrapsychic and sociocultural factors.

Tracing the Intrapsychic Changes of Late Adolescence and Postadolescence

Blos (1962) sees late adolescence as a phase of consolidation, a time of crisis, and a decisive turning point. Changes take place primarily in the ego leading to the elaboration of "a highly idiosyncratic and stable arrangement of ego functions and interests"; an extension of the conflict-free sphere of the ego; a stable and irreversible sexual position; a relatively constant cathexis of self- and object representations; and the stabilization of the mental apparatus. In late adolescence three basic antitheses of mental life are accepted and more or less settled; subject-object, active-passive, and pleasure-pain.

According to Blos, postadolescence is primarily a phase of harmonizing the various parts of the personality so that the components are integrated into a functioning whole. This gradual process proceeds along with vocational choice, courtship, marriage, and parenthood. During this stage of development, internal conflicts which have not already been resolved are rendered specific and are now integrated into the ego as life tasks. Avenues are created to implement these tasks. There is much postadolescent experimentation to try to gratify instinctual needs and ego interests. The moral side of personality emerges with an emphasis on personal dignity and self-esteem. The ego ideal is more in evidence, compared to the idealized parent of the superego of childhood and early adolescence. The postadolescent completes his detachment from parental object representations, comes to terms with this, reaches a lasting settlement with it, and finally is able to integrate ego interests and the attitudes of the parents.

In a paper on the structural criteria for adolescent closure, Blos (1977) returns to the question of when and how adolescence ends. He first acknowledges the more easily recognized phenomenological criteria defining the end of adolescence. These include the relative stabilization of moods; the veiling of emotions; the selected sharing of the self; the attempt to understand oneself; the predictability of behavior and motivation associated with the stabilization of character formation; the achievement of ego autonomy over the childhood dominance of the superego; and the emergence of a lifestyle.

Turning to "the more reliable and crucial psychological criteria," Blos proposes four such interconnected developmental tasks and challenges.

The second individuation process. This refers to object disengagement through individuation at the adolescent level, "especially from the internalized objects of childhood."

Ego continuity. The adolescent is able to use reality testing to develop a sense of his past, present, and future.

Residual trauma. The inevitable accumulation of traumas during infancy, childhood, and adolescence is dealt with and more or less mastered by the adaptive resourcefulness of the late adolescent, promoting a consolidation of adult personality.

Sexual identity. Ideally, in late adolescence, after resolution of the negative Oedipus complex, the infantile narcissistic ego ideal has slowly and laboriously been transformed into the abstracted and desexualized adult ego ideal, making possible the formation of stable, adult object relations.

The "Developmental" Approach

Historically, earlier conceptualizations of adolescence tended to view the period as a new edition of childhood, with the sole addition of sexual maturation. Freud (1905) described the adolescent changes which gave infantile sexual life its final shape. In keeping with the then-current emphasis on id development and the elaboration of the discoveries of the psychosexual stages, early psychoanalytic writers addressed the issues of disruption of latency equilibrium by drive ascendancy in puberty, bisexuality elements in early adolescence, a second confrontation of oedipal conflicts in middle adolescence, and the challenges of heterosexual object choice in late adolescence. Superego and ego ideal transformations were likewise described as they occurred throughout adolescence. With the increasing emphasis on ego psychology initiated by Anna Freud (1936), great strides were made in understanding ego defensive operations and object relations in adolescence. Hartmann (1939) led the way to a deeper appreciation of the adaptive and autonomous functioning of the ego in adolescence. Erikson (1950, 1968) brilliantly extended our views on adolescence into the realm of the psychosocial and problems of identity.

Mahler's groundbreaking observational research and extension of psychoanalytic theory to the symbiotic and separa-tion-individuation stages of development (1963, 1968; Mahler, Pine, and Bergman, 1975) provided a whole new conceptual framework with which to understand adolescence. Blos (1967) quickly saw this and soon spoke of "the second individuation process of adolescence." The American Psychoanalytic Asso-ciation recognized the applicability of Mahler's ideas through-out the entire life cycle and scheduled a series of panels on "The Experience of Separation-Individuation in Infancy and Its Reverberations Through the Course of Life" (Marcus, 1973; Sternschein, 1973; Winestine, 1973) one of which was devoted to adolescence.

Settlage (see Galenson, 1976) and others have been explicit in saying that we must now correlate the psychosexual and the separation-individuation theories. Thus, we are now beginning to glimpse the separation-individuation processes as they evolve in the first three years of life and reverberate in the teen years, and to see the similarities between the issues and crises of the rapprochement subphase and early adolescence, and between self- and object constancy at the end of the separation-indivi-duation phase and personal identity at the end of adolescence. However, Mahler (Mahler and Kaplan, 1977) herself cautions against oversimplification in making such correlations and em-phasizes the possible corrective influences of other subphases. Currently, analysts are working at this integration of classical psychosexual libidinal phases, development perspectives, recent concepts of narcissism, and the psychosocial framework. We shall review, in a highly condensed summary, current concepts of the intrapsychic process.

Intrapsychic Processes

Object Relations and Ego Ideal

Ritvo (1971) has focused on these two principal aspects of development, using the male as model. Their intertwined trans-formations contribute to the greater engagement of the late adolescent with the reality principle and the reality world. Ritvo begins with contributions from Jacobson and Anna Freud.

Through identifications with new, more realistic images, the superego and moral codes are readjusted so that the id is restricted, and there is a shift of power to the ego, to its goals, and to standards of achievement. Compelled to break the libidinal ties to infantile objects by the anxiety created by relibidinization of repressed infantile fantasies, the adolescent libido returns to a narcissistic cathexis of the self.

> In the film *Saturday Night Fever* the central character is depicted as a late adolescent in the process of breaking away from an engulfing mother and an authoritarian father. In much of the movie he primps and adorns himself to prepare for his exhibitionistic solo dancing but remains impervious to the blandishments of the girls he attracts.

Reprojection of this narcissistic libido to new objects, including peers, idealizes them and permits new identifications within the ego ideal. The fact of genital primacy and the importance of orgasm in psychic life now make the adolescent dependent on the body of the new love object. Thus, reality acquires a greater role in pleasure, while the role of fantasy is reduced to a more pragmatic and anticipatory one. However, the possibility of discharge of aggression onto the new object raises the need either to erect new defenses or to flee.

> A young woman, who in late adolescence fled from her strict, narrow-minded, controlling father, successively married and divorced two young men when she developed mounting but unconscious hostility as they became father-figures to her.

Problems center around issues of heterosexual approach-avoidance and homosexual reactions to choices in self-definition. The conditions of pleasure-gain having become more manifest and specific, the adolescent now becomes more aware of the limitations and distortions of his sexual life, and fantasies directed toward his objects may arouse anxiety.

The new central love object is the representation of the old central love object, the mother, and now functions similarly as the organizer of the psyche in effecting new identifications.

Besides rearousing old, repressed oedipal conflicts due to death wishes toward the rival, threats to the self also arise from the regressive merging and fusion fantasies that originate from both narcissistic and anaclitic aspects of object choice. The fear of engulfment as the result of passive wishes, which conflict with phallic active aims, arouses ambivalence and hostility, which, projected, rearouse the phallic woman imago of primitive superego introjects. There is oscillation between the urgency of need for her, the threat of her demands, and the hostility aroused by any narcissistic wound.

The ability to progress from the narcissistic aspects of object choice to toleration of the anaclitic ones marks the steps toward the eventual attainment of intimacy. Attaining both heightens self-esteem, which enhances the consolidation of the ego and the changes in the ego ideal. Through realizing some parts of his own ego ideal in both the self and the love object, and in providing for the loved one, a pleasure-gain is accrued to work functions. The need to commit the self to a love object and the need to prove oneself are links to the tasks of commitment to adult love and work life, and part of the specific delimited identity formation of the self that must replace youth's omnipotentiality (Pumpian-Mindlin, 1965). The problem solving of the new central object love, like that of the old central object love, releases new resources of now neutralized energy. However, the new object has to merge and blend with the old, and early impairment of the ego and of object relationships can cause severe difficulties in making the way back from the ego regression of early adolescence.

One of the main roots of adolescent structuralization of the ego ideal lies in the passive-feminine orientation of the negative Oedipus complex (Freud, 1923; Blos, 1977). Libido, freed from infantile object ties, can be displaced readily from the self to a grandiose compensatory self-image, when feeling failure of other narcissistic wounds, and can easily attach itself to an object who represents his own ideal by regression to the negative oedipal position. Acting out may occur, and identification attempted with the idealized qualities of a homosexual object choice. On the other hand, the adolescent's capacities for abstraction and sublimation permit displacement of narcissistic libido to the idealization of the intellect in general, which may include moral and ethical values and concepts, religious beliefs, philosophies, etc. These idealizations and identifications provide directions for aim-inhibited pursuits, utilizing the neutralized energy thus released, toward choice of work and mastery of other portions of reality.

Recent Theoretical Modifications Regarding Female Development

Psychoanalytic theories of feminine development are undergoing modification from three sources of influence: (1) direct observational studies of early childhood; (2) separation-individuation theories; and (3) changes in women's adult-role expectations caused by reduced procreation and increased career emphasis. Classical analytic theory is being reevaluated in an attempt to integrate these new aspects. Currently there is considerable lack of agreement, but a great deal can be said about the psychology of adolescent female development from the attention recently focused on the whole subject (Galenson, 1976).

What has already been said here about object relations and ego ideal applies to the female, especially as regards reactivation and recapitulation of the Oedipus complex and the regression to pregenital conflicts. Certain features, however, are unique for the female. Whereas the male, in approaching heterosexuality, returns to the original love object, the nurturant female, the girl must make the transition from mother to father as prime object. Classical theory accounted for this as arising during the phallic phase from narcissistic disappointment in the inferior genital, thus making penis envy central to identification with the father both narcissistically and competitively. In order to reach a postambivalent positive acceptance of femininity and childbearing, the resolution of both penis envy and the oedipal rivalry with the mother, with subsequent positive identification with the maternal-receptive orientation, was held to be a prime developmental task of late adolescence and young womanhood.

Current thinking recognizes an early genital stage in toddler girls during the second half of the second year, with penis envy arising then, but very likely resolved by the oedipal period, persisting only pathologically. It is easily reactivated during the early adolescent regression to pregenitality. The place of penis envy in the adult woman is now a controversial idea. Blum (1976) articulates a view that it plays no important part normally. However, separation-individuation theory attributes a greater emphasis to the role of the first heterosexual love object (the father and his successors) as replacements for the mother, to whose tie the libido has been loosened by the threatened regression to pregenitality ushered in by menarche. The principal problems of sexual development for the girl are now seen to lie in the feminine aspects of her self- and body image.

Ritvo (see Galenson, 1976) has reviewed classical analytic understandings of adolescence in general. Among other tasks of the period, he noted, is the need to integrate childbearing functions with other life goals. Ego ideal formation has both a biological and a social aspect; through identification with the mother and through body image experiences, it is related to nuturing, mothering, and comforting. Sociocultural emphasis on careers now puts a strain on the young woman's ego to integrate biological and career roles and timetables. Settlage (Galenson, 1976) has made the point that an adult sense of female gender identity does not require, but is augmented by, the experiences of childhood and mothering. The complexity of achieving psychosexual and social independence within an intimate relationship is a central focus of other writers. These developmental tasks, completed, allow integration and consolidation to occur.

As for the role of masochism, once thought to be crucial to feminine psychology, Blum (1976), among others, rejects the idea completely. Young women have to integrate, with their whole self-accepting maternal images, inner fluctuating feelings and sensations, rhythmicity (Benedek, 1963), their "inner space" (Erikson, 1968), and their "inner genital" (Kestenberg, 1968). Newer concepts recognize that both clitoral and vaguer vaginal sensations are likely to occur early, though either or both may be repressed. Gradual discovery of the vagina, and its blending with clitoral components, is a task of late adolescence. The passive-receptiveness of vaginal sexuality is no longer seen as necessarily rooted in sadomasochism.

Thus, female development is coming to be better understood and more clearly differentiated from its parallels in the male adolescent. Indeed, it is during adolescence and its last phase, youth, that the psychosexual identification as male or female and the capacity for intimacy must be basically established for adulthood to occur.

While this section has focused on the intrapsychic processes of self- and object transformation, none of this takes place without the influence of the sociocultural world in which the evolving personality must find further adult role models and fitting self-roles. We have seen that the new central love object, in reality as well as fantasy, can play an organizing role in this transition. The outcomes of adolescent love are important events for what follows. But there are wider influences that also affect the outcome of development.

Psychosocial Influences and Identity Consolidation

Erikson (1956) speaks of youth as the time of life when there is a simultaneous demand to accomplish commitments to physical intimacy, to decisive occupational choice, to energetic competition, and to psychosocial self-definition. All of these are elements of adult role identity. Keniston (1968) adds that even if all the developmental tasks were accomplished, adulthood would still be lacking without the achievement of a bond to society in some enduring form, whether through a positive identification or a negative, opposing one.

The various identifications must be worked out and consolidated into forms that simultaneously satisfy internal and external needs. They must be internally consistent with each other and with the moral value system that is chosen. Social roles must be adopted that are consistent with the predominant identifications and that provide a fulfilling lifestyle for these identifications and value systems. Moreover, these social roles must provide reality testing of those values and be more or less compatible with them. Youth is a time of encounter with the adult role models available in the external world, to accept, reject, or modify for oneself. Achieving the fit allows resolution of both preoedipal and oedipal ambivalences through conflict-free identifications with role models. One then possesses a form by which to pursue fulfillment of the ego ideal. Finding suitable role models may allow ultimate positive identification with the parent of the same sex. During periods of little historical and technological change, these models change little and are less conflictually cathected than at times like the present.

Erikson (1977) has described how, in times of "historical identity vacua," youth flock to totalitarian movements for ideological renewal. These movements provide the dynamic function of ritualization that youth need to effect an induction into an adult lifestyle. More basically, however, they provide a lifestyle that will perpetuate the certainties and securities of the regressive, pregenital, omnipotent superego while giving the illusion of emancipation. It matters not whether the ideology be one of identification with the society or of rebellion against it. However, in the partial regression to "idolism" there occurs a sustained mutuality in affiliations of work, friendship, and love that merges into the stage of intimacy. Out of a kind of shared narcissism in the form of elitism comes a fitting of respective identities, possibly promising affiliations in productive and procreative life.

When these identifications take place too wholly in positive imitation of parental models, without the self-testing and societal testing that mature identity requires, premature foreclosure may occur, at risk of later vulnerability to stress. Equally compulsive fixation on rebellious negative identity can occur. More healthfully, youths go through a series of temporary identities, not expected to outlast their youthfulness, as part of their means of testing and dealing with their ambivalence toward society (Keniston, 1968). They will ultimately lead to a chosen enduring stance toward that society, whether it be acceptance of the values and lifestyles of the parents, total or partial, and selective modification of it, warfare against it, or some idiosyncratic mode of being adult. The keystone of adulthood is the conscious realization and acceptance of the consequences of that lifestyle and the responsibility of commitment to it in real life.

Societal turmoil distinctly influences individual turmoil of development. Many authors have documented the principal societal changes that have altered the structure of values and roles in America: loss of belief in theological transcendence, the passage of Victorian and Puritan morality, the loss of paternal authority, the separation from the holistic meaning of work in life, the loss of significance of the person in mass society, and the triumph over nature to the point of probable extermination of the species. When society fails to provide supports for future identification, youth's grapplings to find meaningful and gratifying adult roles strain the ego capacities. Deficiencies in ego development from early childhood are then laid bare upon departure from the family structure (Blos, 1967).

Esman (1975) described how changing moral values make the consolidation of psychosexual role and object choice more diffuse and less defined; he cited the value placed on male homosexuality and the corresponding emphasis on female independence in sexuality. He noted also that exotic mystical sects and gurus, when embraced for their often puritanical moral codes that restrict and repress drive impulses, offer a way of avoiding psychosexual definition.

Lifton (1975) characterizes the youth lifestyle of the sixties and seventies as "protean"—an experimenting and questing after psychological patterns in response to the breakdown of forms. It is a struggle for rituals and symbols that allow the experience of primordial emotions that approach the ecstatic rather than the prosaic.

To categorize these radically deviant forms as all pathological or all healthful is to misunderstand the nature of societal forms and to displace to the social sphere, unjustifiably, criteria of health valid only for the individual. Even there, overt behaviors often make it difficult to judge pathological development, since the outward garb of negative identification is so uniform for all. Beneath it, any individual may be anywhere along a range, from very healthy reality testing, making effective use of a moratorium to test oneself and life, to psychotic, borderline, or narcissistic personality structure.

Identity crisis, even with transient anxiety, depression, and confusion, may be normal, as is the moratorium on commitment, whether institutionalized or unique. It is identity diffusion which is pathological. Because choices in sexuality, competition, intimacy, and occupation are required, repudiations must be made. The inability to do so, or excessive avoidance, exposes one to the regressive pull which can become pathological if more than transitory.

Kernberg (1975) emphasizes the sharp delineation between the normal identity crisis and pathological identity diffusion that comes only from early developmental vicissitudes, not from contemporary moral changes. The difference lies in the primitive superego nuclei that are reprojected in borderline and narcissistic structures. He offers the following criteria for discerning the difference: the capacity for experiencing guilt and concern and a genuine wish to repair the damage from aggressive behavior; the capacity for establishing lasting, nonexploitative relationships and the relatively realistic, in-depth assessment of those related to such persons; and a consistently expanding and deepening set of values, whether in conformity with the prevalent culture or in opposition to it. In contrast to those who lack depth but give only lip service, healthy adolescents have an internal consistency between their values, their behavior, and their relationships with others.

Healthy Development

At a later point we will deal with the pathological results of adaptive failures to negotiate this transition. At this point it would be useful to summarize the features of healthy development identifiable from a psychoanalytic perspective, as well as to note the roles of defensive operations of the ego under normal circumstances.

It is not to be expected that anxious and painful periods of separating from parental ties and reinvesting in new loves, friendships, and models should be without traumas. Indeed, depth and growth require some. Optimally, they will not result in lasting regressive retreats or the elaboration of overrestrictive defenses, emphasizing constriction of the ego, repression of drives, narcissistic rescue by excessive projection and rationalization, retreat to sadomasochism, somatizations, or withdrawal to fantasy replacement of the object world. The attainment of gratifying love relationships is crucial to consolidating an identity positively related to the real world. Its achievement frees emotional energy from conflict to address the conflict-free areas of ego development: learning the ways of the world, formal education and apprenticeship, and moral value delineation. This ability to use cognition to learn accurately about oneself and others allows insights that are important in the selection and pursuit of goals relevant to one's future needs. Lack of these capacities is found in instances of identity diffusion.

Defenses are not without a role in attaining this healthy state. Normally the deeper aspects of the regressive pull of adolescence remain unconscious by virtue of protective repressions. Anxieties, depressions, and even somatizations that accompany the transient crises of developmental flux are normally repressed when successful shifts to new objects, identifications, and interests supervene. The late adolescent's capacity to undergo rapid changes of mood with new identifications is legend. In fact, identification is itself one of the principal normal defenses employed, fostering repression and externalization of the old repudiated traits that are superseded.

Likewise needing to be outgrown are anxieties arising not only from separation and castration fears but from associated fears of one's mortality. A comfortable engagement with adult life requires a sense of trust in the future. This is abetted by a certain amount of selective denial of potentially present reminders of mortality, reinstituting, in the service of adaptation, a piece of magical omnipotence in concert with whatever form of transcendental or supernatural omnipotence is most appealing as a superego replacement. Intellectualization, a defense highly developed at this stage, provides a pathway to the normal, ideological, or philosophical sublimation frequently seen at this stage. No doubt reaction-formations closely interdigitate with sublimations in attaining ethical and moral controls over sadistic and narcissistic impulses and in furthering socialization if not altruism. These defenses play their part, along with the capacity for identification, in allowing for compassion and empathy, qualities that ultimately are necessary for a mature loving relationship and parenting, but not possible while narcissistic needs predominate.

Not all regression is pathological. Sufficient flexibility needs to prevail to enjoy healthy regressions, socially sanctioned, to play, relax, and sleep, and to create artistically. All these call upon sublimation to provide the ego with satisfying expressions from the id, lastly, to play with life and self with jest, in forms that outgrow the immature sadomasochism of earlier stages and contribute to the well-being of people at no one else's expense.

There is a psychosocial question regarding identification with the parent of the same sex at the point of completion of late adolescence that calls for some consideration. Earlier we noted the GAP report's criteria for the achievement of adulthood (1968), one of which was a return to the parents in a new relationship of greater equality. It was implied that sufficient resolution of the ambivalence should take place to allow both generations to respect each other's humanity and adulthood, including tolerance for their individual differences and fallibilities. This is a product of the resolution of earlier demands for absolutism, perfection, or sameness, and is part of the capacity to accept people, as well as the world, for what they are. The experiences of "settling down," finding a home, persevering in work, arranging a wedding, mixing socially with older people, etc., all promote greater identification with the parents. Nevertheless, during periods of rapid social change in values, roles, and lifestyle, it becomes an additional problem to accomplish this rapprochement if the younger generation adopts lifestyles too radically different from those of their parents. What seems to be a pivotal time, even then, however, is the experience of their becoming parents themselves, assuming the role responsibilities, cares, and interests of nurturing another generation. This has the effect of integrating part self-images with internalized parental images, both conflictual and conflict-free. Problems thereafter often center around the necessity to resolve whatever internal conflicts remain. The ultimate effect, if successful, is the achievement of a still healthier identity as adult and parent.

Early Adulthood

Several studies have appeared chronicling the longitudinal life courses of people from youth through the various stages of adulthood. These studies are interesting because they are the first systematic long-term clinical studies of "normal" adults. They highlight some of the features of change from youth to young adulthood. In Sheehy's *Passages* (1974) there is a graphic description of the identity struggles of a black ghetto youth as he encounters, accepts, and rejects a multiplicity of identifications and role models, loyalties, and roles until an adult synthesis suitable for him can be created.

Levinson, Darrow, Klein, Levinson, and McKee (1978) find that the process of entering manhood runs from around 17 to around 33. They call this the "novice phase," composed of the "early adult transition" (17 to about 22), "entering the adult world" (22 to about 28), and the "age-30 transition." Four developmental tasks were most important: forming a "Dream"' ("a vague sense of self-in-the-adult-world") and giving it a place in the life structure; forming mentor relationships; forming an occupation; and forming love relationships, including marriage and family. Whether a young man's early life is consonant with, and infused by, the Dream or is opposed to it affects his growth a good deal. If too many forces oppose it, externally or within himself, he may abandon or betray it, but this affects his sense of aliveness and purpose in his vocational life. The mentor is necessary as teacher, sponsor, host, guide, etc., who helps to define the Dream and to create a space for the young man. From the apprentice role he gradually gains a fuller sense of his own authority and capability of autonomous action, gradually transcending the father-son, man-boy division. Lasting from two to ten years or so, the mentor relationship is a love relationship and often ends with strong conflict and bad feeling. As in all object loss there are internalization and identification, furthering adulthood. Even the process of "forming" an occupation is a complex one that extends over the novice phase and often beyond. It requires not only suitable choices and changes but acquisition of skills, values, and credentials. Even for working class men, the same prolonged process was involved, with periods of crisis. By the age-30 transition, more enduring choices must be built on the groundwork established.

Half of the men in the Levinson study married during the early adult transition, having had little experience in forming peer relationships with adult women. The authors describe how the wife of such a man, who was attracted to her in part because she seemed to lack the qualities he feared and resented in his image of his mother, nevertheless became the recipient of various pregenital and genital fantasies he then struggled to both express and control. There are often many aspects of the mother-son interaction which will later become more problematical. Levinson et al. draw attention, however, to the "Special Woman," who is also a mentor, animating the part of him that contains the Dream and helps him attain it. She too is a transition figure he will outgrow as he becomes more complete. A man's wife may be his Special Woman or not. Whether or not their Dreams are the same may well affect their marital future.

While parallel studies of the same sort have not been carried out in women, Sheehy gives us very useful portraits of the course of development in these same periods of life. We see in her writing the continual interplay of what she calls the merger-self vs. the seeker-self, another way of speaking about the fusion-differentiation process of separation-individuation. Unlike the young man, who usually has a societal imperative to define himself occupationally, the young woman is more often provided a structure that is optional, requiring increasingly nowadays a struggle between the goals of career-self and procreative-self. The latter offers itself as a role compatible with the needs for intimacy, fulfilling with greater or lesser ambivalence an identification with the mother but quite possibly at the risk of closure on self-development and displacement of unresolved dependencies onto the man. In Sheehy's cases there is a frequent pattern of dysphasic growth between men, whose occupational life in the world facilitates their adulthood, and wives who take much longer to discover their identity crises, not reacting until their thirties and forties. Again, changes in social attitudes have altered patterns of mating, intimacy, and family life. It is too soon to know what effects these altered adult models will have on the imagos developed by today's young children, affecting their superegos and ego ideals.

In Vaillant's long-term study (1977) of 95 college men from the classes of 1942–1944, success or failure of intimacy again emerged as important for mastery of the next stages of adulthood. He too found the role of the mentor, the successor to the adolescent hero, usually cast aside by age 40 and frequently denied. An interesting finding from this study was that personality traits in adolescence had no predictive value for the future emotional stability of the young adult. Three traits uncharacteristic of adolescence were most often diagnostic, however, of future mental health: adolescents who were seen as "well integrated, practical, and organized" were best adapted at age 50.

Psychopathology

From a descriptive standpoint, the years of late adolescence to young adulthood present a range of maladaptive disorders from mild to severe disability. There are problems of situational maladjustment which may present with anxiety, somatizations, study or work inhibitions, or depression, or may have been acted out with development of secondary situational complications. These situations may have to do with school, work, family, love, or other relationship problems. These are of a relatively acute, short-term nature, and the symptoms may alarm the young person or others out of proportion to their underlying implications for more severe illness. Other conditions of a more chronic nature also appear by virtue of the failure of the adolescent process to resolve more satisfactorily the developmental problems from earlier years. These may take the form of psychoneurosis; characterological disorders; borderline personality with affective, behavioral, or pseudoneurotic symptoms; or frank psychosis. The range of these disorders represents various degrees of adaptive failure to the requirements of psychic development for coping with and mastering life's tasks and challenges in a satisfactory and satisfying way. Some brief clinical examples will be cited to illustrate some typical forms of illness characteristic of this age period, progressing from relatively mild to more severe forms of maladaptation.

Normal Developmental Psychodynamics of Oedipal Resolution: Mild Depression

A 20-year-old male college student, very intelligent, sensitive, and artistic, came for help on the advice of his mother because of his confusion over relationships with girls. It became apparent that certain girls he befriended would cut him down out of their own competitive strivings, but he had accepted their derision as his own defect and had become depressed. He cathected the therapist strongly, utilizing insights and the narcissistic supports from the positive transference to grow in confidence and competence socially. It developed that he was fixated in an unresolved oedipal entanglement which burdened him; he wished his father were stronger, so as to remove the mother's displaced attachments from her son. As the young man gained insight into this situation, his own strivings for masculine ideals attached themselves to athletically potent peers. He identified with them imitatively. In contrast to the denial commonly used, this young man could allow himself to be aware of the sexual tingeing. Identification with more adventurous models enabled him to travel and explore more on his own. He then began to approach girls more assertively, with greater self-confidence.

A Hysterical Somatic Symptom in Avoidance of Adolescence

After a fall, an immature, 23-year-old woman developed paresis and tremor in a lower extremity, diagnosed orthopedically and neurologically as hysterical. She had not progressed developmentally beyond latency. Her parents were quite rigid, repressive, and controlling. She had remained at home, conflicted and financially dependent on them, in a state of relative sexual ignorance and innocence. Her fear of autonomy was mingled with a fear of asserting her wishes for it. When supported toward independence, she was able to leave home and subsequently developed a relationship more typical of late adolescent development.

Psychoneurosis Limiting Successful Consolidation and
Adaptation

A married male graduate student, 22, was self-referred for treatment of an obsessive-compulsive neurosis present since early adolescence. He was compelled to think, "What if I murdered my mother?" Additionally, despite high intelligence and clearly outstanding promise academically, he had failed to achieve in college up to his own reasonable superior expectations, mainly due to examination anxiety. He had had to compensate for these handicaps by very hard work, which itself was compromised by his obsessive, overorganized, and perfectionistic work habits.

Treatment required analysis of lifelong developmental problems. Born into an extraordinarily closely binding family, he had developed an unrecognized and untreated infantile phobic neurosis in early latency, the resolution of which was partially accomplished by repression and the development of an obsessive-compulsive character structure. When, in early adolescence, his parents' opposition to his precocious sexual wishes aroused rage within him, his repressed patricidal wishes were displaced onto the weaker maternal figure but were limited to ego-dystonic obsessive thoughts. It was necessary to work through much unresolved infantile omnipotence, phallic grandiosity, and oedipal material, as well as a narcissistic defense of derogation of authority that, via projection, subjected him to persecutory anxiety, before he could apply himself more freely and self-confidently to his career. While burdened with his neurosis, he could not accept the role of adult, let alone that of parent, to the frustration of his wife, who wanted a child. Only after resolution of the oedipal conflicts, including both the competitive and the negative sides of the oedipal relationship with the father, could he separate from his overidentification with the father imago and individuate himself as an autonomous and different person, his own man, in a new kind of adult relationship with the father. His symptoms subsided, and he then succeeded academically and obtained a good position in his chosen occupation, which originally had been selected unconsciously, as a way of continuing to reexperience (and hopefully master) the residual trauma of his childhood. As the result of treatment, he will not have to go through life acting out his neurosis through his career.

Failure in Identity Consolidation with Adaptive Failure and Depression

A 22-year-old unmarried woman, on finishing college, found herself with mounting anxiety over not wanting to pursue the vocation for which she had trained. At a similar point four years earlier, approaching the end of secondary school, she had had a brief psychosis. She was closely, though ambivalently, identified with both parents and had a religiously moralistic superego that prohibited premarital sex. Faced with the need to terminate her moratorium and assume an autonomy for which she was unprepared, she became mildly hypomanic, fell suddenly in love, and quickly moved to engagement. This flight into premature marriage failed when her fiancé withdrew, and she collapsed into a psychotic depression. During a year of subsequent therapy, she gradually worked out unresolved ambivalences to her parents and separated from them, although utilizing her identifications with them to accept a vocation like theirs. When financially able, she took her own apartment and later dealt with transferred dependencies on men and issues of sexuality.

Eating Disorders

Eating disorders are a particular form of psychopathology frequently occurring from midadolescence to young adulthood. Their severity varies from fairly superficial hysterical problems of adolescence to borderline or psychotic structures. The following two cases illustrate chronic maladaptive forms of illness.

Bulimia. A 15-year-old girl acquired infectious mononucleosis with anorexia and weight loss, secretly prolonging the symptoms thereafter as an ego mechanism to control a ravenous appetite that made her gain weight. A year later she learned to regurgitate her food several times and reingest it, thus satisfying her hunger all the more without weight gain. She preserved the figure and appearance of a prepubertal girl even when she came for treatment, resistively, at age 23. Her parents were highly competitive, successful achievers, and she went through latency and puberty feeling inferior and defective in comparison both to them and to her athletic sister. At 15 she had identified strongly with a rebellious boy who stimulated her secret rebellion against her parents' values and lifestyle. When forced to stop seeing him, she became sick. Her rebellion continued covertly in the form of a retreat into nightly eating binges with regurgitation, a narcissistic withdrawal that constricted her social development and left her very much at the mercy of what became a compulsive ritual. Her search for an omnipotent being, so strong as to enable her to break the compulsion, took her into fundamentalist religion, where she hoped to find in God a love so strong she would always be loved, no matter how many times she failed and disappointed Him. The roots of the problem were evident in her inability to satisfy her parents' narcissistic ambitions through her, and her need to replace them with an unconditionally loving parent whom she would repeatedly test by failing. Her fantasy was that finally He would prove Himself sufficiently that she would love Him unambivalently, identify with His strength, and thereby resist her compulsion and be "born again."

Anorexia nervosa. A 24-year-old childless woman weighing 80 pounds had become anorexic at age 16, but had gone through college and married, her condition worsening gradually. She had always resisted treatment and began it only when threatened with the breakup of her marriage. Analysis revealed a lifelong developmental history, beginning with her mother's postpartum depression and the surrender of this girl to the maternal grandmother, who became the primary mother figure. The mother never recovered her role in the life of this child, who formed a strong oedipal attachment and identification with her father. There had been a religiously repressive upbringing, with adolescent failure to incorporate feminine sexuality. A great deal of rivalry existed toward her two younger sisters, and her personality had acquired a very bossy, controlling character. She remained phobic about heterosexuality, marrying a man she thought she could control verbally. She existed by virtue of a calculated ritual of nocturnal nutrition to maintain a steady weight level, gorging herself with noncaloric foods. The analytic work involved a great deal of oral-aggressive drive and sadistic preoccupation, with infantile terror of abandonment to malevolent nocturnal forces.

Complete Failure of Integrative Capacity: Ego Defect and Psychosis

A 19-year-old boy was referred after two years of hospitalization for psychosis following several years of drug use. He was hyperintellectual and postured constantly as a fighter, a skill his father possessed. History revealed that as an infant he had been terrified by a psychotic older brother, but had in early childhood idealized this brother; between them, they had developed a secret world, private psychotic interpretations of reality, and attitudes about the father. In retrospect, it could be seen that he had had a severe learning problem throughout school, with possible minimal brain dysfunction. At any rate, he learned little and felt progressively inferior. In adolescence he tried to emulate his peers in the neighborhood and sought some self-worth through amateur boxing. Early attempts at sexuality brought rejection from a girl. He began to use drugs and one afternoon suddenly felt that his penis was shrinking and that all his muscles were losing their bulk. These somatic delusions remained for years. Out of his psychedelic experience he acquired an absolute conviction of his own omnipotent power to control the thoughts of others, derived from the universal power of the cosmos. He was unable to sleep because of fear and periodically became suicidally depressed.

Summary

Late adolescence and early adulthood are a phase in the life cycle marked by consolidation and integration of psychic processes and by the stabilization and harmonization of psychic structures. In Eriksonian terms, it is a phase of achieving a sense of identity. Blos paraphrases a well-known statement of Freud to say that "the heir of adolescence is the self."

Late adolescence is a psychosocial phenomenon rather than a physiological stage. Important intrapsychic transformations occur in object relations, conflict resolution, ego and superego functions, ego ideal, defenses, etc. There is a great deal of experimentation of testing and trying out roles, and the beginnings of implementation of goals. In leaving home and family, the late adolescent is influenced by, and influences, the larger social world and current lifestyles.

Cognition does not undergo any further formal change but is deployed toward greater apprehension of the external and internal worlds. New love investments are central to the changes in object relationships, ego ideal, and sense of self, even though they bring the potential for regressive ambivalences associated with the earlier central love object. Earlier developmental failures constitute potential fixation points for pathological courses during this transitional stage. There is a great propensity for the acting out of newly idealized identifications—intellectualized areas of religion, morality, ethics, and philosophy—as well as regressive trends. These all become the arena for repetition and further resolution of both narcissistic and anaclitic problems. Surmounting them enhances self-esteem, while at the same time the need to prove oneself promotes a commitment to the realistic world and a mastery of the tasks it presents.

The principal problems of young womanhood are the consolidation of a feminine sense of self and body image within the context of new intimacy relationships. Expanded role choices for career and for procreation complicate these years of development.

Whereas in stable historical times societies provide rituals for induction into adult lifestyles through education, apprenticeship, military life, courtship, and marriage, in times of "historical identity vacua" youth seek their own forms of ritualization that may embody ideological rebellion. Temporary identifications test the societal reality, contributing to social change, leading ultimately to more enduring chosen stances toward personal and social values and lifestyles. Loss of support from traditional social roles and values puts a strain on young ego capacities. Faced with the necessity of responsibility for self, young people become more vulnerable to pathological regression. While identity crisis at this stage is normal, identity diffusion exposes the

432   HERMAN D. STAPLES AND ERWIN R. SMARR

ego to the pulls of early developmental vicissitudes, and there are potentials for the entire range of pathological conditions. Successful development, however, is accompanied by insights that are essential to selecting and pursuing authentic personal goals and that free emotional energies for the tasks involved.

Defenses play their part in healthy development. Repression of anxieties and denial of existential threats permit a greater sense of safety and confidence. Sublimations most successfully channel drive energy into socialized, gratifying behavior, linking the drives to social reality and allowing healthy forms of regression to contribute. Resolution of narcissistic fixations allows empathic and compassionate identifications with others, including one's parents.

Recent clinical studies have illuminated the central role played by the "special person" and the mentor, who become important love objects in pursuit of a highly individualistic dream. While adulthood is defined by the acceptance of responsibility for an integrated lifestyle and its consequences, psychological development has by now evolved sufficiently stabilized internal structures and object relations to approach these roles. This does not mean the end of development but only a readiness for adult experience.

References

Benedek, T. (1963), An investigation of the sexual cycle in women: Methodological considerations. *Arch. Gen. Psychiat.*, 8:311–322.
Blos, P. (1962), *On Adolescence: A Psychoanalytic Interpretation.* New York: Free Press.
——— (1967), The second individuation process of adolescence. *The Psychoanalytic Study of the Child*, 22:162–186. New York: International Universities Press.
——— (1977), When and how does adolescence end: Structural criteria for adolescent closure. *Adolescent Psychiat.*, 5:5–17.
Blum, H. P. (1976), Masochism, the ego ideal, and the psychology of women. *J. Amer. Psychoanal. Assn.*, 24:157–191.
Erikson, E. H. (1950), *Childhood and Society.* Rev. ed. New York: Norton, 1963.
——— (1956), The problem of ego identity. *J. Amer. Psychoanal. Assn.*, 4:56–121.
——— (1968), Womanhood and the inner space. In: *Identity: Youth and Crisis.*

New York: Norton, pp. 261–294.

—— (1977), *Toys and Reasons*. New York: Norton.

Esman, A. H. (1975), Consolidation of the ego ideal in contemporary adolescence. In: *The Psychology of Adolescence: Essential Readings*, ed. A. H. Esman. New York: International Universities Press, pp. 211–218.

Fountain, G. (1961), Adolescent into adult: An inquiry. *J. Amer. Psychoanal. Assn.*, 9:417–433.

Freud, A. (1936), *The Ego and the Mechanisms of Defence*. London: Hogarth Press.

Freud, S. (1905), Three essays on the theory of sexuality. *Standard Edition*, 7:125–243. London: Hogarth Press, 1953.

—— (1923), The ego and the id. *Standard Edition*, 19:12–66. London: Hogarth Press, 1961.

Galenson, E. (1976), Panel report: Psychology of women: Late adolescence and early adulthood. *J. Amer. Psychoanal. Assn.*, 24:631–645.

GAP (1968), *Normal Adolescence*, Vol. 6. Report No. 68. New York: Group for the Advancement of Psychiatry.

Hartmann, H. (1939), *Ego Psychology and the Problem of Adaptation*. New York: International Universities Press, 1958.

Keniston, K. (1968), *Young Radicals: Notes on Committed Youth*. New York: Harcourt, Brace & World.

Kernberg, O. (1975), Cultural impact and intrapsychic change. *Adolescent Psychiat.*, 4:37–45.

Kestenberg, J. (1968), Outside and inside, male and female. *J. Amer. Psychoanal. Assn.*, 16:457–520.

Levinson, D. J., Darrow, C. D., Klein, E. B., Levinson, M. H., & McKee, B. (1978), *The Seasons of a Man's Life*. New York: Knopf.

Lifton, R. J. (1975), Proteus revisited. *Adolescent Psychiat.*, 4:21–36.

Mahler, M. S. (1963), Thoughts about development and individuation. *The Psychoanalytic Study of the Child*, 18:307–324. New York: International Universities Press.

—— (1968), *On Human Symbiosis and the Vicissitudes of Individuation*. New York: International Universities Press.

—— Kaplan, L. (1977), Developmental aspects in the assessment of narcissistic and so-called borderline personalities. In: *Borderline Personality Disorders*, ed. P. Hartocollis. New York: International Universities Press, pp. 71–85.

—— Pine, F., & Bergman, A. (1975), *The Psychological Birth of the Human Infant*. New York: Basic Books.

Marcus, I. M. (1973), Panel report: The experience of separation-individuation in infancy and its reverberations through the course of life: 2. Adolescence and maturity. *J. Amer. Psychoanal. Assn.*, 21:155–167.

Pumpian-Mindlin, E. (1965), Omnipotentiality, youth and commitment. *J. Amer. Acad. Child Psychiat.*, 4:1–18.

Ritvo, S. (1971), Late adolescence: Developmental and clinical considerations. *The Psychoanalytic Study of the Child*, 26:241–263. New York: Quadrangle.

Sheehy, G. (1974), *Passages: Predictable Crises of Adult Life*. New York: Dutton.

Sternschein, I. (1973), Panel report: The experience of separation-individuation in infancy and its reverberations through the course of life: 3.

Maturity, senescence, and sociological implications. *J. Amer. Psychoanal. Assn.*, 21:633–645.

Vaillant, G. E. (1977), *Adaptation to Life*. Boston: Little, Brown.

Winestine, M. C. (1973), Panel report: The experience of separation-individuation in infancy and its reverberations through the course of life: 1. Infancy and childhood. *J. Amer. Psychoanal. Assn.*, 21:135–154.

18

Personality Development in the Young Adult

GRAHAM B. BLAINE, M.D.

DANA L. FARNSWORTH, M.D.

In this chapter we deal with some aspects of childhood development leading up to the young adult stage. This approach is used to point out the dynamic factors influencing the resolution of the problems and dilemmas facing individuals in the age group from 18 to 23. Psychoanalytic theory proposes that personality growth is determined by events and attitudes experienced over a span of time from infancy through adolescence. We have concentrated on these attitudes and events in order to show their importance and to emphasize the necessity of recognizing and dealing with them in order to promote healthy personality development in the young adult.

Between the ages of 18 and 23 young people experience rapid transition from the status of adolescent to that of adult. The length of time required by this process depends to a considerable extent on the attitudes of parents, teachers, and other important adults around them. Some young people of 18 are as "adult" in their thinking and behavior as others in their mid-twenties. Others seem hardly to have progressed beyond early adolescence. But by the end of this period certain developmental tasks should have been accomplished and early adulthood achieved.

Early adulthood brings a set of challenges which are unique to that stage of life. It is different in many ways from the previous decade. Early adolescent struggles represent attempts to gain freedom from dependence on parents. The often uncon-

scious need to get "out from under" and to feel inwardly motivated rather than outwardly guided often leads to nonconformist
or rebellious behavior during adolescence. Vacillation between
following the crowd (as a substitute for following the parents)
on the one hand and, on the other, trying to resist peer pressure
without regressing to become mother's "model child" characterizes the high school student's attitudes and behavior. Once
in college, however, or living independently in the work world,
new internal and external problems present themselves. One
has to feel at home as an adult in the world. No longer is there
protection from others as expressed in such statements as "He's
too young to understand" or "Leave her alone; she'll grow out
of it." Total responsibility for one's actions must be taken. People in the world outside expect young adults to know where
they are headed and to possess convictions they can define and
defend logically if called upon.

There are many who describe college as a place and a time
to experiment, but most of the students who are there feel
differently. They consider themselves mature, and they look
within themselves for answers to questions about sex, religion,
career, and loyalty to friends, and also about political and cultural morality. They are no longer content to ask advice or
follow the example of others. Disappointment and shame affect
young adults who find themselves floundering over questions
regarding career and marriage. Choices about going home for
Christmas or skiing with friends instead, or whether or not to
date a boyfriend's roommate, for instance, may cause confusion,
and this confusion feels embarrassing. Erikson (1950) postulates
that commitment is the primary task for the young adult. If this
challenge cannot be met an individual feels immature and inadequate and, in our opinion, experiences a developmental lag.

Events in childhood and adolescence bear importantly on
the ability to make healthy commitments as an adult. These
need to be made in many different areas. Among the most
important are (1) problem solving, (2) sexuality, (3) career
choice, and (4) intimacy. Successful commitment in these areas
requires an intellectual and an emotional set of values—a rank-
ing of internal priorities that feels comfortable. This involves

individuals taking into consideration both how they view themselves and how they perceive other's views of them.

Making such commitments and, as a result, achieving a state of internal equilibrium must include a realistic appraisal of what are reasonable goals, for everyone's goals are limited by their capabilities. Many men can be content with a subordinate position at home and at work, for instance, if they are reconciled to the fact that their nature and temperament are best suited to such a position. Many women can become committed to goals involving career or profession exclusively if they are convinced that characterologically they have developed into or have been created in that mold. Young adults should be ready to start moving in whatever direction is right for them. Let us examine in depth each of the four challenges facing the young adult.

Problem Solving

No matter how warm and loving our childhood or how thoroughly we may have been psychoanalyzed, life is bound to present us problems almost daily. Some are soluable, and some are not; the manner in which we face the task of working out a solution for them or bearing the frustration of living with them is a measure of the degree to which we have developed adult maturity. The young adult who runs from a problem, denies it, or poorly defines it has not developed as he should and deserves attention. Rarely does he experience his problem in these terms. Instead, it is depression, anxiety, insomnia, or a psychosomatic symptom such as headache or a knotted stomach which is the presenting symptom.

Preparation in childhood for healthy problem solving as an adult must rely strongly on parental permission to make choices. Areas in which it is safe to allow this are limited, but early in life it is important that a child learn to recognize a problem when one confronts him and that he have the freedom to solve it—correctly or incorrectly. A simple example would be a child standing on the edge of a mud puddle deeper than his rubbers. His mother could carry him over it, pull him around it, or wait for him to solve the problem his own way. Clearly there are alternatives open to the mother after the fact also; these will transmit messages of different qualities to the child. If he puts one foot in the puddle, she might yank him back or let him walk through, after which she might admonish him or simply let him suffer the discomfort of cold wet feet.

Children differ enough in basic nature to make it impossible to make judgments about which of the approaches described above might be the best in terms of training any one of them for problem solving, but it is fair to say that for the average child an opportunity for recognizing the existence of alternatives should be given. The mother might say, "What are you [not 'we'] going to do about that puddle?" It might be necessary to restrain the child from impulsively running through the water, thus giving him a chance to consider alternatives. This would in most cases seem preferable to taking over the decision completely by carrying him across or pulling him around.

Once he has chosen an alternative, it is best to let him carry it out and afterward discuss the consequences and also the other options. If he splashed through the puddle, getting his mother wet, or sat down in it soiling his clothes, it would take considerable parental control not to admonish or punish immediately, but it would be better to point out the consequences and mention the alternatives he had rejected before going on to express righteous indignation. Parental displeasure should be shown clearly to be one of the consequences of the child's decision.

If a child's decision conforms with a parent's expectation (is the "right" decision), the opportunity to point out the fact that a decision had been made and a problem solved should not be lost. It would be a good idea to say something like, "Well, I'm glad you decided to walk around that puddle rather than run through it or try to jump over it." This reinforces a child's sense of self, acknowledges that he has a degree of autonomy, and encourages him to identify ways and means by which he can validate these facts for himself in the future.

Incidents such as the one just described exemplify various parental attitudes. Their influence on the eventual development of a healthy problem solving approach in their children later in life is very significant. Encouragement to make choices and to decide for themselves, after the choice is made, whether or not it was the correct one is the best way for parents to help their children develop skills in dealing with the decisions they will face throughout their lives.

During adolescence it is the personality structure inside the individual, rather than the adults outside, which most influences the building of the elements that will provide a basis for effectively solving problems later in life. An adolescent may deal with a problem using many different behaviors, and he may be unaware of the fact that certain of these are related to this kind of decision or conflict. In other words, the cause of a certain behavior may be unconscious. A high school student who is sleepy all day and unable to go to sleep at night may be unconsciously compelled to behave this way because of her inability to decide on taking a business or a college preparatory degree program. Once forced to confront her own uncertainty about this choice, she may continue her counterproductive behavior and, at the same time, feel anxious and frustrated over her inability to make a decision. Her early training in problem solving may have been inadequate, or she may simply be delayed in her personality development in this area. Whatever the reason, the most effective way of dealing with such a problem in adolescence is to provide help as parents and teachers with, first, the identification of the problem, bringing it out into the light, so to speak, and then to help the individual weigh all the factors involved for herself. Usually, once the pros and cons for pursuing each course are fully realized, a solution appears and can be worked out. If an adolescent becomes more confused as more facts are gathered, a serious disturbance in psychological functioning is likely to be present—either a developmental failure or an obsessive neurosis.

Piaget (1928) has shown that cognitive development in childhood relates importantly to decision making, and his studies indicate that a pragmatic approach to problem solving in early childhood helps the child learn better than does an abstract one. In other words, learning to choose correctly in the puddle example above would be helped more by the direct experience of feeling wet feet than by a discussion of pros and cons. Erikson (1950) makes clear that decision making in adolescence depends on clear definition from significant adults of their own point of view and their own ways of making decisions for themselves—all of this presented in a manner that does not impose a solution but simply offers an example of one person's method. The adolescent may or may not identify with this model, and this is an option which must remain open. In the instance of the girl with sleep problems, discussion of the pros and cons of pursuing a business career as opposed to going to college, rating all the ramifications of sex stereotyping and the choice of motherhood over career, as well as the simpler choice between a prolonged or a more short-term period of education, should help her identify the problem and then solve it.

The method followed by parents, teachers, and therapists in helping adolescents develop successful problem solving must be a subtle one, for one must avoid preaching values on the one hand and being wishy-washy on the other. A conversation that begins "When I was your age. . . ." is doomed from the start. One can see the film cover an adolescent's eyes at such a moment. "Knowing you as I do, I would guess you must be feeling a lot of pressure from lots of directions to do such and such" is often a good opening, or "Decisions! Decisions! You must be facing a lot of them." Either may serve to direct talk away from the presenting problem to what lies beneath it.

Once the problem is identified, the temptation is to offer solutions. While this helps children make up their mind, it only irritates adolescents. One can work a long time trying to tease alternative solutions from the individual. "What comes to your mind? What do you see ahead?" "Tell me what it feels like to see yourself doing this, that, and the other." All these leading questions and statements may lead nowhere or, more likely, to the persistent trap question from the young person, "What do you think I should do?" The answer, "Whatever you want to," begs the question, while "Go to Vassar" starts an argument.

In such instances bringing a third party into the discussion might be helpful. "Joanie Smith went to secretarial school after she got married and had her baby." The latter brings your own values out without imposing them. Of course the adolescent is not going to make her decision on the spot or give you any credit for influencing her solution to the problem if she does solve it later on, but your identification of the underlying conflict and your subtle presentation of solutions with some indication of your own priorities have no doubt been an important contribution to her becoming a mature problem solver.

The emotionally healthy young adult will have had good "training" experiences in childhood and adolescence and, as a result, will be able to make crisp, accurate, clear-cut decisions without experiencing neurotic doubting and obsessive rumination.

Sexual Satisfaction

A second area in which one sees emotional health or its lack is the area of sexuality—in both its broad and its narrow context. For some, gender identity is never fully crystallized. There is discomfort with maleness or femaleness. This represents ill health in the general area of sexuality. Others are unable to obtain satisfying gratification in their genital relationships, and this represents pathology in the specific area.

Young adults who have problems developing a healthy maturity in the general area of sexuality may have experienced problems in childhood or adolescence. Early in life the distinctions between the sexes are defined by parents and other caretakers (nurses, teachers, and babysitters), and the manner and method of this definition have an important impact on how comfortable children will later feel about gender differences. In some families there are two separate value systems for sons and for daughters. What is allowed one and denied the other and what is expected of one and not of the other are clearly defined, and the difference is immediately perceived by the child. It is not simply that boys urinate standing up and girls sitting down, but boys can run around naked, while girls must cover up their torso even before breast development begins. Girls are given dolls, and boys are given trucks. Boys can shout and talk loudly, but girls must speak softly. Girls are expected to be neater and tidier than boys. It seems to us that when these distinctions are made clearly in childhood, there is less concern and anxiety in early adulthood about passivity and aggressiveness and fewer disturbing power struggles between men and women. Divisive competitiveness is unnecessary when the arenas are separate.

There is considerable controversy today about sexual stereotyping. Feminists feel that this practice results in the downgrading of women, but so far the evidence is in favor of helping children develop a clear-cut sense of gender rather than blurring the natural differentiation. Of course, most feminists do not believe in a "natural differentiation" (other than the anatomical one) and attribute all other differences between the sexes to the effects of cultural conditioning (the male "putdown" of women). Most studies, however, whether conducted by men or women, show that there are temperamental, characterological, and sexual arousal differences which are not determined by culture.

Presently there is a greater degree of encouragement for daughters to prepare for careers than was true in the past. Typical American parents do not hold out the prospect of "Kirche, Küche, Kinder" as the most desirable goal for their daughters, as they once did. They indicate that they would be pleased at a daughter's choice of a number of different options, but in regard to dress, manners, sex, and the division of labor within the home, there are still different expectations for sons and for daughters. For healthy personality development these distinctions are necessary.

Treating boys and girls differently in childhood seems clearly indicated, but we are less sure about this when the children become adolescents. The trend now is toward coeducation in private schools and colleges (it has always been more the rule than the exception in public educational institutions), and this can be seen as good evidence that identical curricular and extracurricular programs are preferred for male and female adolescents. Similarity in dress and manners in this age group does seem to foster an ease in relationships between the sexes. While it may be hard for traditionalists to accept women college students as rugby and ice hockey players, so far no harm seems to have come of it, and a great deal of pleasure and companionship between the sexes has apparently resulted. Despite the occasional vituperative outbursts on the part of a few militant feminists, the overall interaction between the sexes at all ages seems to us to be at a higher level of understanding and mutuality than ever before.

Of course, a satisfactory physical relationship between men and women depends almost entirely on the nature of the emotional one. Couples who are angry, distrustful, or afraid of each other are going to engage in mechanical, competitive, mutually demeaning, and unsatisfying sexual relationships. There are other factors which stem from earlier experiences with parents, siblings, and peers which can inhibit the pleasure of sex relations with a partner with whom one has a loving, trusting relationship. Early childhood experiences that can lead to later trouble in this area often involve parental attitudes during toilet training. Emphasis on the dirtiness, foul odor, disgusting appearance, and possible contaminating effect of urine and feces tends to build feelings of revulsion for the sex organs and to lead to excessive shyness and modesty later in life.

Sex play with siblings or incestuous relationships with parents also result in inhibitions which can seriously interfere with healthy sexual relationships in adulthood. There may be little that parents can do in the way of forestalling such incidents other than being aware of their possibility and taking precautionary measures which do not cause unwarranted fears on the part of the child. However, if such incidents do occur (and sex play among siblings or peers is very common in childhood), the attitude taken by parents is usually crucial in determining whether the incident will leave a damaging scar. A thorough discussion of the episode between the child and a parent or therapist, one which includes both the initiator and the complier in separate talks, should take place as soon as possible after the event with the hope that feelings of guilt about the physical enjoyment which occurred and any seduction that might be thought to have played a part will be aired, as well as the shame, fear, and perplexity that usually are involved. Once this kind of catharsis has been achieved, the matter can usually be dropped, and it is unlikely that any inhibiting effect will be seen later.

Positive attitudes toward physical closeness are important also. Simply preventing or dealing with traumatic events is not enough to ensure satisfying sexual relationships in later life. Children need to know that touching, hugging, holding, and kissing between parents is an enjoyable and healthy part of being an adult. A feeling of comfort with physical contact has its developmental origins in the child's observation of what happens between the parents' bodies. Erikson (1950) has written eloquently on this subject, and Harlow's monkeys (Harlow and Zimmerman, 1959) have proven the same thing—not only in terms of the attainment of mutually satisfying sexual relations but also, in the broader sense, in the development of trust in others.

Serious inhibition in sexual function can result from experiences taking place in early adolescence as well as those occurring in childhood. Rape, sexual assault, sex play with siblings, incest, being required to share a bed with a sibling or parent can all happen to a teenager, with the same results described in the child, and the prevention and treatment of such occurrences are much the same. In addition, however, adolescents are forced to deal with their own burgeoning sexual impulses, and the manner in which these impulses are reacted to by parents and significant others influences to a considerable degree sexual adjustment as an adult.

There has been some controversy about where and by whom sex education should be given; we believe there is no clear answer to this question. Schools, churches, physicians, and parents are capable of providing the necessary education, if they are comfortable with the subject, and there are so many variations in this regard that one cannot make a general recommendation. Suffice to say that teenagers do need to know the facts about sexual anatomy and physiology as well as about pregnancy, contraception, and abortion, but these facts have to be accompanied by teaching about their emotional correlates. For instance, boys need to have their feelings about penis size understood, and girls need to have a chance to discuss feelings about breast size and about delayed menarche. Myths which correlate penis size with virility and the ability to give satisfaction and those which suggest that women with small breasts are homosexual create feelings of fear and inadequacy which can seriously cripple sexual performance and enjoyment in early adulthood. They need to be discussed and their influence counteracted. Masturbation, thanks to some of our popular novels and sex manuals, has come to be generally understood for what is is—a healthy release for sexual tension. Nevertheless, there is still an aura of impurity around it which leads some adolescents to suffer inappropriate guilt feelings. These must be dealt with by knowledgeable and understanding parents and teachers. Calderone (1970) has been a pioneer in this field, and her writing and lecturing has gone far toward breaking down mythology and creating relaxed and happy attitudes toward physical sex.

Career

Moving on now to the area of commitment to career —something that has always been the core of most men's midlife existence and is becoming increasingly important also for women, we find here again that occurrences and attitudes experienced in both childhood and adolescence have a significant and often crucial developmental impact. Early in childhood we begin to gain a sense of our own competence and to experience feelings of success and failure. If we grow up feeling inferior and incompetent in comparison with those around us, it becomes more and more difficult to meet the challenges that are part of daily life and in the long run to make the commitment necessary to pursue a career. Often it is children low in the birth order who fail to attain a sense of competence. They have become used to being smaller, weaker, and more stupid than their siblings, and, from the constant frustration of trying to catch up from behind, a feeling of inadequacy and a pessimism about achieving success are created which make them back away from challenges and then avoid commitment to competitive employment throughout their lives.

But it is not only low birth order that may cause children to have problems with their careers in later life. Young people whose parents' expectations are so narrow that they can praise their children for success in a very limited number of areas also fail to gain the courage and feeling of optimism which allow them to compete and to commit themselves to careers that are demanding. It is incumbent on parents to compensate in whatever ways they can for the feelings of smallness in their later-born children, taking them away on trips without the older children, for instance, or having them visit relatives by themselves where they will be out from under the domination of their brothers and sisters. Parents should also seek out areas of competence and interest in their children and foster them. Sometimes these areas may seem "far out" or perhaps even unacceptable, but the advantage of doing something right and feeling pleased with the achievement, as well as gaining some praise from respected elders means so much to the child, both in the present and for the future, that mothers and fathers should be able to broaden their focus and, in some instances, swallow their pride in the best interests of their children. We know of one individual who gained a sense of pride in himself from being the local tiddlywinks champion, another from collecting butterflies, and another, a girl, who found a new sense of self-worth from having more freckles than any other person, boy or girl, in the county!

Another important factor in the development of the ability to commit oneself to a career is the image of the work projected by those in the family who are employed. Sometimes parents will blame their jobs for taking them away from home and causing them to be less adequate mothers, fathers, or spouses than they want to be. This casts careers in the role of enemy and leads to feelings in the children that they should be avoided rather than sought after. To adults, such an assumption seems silly and irrational, but we must never forget that young children are much more in tune with the feelings embodied in situations in their environment than they may be with the logic involved.

Parents who are able to give their children a sense of the value of the jobs they are working at and, if at all possible, a sense of the enjoyment and gratification which come from their employment are parents who are cultivating in their children the roots of a later ability to commit themselves to a career.

For the adolescent, the problems that arise to interfere with such a commitment are different from those we find in the child. Young men and women from about 15 on begin to look within themselves for incentive and motivation. They tend to be suspicious of suggestions and even of encouragement from adults about where they should go and what they should do. The primary need in adolescence is to be sure that one's goals and ambitions are independently chosen and are unique to themselves. Often they experience an interim of neutrality, labeled by Erikson (1950) a psychosocial moratorium, during which they are against everything and for nothing. This is often very distressing to adolescents, but at times they seem oblivious of it or even happy with it. It is almost always frustrating and irritating to parents, teachers, and therapists, and they tend to moan about "wasted lives" and "unfulfilled potential." There is little they can do except wait until it passes—which it almost always does after a few months or perhaps a year or two. At this time in the lives of their children, parents must be tolerant of experimentation and not preach the old saw, "Anything worth starting is worth finishing." They must also be careful not to take over when a flash of enthusiasm appears in their young son or daughter. This almost always results in an immediate dropping of the project, whatever it may be. Former President Eliot of Harvard once said regretfully, "Whenever we see a spark of genius around here we water it!" Appropriately supporting an adolescent's interest in something without taking it over through enthusiasm and a wish to participate may be difficult, but it is an important responsibility of parenthood.

Models are important to adolescents, more than to children, for they are aware of the action and attitudes of the adults they respect and admire. They rarely can acknowledge this for, as we said before, they very much want to feel that their values and goals spring from within. But unconsciously they are identifying with those they respect. Over and over again we see young people lose their zest for life and become lethargic and unmotivated following the death of an older family member or admired teacher. Their reason for succeeding is suddenly gone, without their even knowing it. No longer can they unconsciously work toward emulating such persons and gaining their praise and respect. This is beautifully illustrated in Arthur Miller's *Death of a Salesman* (1949) when Biff, shortly after surprising his father in a hotel room with a prostitute, says to his mother, "Gee, Mom, I can't seem to take hold. I can't get hold of a way of life."

One other eventuality that may have a deleterious effect on an adolescent's ability to commit himself to the idea of working is the death of a parent which may be attributed to overwork or pressures on the job. Such an event may set up an unconscious association between death and dedication to a career. Parents need to be careful what they say about the influence of work on their health. Sometimes its effects are exaggerated, and this may adversely influence a child's ambition. By careful encouragement of young people to seek their own ego-syntonic means of expression and an enthusiastic and optimistic attitude toward their own work, parents can help their children develop a healthy commitment to careers when they become young adults. Later this same attitude on the part of teachers will be very important. Erikson (1950), White (1975), and Vaillant (1977) have made important contributions to our understanding of what embraces the development of feelings of competence, commitment, and success in the world of work.

Intimacy

Intimate relationships with others are the healthy expression of commitment in the interpersonal area. An infant's experience of being touched, held, carried, and hugged has been found to be related to the development of trust, which as contrasted to suspiciousness is the basis of healthy relationships throughout life. If an infant has obtained a sense of trust by feeling his body being supported and nourished by another, he has a good start toward developing intimate feelings as an adult, but factors in later childhood and adolescence play a role also.

In addition to loving acceptance at home, children need to attend to developing close relationships to peers in play groups and at school. The importance of these friendships is often minimized by the child, either because he does not recognize them for what they are or because he does not have the vocabulary to describe his feelings. Parents must be careful to foster such friendships and do their best not to disparage these friends or to fail to take the trouble to arrange opportunities to meet and play. They must also be alert to the trauma involved when playmates are separated by a family's moving away. Special efforts must be made in such cases to find new companions and to help the child overcome any shyness or reluctance in reaching out or responding to new friends. Attempts to help the child verbalize his sadness and his sense of loss, though not often very successful, should be made.

Adult figures need to be as consistent and as constant in the child's life as is possible. Revolving babysitters or a changing cast of spouses or lovers tends to build distrust of people in young children. It is hard for them to tolerate the disappointment which follows the disappearance of a person they have come to trust, and a multiplicity of such disappointments can leave vestiges of uncertainty about relationships which may inhibit the development of deep relationships later in life.

Intimacy includes a deep trust and a mutuality of feeling which allow for and even enjoy differences in opinions, taste, and values. Many experts, specifically Erikson (1950), believe that intimacy can come only after the solidification of identity, for intimacy is thought to threaten identity—the closeness one feels to another brings to mind the possibility of merger into the other and thus losing one's individuality. Whether this is true or not, there are many adolescent experiences which can work against the development of a capacity to be intimate. One has already been discussed in the context of career commitment—loss of or disillusionment in a respected and admired adult. As does a child, an adolescent feels angry and resentful when a loved one dies. Although this is irrational, there is always a sense that the person who has died has deserted the one left behind and that this is a breach of faith. It becomes more difficult after such a loss to love and become intimate with another.

Behavior on the part of one person toward another which breaks trust (or seems to) and thereby interferes with the ability to become intimate is all too common, and much of it is not preventable. Fractured romances seem to be part of growing up, and, all too often, a truly one-sided defection on the part of a lover leads to the development of a callousness and a defensive burying of tenderness which may never change. Fortunately, the trite saying "Time heals all wounds" has (as have so many trite sayings) a germ of truth, and the individual who is hurt recovers, at least to some degree, and is once more able to feel lovingly enough toward another to develop intimacy after a period of numbness. Helping adolescents to grieve for a lost parent or lover is one of the most frequent tasks challenging therapists and counselors of adolescents. Their help can often make the difference between permanent scarring and temporary withdrawal. Intimacy can follow successful recovery from rejection or loss, but such a recovery often requires help from older and wiser confidants.

Conclusion

The goals of the young adult should be to work out a stable identity, decide what one wants to do, develop independence from one's family while retaining good relationships with them, develop appropriate sexual attitudes, and adopt or reject, if necessary, the ethical and moral values consistent with the well-being of one's society.

As we have said, the transition from adolescence to adulthood, or maturity, can be quite difficult or even impossible if the developing person has not been helped to know what to expect and what society expects of the individual. This depends on a value system being clearly defined. It is here that one all too often finds much uncertainty on the part of older people. Young adults tend to admire and respect, as well as emulate, older persons whom they observe engaging in pleasant and rewarding activities, particularly those that help others or the general community culture. Unfortunately, many ideas being promulgated are destructive rather than constructive. This is especially true of the content of many recreational mediums, most notably television. In many programs the ideals expressed in action, speech, dress, and thought tend to exploit young adults rather than encourage them to develop patterns of living that are conducive to the betterment of society.

The developmental period of young adulthood is the culmination of much nurturing, teaching, and coaching by a wide variety of significant persons: parents and other relatives, teachers, classmates, neighbors, religious authorities, and those the young person encounters through books, magazines, and television. Fortunately, the resiliency of late adolescents and young adults is such that early positive influences can have a dramatic effect in overcoming difficulties encountered in this age span, and thereby enabling them to live satisfying lives.

References

Calderone, M. S. (1970), *Manual of Family Planning and Contraceptive Practice.* Baltimore: Williams & Wilkins.

Erikson, E. H. (1950), *Childhood and Society.* Rev. ed. New York: Norton, 1963.

Harlow, H. F., & Zimmerman, R. R. (1959), Affectional responses in the infant monkey. *Science,* 130:421–432.

Miller, A. (1949), *Death of a Salesman.* New York: Viking.

Piaget, J. (1928), *Judgment and Reasoning in the Child.* London: Harcourt, Brace.

Vaillant, G. E. (1977), *Adaptation to Life.* Boston: Little, Brown.

White, R. W. (1975), *Lives in Progress.* 3rd ed. New York: Holt, Rinehart & Winston.

19

The Second Separation Stage of Adolescence[1]

RICHARD A. ISAY, M.D.

The onset of adolescence is accompanied by an upsurge of libidinal and aggressive impulses, propelled largely by the physiological changes that initiate puberty. Adultlike sexual and aggressive capacities are now better organized than the instinctual impulses of childhood, which were more diffuse with regard both to aim and origin. Puberty, following a latency period in which there has been consolidation of the developmental gains of childhood, finds an ego becoming more capable of tolerating, as well as controlling, an increase in drive strength. Accompanying these strong sexual and aggressive impulses (and occasioning a fear of retaliation) are recrudescent incestuous fantasies and, by heterosexuals, hostility directed toward the same-sex parent. A need for distance from both parents thereby arises. We might think of the separation that the early adolescent imposes between himself and his parents in order to achieve this distance as constituting a first separation stage of adolescence.

Unlike the onset of early adolescence, marked by physiological and psychological changes and a consequent need for emotional distance, the onset of late adolescence is initiated by a cultural expectation of independence and developmental progression. In American society this usually occurs at about the

[1] This chapter, written in 1977, is about the development of heterosexuals in late adolescence. It does not reflect my views about the normal development of gay adolescents of which some views are set forth in chapter 20 and further elucidated in Isay (1989).

age of 17 or 18 and often coincides with the departure for college.[2] This cultural expectation of independence initiates the second separation stage of adolescence. In this developmental stage there is a further mitigation of the restraining parental ego and superego, in large measure a result of the loosening of parental ties. While the core superego remains, an extensive modification or revision of values often occurs through the influence of peers and of adults outside the immediate family. During late adolescence there occurs another increase in sexual and aggressive wishes and impulses—this time, largely as a result of the separation and not as its cause—with greater opportunity than in early adolescence to express these impulses through diverse experiences in an enlarged sphere of relationships.

The separation and increased emotional distance from parents that mark the onset of this stage of adolescence normally result in some subjectively experienced depression and anxiety; however, the mood swings are neither as abrupt nor as pronounced as in early adolescence, when what has been compared to a mourning process occurs (Jacobson, 1961). Nor is the discomfort usually as severe, since a partial working through of the loss has already been accomplished and the ego is better equipped to cope with anxiety and trauma, both factors enhancing the adolescent's capacity to deal with the separation.

With menarche the pubescent girl, confronted by her separateness and the need to care for herself, has had separation forced on her by her physiology at the earliest stage of adolescence. A boy in early adolescence has had no comparable physiological confrontation with his own separateness, for while masturbation with ejaculation is a physiological landmark that

[2] In Israel the separation that marks the onset of late adolescence also occurs at 18, imposed by military training rather than by advanced education. In Israeli society this period is consciously and clearly acknowledged as an opportunity for growth and independence, although it is also a time fraught with realistic anxieties. The demarcation between the early stages of adolescence and late adolescence is not so clear in America. Physical separation is neither enforced nor universal; although the 18-year-old now has most of the legal prerogatives of the adult, most middle-class American adolescents are still dependent for support on their parents and are not perceived as adults or treated as such within the family.

may cause anxiety because of the new sexual and competitive prowess it represents, it does not evoke comparable feelings of separateness and aloneness; it lacks the regularity, automaticity, and total body involvement of menstruation. Some adolescent boys attempt to control their anxiety by being abstemious, thereby attempting to assert the efficacy of mind over a body whose impulses and responses to impulses appear to dominate. The adolescent girl has no such option; the onset of menstruation demands of her that she regularly take care of the needs of her body by herself, evoking a sense of abrupt and often profoundly painful separation from the mother.

It is this abrupt and more painful separation that may contribute to making early adolescence more traumatic for girls than for boys. Feelings of depression caused by the girl's sense of separateness, as well as anxiety evoked by the ensuing regressive pulls, may be major causes of the early adolescent girl's seeking psychological assistance. It is my impression that girls are more likely than boys to seek psychological help at this age for problems involving separation and the recrudescence of childhood separation conflicts. The mother's identification with her daughter, the mother's own anxiety, and her ambivalent involvement in her daughter's maturation often make the progress through this first adolescent separation phase particularly difficult.

We might think that, because of their relatively more profound and extensive experience with feelings of separateness, girls would be less distressed than boys are by the separation of this later developmental stage. It is my impression, however, that this is not the case. I believe this to be explicable by a girl's identification with and attachment to her mother, which to some extent must be surrendered to form the deeper and more complex heterosexual attachments of late adolescence, thereby contributing to her sense of loss at this stage. We are also aware of variables that may make the separation of late adolescence especially difficult for a girl, such as an intense symbiotic relation with her mother or attending a male-dominated college that may lack maternal surrogates and role models and thereby increase her longing and loneliness.

All of us who work with late adolescents in analysis or

psychotherapy frequently see depression, overt and masked, in both boys and girls during the first year in college. It may take the form of doleful, repetitious complaints about classmates, roommates, living accommodations, or other aspects of college life, a displacement of the anger associated with longings, loneliness, and anxiety caused by the separation. A new school for the second year may be sought—one that may be either very close to home or very distant—in an essentially futile attempt to escape these painful longings.

The increased psychological and physical space for the expression of libidinal and aggressive impulses, along with the forceful aggressive push of physiological maturation, may be frightening to many adolescents, and their behavior often demands external intervention as an unconsciously imposed means of constraining or containing these impulses. What we consider the testing of limits to help him contain impulses may also have the function of providing an external authority as a substitute for the ego and superego function of the longed-for parents. Such "limit testing," then, may be another expression of the late adolescent's mourning process, and these self-imposed external constraints may be unconsciously sought-after substitutes for the missed and missing parents (also see Blos, 1963).

The intensity of competitive strivings with the parent of the same sex evokes in many heterosexual late adolescents the resurgence of enormous anxiety, often caused by fears of retaliation (Isay, 1989, chapter 7). Various forms of self-injurious or self-destructive behavior may occur as a means of controlling, or magically attempting to ward off, the feared retaliation for the expression of these aggressive and sexual strivings. What appears, however, to be simply self-destructive behavior may also be an expression of the late adolescent's need to examine and test his or her own capacities in an effort to learn to deal more effectively with new aspects of external reality, a need arising from the separation and increased psychological distance from parents. A variety of experiences and relationships with peers serves this function of testing the viability and solidity of certain functions of the ego, especially those "autonomous characteristics," such as motor, language, and thinking skills that are primarily concerned with increasing mastery over the environment. These aspects of the ego, of course, do not necessarily remain untouched by conflict (Hartmann, 1958, p. 9). Any analyst working with adolescents can attest the severe disruptions, distortions, and inhibitions that occur at times, especially in the spheres of language and thinking, because of conflict.

Adolescents may form close attachments to peers who they anticipate will be unacceptable to their parents or whom they experience as being unlike anyone they have previously associated with. These relationships, "spite and revenge attachments," may be a means of placing a barrier between the adolescent and his parents. In this manner, he attempts to force a separation by causing a rupture in a relationship in which he unconsciously feels his dependency longings to be too great, or in which he experiences, again usually unconsciously, the parental attachment to be frightening. This is seen relatively frequently when a late adolescent, spending his college years at or near home, experiences the continued attachment to be too uncomfortable.

Not all late adolescents who live at home, of course, need to expand their psychological space in this manner, as the psychological distance and the independence necessary for developmental maturation at this stage may be achieved even though there is physical proximity. There are, furthermore, late adolescents who leave home during the college years, forming vindictive attachments in order to establish greater independence, and sever what is perceived as a burdensome emotional attachment to either or both parents. Physical separation itself does not insure the necessary independence for maturation at this stage, any more than physical proximity necessarily limits the capacity for emotional growth.

This traditional way of viewing such relations does not, however, do justice to their complexity. For, while their aim may be, in part, to aggravate parents and to enhance separation, they are also a means the adolescent has of testing his capacity to deal effectively with unfamiliar types and groups of people in new and unfamiliar circumstances, just as he tests his capacity to deal with unfamiliar and at times dangerous situations. Such apparently vindictive attachments are thus formed not only to compel the rupture of a relationship with parents, but to test and enhance the adolescent's social competence after he has achieved a degree of separation and independence.

The late adolescent's testing of society's limits, his reckless and sometimes even dangerous behavior, and his seeking out of relationships that may appear dangerous, unwise, or unhealthy do express the wish to have external forces intervene to help contain frightening internal pressures. But all these experiences also test and expand the ego's capacities to contain, control, organize, and cope with a variety of new and variegated reality situations. Largely because of such experiences, along with enhanced intellectual and motor skills that appear as a result of physiological maturation, there occurs during late adolescence a further increment in ego assets, particularly in the coping devices that enhance the capacity to deal more effectively with external reality and, in turn, with instinctual impulses.

Developmental Goals

According to Laufer (1976), the developmental tasks of late adolescence are "the change in relationship to contemporaries; and the change in attitude to his (the adolescent's) own body"; the main developmental function of adolescence, in his view, lies in the "establishment of a final sexual orientation (p. 298).[3]

Blos (1962) understands late adolescence as a stage of consolidation whose goals and tasks are the "elaboration of a highly idiosyncratic and stable arrangement of ego functions and interests; an extension of the conflict-free sphere of the ego; an irreversible sexual position (identity constancy); a relatively con-

---

[3] My clinical experience with late adolescents and adults who are homosexual has convinced me that their sexual orientation is established by the earliest years of childhood. Only the consolidation and integration of the sexual orientation remain as developmental functions of adolescence (see chapter 20). Laufer's views might encourage therapists to attempt to change the sexual orientation of a gay adolescent or adult. It is my experience that such efforts usually result in symptoms of anxiety and depression due to self-esteem injury (Isay, 1985).

stant cathexis of object and self representations; and the stabilization of the mental apparatuses . . ." (p. 129).

Aarons (1970), Ritvo (1971), and Blos (1974) all stress that
a final structuralization and organization of the ego ideal occurs
as an outcome of the psychic reorganization of late adolescence.
They see many major conflicts and difficulties of late adolescence arising out of an insufficient and inadequate ego ideal.
The final structuralization of the ego ideal corresponds to the
final resolution of the negative oedipal complex by freeing up,
for the heterosexual boy, his libidinal tie to the father and, for
the girl, the libidinal attachment to the mother. Laufer (1964,
1976) feels that it is more accurate to say that the ego ideal is
fixed as a more or less permanent structure from the immediate
postoedipal identifications, but that there are some "realign-
ments" and additions to the ego ideal occurring during late
adolescence that reflect "the demands and expectations of contemporaries" (1964, p. 197).

My clinical work has suggested two developmental goals
(or tasks) of late adolescence: (1) the consolidation and integration of a final sexual orientation, so that there is at the
conclusion of this developmental stage a reasonably consistent
heterosexual or homosexual identity, and (2) the consolidation
of a vocational goal, so that there is more or less consistent
vocational identity which is not subject to change with the tentative vacillations and shifts of interests that may occur at times
of crisis, such as unexpected loss or trauma. This does not mean
that for adolescence to be completed one must have selected
a vocation. I am suggesting, however, that by the conclusion of
adolescence, the individual has a vocational as well as a firm
sexual orientation.

The successful accomplishment of these goals depends on
the adolescent's capacity to effect the psychological separation,
and to gain the necessary distance from his or her parents, to
permit the expression of sexual and aggressive needs in a broadened scope of relationships and experiences, leading to an ever
increasing specificity in love object and career choice. If difficulties in early relations with parents continue to make separation difficult, then one may expect to encounter at this age
symptomatic disturbances that interfere with both goals of late

adolescence. If there is not therapeutic intervention during this period of consolidative development, then a symptomatic adult neurosis is likely to develop (see also Blos, 1972a, p. 110).

The process leading to the consolidation of a vocational identity is inextricably tied to the formation of the ego ideal. Early ego ideal precursors lie in the fantasies the 2-, 3-, or 4-year-old uses to heal wounded self-esteem and to achieve a sense of security, as he or she attempts to maintain an equilibrium between desires and reality. Lampl-de Groot (1962) gives the engaging example of John, 2 years and 10 months old, who told his mother that "his penis would grow to be as big as the garden hose; he would fill the ocean and a big steamer would take him overseas" (p. 97). As a result of identifications and internalizations that are the outcome of the oedipal rivalry in heterosexuals, the ego ideal later becomes less exclusively an agency for the healing of narcissistic wounds. It becomes the agency that contains wishes to be like the parents, especially the same-sex parent.

The late adolescent's testing of external reality, mentioned previously in the context of enhancing and strengthening the ego, also contributes to accretions in those aspects of the ego ideal that contribute to vocational interests, and to their modification and solidification. This occurs through identifications with an extended group of peers and parent surrogates and the adolescent's increased understanding of cultural expectations.

On the basis of clinical work with adults as well as adolescents, it is clear that the ego ideal of the late adolescent contains identifications, not only with the same-sex parent, but with the opposite-sex parent as well. In part, this may represent residuals of the archaic, need-fulfilling, preoedipal ego ideal precursors; restitutive identifications with the lost parent of the oedipal period (aspects, for example, for the boy of his mother's vocational ambitions that are part of the father's wishes and ambitions); and identifications with valued vocational interests and activities of the mother. There are also identifications with the opposite-sex parent's interests that are, of course, caused during the oedipal period by regressive solutions of castration fears or envy of such maternal functions as childbearing. However, the boy's identification with the vocational interests of his mother have become increasingly common as a reflection of society's greater appreciation of the professional and working woman in the family.

As with the boy, a girl's vocational ambitions are in part derived from that part of the ego ideal that is formed through attempted resolution of early narcissistic injuries. In addition, one finds identifications with the father's vocational aims and aspirations, which may be emphasized if she has a sense of not being equal to her brother or father or of not having the body completeness of a man. One may find, at the end of the oedipal period, a strengthened identification with the mother, which is in part an attempt to restore a sense of closeness to the lost father as well as to the mother, thereby maintaining contact with both parents. The demands and expectations of peer groups and parent surrogates, along with social expectations, lead to increments in the girl's ego ideal. Since one aspect of the solidification of the ego ideal that is concerned with vocational interest occurs through the restitutive identification with both parents, the accepted role of the working mother may make the achievement of a reasonably stable vocational identity less conflicted for many female college students who have two working parents. However, this increased freedom of vocational choice may evoke a conflict in a girl from a more traditional middle class family, in which only the man works, as she may feel that by selecting a vocation she surrenders the closeness derived from identification with her mother, entering into what may be a frightening rivalry with her father (and/or brothers). (For further elaboration of ego ideal formation in girls, see Jacobson, 1954; Blos, 1974.)

I have focused on the development of vocational identity in an attempt to emphasize an important developmental goal of late adolescence that has been attended to less than the attainment of a stable sexual orientation. For heterosexual boys and girls, the consolidation of sexual identity follows a similar developmental course. It is clear that for both there must be sufficient resolution of oedipal conflicts to permit a core identification with the same-sex parent. If there is inadequate resolution of preoedipal issues, especially during the separation-individuation stages, then anxiety may be so disabling as to interfere with establishing a stable vocational identity or consolidating a sexual orientation. This is the implication of Blos's statement that "only after the analysis of the fixation in the negative oedipal complex has been accomplished, can the formation of an age-adequate, workable ego ideal take its normal course" (1974, p. 46).

One indication for the psychoanalytic treatment of the late adolescent is the presence of conflict that results in painful symptoms that interfere with the attainment of either of these developmental goals. I am stressing here not only the presence of conflict that may result in the failure of developmental progress, but the experience of pain. For, unlike the child who can be brought to the office and whose motivation can largely be supplied by the parents' distress, concern, and exhortation, the adolescent must proceed of his own volition, participating in a process that demands, among other things, passivity, acquiescence, and verbalization. All of these at times run counter to peer pressure and other social and developmentally appropriate growth forces that demand activity in the service of mastery. I am using the following cases to illustrate the types of developmental conflict that make it both difficult and painful for a late adolescent to accomplish these tasks satisfactorily, necessitating psychoanalytic intervention to free up and facilitate development into adulthood.

Clinical Illustrations

Adam

Adam was 19 when he was referred for analysis, at the end of his freshman year of college. Although his college work had been fair, he had the continued, painful recognition that his performance was not as good as he wished, and he feared that he would be unsuccessful in any attempted vocational endeavor. He was concerned about a stammer and what he thought was a small and inadequate penis.

Adam's father was very competitive and very successful. Adam viewed him as a ruthless man, ruling a vast business empire by humiliating subordinates, just as he had humiliated Adam as a child. Adam adored his mother, and they shared an articulated fear and ambivalence toward the father. Adam had no recollected overt symptomatology or significant distress as a child. Although he was compliant and agreeable at home in order not to anger his father, he was successful and popular in school and in his social relations.

It is, however, important not to confuse the absence of recollected subjective distress, or of symptoms, with the absence of neurotic conflict. It is clear that there was massive inhibition of rage and of competitiveness with his father, which was expressed in compliance. Agreeable environmental factors, especially the favored support of his mother, made it possible for Adam to succeed despite these inhibitions. However, the fear and hostile ambivalence toward the father, along with the closeness to his mother, made successful identification with his father impossible. While the origin of his neurotic conflict clearly lay in childhood, he did not become symptomatic until the onset of adolescence.

It was with the onset of pubescence, at age 12 or 13, that Adam became preoccupied with the small size of his penis and his general inadequacy. A painful and transiently immobilizing hip dislocation in early adolescence, along with a frightening upsurge of heterosexual impulses, increased his need to maintain a passive posture and helped to explain the onset of symptoms at this time. He began to stammer in class. Athletically inclined, he now failed where previously he had known only success. Academically he seemed to thwart his every effort to be successful. Although admitted to a major university, he felt, and he may have been correct, that this was the result of his father's connections or even his active intervention. He was totally unable and unwilling to make up his mind about what to do upon graduation or to entertain serious vocational alternatives.

In the analysis the transference took the form of Adam's needing to appear stupid in order to protect himself from any retaliation from me for his competitive and at times murderous impulses. He hid his ambition and rage in part behind ambiguities and obscurities of speech (Isay, 1977). At the same time he made himself look small and inadequate, which gave expression to the intense but repressed passive longings he had toward his father, whom he was fearful of getting close to. His difficulty in studying, his inability to decide on a vocation, his feeling of sexual inadequacy, and his occasional impotence protected him from feared retaliation for his anger and competitiveness, expressed in an unconscious desire to be taken care of by his father and a related desire to remain close to his mother. To do nothing, to be nothing, was not only safe vis-à-vis his father: it was to remain his mother's child. The distance imposed by the separation of early pubescence, and now by late adolescence, entailed activity, decisions, experiences, and relationships that were perceived as dangerous.

On one occasion during his third year of analysis, after I had attempted to help him understand some aspect of his complex work and sexual inhibitions, he had the following dream:

> I am driving down a highway with you. You are in the back seat. I'm driving about ninety miles per hour. There is a lot of oil on the road. All the cars in front of me begin to fishtail, slide, and crash into each other. My car is traveling straight and fine. I apologize for not slowing down, but I really didn't want to. You then point out the window and say, "Look, there's a growing tree."

His association to this dream centered about the discovery of his capabilities in the analysis. He had an occasional desire to be a race car driver, which his father viewed as one of his many "mindless preoccupations," but he also liked the skill and challenge of successfully maneuvering through a dangerous course of action, which can be understood as the beginning enjoyment of attempts to cope with and master a frightening and dangerous external reality. Of course, he also felt that if he permitted himself to pursue a vocation or to enjoy sexual potency, he would unleash a terrible rage and either kill or be killed; he did not want to be violent and competitive like his father, whom he felt and hoped his mother could not love.

The completion of his college career terminated our work after just under three years of analysis. This was not a complete analysis, for while we touched on most of the areas of conflict, there was not enough time for an optimal amount of working through of his conflicts in the transference, in dreams and associative material. Nevertheless, he became aware enough of many of the unconscious determinants of his inhibitions to decide upon a career related to his father's, and he experienced mitigation of his sexual inhibitions and consequent improvement in his self-perception. He also intended to continue his analysis in the city where he had taken a job.

Benjamin

This boy entered analysis when he was 19, at the beginning of his sophomore year of college. He felt he was inadequately masculine, was consequently fearful of homosexual impulses, had distressing and painful psychosomatic complaints, and was unable to do his work adequately. He had had one year of previous psychotherapy.

Benjamin was an only child. His mother was perceived as obtrusive, overwhelming, and devouring; his father, as weak, submissive, and impotent. He was first symptomatic in early childhood as a fussy, poor eater, and later with a stutter, for which his parents sought assistance when he was 6 or 7. The early disturbances in Benjamin's relationship with his mother caused him to seek comfort and security from a less obtrusive, probably seductive father, and in later childhood he seemed comfortable only in his father's presence.

With the onset of early adolescence, Benjamin veered violently away from both parents and began to view them with contempt. His relationships with boys who were older and admired had a hero-worship quality. His intimate physical relationships with girls were terrifying from the time of his earliest sexual experiences at 16. His intense castration fears were aroused by the female genitals, which repulsed him and filled him with anxiety. On many occasions he was impotent. Although his grades were adequate, this seemed mainly the result of his high intelligence, for it took him enormous effort and inordinate amounts of time to complete his assignments.

In his analysis, the transference first took the form of his viewing the analyst as holding him back, interfering both with his work and with satisfying sexual encounters. In a later aspect of the transference, he somewhat resembled Adam: looking silly or inadequate when his angry, competitive feelings manifested themselves. This was, as with Adam, a means of warding off retaliation, of acting out passive wishes toward the father and the desire to be the mother's child again. For both Adam and Benjamin the conflicts that made postoedipal identifications with their fathers difficult and core ego ideal formation inadequate resulted in passive fears, longings, and anxiety that interfered with scholastic performance, vocational goals, and sexual functioning.

Benjamin's analysis, like Adam's, terminated after approximately three years of work—four months after his graduation. It helped him to establish more satisfying relationships with women, much freer of the terrors characteristic of his previous relations; to become less passive and more mutual in his relationships with male peers; and to achieve some mitigation of psychosomatic complaints, which had interesting and complicated unconscious determinants. Both analyses were technically incomplete, as they are for many late adolescents for whom college graduation and vocational requirements necessitate a move. Benjamin terminated his analysis after three years in order to pursue, in another state, a vocation in which he had become increasingly interested. For some late adolescents termination before completion of the analysis may be a resistance; for others, such as Adam and Benjamin, immediate continuation of the analysis might have been a resistance to continued growth and progression by impeding heretofore inhibited vocational aspirations.

At the time of the onset of late adolescence, both Adam and Benjamin had been unable to achieve satisfactory emotional distance from either parent, particularly their fathers. The result was not an expanded sphere of social relations and experiences but a world narrowed by their fears and longings. This made the testing and mastery of new social skills, including the establishment of heterosexual attachments, extremely difficult and painful. It also limited their capacity to test and examine fantasies and wishes related to vocational ambitions, making academic success difficult and the discovery of a vocational direction temporarily impossible. Analysis resulted in sufficient conflict resolution to enable them to deal more effectively with frightening aspects of an extended reality, which in turn made further developmental progression possible.

References

Aarons, Z. A. (1970), Normality and abnormality in adolescence. *The Psychoanalytic Study of the Child*, 25:309–339. New York: International Universities Press.

Blos, P. (1962), *On Adolescence: A Psychoanalytic Interpretation*. New York: Free Press.

——— (1963), The concept of acting out in relation to the adolescent process. *J. Amer. Acad. Child Psychiat.*, 2:118–143.

——— (1972a), The epigenesis of the adult neurosis. *The Psychoanalytic Study of the Child*, 27:106–135. New York: Quadrangle.

——— (1972b), The function of the ego ideal in late adolescence. *The Psychoanalytic Study of the Child*, 27:92–98. New York: Quadrangle.

——— (1974), The genealogy of the ego ideal. *The Psychoanalytic Study of the Child*, 29:43–88. New Haven: Yale University Press.

Hartmann, H. (1958), *Ego Psychology and the Problem of Adaptation*. New York: International Universities Press.

Isay, R. A. (1977), Ambiguity in speech. *J. Amer. Psychoanal. Assn.*, 25:427–452.

——— (1985), On the analytic therapy of homosexual men. *The Psychoanalytic Study of the Child*, 40:235–254. New Haven, CT: Yale University Press.

——— (1989), *Being Homosexual: Gay Men and Their Development*. New York: Farrar, Straus & Giroux.

Jacobson, E. (1954), The self and object world: Vicissitudes of their infantile cathexes and their influence on ideational and affective development. *The Psychoanalytic Study of the Child*, 9:75–127. New York: International Universities Press.

——— (1961), Adolescent moods and the remodeling of psychic structures in adolescence. *The Psychoanalytic Study of the Child*, 16:164–183. New York: International Universities Press.

Lampl-de Groot, J. (1962), Ego ideal and superego. *The Psychoanalytic Study of the Child*, 17:94–106. New York: International Universities Press.

Laufer, M. (1964), Ego ideal and pseudo ideal in adolescence. *The Psychoanalytic Study of the Child*, 19:196–221. New York: International Universities Press.

——— (1976), The central masturbation fantasy, the final sexual organization, and adolescence. *The Psychoanalytic Study of the Child*, 31:297–316. New Haven: Yale University Press.

Ritvo, S. (1971), Late adolescence: Developmental and clinical considerations. *The Psychoanalytic Study of the Child*, 26:241–263. New York: Quadrangle.

20

The Development of Sexual Identity in Homosexual Men

RICHARD A. ISAY, M.D.

In this chapter I will draw on my clinical work to discuss some of the developmental issues that lead to the acquisition of sexual identity in homosexual men and to the healthy consolidation and integration during adolescence and early adulthood of this identity as part of a positive self-image. My intention is to contribute to our further understanding of homosexual men in general; specifically, I discuss issues which may act as guidelines in our assessment of their development. By presenting an outline of a normal developmental pathway for the establishment of a positive identity, I am hoping that we will be better able to conceptualize some of the impediments that may interfere with the formation of a gay man's positive self-image and with the full and gratifying expression of his sexuality. In viewing identity formation as a life-long process that commences in early childhood, I hope to provide a framework for understanding why the attempt to change his sexuality, either explicitly stated or implicitly guiding the therapy, will inevitably be injurious to a homosexual man's self-esteem.

Analysts view normality as a never obtainable ideal (Offer and Sabshin, 1966). Freud (1937) felt that the distinction between a "normal" mental life and an "abnormal" one is only a matter of degree: "Every normal person, in fact, is only normal

A version of this paper was originally published in *The Psychoanalytic Study of the Child*, edited by A. J. Solnit, R. S. Eissler, and P. B. Neubauer, Yale University Press, New Haven, Vol. 41, 1986. Reprinted by permission of the editors and publisher.

on the average. His ego approximates to that of the psychotic in some part or other and to a greater or lesser extent" (p. 235). Jones (1931) wrote that the normal mind does not exist, and Eissler (1960) that "health is a fictitious concept in the psychic stratum." When speaking from the point of view of intrapsychic conflict and the balance of intrapsychic structures, most analysts agree that we are all relatively neurotic and that there is no such thing as a "normal" person. (For a review of analytic views of health and normality see Hartmann, 1939; Abrams, 1979.)

Although I am aware that in theory analysts do not feel that adaptation should be at the expense of "critical aspects of the internal world" (Abrams, 1979, p. 829), when it comes to our patients acting in the world, psychoanalysts and other dynamically oriented therapists tend generally to be governed by social values and social morality and by the concept of instinctual renunciation as the price of being civilized (Freud, 1930). "Acting out" has a pejorative ring in our literature and those who consistently "act out" their impulses are traditionally viewed as not being good analysands (A. Freud, 1968). I feel that homosexuals are viewed as abnormal not only because of social bias (Isay, 1985) and because of the theoretical perspective that maintains they have failed to meet the developmental task of achieving heterosexuality (Isay, 1986), but because they are viewed as "acting out" sexual impulses rather than containing them, and therefore as not having sublimated their sexuality for the sake of social adaptation.

In this chapter I use "healthy" and "normal" interchangeably. By these terms I refer to the gay man's potential to have a well-integrated personality (Klein, 1960); that is, a personality in which there is reasonable intrapsychic harmony, so that he may feel positively about his personal identity as a homosexual and may work and live without significant hindrance from intrapsychic conflict.

I define as homosexual one who has a predominant erotic preference for others of the same sex—i.e., one whose sexual fantasies are either exclusively or almost entirely directed toward others of the same sex. Most homosexuals do engage in sexual activity. However, by this definition one need not do so to be considered homosexual because of the inhibition of sexual behavior due to societal pressures or intrapsychic conflict. There are also those who may be homosexual but are unaware of their sexual fantasies because of repression, suppression, or denial of these fantasies. There are also homosexual men who are conscious of their homoerotic fantasies, arousal patterns, and even behavior, but cannot acknowledge their homosexuality because of censurious social and/or intrapsychic pressures. In adults, homoerotic preference can initially be recollected as present from the latency years, preadolescence, or early adolescence—i.e., from ages 8–13—and sometimes even earlier. There are, of course, heterosexuals who for developmental reasons (some adolescents), for opportunistic motives (some delinquents), for situational reasons (some prison inmates), or to defend against anxiety may engage in homosexual behavior for varying periods of time and yet not be homosexual (see Isay, 1986).

The Experience of Being Different

Each of the approximately forty gay men I have seen in psychoanalysis or analytically oriented therapy has reported that starting from age 4 or 5 he experienced that he was "different" from his peers. Being different is described as having been more sensitive than other boys, crying more easily, having one's feelings hurt more easily, having more aesthetic interests than other young boys, enjoying nature and music more, preferring "soft" objects to "hard" ones, and being drawn to other "sensitive" boys, girls, and adults. They felt less aggressive than others their age and did not enjoy participating in athletics and other "rough and tumble" activities (Green, 1979; Friedman and Stern, 1980; Bell, Weinberg, and Hammersmith, 1981). These differences make these children feel like outsiders in relation to their peers and often to their family as well. Extensive longitudinal studies by Green (1979, 1985) and by Zuger (1978, 1984) corroborate earlier studies by Saghir and Robins (1973) that reveal a high incidence of adult homosexuality in individuals who as children display effeminate behavior. These studies suggest that gender identity disorders and cross gender behavior in childhood may be indicators of the later development of homosexuality, but it is unclear from these studies what proportion of adult homosexuals have gender disorders in adulthood. In my smaller clinical sample I have found that many of the same characteristics described in these studies of effeminate boys, except for the cross dressing, are recollected in gay men whom I do not consider to have gender identity disorders—i.e., they experience and perceive themselves as men rather than as women. I have not observed a qualitative distinction in the early experiences described by men who as adults are more conventionally masculine and those whose behavior and appearance are more conventionally feminine. However, a closer, quantitative evaluation that is not readily afforded in a clinical setting may reveal some distinctions in early behavior between these groups of gay men.[1]

Part of the experience described by these men as being "different" from their peers appears to have been the perception of same-sex fantasies and early homoerotic arousal patterns. The childhood feeling of being different, consistently acknowledged by gay men, may be unconsciously used as a screen for these earlier repressed childhood memories of sexual arousal by others of the same sex. Although the childhood fantasies may be recalled by the adult, they are, like the childhood sexual fantasies of heterosexuals, most often reconstructed as they manifest themselves in the transference and other current relationships. I will briefly describe three men who illustrate how the child's actual experience of being different from peers in the early latency years from 6 to 8 may act as a screen for these early sexual feelings.

Alan, 32, a handsome man with a small, neat mustache, is masculine-appearing, but somewhat tight and rigid. He initially entered psychotherapy because of feelings of loneliness, dysphoria, anxiety, and dissatisfaction with the quality of his re-

---

[1] In my clinical sample, I would not consider anyone to have had a gender identity disorder as an adult. However, my experience, in general, has been with highly functioning professional men who tend to be masculine in appearance and behavior and to be integrated into heterosexual vocational settings. It may be that my sample is skewed and that these men have less gender disturbances than gay men in the general population.

lationships. He seemed moderately depressed and distressed over the breakup during the previous month of a one-year relationship. He had no apparent conflict over his homosexuality, easily speaking in the initial sessions of his attraction to other men but also of his difficulties in feeling close to them. He had had a five-year relationship with one man that was "tempestuous" and described as sexually one-sided. He had had a similar experience during a more recent relationship in which he had felt too much in the role of pursuer. Being the pursuer in some relationships made him feel sexually alive and more attracted to his lovers than when he was pursued. However, being the pursuer also made him feel unloved and unlovable.

Early in therapy he spontaneously recollected having felt different from his peers during his childhood. He described this in part as "not liking to hit people or rough stuff. I was more sensitive. I never liked being demanding. I liked playing the piano." He believed that his sense of inadequacy derived from his feeling like a perpetual outsider. Peer recognition in adolescence, occurring readily because of his intelligence, good looks, and muscularity, could not enhance his self-esteem. "I never could understand why I was selected for the honor society. When I was chosen, I thought they were talking about someone else and not me."

Alan's father was described as being somewhat distant, a man of few words and fewer feelings. His work was viewed by the patient and his mother as being demeaning, although he always earned a reasonable living. His mother was described as clinging, depressed, and needy, but also as the dominant force in this family, in which Alan was favored by both parents over a brother two years older. In his artistic and musical interests, Alan perceived himself as being like his mother. His acquiescence, nondemandingness, passivity, and emotional distance he viewed as traits similar to his father's.

Early in treatment the transference took the form of indifference toward the therapist, which suggested a need to deny my importance to him. As our work progressed, he met and moved in with a new lover, who was comfortably open in his expression of affection and tenderness toward the patient. Alan became somewhat less frightened of his feelings within the transference and much more open and giving in this new relationship. It was during this period of gradually increasing comfort with the expression of his sexual feelings that he recalled sexual fantasies from when he was 3 or 4 that were centered on muscular comic book heroes. Many of his therapy hours dealt with a longing for the father he perceived as being weak. He also recollected that from about 9 or 10 he began to notice his interest in other boys in his class. During the course of therapy, as his childhood sexual feelings became more accessible, he became less preoccupied with feelings of being "different" and less critical of his sexual fantasies and feelings in the present. It seemed likely from our work, especially from the nature of the transference, that these early sources of sexual interest and excitement were displacements and expressions of his repressed sexual feelings toward his father.

Another patient, Benjamin, entered analysis because of very low self-esteem, severe dysphoria, discontent with his work, and with his life in general. He readily acknowledged that he was homosexual but, unlike Alan, in the earliest hours wished he were not. His fears of closeness to men were intense. His mother was described as intrusive and cloying; his father as gruff and harsh but always available. He always felt different as a child—in fact, he could not recall ever feeling any other way. He described having had no interest in sports but being interested in artistic and musical endeavors. He did not enjoy playing with children his own age—whether girls or boys—and felt isolated and lonely.

During the first months of his analysis he could not recall or had suppressed the memory of any sexual experiences before college. By the second year he was able to speak of sexual experiences that had occurred when he was 11 or 12, when he went to New York's West Village and was picked up by a college student who "taught" him to masturbate. Forays to the West Village continued throughout his adolescence. His typical masturbation fantasies were of being picked up by a dark, muscular man and being dominated by him. One aspect of the evolving transference over several years was first defense against, then indirect manifestations of, and finally direct expressions of the wish to be dominated and sexually penetrated by me. This was accompanied by recollections of feelings of great warmth and comfort lying in bed with his father on weekend mornings while being told stories, then of some vague childhood memories of sexual thoughts about his father and about boys his own age. These recollections date from about age 4, when he also began to feel he was different from his peers. As was true of Alan, his preoccupation with being "different" as a child eased considerably as these early sexual feelings were recollected.

Another patient, Carl, was a slender and clean-shaven young man who entered treatment while in college. His analysis continued for six years, with one brief interruption that occurred between the end of college and the start of graduate school. He entered therapy initially because of low self-esteem and an inability to form meaningful relationships. His sexual activity had been confined largely to the bathroom of the college library and to the stalls of pornographic bookstores. His mother had been extremely attentive until the birth of his younger brother, when he was abruptly sent to prenursery school at the age of 3½. She was always ambitious for Carl, and he felt like an extension of her. His father, whom he perceived as unsuccessful and demeaned by her, was also seen as warm, kind, and loving.

Carl said he felt estranged from other boys throughout his childhood. Like the men described previously, he had had no interest in athletic activities, enjoyed nature, and felt he was more sensitive than his peers. He, like the others, believed these early feelings contributed to his current poor self-image and low self-esteem.

Again, as with Alan and Benjamin, the transference initially was one of feeling indifferent to me. Yet he also seemed devoted to our work and rarely missed an appointment. Throughout the first years he stressed that he was not attracted to "older men in their forties," feeling they were "lecherous" and would take advantage of him. He suffered intense anxiety about being the recipient of anal sex and often was too tight to permit anal penetration, especially if he felt affection for his sexual partner. He was attracted mainly to passive, androgynous appearing young men, but had masturbation fantasies of powerful black men with large penises.

The very slowly evolving sexual transference was manifested largely in dreams of being passively dominated by me.
As these wishes became clearer to him, he also began to have
vague recollection of sexual feelings toward other boys in the
early years of grade school. Deeply repressed and conflicted
wishes to be dominated and penetrated by older men became
clear from dreams and from the transference, although no
childhood attraction to his father was directly recollected. These
repressed wishes appear to stem from the same period in early
childhood in which he places his feelings of being different
from other children.

To summarize, it has become clear from my analytic and
psychotherapeutic work with many adult homosexual men that
some homoerotic fantasy is present in the period between 3 and
5. I conceptualize this period as being analogous to the oedipal
stage of male heterosexuals, except that the primary sexual
object in these homosexual men appears to be their fathers
(Isay, 1987). I see no evidence, either in the nature of the
transference or in the nature of the sexual object choice of these
men, of a defensive shift in erotic interest from their mothers
to their fathers. The experience of being different, which may
be concurrent with the homoerotic fantasies or follow somewhat
later, commences during the early phases of peer socialization.
This experience appears to include a preconscious perception
of same-sex fantasies.

The period of childhood homoerotic sexual attachment to
the father, with its derivative fantasies and sexual arousal pattern, is the first stage in the acquisition of a homosexual identity.
The experience of being different and of in fact being an "outsider" in relation to peers (Bell, Weinberg, and Hammersmith,
1981) often becomes a screen for conflicted sexual feelings.
Both the guilt around early homoerotic fantasies and the experience of being different from peers may contribute to the
low self-esteem and negative self-percepts of many gay men.

I turn now to the stage of consolidation of a homosexual
identity in adolescence and then to some of the developmental
impediments that may hinder the healthy consolidation and
continuing integration in adulthood of a homosexual orientation as part of a positive identity.

Consolidation of Sexual Identity

Alan, at the age of 31, was open about his sexuality and had acknowledged that he was homosexual during his first year of graduate school. As noted above, this man had little difficulty in recollecting that he had same-sex fantasies and feelings from the ages of 3 or 4. Fantasies about male classmates, and an attraction to them, continued throughout grade school and high school without abating, but also without his having had any sexual experience. He had been very popular with his peers in high school because of a combination of masculine appearance, intelligence, sensitivity, and good looks. Though he had always felt like an outsider, like most adolescents he cultivated and appreciated peer group recognition. In order to "fit in" he dated one girl steadily throughout high school, but he was so apprehensive that she might want sex that he would have diarrhea before dates. Because they never did have sex, she broke off the relationship after several years. Throughout this period he continued to deny that he was homosexual.

In college his closest friend was gay. This friend had wanted to have sex with Alan, but, although the attraction was mutual, Alan still could not associate this attraction with a sexuality that was unacceptable to him. "It was okay for him, but not for me. I was a liberal before I knew I was gay." It was in his first year of graduate school, when he was about 23, that he fell in love and then suddenly recognized and acknowledged to himself that he was homosexual. After that recognition he had sex for the first time. He has been relatively and appropriately open about his sexuality ever since.

Alan's experience was similar to that described by others who acknowledge their sexual orientation after a relatively sudden and dramatic breakthrough of barriers of denial, repression, and suppression. This "aha" experience, caused by the coming together of a long-established sexual arousal pattern and a sexual object, feels like the pieces of an old puzzle falling into place. "Until then I had felt I could never fall in love, that I had no sexual feelings, and that they weren't what they should be." A sense of relief, well-being, and "rightness" follow. This experience is similar to what occasionally happens in analysis or psychotherapy following an interpretation that may have been made many times before and is, at last, cognitively and affectively comprehended. In the gay man this experience signifies both the conscious recognition of his sexuality and the beginning of its acceptance as part of his identity. The process of recognition and beginning consolidation is an expectable and normal occurrence in the development of gay men during late adolescence, although the experience is not always as dramatic as with Alan. The initial stage of consolidation of sexuality does not often occur as early in adolescence as it does in heterosexual boys because internalized social constraints and prohibitions confronting the homosexual cause him to suppress and deny his sexuality with greater vigor. Alan's development in this regard was essentially normal. The delay in acknowledging his sexual orientation until age 23 and his degree of denial in the face of early conscious sexual fantasies were attributable to the adolescent wish for peer recognition and to the fear that he would fall out of favor with his parents if he were gay.

I will illustrate the process of recognition and the beginning integration of the homosexual orientation with the experience of another man seen in a two-year analysis following a lengthy previous analysis. With this man the acceptance and consolidation of his sexuality was delayed long beyond late adolescence because of severe conflicts both social and internal.

Donald was in his late thirties before being able to acknowledge his homosexuality. He had been aware of exclusively homoerotic fantasies since early childhood and of arousal by male classmates in grade school. Although it is always difficult to assess patient reports of a previous analysis, he perceived that there had been an unconscious collaboration between his previous analyst and himself around a shared need for the patient not to be homosexual. His analyst attempted over many years to analyze the always present homosexuality as a defense against conflicted competitive and heterosexual wishes and did not analyze the transference aspects of Donald's unsuccessful and painful attempts at heterosexuality, which stemmed from his need to be perceived by his analyst, like his parents, as a "good" boy. Donald married during this first analysis, a marriage that lasted three years, followed by a divorce and the termination of this first treatment.

After completion of that analysis Donald unconsciously felt released from the confinement of his transference need to please his analyst, and within a month had an anonymous homosexual encounter, followed by the "click" of recognition of his sexuality and an enormous feeling of relief. For the first time in his life he felt "sexual, vital, and alive." The low self-esteem and depression that had plagued him for many years began to lift spontaneously. Further analytic work over a two-year period was focused by the patient on his feelings of rage toward the first analyst, a rage which had childhood antecedents, on the previously unanalyzed transference need to please, and on the genetic and developmental origins of the early homosexual arousal patterns. This analytic process further contributed to the integration of his sexuality as part of his identity, mitigating the image he had of himself of being bad, which derived in part from his misunderstood, unrecognized, and disowned sexual impulses. A recent two-session follow-up three years after termination revealed that he had been involved for the past several years in a gratifying relationship with another man.

Not all homosexual men "come out" to themselves with the suddenness and unexpected great relief experienced by the two men just described. In those who have less need for peer recognition than Alan and less hunger for parental love than Donald, there may be a healthy recognition and integration that occurs more gradually, with less suppression and denial of their sexuality during adolescence.

Edward, for example, sought therapy for some depression and general dysphoria as he was about to enter graduate school. The depression in large measure was associated with difficulties in dealing with rage at his father, who had left the family when the patient was 7. His relationship with his mother, described as an intelligent, warm, and loving woman, was generally good, as it was with his stepfather and siblings. He matter-of-factly acknowledged his sexuality during our first hour, when he spoke of his relationships and of looking for, but not yet being able to find, the "right man." Like every gay man, he at times had periods of regret, confusion, and even despair about his sexuality, but there was no ambiguity in his mind about the nature of his sexuality.

His first recollected sexual experience was at the age of 8 or 9, when he was fondled by an older man. He was uncertain how this had occurred, but he felt that he had been a reluctant accomplice in an event remembered with considerable anxiety and guilt. This memory has the qualities of condensation, clarity, and affective investment characteristic of a screen memory, but, while I am certain the event did in fact occur, it is still unclear to me if it was used as a screen for earlier sexual memories.

At 12 or 13 Edward became aware of his attraction to some of his teachers, whom he had identified as being gay. He recognized a strong wish to be close to them, although not specifically to be sexual with them. His adolescent masturbation fantasies were of a man lying on top of him, making him feel submissive and cared for. He traveled abroad when he was 15 or 16 and had his first mutual sexual contact with a man working in a hotel. It was in his second year of college that he acknowledged he was homosexual, in a conversation with a friend. There was no rush of relief following this recognition, as was seen with Alan and Donald, for his acknowledgment of his sexuality had previously been at a preconscious level and the process of integration had been going on over the preceding years of early and middle adolescence. What self-esteem problems this young man had stemmed much less from the early experience of being an outsider or from a conflicted sexual identity than from his identification with an ambivalently viewed father and the injury sustained by the early separation from him.

Edward had acknowledged his sexual orientation more gradually and earlier than either Alan or Donald. His more nourishing maternal environment enabled him to rely less on peer and social conformity in adolescence for self-esteem enhancement, and this made it less necessary for him to please in order to feel lovable. As Erikson (1959) wrote, such a maternal environment "assures the child that it is good to be alive in the particular social coordinates in which he happens to find himself" (p. 39).

The development of a homosexual identity is, as we have seen, normally a gradual one beginning in childhood with the occurrence and preconscious or conscious recognition of same-sex fantasies and same-sex attraction. There is increasing consolidation of this sexuality with the preponderance of homoerotic masturbation fantasies and sexual arousal patterns during adolescence. There usually is some homosexual activity during this developmental period. But, because of the perception of a "different" sexual orientation, and a sense of shame due to perceived social intolerance in general and to adolescent peer intolerance of homosexuality specifically, there may be surprisingly little overt sexual activity in many normal homosexual adolescents.

When there is sexual activity, it can be distinguished from the homosexual activity of heterosexual boys. It has less of the experimental, accidental, and playful quality of the homosexual activity of heterosexual adolescents. The sexual activity feels "for real," because it usually has a strong affective component, either a passionate feeling of being in love or a longing for love from the sexual partner. This is more like the initial sexual encounters of heterosexual adolescents with girls than the sexual play of these adolescent boys with other boys. Heterosexual boys may, of course, have powerful "crushes" on idealized older men or peers, but these are not usually sexually acted on. When they are, a strong bisexual or homosexual orientation is almost certainly present (Fraiberg, 1961). The heterosexual activity of homosexual adolescents usually has the quality of experimentation seen in the heterosexual boy's homosexual activity, and it is usually accompanied by a good deal of anxiety.

The powerful peer and social pressure during adolescence often delays the conscious recognition and acceptance of a homosexual orientation until late adolescence or early adulthood, even in gay men who seem otherwise to have a positive image of themselves. The conscious recognition and subsequent continuing integration of the homosexuality lead to enhanced self-esteem, to a greater sense of well-being, to a greater capacity to love more confidently, both in sexual relationships and in friendship with both men and women, and, usually, to increased productivity.

The integration of one's homosexuality into a cohesive and positive self-image is part of the normal development of a healthy homosexual man. However, not all men who are homosexual are able to accept their sexuality. My clinical experience suggests that early developmental problems related to the maternal relationship may interfere with this normal process. To illustrate, I return to Benjamin, who, it may be recalled, entered analysis because of extremely low self-esteem. He searched for men who could dominate him and, as an early adolescent, had had frequent homosexual experiences in the West Village. Such extensive sexual experience, as I have indicated before, is not customary in early adolescence. He entered analysis with me after an extended consultation with another analyst, whom he knew by reputation to specialize in changing the sexual orientation of homosexuals. Though he left this man after a few sessions, he sought help both from him and then from me to alter his sexuality, which he believed accounted for his low self-esteem and depression. In his initial interview with me he spoke of his sexuality as though it were a foreign appendage that he would like to have excised. He was very fearful that his homosexuality would be discovered at work, and he would go out of his way not to associate with other homosexual men.

Benjamin appeared driven to have sex frequently. He could not tolerate the anxiety generated by being alone and feeling separated from his mother. In his nightly forays into dangerous areas of the city, he would have sex indiscriminately with hustlers and drug abusers, at times risking robbery, physical injury, and sexually transmitted diseases.

The intense masochism and the narcissistic injuries that determined the manner in which Benjamin selected his partners and expressed his sexuality were determinants also of the difficulty he had in accepting himself as a homosexual man. His mother, he felt, perceived him as an extension of herself and never conveyed to him a sense of his separateness. Because he had an unconscious perception of her hatred of him, and strongly identified with it, he had little capacity to feel lovable or to accept any aspect of himself without either compensatory inflation or intense hatred. His sexuality, known to his father but secret to his mother, became a focus and displacement of aspects of himself that made him feel hated and hateful, and he had no capacity to sustain a sense of himself as a good person in a society that was inimical and censorious toward his sexuality.

Carl is another man who sought analysis because of low self-esteem. Unlike Benjamin, he had some concern about his inability to form meaningful relationships and some wish to improve this aspect of his life. Carl had a few incidental sexual experiences in his last two years of high school, and in college had anonymous sex or one-night stands, a pattern that continued during the early years of his analysis. He seemed invariably attracted to men who would not like him; those who might he either would not be attracted to or would drive away. He had little or no interest in girls but dated occasionally in college in order to please his mother, who spoke often to him about her wish for grandchildren. He readily acknowledged his homosexuality in the early interviews, but also spoke of how he hated himself for being gay. During his analysis he would occasionally speak of going to "one of those shrinks" who would change him. This would follow his feeling particularly close to me and threatened by both the closeness and well-defended sexual feelings. Early in analysis he, like Benjamin, tended in school or work situations to avoid being seen with other gay men.

Carl's low self-esteem appeared to be associated with his early relationship with his mother. Like Benjamin's mother, she appeared to treat her son as an extension of herself, and conveyed in many ways that her goals and gratifications were to be accomplished through his achievements and that his failures and unhappiness would result in her disappointment. Having little sense of himself as a separate person or of his own goals, Carl was very dependent on peers and on social approval generally for self-esteem regulation, and censorious social attitudes toward homosexuality weighed heavily on him. Although there is no suggestion that Carl's aggression toward his mother was a primary determinant of his sexual orientation, both this aggression and his masochism played a large role in the manner in which he expressed his homosexuality and the tenuous quality of his relationships. His feelings about his sexuality acted as a displacement from other sources of self-hatred, especially at his rage toward his ambivalently viewed mother. The binding relationship with an impaired and hostile mother, which filled him with rage and self-hatred, eventuated in a profound difficulty in permitting himself any pleasurable sexual activity in the context of a gratifying, loving relationship. As with Benjamin, sex was masochistically tinged, contributing to the feeling that his sexual orientation was bad and dirty, and to his failure to integrate it as part of a positive identity.

As Carl's self-image improved through the recognition of the early humiliations and rejections that contributed to his feeling unlovable, the quality of his object relations also improved. He was able to have two sustained relationships with people who cared about him. These more nourishing relations in turn enhanced his self-esteem and his image of himself as a gay man.

With both Benjamin and Carl one aspect of the transference in the middle phase of their analyses was a concern that, if I were accepting of them and did not appear to have any intention of converting their homosexuality to heterosexuality, I must myself be homosexual. I therefore became degraded and denigrated like themselves. This important aspect of the transference was a defense against an early and conflicted erotic attachment to their fathers and a reflection of their later perception and experience of them (Isay, 1987). As Benjamin's and Carl's conflicts about their sexuality became better analyzed, and the inhibitions preventing more gratifying relationships were lifted, both men became better able to experience themselves and the analyst in a less deprecatory manner, leading in the latter stages of our work to the less inhibited and less defended expression of the wish for closeness and love both inside and outside their analyses.

I will present one further illustration of delay and disruption in the process of consolidating a homosexual identity. Fred, whom I initially saw during his first year of college, when he was 17, had left his previous therapist, who had begun to encourage him to date and who appeared oblivious or hostile toward his being homosexual. Fred had experienced the feeling of being "different," along with a conscious perception of early homoerotic fantasy and arousal, and had a clear memory of homosexual fantasy from the age of 8 or 9. His masturbation fantasies had always been exclusively homosexual. When he initially consulted with me he had no question about his sexual orientation, although he was fearful of sexual contact or emotional closeness with another boy. We both considered this to be a neurotic inhibition that was interfering with his sexual expression and, therefore, with his capacity to consolidate his identity as a homosexual.

Fred was concerned about the intensity of his homosexual arousal at college. He felt attracted to many boys, most of whom were openly gay. Because of the possibility that there would be a mutual attraction and the potential for consummation of his desire, this made him particularly anxious. He was inhibited from expressing this desire; if he were cruised, he refused to return the gaze. In his second year of therapy he fell in love with a classmate and had a brief sexual experience, which he had enjoyed, but he found himself so "embarrassed" when he saw his new friend that he could not maintain the relationship. His sexual life became exclusively one of solitary masturbation, with increasing pot smoking in an effort to dull his sexual excitement and his self-consciousness about it.

Fred's sexual inhibition stemmed from a fear of humiliation that by and large derived from his mother's expressed ambivalence toward him and his father. The constantly chaotic relationship between his parents, and his mother's denigration of his father, made the love and erotic attachment he felt toward his father a source of humiliation and shame. Out of rage at both parents, and for purposes of self-protection, Fred became intent on not exposing himself to his mother's humiliating rejection by refusing to become attached to another man and by rejecting any man's interest in him with dismissive contempt. For Benjamin and Carl, the severe narcissistic injury that occurred from their experience of being little more than extensions of their mothers, along with the perception of their mothers' ambivalence and their own rage turned against themselves, neurotically distorted the erotic attachment to their father and made emotional intimacy with other men terrifying. The inability to have gratifying relationships kept each of these men from having a positive identity as homosexual men. Injured self-esteem, fears of intimacy, and the inability to accept a homosexual orientation or to express it in a manner that is emotionally fulfilling appear to have gone together in each of these three men.

Integration of Sexual Identity

The process of developing a sexual identity as a homosexual man is of course lifelong. Acquisition of the sexual orientation occurs in childhood, as does the beginning of sexual identity formation, with the feeling of being different and a preconscious recognition of same-sex fantasies. Consolidation occurs during adolescence and early adulthood, with the expression of sexuality motivated by the surge of sexual needs. However, continuing integration of the sexual identity occurs throughout adulthood, through both sexual and social relationships with other homosexual men and through varying degrees of involvement in gay social networks (Troiden, 1979).

The process of "coming out" to other gay men usually leads to "homosocialization," by which I refer to nonsexual contacts with other gay men either within or without an established gay community. This aspect of the life of the homosexual man has received little attention from psychoanalysts. Some hold that "social acceptance," by reducing a homosexual's feeling that he is "ill," increases the difficulty he may have in being motivated for treatment and so should be discouraged as not in his interest (Socarides, 1963). Others are quoted as stating that the issue of narcissism is more pervasive in the "sociosexual than in the sexual homosexual groups," and that investment in the homosexual world compensates for maternal deprivation and is an expression of rage (Payne, 1977, p. 190). In the social psychological literature, there are those who argue the opposite position, namely, that a nearly exclusive association with other gay men is a necessary component of the consolidation of normal identity as a homosexual (Cass, 1979).

None of these positions conforms to my clinical experience. There are homosexual men with a relatively healthy and comfortable acceptance of their homosexual orientation who do not have extensive gay social networks. The degree and nature of involvement in the gay community usually are determined by social and vocational needs, by marital status, and by the availability of other gay men (Weinberg and Williams, 1974, p. 11). The support provided by having many gay friends or by living in a gay community, when this is available, may be unnecessary for those, for example, who receive adequate gratification from social and vocational activities within the heterosexual community. It is also easier for a homosexual man in our society to be integrated into a heterosexual community when he is not coupled and has not "come out." Those who are coupled generally find it more comfortable and better for the stability of the relationship to have the support and relatively unprejudiced structure offered by a gay community or gay friends.

The freedom to be homosocial may also be related to one's having less need for support from heterosexually oriented peer and social organizations, and so is often indicative of a healthy acceptance of one's sexual orientation and of a self-assurance that precludes the necessity for traditional sources of support. Of course, extensive homosocial involvement may also suggest a rageful need to reject these conventional sources (Payne, 1977). However, as I have indicated in my descriptions of the nonsexual gay relationships of Benjamin, Carl, and Fred, there was a connection between their low self-esteem, the consequent inability to have a positive image of their sexuality, and their need to avoid contact with other gay men. As their self-esteem improved through the analysis of the early conflict, especially around the problematic relation with their mothers, the transference evolved into one of decreased self-imposed distance, and homosocial contacts increased extensively. For these men homosociability further increased the acceptance of their sexuality and enhanced their feeling of self-worth. For Alan and Edward, whose self-esteem had not been severely disturbed by early conflict, there was always a capacity for and an interest in nonsexual social relationships with other gay men. Insofar as availability and other obligations permit, homosocial relationships are necessary for the continuing consolidation and integration of identity, and the capacity for such relationships is a sign of a relatively positive self-regard. Conversely, the

inability or unwillingness to have such relationships suggests
impaired self-esteem.

Discussion

It would be inaccurate to conclude from what I have written
that all homosexual men who engage in random sexual encounters are beset by neurotic difficulties and that only those
who have sustained relationships are "healthy." The selection
of multiple partners is best understood as being determined by
a number of interactive issues that include social as well as
dynamic factors. For example, furtive, anonymous sexual activity in public rest rooms is more likely to be carried out by
homosexual men who cannot risk discovery and disclosure and
who are well integrated into a heterosexual community by virtue
of religious affiliation, marriage, or vocation (Humphreys,
1972) than by those integrated into a gay subculture. For the
same reasons such men may not have a sustained relationship,
even though they may be capable or even desirous of having
one. The expression of defiance of antihomosexual attitudes
(Altman, 1973), the lack of legal and social sanctions for homosexual relationships, the absence of children to bind these relationships, and the availability of partners are some of the
other social factors that may play a role in the selection and
nature of sexual partners. Foucault (1982–1983) was possibly
also correct when he wrote that interdictions of our society
foster furtive, random sexual encounters. Further, there is evidence to suggest that biological factors related to male sexuality
play a role in the nature of the homosexual man's sexual activity.
Human males in general are more promiscuous than females
if left to their own devices and when there are opportunities
for such behavior. "This is the history of his anthropoid ances-
tors and this is the history of unrestrained human males every-
where" (Kinsey, Pomeroy, and Martin, 1948, p. 589). The
human male is in general less object directed than is the human
female, who appears to be less interested in a variety of partners
(Kinsey, Pomeroy, and Martin, 1948; Ford and Beach, 1951).
By noting these social and biological issues I am not min-

imizing the importance of the intrapsychic factors that motivate different types of sexual behavior in human beings. Nor am I underestimating the difficulties some gay men have in maintaining sustained long-term relationships, which may be caused by both social and dynamic factors.[2] I do believe, however, that to view the sexual behavior of homosexual men as being unconnected to an external social reality leads to simplistic, unifactorial, dynamic explanations of such behavior (see, e.g., Calef and Weinshel, 1984). In the homosexual man social factors interact with, help to shape, and even modify intrapsychic forces based on early developmental factors. Understanding and attending to such issues provides the analyst or dynamic therapist a more complete explanation of sexual behavior. Understanding some of the developmental issues that confront every gay man in the acquisition, consolidation, and integration of his identity will, it is hoped, deepen and enhance the therapist's understanding of his patients' lives.

Summary

I have outlined three broad stages in homosexual identity formation: a childhood acquisition stage, the consolidation stage of adolescence and early adulthood, and the integration stage of adulthood. The stage of acquisition is characterized by same-sex fantasies and impulses in early childhood. Memories of these early arousal patterns may be repressed, but do become more accessible through the analysis of the indirect memories that are manifested in the transference and in the nature of the choice of sexual objects. They may, of course, also be directly recalled. The experience during early peer socialization of being "different" appears to include the preconscious recog-

[2] Homosexuals cannot be stereotyped with regard to either the nature or the frequency of their sexual behavior. Sustained relationships are more extensive than generally believed (Bell and Weinberg, 1978; McWhirter and Mattison, 1984), and the view that all homosexuals are promiscuous, fueled further by the AIDS epidemic, is a pernicious stereotype prominently directed against all minority groups who are feared because of their differences. This includes not only gays, but blacks, Puerto Ricans, and Jews as well, the latter association having been particularly prominent during the Nazi era.

nition of same-sex arousal. Other recollected aspects of being different from peers may act as a screen for these repressed sexual memories.

The consolidation and integration of the homosexual orientation appear to be enhanced by a warm and loving mother who permits the child to have an accepting image of himself and of his father. Homosexual men who have been used by their mothers as narcissistic extensions of themselves, and who have unconsciously perceived their mother's ambivalence toward them, tend to have more masochistic tendencies and poorer self-images due to their early narcissistic injuries. They feel greater need for social conformity because of their reliance on peer and social approval for self-esteem maintenance. They are more likely to despise their homosexuality as they do other aspects of themselves, to avoid the companionship of other homosexual men, and to fear intimacy with them. The negative perception of their sexuality is manifested in and reinforced by the ungratifying nature of these relationships.

The expression of the homosexual orientation in adolescence and early adulthood within the context of warm sexual relationships and the capacity to form loving sustained relationships later in adulthood enhance the consolidation and integration of this sexuality as part of a positive identity. This process continues throughout adulthood both through loving relationships and, insofar as social circumstances permit, through sustaining nonsexual relationships with other gay men.

References

Abrams, S. (1979), The psychoanalytic normalities. *J. Amer. Psychoanal. Assn.*, 27:821–835.

Altman, D. (1973), *Homosexual*. New York: Avon Books.

Bell, A. P., & Weinberg, M. S. (1978), *Homosexualities*. New York: Simon & Schuster.

———— ———— & Hammersmith, S. K. (1981), *Sexual Preference*. Bloomington: Indiana University Press.

Calef, V., & Weinshel, E. (1984), Anxiety and the restitutive function of homosexual cruising. *Internat. J. Psycho-Anal.*, 65:45–53.

Cass, V. C. (1979), Homosexual identity formation. *J. Homosexual.*, 4:219–235.

Eissler, K. R. (1960), The efficient soldier. *Psychoanalytic Study of Society*, 1:39–97. New York: International Universities Press.

Erikson, E. H. (1959), Identity and the life cycle. *Psychological Issues*, Monograph 1. New York: International Universities Press.
Ford, C. S., & Beach, F. A. (1951), *Patterns of Sexual Behavior*. New York: Harper.
Foucault, M. (1982–1983), An interview with Michael Foucault. *Salmagundi*, 58–59:10–24.
Fraiberg, S. H. (1961), Homosexual conflicts. In: *Adolescents*, ed. S. Lorand & H. I. Schneer. New York: Hoeber, pp. 78–112.
Friedman, R. C., & Stern, L. O. (1980), Juvenile aggressivity and sissiness in homosexual and heterosexual males. *J. Acad. Psychoanal.*, 8:427–440.
Freud, A. (1968), Acting out. *Internat. J. Psycho-Anal.*, 49:165–170.
Freud, S. (1930), Civilization and its discontents. *Standard Edition*, 21:64–145. London: Hogarth Press, 1961.
——— (1937), Analysis terminable and interminable. *Standard Edition*, 23:216–253. London: Hogarth Press, 1964.
Green, R. (1979), Childhood cross-gender behavior and subsequent sexual preference. *Amer. J. Psychiat.*, 36:106–108.
——— (1985), Gender identity in childhood and later sexual orientation. *Amer. J. Psychiat.*, 142:339–341.
Hartmann, H. (1939), Psychoanalysis and the concept of health. In: *Essays on Ego Psychology*. New York: International Universities Press, 1964, pp. 1–18.
Humphreys, L. (1972), *Out of the Closets*. Englewood Cliffs, NJ: Prentice-Hall.
Isay, R. A. (1985), On the analytic therapy of homosexual men. *The Psychoanalytic Study of the Child*, 40:235–254. New Haven: Yale University Press.
——— (1986), Homosexuality in homosexual and heterosexual men. In: *The Psychology of Men*, ed., C. Fogel, F. Lane, & R. Liebert. New York: Basic Books, pp. 277–299.
——— (1987), Fathers and their homosexually inclined sons in childhood. In: *The Psychoanalytic Study of the Child*, 42:275–294. New Haven: Yale University Press.
Jones, E. (1931), The concept of a normal mind. In: *Papers on Psycho-Analysis*. Baltimore: Williams & Wilkins, 1948, pp. 201–216.
Kinsey, A. C,. Pomeroy, W. B., & Martin, C. E. (1948), *Sexual Behavior in the Human Male*. Philadelphia: Saunders.
Klein, M. (1960), On mental health. *Brit. J. Med. Psychol.*, 33:237–247.
McWhirter, D. P., & Mattison, A.M. (1984), *The Male Couple*. Englewood Cliffs, NJ: Prentice-Hall.
Offer, D., & Sabshin, M. (1966), *Normality*. New York: Basic Books.
Payne, E. C. (1977), Panel report: The psychoanalytic treatment of male homosexuality. *J. Amer. Psychoanal. Assn.*, 25:183–199.
Saghir, M. T., & Robins, E. (1973), *Male and Female Homosexuality*. Baltimore: Williams & Wilkins.
Socarides, C. W. (1963), *New York Times*, December 17, page 33.
Troiden, R. R. (1979), Becoming homosexual. *Psychiatry*, 42:362–373.
Weinberg, M. S., & Williams, C. J. (1974), *Male Homosexuals*. New York: Oxford University Press.
Zuger, B. (1978), Effeminate behavior in boys from childhood. *Comprehensive Psychiat.*, 19:363–369.
——— (1984), Early effeminate behavior in boys. *J. Nerv. Ment. Dis.*, 172:90–96.

21

The Phase of Young Adulthood, Age Eighteen to Twenty-Three Years

MELVIN LEWIS, M.B., B.S., F.R.C.PSYCH., D.C.H.

The phases of development that commonly occupy the years 18–23 may include late adolescence (Blos, 1962), youth (Keniston, 1970), the periods of "Intimacy and Distantiation versus Self-Absorption" and "Generativity versus Stagnation" (Erikson, 1959), and young adulthood (Lidz, 1968). Indeed, the word "adolescence" means becoming an adult and was first used in the English language in 1430, when it referred to ages 14–21 in males, and 12–21 in females. These phases of development in turn have biological, psychological, and social correlates and are viewed differently by society as the individual matures from a juvenile to an adult. Lastly, there are sex differences as well as sociocultural variables.

Developmental Tasks

Just as there is a stabilization of biological maturation as epiphyses close, adult stature is achieved, and drive upheaval settles, so there is an increasing stabilization of the personality. Conflict between the self and the changing milieu intérieur abates and is displaced by conflict within the self and between the self and the external world. Thus, consolidation and integration of one's personality and the adaptation to a changing and unfamiliar society become the pivotal "developmental tasks" at this stage. Specific developmental tasks include the achievement of gratifying heterosexual relationships, deciding upon a career, and committing oneself to marriage or an alternative lifestyle.

Failure to resolve any of these developmental tasks may occur because of persisting difficulties arising from unresolved earlier conflicts. Moreover, current conflicts may be heightened by interaction with the existential anxiety that arises when one is confronted with certain challenges of society. These societal challenges, at least in Western society, include attitudinal and technological confrontations. For example, changing attitudes toward sexual intercourse have been accelerated by the reduced fear of pregnancy. Instantaneous mass communication has enabled young people to realize that they have much in common and that they constitute a large group in our population. The precarious control of destructive violence of a magnitude far greater than ever before possible may engender or aggravate a high level of anxiety in the adolescent, particularly at times of international crisis accompanied by the threat of nuclear attack.

Another, more immediate variable is the socioeconomic status of the individual (Esman, 1977). For example, a white middle-class professional has an experience entirely different from that of a native American Indian. Additional variables are sex and parenthood. Psychoanalytic investigations of this developmental period, however, have focused for the most part on the affluent individual. For example, Ritvo (1971) concentrated mostly on college students and college dropouts. Yet even among this group there is change. Thus, the striking difference between the behavior of students in the late 1960s and that seen in the early 1970s seems to reflect both intrapsychic development and the individual's responsiveness to a particular historical context.

Yet the basic developmental tasks remain to be resolved, even if they are influenced by immediate or global social factors.

Identity, Intimacy, and Society

By the age of 18–23, a sufficient history of personality traits and intellectual development has occurred to enable the individual to observe his or her own behavior in response to internal urges and external demands. This conscious identity, including a new decision-making capability, is now more fully integrated into the ego and is more or less independent of superego reinforcement. Moreover, decisions can now be made in the context of lengthier commitment rather than immediate wishes or superego sanctions. In addition, a greater degree of intimacy now becomes possible, as independence from the family is established and a conscious sense of identity is achieved. Further, a new relationship with society emerges as the individual's horizons widen and the inequalities of society are recognized, if not tolerated. In some young adults there is an acute disillusionment with society, reminiscent of the disillusionment with parents that occurs in the postoedipal phase. Disillusionment with society may be an extension of, or a displacement from, that earlier disillusionment. However, in most instances it is a true recognition of human frailty and social reality. Thus, identity is a complex achievement, involving a sense of one's personal sameness within a comprehensible social reality and having both conscious and unconscious aspects.

Dyadic Love Relationships

Both males and females in this period are on the threshold of establishing new, long-lasting relationships based primarily on reality considerations. The short-lived relationships based on replication of original objects, or on part-identification or overidealization, that characterize earlier adolescence are now replaced by a full sense of identification and the need to form realistic and lasting relationships that "fit" the now-consolidated identification. The motivations and forces acting on the formation of long-term heterosexual relationships (including marriage) are early conscious and unconscious need fulfillment, unconscious incestuous fantasy wishes, the need for intellectual stimulation, sexual pleasure, self-esteem and narcisstic gratification, the influences of family and peer relationships, social striving, neurotic role interlocking, the wish to have children, and desire for complementarity. The degree to which any one of these components overrides the others will determine whether the relationship will succeed or fail. Since few, if any, relationships stay the same, a strong conscious commitment is usually required to resolve difficulties and misunderstandings arising from these factors. Young adults are generally capable of making this kind of commitment, particularly as they approach their midtwenties. A failure to make this kind of commitment or an overriding and interfering unconscious motivation, or even preconscious motivation that is not allowed recognition or expression, is likely to result in a failure or radical change in such relationships.

Early Parenthood Phase

During this phase the individual also becomes capable of parenthood, during which the individual's own childhood experiences are reworked (Benedek, 1959). The individual's children act as stimuli and provide opportunities for this development. This in turn is a part of the individual's growing capacity for mutuality during what Erikson calls the stage of "Generativity versus Stagnation." Parenthood, however, is more than a single developmental phase; it is a series of interconnected subphases, beginning with fantasies of parenthood, through the psychological process for man and woman during pregnancy, labor, and childhood (Bibring, Dwyer, Huntington, and Valenstein, 1961), to the identity changes in the parents as they experience changes in their relationship with each other and with their children as their children move from phase to phase in *their* development.

Intergenerational Experience

The period between 18 and 23 is often the beginning of the experience of being between two generations, one's parents and one's children. While emancipated from parents, there is a concern that one will be pulled back into the family of origin as a child and not as an adult (Gould, 1972). Consequently, there is a tendency to intensify peer relationships, provided such relationships, especially in the aggregate, do not in turn threaten one's autonomy and individuality. Life is viewed mostly in terms of present and future, as the individual sets on a course that involves mastering a work skill, profession, or lifestyle.

Work

Sociocultural and family influences, sex, economic conditions, physical status, cognitive abilities, education, job opportunities, personality type and needs, and specific conscious and unconscious motivations, identifications, talents and skills are some of the factors that determine an individual's work. Sometimes the choice of a particular career provides an environment in which group values can take the place of individually derived moral and ethical values. The individual superego may become dissolved in the group superego or may be reinforced by the group ego ideal. Repetition compulsion may be another factor in determining not only the individual's choice of work but also the degree of success or failure in it. Work may thus be an end in itself, a means of satisfying old urges, or a force acting upon the young adult—or all three.

Intellectual Function

By 18 the individual should be capable of formal operations (Piaget, 1969); now intellectual thought can begin with a theoretical synthesis of certain relations and then proceed to empirical data, instead of vice versa. This intellectual ability enables normal individuals to take distance on their thoughts, feelings, and behavior, and to influence the direction of all three. Cognitive fixation, on the other hand, interferes with this capacity and leaves the individual vulnerable to the repetition compulsion mentioned earlier.

Concluding Remark

Ideally, the normal individual between 18 and 23 years of age is experiencing for the first time the consolidation of identity, the mastery of drives, the achievement of unfettered, true heterosexual object relationships, and a realistic view of the world as he or she enjoys new heights of intellectual activity. Few achieve this ideal state. Indeed, even were this state achieved, it would not last; the next phase of development would once again demand change.

References

Benedek, T. (1959), Parenthood as a development phase. *J. Amer. Psychoanal. Assn.*, 7:389–407.

Bibring, G. L., Dwyer, T. F., Huntington, D. S., & Valenstein, A. F. (1961), A study of the psychological processes in pregnancy and of the earliest mother-child relationship. *The Psychoanalytic Study of the Child*, 16:9–44. New York: International Universities Press.

Blos, P. (1962), Phases of adolescence. In: *On Adolescence: A Psychoanalytic Interpretation.* New York: Free Press, pp. 52–157.

Erikson, E. H. (1959), Identity and the life cycle. *Psychological Issues*, Monograph 1. New York: International Universities Press, pp. 50–100.

Esman, A. H. (1977), Changing values: Their implications for adolescent development and psychoanalytic idea. *Adolescent Psychiat.*, 5:18–34.

Gould, R. I. (1972), The phases of adult life: A study in developmental psychology. *Amer. J. Psychiat.*, 129:521–531.

Keniston, K. (1970), Youth: A new stage in life. *American Scholar*, 39:631–653.

Lidz, T. (1968), The young adult. In: *The Person.* New York: Basic Books, pp. 362–367.

Piaget, J. (1969), The intellectual development of the adolescent. In: *Adolescence: Psychosocial Perspectives*, ed. G. Caplan & S. Lebovici. New York: Basic Books, pp. 22–26.

Ritvo, S. (1971), Late adolescence: Developmental and clinical considerations. *The Psychoanalytic Study of the Child*, 26:241–263. New York: Quadrangle.

Name Index

Subject Index